A BIRDER'S GUIDE
TO
VIRGINIA

David W. Johnston, compiler

American Birding Association, Inc.

Library of Congress Catalog Number: 97-71776
ISBN Number: 1-878788-12-4
First Edition
    2   3   4   5   6   7   8
Printed in the United States of America

Publisher
    American Birding Association, Inc.
Series Editor
    Paul J. Baicich
Associate Editors
    Cindy Lippincott and Bob Berman
Copy Editor
    Hugh Willoughby
Layout and Typography
    Bob Berman; using CorelVENTURA, Windows version 5.0
Maps
    Cindy Lippincott and Eng-Li Green; using CorelDRAW version 5.0
Cover Photography
    front cover: *Belted Kingfisher;* Brian E. Small
    back cover: *King Rail with chicks;* Fred Siskind
Illustrations
    Georges Dremeaux
    Ali Wieboldt
    Gail Diane Yovanovich
Distributed by
    American Birding Association Sales
    PO Box 6599
    Colorado Springs, Colorado 80934-6599 USA
    phone: (800) 634-7736 or (719) 578-0607
    fax: (800) 590-2473 or (719) 578-9705
European and UK Distribution
    Subbuteo Natural History Books, Ltd.
    Treuddyn, Mold, Clwyd
    CH7 4LN UK Tel: 1352-770581; fax: 1352-771590

Dedicated

to

F.R. Scott,

a long-time leader

in observing

Virginia's birdlife.

ACKNOWLEDGEMENTS

Compiling data for this guide was made possible only by the input of dozens of birders from all parts of the state over a three-year period. The Virginia Society of Ornithology, through its Executive Committee and Board of Directors, provided guidance and financial support to me as Chairman of its Publications Committee. Financial assistance also came from the Monticello Bird Club.

Many people helped to review site information or to write new site descriptions. They included Mary Arginteanu, Henry T. Armistead, Ken Bass, John Bazuin, Jr., Ruth Beck, Stan Bentley, Jeffrey Blalock, Ned Brinkley, Roger Clapp, John and Thelma Dalmas, Paul DuMont, Mark Farmer, Charlotte Friend, Ken Hollinga, Teta Kain, Valerie Kitchens, Kerrie Kirkpatrick, George Larkins, YuLee Larner, Clair Mellinger, Norwood Middleton, Darrell Peterson, Richard Peake, Bill Portlock, Dan Puckette, Mike Purdy, Larry Robinson, Paul Saunier, Jr., Donald Schwab, Charles Stevens, Ruth Snyder, Brian Taber, Leonard Teuber, Robert Watson, Carter Whatley, Bill Williams, and Erika Wilson. Comments, additions, and deletions for the annotated list were ably provided by David Abbott, Robert Ake, John Bazuin, Jr., Ned Brinkley, Roger Clapp, John and Thelma Dalmas, Fenton Day, Charlotte Friend, Teta Kain, YuLee Larner, Norwood Middleton, Brian Patteson, Richard Peake, Brian Taber, Leonard Teuber, Claudia Wilds, and Erika Wilson.

John and Thelma Dalmas have birded all over the state for many years; their intimate and broad experiences with birdlife are reflected in their introduction to this guide. Both Teta Kain and Charlotte Friend shared recent results of VARCOM (Virginia Rare Birds Committee) actions and reviewed rare and unusual bird records in the annotated list. Others deserving special gratitude for their help in particular sections are Myriam Moore and Kerrie Kirkpatrick (hawk-watching), Brian Patteson (pelagic birding), Lisa Hamilton (Eastern Shore Birding Festival), Teta Kain (Christmas Bird Counts), Marcus Simpson, Jr. (Blue Ridge Parkway), Paul Opler (butterflies), Joseph Mitchell (amphibians and reptiles), and Charles Handley, Jr. (mammals).

Very special thanks are due to Jeffrey Blalock, who undertook the time-consuming task of soliciting revisions of the sites published in an earlier site guide published by the Virginia Society of Ornithology (VSO).

Final drafts of large portions of the guide were carefully reviewed by John and Thelma Dalmas and David Abbott, all long-time birders in the state.

I also wish to thank Teta Kain, former editor of the *Raven* and a person intimately familiar with the state's bird records, for her unflagging support and morale boosting in difficult times.

The work of the two cover photographers, Brian Small and Fred Siskind, is much appreciated, as is that of the habitat photographers, Adrian R. Davis, W. Juergen Schrenk, and Rob Simpson, and the three artists, Georges Dremeaux, Ali Wieboldt, and Gail Diane Yovanovich. The ABA support-staff for this book organized the production admirably: Paul Baicich, the series editor; Cindy Lippincott, associate editor and map-maker; Eng-Li Green, who also did maps; Bob Berman, the technical associate editor; and Hugh Willoughby, the copy-editor.

David W. Johnston
Fairfax, Virginia, February 1997

TABLE OF CONTENTS

Introduction 1

Virginia Sites: 24

Eastern Shore 24
1.   Chincoteague National Wildlife Refuge 27
2.   Virginia Coast Reserve Barrier Islands 32
3.   Kiptopeke State Park and Vicinity 35
4.   Chesapeake Bay Bridge-Tunnel Islands 39

Coastal Plain 44
5a.   Harrison Lake National Fish Hatchery 48
5b.   Point of Rocks Park 50
5c.   Presquile National Wildlife Refuge 51
6a.   Stumpy Lake 52
6b.   Great Dismal Swamp National Wildlife Refuge 55
6c.   Ragged Island Wildlife Management Area 56
6d.   Craney Island Landfill 58
6e.   First Landing/Seashore State Park and Natural Area and Fort Story   59
6f.   Back Bay National Wildlife Refuge 61
6g.   False Cape State Park 64
7a.   Grandview Beach 66
7b.   Jamestown Island 68
7c.   Jolly Pond 70
7d.   York River State Park 71
7e.   Colonial Parkway 72
7f.   Newport News City Park 74
7g.   Hog Island 75
8a.   George Washington Birthplace National Monument . . . 76
8b.   Westmoreland State Park 78

Northern Virginia 80
9a.   Long Branch Nature Area/Glencarlyn Park 83
9b.   Potomac Overlook Regional Park 85
9c.   Lubber Run Park 86
10a. Chinquapin Park 88
10b. Monticello Park 90
10c. Hunting Creek/Bay,Belle Haven, Dyke Marsh, and Jones Point Park   91
10d. Huntley Meadows Park 95
11a. Accotink Bay Wildlife Refuge and Fort Belvoir 97
11b. Mason Neck State Park and National Wildlife Refuge . . 100
12a. Scotts Run Nature Preserve 103
12b. Great Falls National Park and Riverbend Park 105
13.   Lucketts Area 106
14a. Snickers Gap 109
14b. Sky Meadows State Park 110
14c. Linden Fire Tower 113

Central Virginia 114
15.   Lake Anna 117
16.   Shenandoah National Park 120
17a. Ivy Creek Natural Area 126

17b.	Observatory Mountain	128
18a.	Grand Caverns Regional Park	129
18b.	Montgomery Hall Park	129
18c.	Natural Chimneys Regional Park	131
18d.	Silver Lake	132
19a.	Highland County	134
19b.	Ramseys Draft and Shenandoah Mountain	137
20.	Lake Moomaw	138

Southern Piedmont 140

21.	James River Park	143
22a.	Pocahontas State Park and State Forest	146
22b.	Swift Creek Reservoir	148
23.	Red Hill Shrine	149
24.	John H. Kerr Reservoir	151
25a.	Staunton River State Park	156
25b.	Staunton River Battlefield State Park (Fort Hill)	158

Southern Mountains and Valleys 160

26.	The Blue Ridge Parkway	164
27a.	Roanoke Sewage Treatment Plant	174
27b.	Carvins Cove Reservoir	176
27c.	Daleville Ponds	177
28.	Mountain Lake	178
29.	Shot Tower and New River Trail State Parks	180
29a.	Burkes Garden	182
30a.	Mount Rogers	184
30b.	Whitetop Mountain	186
30c.	Grayson Highlands State Park	187
30d.	Laurel Bed Lake	188
30e.	South Holston Lake	189
31.	Mendota Fire Tower	191
32a.	Clinch Valley College Campus	192
32b.	Flag Rock Park	193
32c.	High Knob Recreation Area	194
32d.	Breaks Interstate Park	195

Hawk-Watching in Virginia 198

Pelagic Birding in Virginia 203

An Annotated Checklist of Birds Found in Virginia 210

Specialties of Virginia 249

Other Animals of Virginia 260
- Butterflies 260
- Amphibians 263
- Reptiles 265
- Mammals 267

Suggested References 270

The Virginia Society of Ornithology 275

American Birding Association 277

Index 279

AMERICAN BIRDING ASSOCIATION
PRINCIPLES OF BIRDING ETHICS

Everyone who enjoys birds and birding must always respect wild-life, its environment, and the rights of others. In any conflict of interest between birds and birders, the welfare of the birds and their environment comes first.

CODE OF BIRDING ETHICS

Promote the welfare of birds and their environment.

a) Support the protection of important bird habitat.

b) To avoid stressing birds or exposing them to danger, exercise restraint and caution during observation, photography, sound recording, or filming.

Limit the use of recordings and other methods of attracting birds, and never use such methods in heavily birded areas or for attracting any species that is Threatened, Endangered, or of Special Concern, or is rare in your local area.

Keep well back from nests and nesting colonies, roosts, display areas, and important feeding sites. In such sensitive areas, if there is a need for extended observation, photography, filming, or recording, try to use a blind or hide, and take advantage of natural cover.

Use artificial light sparingly for filming or photography, especially for close-ups.

c) Before advertising the presence of a rare bird, evaluate the potential for disturbance to the bird, its surroundings, and other people in the area, and proceed only if access can be controlled, disturbance can be minimized, and permission has been obtained from private land-owners. The sites of rare nesting birds should be divulged only to the proper conservation authorities.

d) Stay on roads, trails, and paths where they exist; otherwise keep habitat disturbance to a minimum.

Respect the law and the rights of others.

a) Do not enter private property without the owner's explicit permission.

b) Follow all laws, rules, and regulations governing use of roads and public areas, both at home and abroad.

c) Practice common courtesy in contacts with other people. Your exemplary behavior will generate goodwill with birders and non-birders alike.

3. Ensure that feeders, nest structures, and other artificial bird environ- ments are safe.

3(a) Keep dispensers, water, and food clean and free of decay or disease. It is impor- tant to feed birds continually during harsh weather.

3(b) Maintain and clean nest structures regularly.

3(c) If you are attracting birds to an area, ensure the birds are not exposed to predatic from cats and other domestic animals, or dangers posed by artificial hazards.

4. Group birding, whether organized or impromptu, requires special care.

Each individual in the group, in addition to the obligations spelled out in Items #1 and #2, has responsibilities as a Group Member.

4(a) Respect the interests, rights, and skills of fellow birders, as well as those of peo- ple participating in other legitimate outdoor activities. Freely share your know edge and experience, except where code 1(c) applies. Be especially helpful to beginning birders.

4(b) If you witness unethical birding behavior, assess the situation and intervene if you think it prudent. When interceding, inform the person(s) of the inappropri- ate action and attempt, within reason, to have it stopped. If the behavior contin ues, document it and notify appropriate individuals or organizations.

Group Leader Responsibilities [amateur and professional trips and tours].

4(c) Be an exemplary ethical role model for the group. Teach through word and ex- ample.

4(d) Keep groups to a size that limits impact on the environment and does not interfere with others using the same area.

4(e) Ensure everyone in the group knows of and practices this code.

4(f) Learn and inform the group of any special circumstances applicable to the areas being visited (e.g., no tape recorders allowed).

4(g) Acknowledge that professional tour companies bear a special responsibility to place the welfare of birds and the benefits of public knowledge ahead of the co pany's commercial interests. Ideally, leaders should keep track of tour sighting document unusual occurrences, and submit records to appropriate organization

PLEASE FOLLOW THIS CODE— DISTRIBUTE IT AND TEACH IT TO OTHERS.

Additional copies of the *Code of Birding Ethics* can be obtained from: ABA, PO Box 6599 Colorado Springs, CO 80934-6599, (800) 850-2473 or (719) 578-1614; fax: (800) 247-332 or (719) 578-1480; e-mail: member@aba.org

This *ABA Code of Birding Ethics* may be reprinted, reproduced, and distributed without restriction. Please acknowledge the role of ABA in developing and promoting this code.

7/1/

INTRODUCTION

John and Thelma Dalmas and David W. Johnston

Virginia is a state remarkably rich in history and tradition. First settled by the English in 1607 at Jamestown, the area was prominent in colonial life. Major battles in the Revolutionary War and in the War between the States were fought on the Commonwealth's soil, and today many of these historic battlefield sites are preserved. Four of the first five U.S. Presidents came from Virginia. Plantations, some retained today by descendants of the original families, dotted the lower James River. Later, Richmond served as the capital of the Confederacy, and the graceful statues along Monument Avenue serve as reminders of that city's heritage. The state boasts many other historic sites, such as mansions and large plantations, some of which, not surprisingly, still have magnificent gardens and wild areas attractive to birds.

Unique natural features are scattered over the state and are notable tourist attractions. These include caverns (such as Luray, Endless, Shenandoah, Dixie), Natural Bridge, Natural Chimneys, waterfalls (such as White Oak Canyon, Apple Orchard, Great Falls), scenic drives (such as Colonial Parkway, Blue Ridge Parkway, Skyline Drive, Chesapeake Bay Bridge-Tunnel), Mount Rogers (the highest point in the state), Great Dismal Swamp, Seashore State Park, and numerous smaller attractions. Major rivers traverse or border the state: New, Roanoke, James, York, Rappahannock, and Potomac. They provide special riparian habitats for birds as well as waters popular for fishing, boating, canoeing, and birding.

GENERAL GEOGRAPHY AND TOPOLOGY

Virginia is fairly large, as eastern states go, covering approximately 40,000 square miles. A drive from the northernmost point on the Eastern Shore to western Lee County would cover a distance of well over 600 miles. Elevation ranges from sea level to 5,729 feet on Mount Rogers. In spite of a population of more than six million, Virginia still has sections with strong rural character. Away from the Northern Virginia and Tidewater urban centers, the state is largely agricultural. The state is broadly divided into three physiographic provinces, each of which contains geologic, edaphic (soil-related), and climatic features influencing the distribution of plants, birds, mammals, and other life-forms.

(Note: These physiographic provinces are not the same as the six regions in the birdfinding section of this book. The two types of categories actually overlap each other.)

Rob Simpson
Chincoteague National Wildlife Refuge—Black Duck Marsh with Loblolly Pines.

Coastal Plain - This province is bordered on the east by the Eastern Shore, the Barrier Islands, the Chesapeake Bay, and beaches of the Atlantic Ocean. The Chesapeake Bay, with its miles of shoreline, is one of the richest estuaries on earth and is home to a great variety of birds. From Smith Point at the mouth of the Potomac River southward, Chesapeake Bay waters are in Virginia. The Coastal Plain extends west to the Fall Line, which marks the boundary between the hard metamorphic rocks of the Piedmont and the sedimentary rocks of the Coastal Plain. Because of many rapids and falls on major rivers along the Fall Line, it has always been a natural barrier to sea-going vessels. Lying along the Fall Line are such cities as Alexandria, Fredericksburg, Richmond, and Petersburg. Soils are usually sandy, and (geologically speaking) this is the youngest portion of the state. Both oak/pine and southeastern evergreen forests are found here.

The configuration of the Coastal Plain and of the Eastern Shore is complex, providing a wide spectrum of habitats for birds. These include beach, dunes, dune forest, salt marsh, freshwater marsh, pine barrens, mixed forest, oak flats, juniper woodlands, and cypress swamps. Predominant in the dune forest are scattered live-oaks, Loblolly Pine, American Holly, and junipers.

Piedmont - This term literally means 'the foothills.' It is comprised of the area west of the Fall Line to the eastern flank of the Blue Ridge. The underlying rock is ancient, greatly metamorphosed, and heavily eroded. Much of the Piedmont is a mosaic of rolling farm land, small woodlots, and some extensive forested tracts, which are classified as oak/pine or mixtures of other deciduous types (oaks, hickories, Tulip Poplar, and others).

Mountains and Valleys - For the purposes of this book, we combine the Blue Ridge and Appalachian mountains, Shenandoah (Great) Valley, and Appalachian Plateau. The underlying rock of this area is highly variable, and geologists consider the mountains and valleys to be three or more geologic divisions. The rocks include the igneous granite of the Blue Ridge, sedimentary limestones of the Great Valley, and sandstones of the Appalachian coal region. Mountainous portions are generally covered with deciduous forests, whereas valleys are dominated by agricultural fields and woodlots. In mountainous sections an oak/chestnut forest once prevailed, but with the loss of the American Chestnut early in this century, the forests today are complex mixtures of deciduous trees, with hemlocks in moist ravines and remnants of spruce/fir forests on some mountain-tops.

Since early colonial times, settlers and their successors have drastically altered the Virginia landscape, from seacoast to mountains. Clearing and burning forests provided habitats for house sites and agricultural fields. Lumbering activities removed most of the original trees, so that existing forests, although perhaps classified as "mature," are nonetheless largely second-growth. Natural plant succession of abandoned farmland and fields has produced a patch-work of intermediate communities, from grasslands dotted with growing pines and junipers to pine-dominated woodlands to deciduous forests. Each of these forest and successional types has its own complement of bird species: Red-eyed Vireos, Scarlet Tanagers, and Black-throated Green Warblers in the older deciduous forests; Pine Warblers, Brown-headed Nuthatches, and Summer Tanagers in pine forests; Prairie Warblers, Eastern Towhees, and Indigo Buntings in overgrown fields; and Grasshopper and Field Sparrows and Eastern Meadowlarks in grasslands.

SOME ORNITHOLOGICAL HISTORY

In addition to its rich cultural, societal, and economic history, Virginia can boast a remarkable record of early natural history observations, including birds. Initiated first in the Jamestown area, the earliest published colonial bird records were those of George Percy (1607), Thomas Studley (1607), Capt. John Smith (1608, 1612), and William Strachey (1612). In most cases their bird reports were general—"divers other fowls," "swans, geese, duckes, and cranse," "divers sortes of Haukes." However, some of their bird names are easily recognizable—"blackbirds with crimson wings," "Osperayes," Mallards, and Wigeons. Strachey in particular gave early descriptions of the greenish "Parakitoes with forked tayles" and the "thousands of wood-pidgions," indicating the Carolina Parakeets and Passenger Pigeons, now gone forever from Virginia skies.

Further into the 17th century in colonial Virginia, other observers were more specific. Thomas Glover (1676) reported "Turkie Buzzards, Mockingbird, Red-bird, and Humming-bird." The Rev. John Clayton (1684-1686) added still others to the growing list of birds seen in the colony—"Kings-fisher, Barn Owl, Raven, Patridges, Blew-bird, and Snow-bird." He was one of the first naturalists to report in some detail avian behavioral traits, such as hummingbirds feeding on the "Honey" of flowers, Mockingbirds "imitating the Notes of all Birds that it hears," fishing-Hawks being pursued by eagles," and martins "constantly come thither upon the Tenth of March." The famous naturalist John Banister also mentioned many birds from 1678 to 1692 in his *Natural History*: Passenger Pigeons, "rivers & Creeks ...covered with swans, Geese, Ducks, & several other kinds of waterfowle."

In 1712 the Englishman Mark Catesby came to visit relatives in Virginia and stayed for seven years. While there, the wealthy planter/politician William Byrd II introduced Catesby to many of the common colonial birds, including a nesting Ruby-throated Hummingbird. Catesby returned to America (South Carolina) in 1724 and spent several years studying natural history as far south as Florida. Although he was principally interested in plants, his *Natural History of Carolina, Florida, and the Bahama Islands* (1731-1743) included birds, about 33 species of which he reported from his earlier stay in Virginia. These included American Kestrel, Killdeer, Chimney Swift, Northern Cardinal, and Dark-eyed Junco. Today, Catesby is remembered as the first to describe many of our common birds, including some from Virginia: Gray Catbird, Northern Mockingbird, American Redstart, and Baltimore Oriole.

When the dividing line between Virginia and North Carolina was surveyed in 1728, one of the party, William Byrd II, made some notes of birds seen along the boundary: Blue-winged Teal, Sandhill Crane, Ruffed Grouse, and Carolina Parakeet. His diaries written at his plantation along the James River reveal the presence there of Canvasback, Common Snipe, Northern Bobwhite, and other birds.

Early explorers into the western Piedmont (John Lederer, 1670), Blue Ridge Mountains and Shenandoah Valley (Thomas Batts, Abraham Woods, Robert Fallam, 1671; Alexander Spotswood, 1716), and the southwestern mountains (Thomas Walker, 1750) left few bird records of any note except for the ubiquitous Wild Turkey, the occasional flock of geese, and vultures. Much later, specific birds were observed in the southern and western mountains (Rives: Mountain Lake, 1886, and Whitetop Mountain, 1889; Harold Bailey, *Mountains of Virginia*, 1912). In these reports, the authors documented at high elevations breeding birds such as Winter Wren, Carolina (Dark-eyed) Junco, Chestnut-sided and Black-throated Blue Warblers, Golden-crowned Kinglet, Red-breasted Nuthatch, and Brown Creeper.

In 1787, Thomas Jefferson published *Notes on the State of Virginia*. Therein he included a list of 93 birds, these taken largely or entirely from Mark Catesby's famous book. Jefferson probably assumed that these birds also occurred in Virginia; in fact, he had personally observed many of them. To this list, Jefferson added 33 more, but some, such as "crane," "greatest grey eagle," and "squatting snipe," are not easily identifiable.

The famous ornithologist/artist Alexander Wilson, often called the "Father of American Ornithology," passed through Virginia in the winter of

1808-1809. President Jefferson received him warmly and took out a subscription to Wilson's new *American Ornithology*. While in the state Wilson made notes on "the towhe bird," "Great Carolina Wren," and "Ferruginous Thrush" (Brown Thrasher), and gained knowledge of other species at other seasons. Notable was his visit with Bishop Madison, President of the College of William and Mary, from whom he learned of the abundance of "soruses" (Sora) in nearby marshes.

In the 1830s and 1840s, another famous naturalist/artist, John James Audubon, also visited Virginia. He spent most of his time in Richmond seeking subscribers to his *Birds of America*. Apparently he painted no birds in Virginia, but he wrote that in the environs of Richmond he "had seen several Hum birds and heard the ever-pleasing notes of 'Sweet-William' from the Carolina Wren."

Toward the end of the 19th century, people became aware of rich birdlife at two specific sites, the Dismal Swamp and Cobb's Island. Traveling through or around the swamp in 1728, William Byrd II reported "Not even a Turkey-Buzzard will venture to fly over it." After several trips in the 1890s by ornithologists from the National Museum, however, it soon became clear that the swamp housed a large diversity of birds, from cormorants to eagles to Prothonotary and Swainson's Warblers. (Based in part on his observations in the swamp, Brooke Meanley published in 1971 the only definitive life-history study of the Swainson's Warbler.)

Following the publication of a list of breeding birds of Cobb's Island in 1876 by Harry B. Bailey, that island, a narrow sand-spit only five miles long and eight miles off the Eastern Shore, became the focus of some bird observations. For many years egg- and bird-collectors for the plume trade had ravaged the breeding sea birds of Cobb's Island, but pressures from the fledgling Audubon movement and others led to active protection of the birds by positioning Audubon wardens on the island. (By 1901 up to eight Audubon wardens were employed in protecting nesting colonies in the state.) So celebrated was the birdlife of Cobb's Island that the American Museum of Natural History in New York used the island as the site for its habitat exhibit of coastal breeding birds. (Since 1976, Bill Williams and his colleagues have monitored bird populations on this and other nearby barrier islands, where some species of gulls and terns have decreased, whereas Brown Pelicans have increased in numbers.)

The bird-protection movement grew, and within a few years Audubon field agents dotted the south, including Katherine H. Stuart in Virginia. Through her efforts, Virginia Audubon won specific legislation out of Richmond to protect the American Robin. This accomplishment, won in part by mobilizing a battalion of school children and presenting a petition in Richmond with 10,000 names, was no small feat at the time.

Meanwhile, in the late 1800s and early 1900s, both bird- and egg-collectors added important records. Among these collectors were William Palmer, who added or reported Scissor-tailed Flycatcher, Ruff, Wood Stork, and Bachman's Warbler, and Fred M. Jones, whose large egg collections contained

Rob Simpson
Shenandoah National Park—Central District—view into hollows.

valuable life history notes (nest heights, clutch sizes, distribution). During this same period ornithologists of the National Museum and the U.S. Biological Survey covered parts of northern Virginia as well as the District of Columbia. Many of their reports have appeared in several accounts of the birds of Washington, D.C., and vicinity.

In addition to Jefferson, at least one other President made a unique contribution to Virginia ornithology. Theodore Roosevelt had a hide-away near Charlottesville (Pine Knot) where he made a list of birds, including a sighting of a flock of Passenger Pigeons on May 18, 1907, one of the last reports of this now-extinct bird.

Although Jefferson listed birds found in the state, it was William Cabell Rives whose *Catalogue of Birds of the Virginias* (1890) was the first scientific attempt to list all birds in Virginia, approximately 305 species. Rives also introduced the concept of major faunal zones and birds associated with them. Then, in 1913, Harold Bailey's *Birds of Virginia* mentioned 170 species "that breed in the state," although the listings clearly did not include all of the state's breeding birds.

Local lists identifying birds at specific sites began to appear in the late 19th and early 20th centuries. These included Amelia County (1881, Percy Freke), Cobham (William C. Rives, 1884), Mountain Lake (Rives, 1886), Ashland (G. C. Embody, 1910), Montgomery County (Ellison Smyth, 1912), and Goochland County (Robert Williams, 1922-1923).

In 1929 the Virginia Society of Ornithology was founded at Lynchburg College by a handful of ornithologists. Its purpose was to gather all possible information on the distribution of birds in the state. Shortly thereafter, several well-known ornithologists led the way in making important observations from various parts of the state—John B. Lewis, Charles O. Handley, Sr., J. J. Murray, Sr., and Ruskin Freer, to mention a few. Their reports, many appearing in *The Raven*, the state's bird journal, greatly enhanced our knowledge of bird distribution at that time.

The ensuing years have witnessed the vast increase of serious bird students in the state, the growth of Christmas Bird Counts, co-ordinated banding (on the Eastern Shore in particular), the start of pelagic birding off the Virginia coast, and accessibility to sites only dreamt of by past ornithologists.

The state's list also grew. By 1931 a consolidated list from nine local regions totaled 279 forms. By 1938 the list of Virginia birds stood at 369 species and subspecies. In 1952, thanks to the meticulous documentation and research of J. J. Murray, Sr., the total number of full species was 343. Efforts of the Virginia Society of Ornithology produced two compilations (check-lists) in 1980 and 1987, respectively, the latter documenting the presence of 390 species. By 1999, the total number was 431.

VIRGINIA'S WEATHER

Virginia's climate is considered temperate, but depending on elevation and distance from the coast, annual temperatures can be extreme, from the hotter areas in the Coastal Plain to the cooler climate of the mountainous regions. Indicative of temperature ranges in the state is the length of the growing season, which varies from 135 days in the mountains to 178 days in the Shenandoah Valley to 250 days on the Coastal Plain.

Prevailing winds are generally from west to east, these bringing fronts that trigger summer rains and rapidly changing temperatures. Average annual rainfall is about 45 inches, varying according to season and topography. Heaviest amounts of rain are received on the Blue Ridge Mountains where the north-south orientation of the mountains intercepts the generally westerly airflow. In something of a rain-shadow, the northern Piedmont and Shenandoah Valley receive the smallest rainfall amounts.

Winter ushers in cold weather, often near or below freezing. In some years snowy spells are frequent and snow depths heavy; at these times access to prime birding areas in mountainous areas is usually restricted. But at these times "northern" birds can be found scattered over the state: Snow Buntings, Lapland Longspurs, Golden Eagles, Snowy Owls, Northern Shrikes (the latter two rare), and, in some years, erratic flocks of Evening Grosbeaks, Pine Siskins, and Common Redpolls. Mild winters in coastal areas can, and often do, present unusual bird finds: Cape May Warbler, Yellow-breasted Chat, Painted Bunting, and even a Rufous Hummingbird.

Spring can be dramatic in Virginia, with warm southerly breezes and pleasant temperatures. Early mornings may be cool, or even cold in the mountains, but by mid-day the temperatures rise to comfortable levels. As the deciduous trees begin to leaf out, migrating landbirds begin to search the forests for newly hatched insects, and, along the ocean beaches and water-ways, migrating waterfowl and shorebirds become abundant. The warmer weather and longer days seem to stimulate male song, territorial defense, and nesting activities.

Summer is a time of heat and humidity, as is true for other southern states. Combined with temperatures in the 90s in the middle of the day, summer humidity can be oppressive to birders almost anywhere in the state. At this time birders usually opt for early-morning hikes. Afternoon thunder-storms are both frequent and widespread, these often being accompanied by strong winds and lightning. By the end of summer, tropical storms and hurricanes may occasionally severely impact the state, especially in the coastal areas. Such storms bring heavy rains and strong onshore winds. They also bring unusual pelagic birds to Virginia, even far inland, where Black-capped Petrels and Sooty Terns have been recorded.

Fall is a delightful time to go birding. Although the occasional advancing cold fronts can bring cool and blustery weather, usually fall weather conditions are quite enjoyable. The famous fall foliage colors in the mountains peak around the first week of October, and fall flowers and migrating butterflies add to the ambiance of the season. This is the time when, of course, those "confusing fall warblers" challenge the best of the birders and when hawk-watching stations are in full swing.

BIRDS AND WHERE TO FIND THEM

Virginia's avifauna presently includes approximately 425 species. Of these, about 390 occur regularly and two have become extinct. Others are rare or considered to be hypothetical, i.e., observations of them lack sufficient documentation. Exclusive of pelagic species, approximately 60 species are permanent residents (found at all seasons somewhere in the state; most are known to breed); 75 are summer residents (found only or chiefly during migration and the summer months; breeding); 67 are chiefly found only in winter months; and 43 are transients or migrants. These numbers support the statement that Virginia can be an exciting state for birding at any season.

Some species (e.g., permanent residents) are more common in one physiographic province than in another (see the Annotated Checklist begin-ning on page 210). Numbers of individuals also may vary seasonally. For example, American Crows and mixed species of blackbirds apparently flock into the state in winter and occupy large roosts. Chipping Sparrows, on the other hand, although relatively common and widespread in summer, are much less common in winter when, we believe, most individuals migrate southward.

Spring and **fall** are the times when migrants flood through the state. Along the coastal areas, migrating shorebirds (plovers and sandpipers), larids (gulls and terns), and waterbirds (cormorants, ducks, and loons) can often be found in large numbers and in a great variety. Farther inland, migrating passerines (warblers, vireos, thrushes, and sparrows) begin arriving in April and tend to peak in numbers by the first or second week in May. Through the mountainous portions, peak migration is usually a week or two later. Frequently, on a "good day", 20 or more species of warblers have been found on a single morning in May. Migrants may include species that remain to nest or others, such as Bay-breasted and Blackpoll Warblers, that pass through the state on the way to more northerly breeding sites. In the autumn, so-called "confusing fall warblers" are particularly common, especially along migratory corridors such as the Eastern Shore. August and September are the best months for viewing the shorebird migration, whereas mid-September to October is the peak for passerines. The Broad-winged Hawk migration is best over the Blue Ridge during mid-September. Sharp-shinned Hawks reach highest numbers on the coast in October. (For details, see the chapter on Hawk-watching, beginning on page 198.)

Summer is the time to find nesting birds, these including the permanent residents as well as many migrants. Nesting activity for most species peaks from early to mid- June. This is the time that male warblers, tanagers, orioles, and other birds are in breeding plumage and advertise their territories with loud and beautiful songs. Once nesting is over, males sing much less often, parents tend to raising their young, and an annual molt begins. Toward the end of July and August when the weather is usually hot and humid, relatively little bird activity occurs; birds tend to be more secretive as they molt and move away from established territories. Then the fall migration commences as the Neotropical migrants head toward their tropical wintering grounds and other migrants move into more southerly states.

Winter is an exciting time for finding birds arriving from the north and west to spend the colder months in the state. Many waterbirds fall into this pattern: loons, grebes, ducks, geese, and swans. In fact, along the coast, in places such as the Chesapeake Bay and Back Bay National Wildlife Refuge, waterfowl concentrations are greatest at this time. But landbirds of a considerable variety also invade the state for the winter months: White-crowned and White-throated Sparrows, Yellow-rumped Warblers, American Pipits, and others. It is also at this time that several rarities have been observed: Iceland Gull and Snow Bunting, and very rarely, Snowy Owl and White-winged Crossbill, as well as many pelagic species. (See the chapter on Pelagic Birding, beginning on page 203.)

CHRISTMAS BIRD COUNTS

Between 45 and 50 Christmas Bird Counts are conducted in Virginia each year. They are somewhat evenly distributed over the three physiographic regions of the state. Fully 50% of today's counts have been conducted for at least two and a half decades, and six boast histories of more than 50 years each.

Nearly every conceivable habitat that the state has to offer is included in one count or another, with many counts held within or near major metropolitan areas, whereas others are conducted in distinctly rural settings. Participants on the coastal counts and on those bordering the Chesapeake Bay often enjoy mild weather conditions and routinely chalk up the highest species totals. Many unusual waterfowl, shorebirds, and gulls appear frequently in those areas, ensuring exciting birding. On the other end of the scale, difficult weather conditions and rugged terrain encountered on the mountainous counts provide unusual challenges for participants willing to hunt for the few species that winter in the harsh environment of the higher elevations.

Participants on other counts may find themselves enjoying the serene beauty of the Shenandoah Valley or meandering through the gently rolling hills of the Piedmont. A few counts are located at or near some of America's best-known historical sites, including Civil War battlefields, famous Revolutionary War locations, and old Indian and colonial settlements.

Approximately 1,000 people participate in the Virginia counts each year; they find a total of about 200 species statewide. Among the more unusual wintering birds which they record with some frequency are: American White Pelican, Ross's Goose, Eurasian Wigeon, Common and King Eiders, Harlequin Duck, Northern Goshawk, Golden Eagle, Marbled Godwit, Iceland, Lesser Black-backed, and Glaucous Gulls, Black Skimmer, Long-eared, Short-eared, and Northern Saw-whet Owls, Ash-throated Flycatcher, White-eyed and Blue-headed Vireos, Dickcissel, Lark and Le Conte's Sparrows, Lapland Longspurs, and Brewer's and Yellow-headed Blackbirds.

Information about individual counts at specific localities can be obtained by writing to the compiler listed in the current Christmas Bird Count issue of *National Audubon Society Field Notes* or in the latest edition of the VSO's journal, *The Raven*.

VIRGINIA BIRDING TRAIL

The Virginia Department of Game and Inland Fisheries has launched an exciting initiative designed to tie together many of the individual locations mentioned throughout this book, and nature-viewing sites, into a comprehensive *Virginia Birding Trail*. Related sites, organized into loops, are generally being designed to accommodate a three-day trip, but visitors may choose the length of time they wish to spend at any particular site and on the Trail. Maps will guide the visitor from one site to the next with descriptions of sites and their wildlife viewing opportunities. The Trail is a statewide project, with the first phase through eastern Virginia to be completed by 2001, and future phases to include a Mountain Trail through western Virginia and connecting Central Trails. Information about the Trail can be obtained from the Department's web site, www.dgif.state.va.us, or from the agency at 4010 W. Broad St., Richmond, VA 23230, (804) 367-4335.

EASTERN SHORE BIRDING FESTIVAL

Located on the southernmost tip of the Delmarva Peninsula, the Eastern Shore Birding Festival at Kiptopeke is an annual celebration of the fall migration of songbirds, raptors, and other birds. It has proven to be a major conservation and birding attraction in the mid-Atlantic states, and includes activities at the Eastern Shore of Virginia National Wildlife Refuge, Kiptopeke State Park, and cooperating privately owned lands. In previous years, the festival has been attended by some 2,000 people, with birders recording about 170 species annually. In recognition of the ecological, conservation, and educational significance of migrants in the region, the event is sponsored by the Eastern Shore of Virginia Chamber of Commerce with the help of the Virginia Society of Ornithology, The Nature Conservancy, the newly formed KESTREL (Kiptopeke Environmental Station; Research and Education Laboratory) Foundation, and numerous local, state, and federal agencies and organizations.

The Eastern Shore peninsula creates a geographic funnel which concentrates large numbers of south-bound migrants at the southern tip, at Cape Charles. This natural phenomenon provides excellent birding opportunities, from shorebirds and raptors to Neotropical migrant songbirds. In addition to scheduled field trips to a variety of Eastern Shore habitats, the Festival includes ongoing activities at the Kiptopeke Bird Banding Station and the Kiptopeke Hawk Observatory, located at the nearby state park. The Eastern Shore Birding Festival is also the site of numerous exhibits, workshops, guest speakers, and children's activities.

The Festival is held the first or second weekend in October at the Sunset Beach Inn located just north of the Chesapeake Bay Bridge-Tunnel. Additional information on the Festival, area lodging and reservations, camping, and restaurants may be obtained by contacting:

Eastern Shore of Virginia Chamber of Commerce,
   P. O. Box 460, Melfa, VA 23410
   757/787-2460

PUBLIC AREAS OF INTEREST TO BIRDERS

The State Parks

Virginia has some 28 state parks, 6 state historic sites, and 18 state natural areas. These are all under the jurisdiction of the Department of Conservation and Recreation. Although a principal purpose of these parks is to protect animals, plants, and natural communities, they also offer excellent opportunities for hiking, birding, and family gatherings. Most park facilities and services are operated on a seasonal basis. Campgrounds are found in 18 parks; housekeeping cabins of various sizes are found in 7 parks.

For camping and related information at the state parks, contact the following:

Virginia Department of Conservation and Recreation
    203 Governor Street (Suite 302), Richmond, VA 23219
    (804/786-1712) (800/933-7275 for reservations)

The following state parks are covered in this book: Kiptopeke (site #3), First Landing/Seashore (site #6e), False Cape (site #6g), York River (site #7d), Westmoreland (site #8b), Mason Neck (site #11b), Sky Meadows (site #14b), Lake Anna (site #15), Pocahontas (site #22a), Occoneechee (within site #24), Staunton River (site #25a), Staunton River Battlefield (Fort Hill)(site # 25b), Shot Tower (site #29), New River Trail (site #29), and Grayson Highlands (site #30c).

Virginia Department of Game and Inland Fisheries

VDGIF is the state's regulatory and management agency for all wildlife. It conducts programs for managing and protecting species and their habitats, for public education, and for recreational enjoyment of Virginia's wildlife resources. The department publishes a monthly magazine, *Virginia Wildlife*, which contains current information about birds and other wildlife. VDGIF serves as the state's lead agency in the Partners in Flight program with its efforts to protect nongame birds, their habitats, and their migratory pathways. For additional information about VDGIF, call 804/367-1000 and ask for the Nongame Wildlife Program.

The Commonwealth of Virginia has designated numerous Wildlife Management Areas which are managed by the Nongame Wildlife Program and are open to public hunting with a minimum of restrictions. As the name implies, the WMAs generally serve the purpose of preserving lands for wildlife management. Ostensibly they are managed for wildlife such as deer, turkeys, fishes, and natural vegetation. Forest management practices are also implemented to enhance wildlife habitats. These areas vary widely in their locations, their constituent habitats, and their flora and fauna. Some, such as the Thompson WMA in northern Fauquier County, are noted for their abundant crop of wildflowers, whereas others are known for waterfowl abundance. The WMAs provide myriad outdoor activities through the seasons, which often include hunting and fishing, hiking, camping, sightseeing, horseback riding, and birding. The WMAs also include some of the best birding sites in the state and are listed at the beginning of the book's six regions.

An excellent guide to all of the wildlife management areas, as well as other game department facilities, is available free of charge by writing to:

Virginia Department of Game and Inland Fisheries
    4010 West Broad Street, Richmond, VA 23230

National Wildlife Refuges

National Wildlife Refuges, managed by the U.S. Fish and Wildlife Service, serve several purposes. Most were established to protect and enhance wetlands for the conservation of migratory birds, whereas others provide essential habitats for endangered species. All seven National Wildlife Refuges in Virginia are found in the eastern part of the state. Each is covered in this book.

The "jewel in the crown" for birders is probably Chincoteague National Wildlife Refuge (site #1). It is one of the nation's most popular refuges because of its beauty and its wildlife diversity. It provides resting places for large numbers of migrating waterfowl, shorebirds, raptors, and landbirds. The Eastern Shore of Virginia National Wildlife Refuge (covered under site #3) is rapidly developing a reputation as a hot-spot, particularly during fall migration. (A nearby additional staging area for southbound migrants is Fisherman Island National Wildlife Refuge, to which access is gained only through pre-arranged tours.) Presquile National Wildlife Refuge (site #5c) consists of 1,400 acres of upland farm fields, tidal woodland, and marsh. It is known for its Bald Eagles and large numbers of wintering waterfowl. The Great Dismal Swamp National Wildlife Refuge (site #6b), located in Virginia's southeastern corner, is a 100,000-acre swampland, a unique ecosystem supporting a great diversity of plant and animal life. Back Bay National Wildlife Refuge (site #6f) abuts the Atlantic Ocean on one side and Virginia's Back Bay on the other. In the refuge are several thousand acres of fragile dunes, shrub communities, upland woods, bay habitats, marshes, and swamps. Mason Neck National Wildlife Refuge (site #11b) is a peninsula jutting into the Potomac River just 18 miles from Washington, D.C. It was originally set aside in 1969 under the federal Endangered Species Act to protect the Bald Eagle. The large acreage of woods, marsh, and shoreline includes one of the last large marshes remaining in otherwise urbanized and crowded Fairfax County.

Each of these refuges usually includes a visitors center, refuge literature (e.g., lists of birdlife), wildlife viewing sites, hiking trails, educational programs, hunting and fishing information, and directions to nearby food and lodging. The Fish and Wildlife Service is in the process of removing barriers to accessibility for disabled visitors. Additional information about these refuges can be obtained by writing to:

U.S. Fish and Wildlife Service, Region V,
    300 Westgate Center Drive, Hadley, MA 01035-9589.

National Park Service Areas

The following lands are under National Park Service jurisdiction and are covered in parts of this book: Assateague Island National Seashore (site #1), Jamestown Island National Historic Park (site #7b), Colonial Parkway (site #7e), George Washington Birthplace National Monument (site #8a), Dyke Marsh (along the George Washington Memorial Parkway) (site #10c), Great Falls National Park (site #12b), Shenandoah National Park (site #16), Blue

Ridge Parkway (site #26), and Mount Rogers National Recreation Area (Mount Rogers and Whitetop: sites #30a and #30b).

Some of these sites permit camping; others do not. Check the individual birdfinding site details for appropriate information.

National Forests

Both the 1.8-million-acre George Washington National Forest and the 575,000-acre Jefferson National Forest are located in Virginia's western mountains and valleys. They have extensive forest tracts and other habitats that attract a great variety of birds. Maps can be obtained by writing to:

George Washington National Forest and Jefferson National Forest
5162 Valley-pointe Parkway, Roanoke, VA 24019
540/265-5100

There are a few sites in the George Washington National Forest that are covered in this book. For example, Ramseys Draft and Shenandoah Mountain (site #19b) are in the George Washington National Forest, as are parts of the sites covered under Highland County (site #19a) and Lake Moomaw (site #20). Two sites are also in the Jefferson National Forest: Laurel Bed Lake (site #30d) and High Knob Recreation Area (site #32c).

Locations of campgrounds and other facilities in the state's National Forests may be obtained as follows: Jefferson National Forest Glenwood Ranger District (P.O. Box 10, Natural Bridge, VA 24579, 540/291-1759); Wythe Ranger District (155 Sherwood Forest Road, Wytheville, VA 24382, 540/228-5551); George Washington National Forest Pedlar Ranger District (2424 Magnolia Avenue, Buena Vista, VA 24416, 540/261-6105); Mount Rogers Recreation Area (Route 1, Box 303, Marion, VA 24354, 540/783-5196).

OTHER BIRDING OPPORTUNITIES

For those who prefer to do their birding exclusively on foot, many well-kept trails are scattered over the state; these often traverse excellent birding spots. The most popular of these is the Appalachian Trail, which winds through Virginia from Harpers Ferry south to the Mount Rogers area at the Tennessee border. In fact, nearly one-fourth of the 2,159-mile trail is in Virginia. For the most part the trail winds through forests and fields, most often in mountainous terrain. Many side trails lead to beautiful waterfalls, especially in Shenandoah National Park. For maps or other information about the Appalachian Trail, contact:

Appalachian Trail Conference
P. O. Box 807, Harpers Ferry, WV 25425-0807
304/535-6331

A number of other interesting birding sites are managed by The Nature Conservancy. Perhaps the most interesting is the Virginia Coast Reserve (site #2). The Conservancy manages over 25 other Preserves, and has cooperative projects and managed areas in about 50 locations. For information on TNC throughout the state, contact:

TNC Virginia Chapter
1233A Cedars Court, Charlottesville, VA 22903-4800
(804/295-6106)

Finally, some casual birding can be done from a bicycle (as, of course, it can be done from a canoe or other small boat). There are about nine rails-to-trails conversions in Virginia, including the 34-mile-long Virginia Creeper Trail in Abingdon, the 45-mile Washington and Old Dominion Railroad Trail in Northern Virginia (see site #9a), and the 57-mile linear New River Trail State Park, formerly the Cripple Creek Branch of the Norfolk and Western Railroad (site #29). Other biking/birding opportunities exist in the state, some of which are mentioned in this book. For more bicycling information, maps, and a copy of "Virginia, A Great Place to Bike" brochure, contact:

State Bicycle Co-ordinator
Virginia Department of Transportation ,
1401 E. Broad Street, Richmond, VA 23219

Virginia Society of Ornithology

Since its founding in 1929, the Virginia Society of Ornithology has broadened its purposes to encourage systematic studies of birds in the state, to stimulate interest in birds, and to assist in the conservation of wildlife and other natural resources. All persons interested in these objectives are welcome as members. Present membership includes every level of interest, from professional scientific ornithologists to enthusiastic amateurs.

Through its Records Committee (VARCOM), the VSO reviews observations of rare, unusual, and out-of-season birds for official acceptance on the state's list. In addition to passing information to the several bird-lines (see below), observers should send complete documentation of a sighting (including copies of sketches, field notes, and photographs) to VARCOM c/o the VSO office in Lynchburg. Forms specifically designed for this purpose are available from the VSO or the VARCOM chairman. Following committee review, the VARCOM will notify the observer of the committee's evaluation. Anyone seeking information about sightings of species in the state should contact the VSO office.

Local chapters of the VSO are geographically scattered over the state in some of the larger cities and towns. These chapters conduct their own programs of meetings, field trips, Christmas counts, and other projects. To find the current contact person for a local chapter and information about their local birding activities, write to the VSO, whose address is listed on page 275 of this book.

Augusta Bird Club, Staunton/Waynesboro, VA
Bristol Bird Club, Bristol, TN
Cape Henry Audubon Society, Norfolk, VA

Clinch Valley Bird Club, Tazewell, VA
Cumberland Nature Club, Wise, VA
Eastern Shore Bird Club, Accomac, VA
Fairfax Audubon Society, Vienna, VA
Foothills Bird Club, Martinsville, VA
Hampton Roads Bird Club, Newport News/Hampton, VA
Lynchburg Bird Club, Lynchburg, VA
Margaret H. Watson Bird Club, Farmville, VA
Marion Bird Club, Marion, VA
Monticello Bird Club, Charlottesville, VA
New River Valley Bird Club, Blacksburg, VA
Northern Neck of Virginia Audubon Society, Kilmarnock/White Stone, VA
N. Shenandoah Valley Audubon Society, Winchester/Strasburg/Front Royal, VA
Northern Virginia Bird Club, Arlington/Fairfax, VA
Richmond Audubon Society, Richmond, VA
Roanoke Valley Bird Club, Roanoke/Salem, VA
Rockbridge Bird Club, Lexington, VA
Rockingham Bird Club, Harrisonburg, VA
Virginia Beach Audubon Society, Virginia Beach, VA
Westmoreland Bird Club, Montross, VA
Williamsburg Bird Club, Williamsburg, VA

Those wishing to participate in any of the above groups, or in working to advance the objectives of the Society, are cordially invited to join. See pages 275-276 on the Virginia Society of Ornithology (with a membership form) at the end of this book.

Migratory Bird Conservation Program (Partners in Flight)

In recent years the plight of Neotropical migrant birds has attracted the attention of ornithologists, conservationists, and regulatory agencies all over the country. These birds breed in temperate North America and then migrate long distances to overwinter in the New World tropics, from Mexico to southern South America. In an effort to focus on species' declines and to work together on efforts to identify their causes and to promote appropriate management programs, a Neotropical Migratory Conservation Program (now an international project called Partners in Flight) was formed in 1990. Since that time, Virginia has been a participant in the program because 71% of the Neotropical migratory species in the state declined in numbers between 1980 and 1989. These include Black-billed Cuckoo, Golden-winged and Hooded Warblers, and many others.

Efforts are underway in the state to monitor bird populations and their habitats, to manage habitats for maximum biological diversity, and to educate the public on the need to conserve migratory birds. For further information on Partners in Flight and how you can help in these conservation efforts, contact:

Center for Conservation Biology,
  College of William and Mary, Williamsburg, VA 23187-8795
  804/221-1645

Virginia Department of Game and Inland Fisheries,
  Box 11104, Richmond, VA 23230-1104
  804/367-1000

Birding Ethics

Some of the most interesting birding areas in the state are not generally open to public access, but the agencies controlling these sites have usually let birders in. *Please observe the regulations governing the use of these facilities so that we will not wear out our welcome.* For example, if you want to stop on any of the three northernmost islands of the Chesapeake Bay Bridge-Tunnel, you must secure permission ahead of time and in writing. Craney Island Landfill is open only during weekdays, and areas of particular sensitivity will be roped off during the breeding season. Respect the barriers and give the rare and endangered species privacy and protection. Be judicious with the use of tape recorders. It should go without saying that birds restricted to only a few well-known spots, such as Swainson's Warbler in Great Dismal Swamp, should not be harassed by the playing of tapes. Respect private property and posted signs. The mountains of Virginia have been home to moonshiners for generations, and the last thing a birder wants to do is to stumble across somebody's still.

The American Birding Association has a "Code of Ethics." It is printed on pages *vii-viii.* You would do well to take this code to heart.

What to Wear Afield

Birders are known for their considerable individuality in clothing regardless of the weather and location. The general rule-of-thumb is to be comfortable, while maintaining the ability to locate, observe, and identify birds. Winter is an especially crucial time for appropriate cold-weather clothing. In coastal areas and along waterways, especially when the wind-chill factor is extreme, birders often resort to the use of telescopes from a car window.

The heat and humidity of summer demand loose-fitting clothing, except around the ankles, where protection against ticks and chiggers is highly recommended. Be prepared for an afternoon thunderstorm. It is often cool in the mountains, even in July and August, and a light jacket may be necessary in the evenings. If you plan to be out during the hunting season, a blaze-orange vest or hat is a good idea. Hunting is prohibited on Sundays.

Outdoor Pests

In part because of its relatively mild climate, Virginia has its share of plants and critters to avoid. Widespread over the state is Poison Ivy, to which many people are allergic. It is especially common along old roadsides, where the vines often grow in profusion along fence posts. One has to learn to recognize the leaves and simply avoid contact with any part of the plant. Another precaution is to wear long-sleeved shirts and long pants when walking in an area where Poison Ivy is growing. If you do happen to brush against this plant, rinse the affected portions of your anatomy with water as soon as possible; soap helps, too. Stinging Nettle is common is summer near seepages and springs in the mountains.

Mosquitoes can be a problem almost anywhere in the state except at high elevations. Particularly are they bothersome in wet areas. Again, covering arms and legs can help, but liberal use of a name-brand insect repellent is highly recommended. At times and in some places, ticks are pests frequently encountered by birders, especially in grassy areas and in places frequented by cattle, deer, and other mammalian vectors. In such areas, be sure to tuck your pants into your socks, and periodically examine your clothing for ticks. (Light-colored clothing makes the dark ticks easier to see.) When coming in from the field where ticks might be found, examine not only your clothing but also your body to detect any of these pests. (Usually the ticks are just an annoyance. However, watch for a "bulls-eye" blotch on your skin or the onset of fever after tick removal, both signs of possible Lyme disease. Under these circumstances you will want to consult a doctor. Early treatment avoids serious complications later.)

Virginia is far enough south to support a healthy population of chiggers. If you spend much time off the trail in the Coastal Plain or the Piedmont, take precautions or be prepared to scratch a lot.

Poisonous reptiles, such as Timber Rattlesnakes and Copperheads, although widespread over the state, are rarely encountered by birders. Of course, such snakes should be avoided, and birders should be careful where they tread. A good rule is never to put your hands or your feet into places that you cannot see first. Snake-bite can be treated in a variety of ways, but the best advice is to get the victim to medical assistance as soon as possible.

Virginia's Museums, Libraries, Colleges, and Universities

Local, regional, state, and college libraries can be tremendous resources for information about birds. In addition to maps, climatic data, books, popular and professional journals, and other publications, most libraries can help to find local bird experts and groups, as well as local parks or preserves where birding activities are conducted. Museums are also excellent sources of information on birds, especially in their public displays and educational materials. Many are scattered over the state. Try the Mountain Lake Biological Station, Virginia Museum of Natural History (Blacksburg), National Museum of Natural History (Smithsonian Institution, Washington, D.C.), National Wildlife Federation (Vienna), D. Ralph Hostetter Museum of Natural History (Eastern Mennonite College, Harrisonburg), Bedford City/County Museum (Bedford), Science Museum of Western Virginia (Roanoke), Virginia Living Museum (Newport News), and Virginia Marine Science Museum (Virginia Beach).

Many colleges and universities in the state offer courses dealing with birds and have faculty members who are trained in ornithology. These include the University of Virginia (Charlottesville), Bridgewater College (Bridgewater), Clinch Valley College (Wise), College of William and Mary (Williamsburg), Eastern Mennonite College (Harrisonburg), James Madison University (Harrisonburg), Lord Fairfax Community College (Middletown), Longwood College (Farmville), Mary Baldwin College (Staunton), Northern Virginia Community College (Annandale), Old Dominion University (Norfolk), Randolph-Macon Women's College (Lynchburg), University of Richmond (Richmond), Virginia Commonwealth University (Richmond), and VPI & State University (Blacksburg).

Where to Stay

You are never too far from food and lodging in Virginia. Once you get away from the major metropolitan areas, nationally known motel chains or five-star restaurants may be scarce. However, even the smaller towns usually have some type of tourist accommodations. We do have many excellent bed-and-breakfast establishments, but most of them require advance reservations. It would also be wise to plan ahead for accommodations during the summer months at popular resort spots, such as Chincoteague and Williamsburg.

Private, federal, state, and local campgrounds dot the state, and are often located near good birding areas. Especially during peak seasons, it is best to call ahead and make reservations. A list of many privately owned campgrounds can be obtained from the American Automobile Association (AAA); a partial list is included in the DeLorme atlas for Virginia.

For information about camping, cabins, and other activities in state parks and National Forests, see the previous pages (11-12 and 14) under those topics.

MAPS AND DIRECTIONS

General Information from the State

You can get an Official State Map, listing historic points of interest, parks, outdoor recreation resources, and other visitor information, as well as intelligible map details. These maps are available at Welcome Centers along the Interstates, at any Department of Transportation office, or by writing to:

Virginia Department of Transportation
1401 E. Broad Street, Richmond, VA 23219

You may also want a free copy of the *Virginia Travel Guide*, which includes information on accommodations, scenic attractions, festivals, and other events. It is available from:

Virginia Division of Tourism
Bell Tower, Capitol Grounds

P. O. Box 798, Richmond, VA 23219
(1-800/VISIT-VA)

DeLorme Virginia Atlas and Gazetteer

This is an invaluable guide for navigating through Virginia's state highway system. This handy and large-format paperbound book is available in many book and sporting goods stores, or can be ordered through:

DeLorme Mapping
P. O. Box 298, Freeport, ME 04032

Topographic Maps

For topographic maps of specific areas of interest, write to:

USGS Branch of Distribution
Box 25286, DFC, Bldg. 810
Denver, CO 80225

General Travel

For detailed information in an attractive format, with particulars on individual streams and parks, try the *ADC State Road Atlas of Virginia*. The ADC company also produces detailed individual county maps:

Alexandria Drafting Co.
6440 General Green Way, Alexandria, VA 22312
(1-800/ADC-MAPS)

WHAT TO DO IF.......

You see a rare or unusual bird or one out-of-season or out-of-place

First and foremost, while observing the bird(s) take copious notes on the location, date, and time, the bird's description (especially distinctive field marks), habitat, behavior, call notes or song, and any other information that was used in identifying the bird. Photographs and sketches should be made if possible. If possible, enlist the aid of another birder to confirm the identify of the bird.

Contact the "Virginia Birdline," which is the state's rare bird alert sponsored by the Virginia Society of Ornithology. You will hear a tape which is made weekly to disseminate rare bird information to Virginia birders and to birders from other states as well. Highlights include great birds seen throughout the state—with detailed directions for rare birds. Thanks go to all birders who call and leave bird sightings, field-trip details, or other general information for Virginia birders. Updates are made of the tape on Tuesday evenings, with special reports of "show-stopping" birds made on Fridays and Saturdays.

To report birds or listen to up-to-date statewide observations:
Voice—757/238-2713
FAX—757/238-9145

Hours—24 hours, 7 days

You can also listen to and make reports to "The Voice of the Naturalist," which is geared more toward the Mid-Atlantic region in general (301/652-1088). Both of these tapes will carry information about any upcoming pelagic trips, also.

When you dial the Virginia Birdline, birds of varying status will be reported, with preference given to the importance of the sighting, while also being limited somewhat by the length of the recorded announcement. A slow week may bring only reports of seasonal movements of birds. An exciting week may devote most of the tape to one rare bird. The Virginia Birdline is not part of the Virginia Records Committee. The function of the Birdline is to serve as a medium for the distribution of current bird sightings in Virginia.

Remember, all unusual birds that are out of place, out of season, etc., should be called in for the enjoyment of other birders. A report of a bird that *you* may see frequently but which may be of interest to others will be welcomed. You would be surprised at the birds needed by listers in the state and of the importance of out-of-place bird sightings. Don't be discouraged if your sighting doesn't get on the tape because of the presence of many other sightings and reports. The next time you call, it may be a slow week—and yours may be the *only* report. *A record is being kept of all calls, so it won't be a waste to report in. The basic request is to call!* This is the only way in which we can keep the Birdline fresh and current.

You find a sick or injured bird

Make an effort to get it to a licensed rehabilitator. Call the Wildlife Center of Virginia at Waynesboro: 540/942-WILD (staffed seven days a week, from 8-5 on weekdays, 8-4 on weekends). The Center (P.O. Box 1557, Waynesboro VA 22980) is one of the nation's leading teaching and research hospitals for native wildlife. In operation since 1982, the Center provides injured birds and other native wildlife with state-of-the-art veterinary care, free of charge, with the goal of returning the victims to the wild as soon as possible. In addition to outdoor environmental education workshops, the Center has an excellent referral service to rehabilitators strategically located all over the state.

You find a banded bird

Write down the bird's identification, sex and age, band number, its location, date, how it was recovered (e.g., dead, injured, shot, etc.). If possible, remove the band and have another person confirm the number. With this information in hand, either call the Bird Banding Laboratory at Laurel, MD (800/327-2263) or send the band and information to BBL, 12100 Beech Forest Road, Laurel, MD 20708-4037. Once the band recovery information has been processed by BBL, you will receive a Certificate of Appreciation and information as to where and when the bird was banded.

You find an injured or dead threatened or endangered species

Following is a list of state and federal threatened and endangered species. Contact the state (804/367-1000) or federal authorities (804/771-2883) with particulars about the bird, especially if its death might have been caused by a suspicious circumstance (shot, trapped, poisoned). Codes below indicate the following status: FE=federal endangered; FT=federal threatened; SE=state endangered; ST=state threatened.

Bald Eagle—FT
Peregrine Falcon—FE
Wilson's Plover—SE
Piping Plover—FT
Upland Sandpiper—ST
Gull-billed Tern—ST
Roseate Tern—FE
Red-cockaded Woodpecker—FE
Bewick's Wren—SE
Loggerhead Shrike—ST
Bachman's Warbler—FE
Kirtland's Warbler—FE
Bachman's Sparrow—ST
Henslow's Sparrow—ST

HOW TO USE THIS BOOK

In addition to the three major physiographic provinces identified at the beginning of this Introduction (Coastal Plain, Piedmont, and Mountains and Valleys), the state has been divided into six geographic birding areas in this book. For ease in locating good birding sites, the areas are as follows: (1) Eastern Shore, (2) Coastal Plain, (3) Northern, (4) Central, (5) Southern Piedmont, and (6) Southern Mountains and Valleys. Within each area are prime birding sites which have provided exciting bird records for many years and which are highly recommended to the interested birder.

Each of the birdfinding site descriptions is organized similarly. For each site there are details on the background, directions to the site (from major and minor roads), a map, habitat description, occurrence of the birds by season, any rarities found (sometimes even if they were found there just once or twice), and special comments on the birds or the site. For many sites (especially those away from obvious population centers) towns with nearby accommodations are listed. By examining the maps and the descriptions for each area, and depending on the time available, a birder can plan visits to sites to see the greatest variety of birds.

Following the birdfinding sites in this guide, you will find valuable sections on hawk-watching and pelagic birding in the state. An annotated list of Virginia's bird species follows, where you will find information on distribution and abundance. A listing of Virginia "specialties" and details for finding them concludes the major bird portion of this guide.

Additionally, for those interested in other animals of Virginia (butterflies, amphibians, reptiles, and mammals), there is a series of helpful listings following the bird "specialties."

SUMMARY

B ecause of its relatively mild climate, topography, and great variety of plant communities, Virginia boasts a high diversity of birdlife in nearly all seasons and in all sorts of habitats. For birders in Virginia, there is almost always some wonderful new location to visit and some fascinating bird to pursue. This can be a solitary pastime, or it can be one enjoyed with friends old and new.

Moreover, birders interested in the plight of the Neotropical migrant landbirds, or the parade of migrating raptors, can find immediate study subjects in Virginia. Censuses, breeding bird surveys, and other counts have helped to identify declining species, and conservation-minded birders and professionals are seeking appropriate management strategies.

Virginia has a promising future for birders. Each year new species are found in the state, especially in offshore waters; others can be expected. Ongoing studies of rare, threatened, and endangered species continue to pinpoint crucial requirements for successful breeding and survival. And, finally, a new ethic is developing among birders: a pro-active concern for the environment, addressing the effects of development and pollution on birdlife, educating the public, and involvement in decision-making processes that affect birds and other wildlife.

You can become a part of these birding possibilities; enjoy Virginia birdlife!

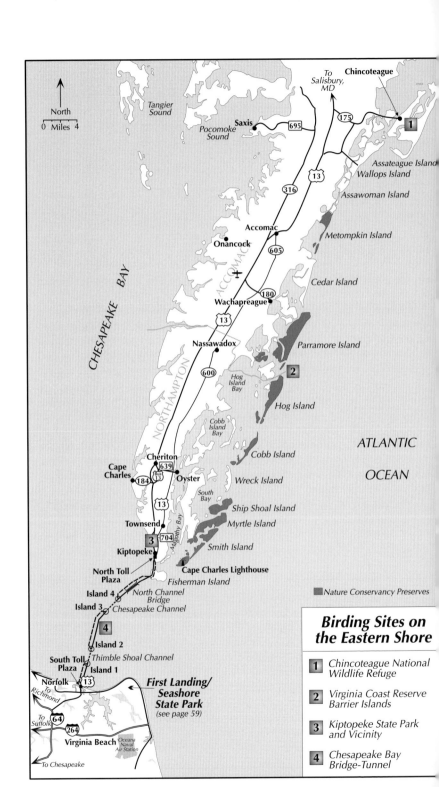

North

0 Miles 4

Tangier
Sound

To
Salisbury,
MD

Chincoteague

175

Saxis

695

Pocomoke
Sound

Assateague Island
Wallops Island

13

316

Assawoman Island

Metompkin Island

Accomac

Onancock

605

ACCOMACK

Cedar Island

180

Wachapreague

13

Parramore Island

Nassawadox

600

Hog
Island
Bay

NORTHAMPTON

Hog Island

Cobb
Island
Bay

ATLANTIC

Cheriton

639

Cobb Island

**Cape
Charles**

Bus
13

184

Oyster

Wreck Island

OCEAN

South
Bay

13

Ship Shoal Island

Townsend

704

Myrtle Island

Magothy Bay

Kiptopeke

Smith Island

**North Toll
Plaza**

Cape Charles Lighthouse

Island 4

North Channel
Bridge

Fisherman Island

Nature Conservancy Preserves

Island 3

Chesapeake Channel

Island 2

Thimble Shoal Channel

**South Toll
Plaza**

Island 1

Norfolk

13

*First Landing/
Seashore
State Park*
(see page 59)

To
Richmond

To
Suffolk

64

264

Oceana
Naval
Air Station

Virginia Beach

To Chesapeake

CHESAPEAKE BAY

*Birding Sites on
the Eastern Shore*

1 *Chincoteague National
Wildlife Refuge*

2 *Virginia Coast Reserve
Barrier Islands*

3 *Kiptopeke State Park
and Vicinity*

4 *Chesapeake Bay
Bridge-Tunnel*

EASTERN SHORE

The Eastern Shore is essentially the southernmost part of the Delmarva Peninsula, bordered on the east by the Atlantic Ocean and its barrier islands and on the west by the Chesapeake Bay. Although this region is flat, its soils and water-drainage systems have produced a wide spectrum of habitats for birds. These include fresh-water and salt-water marshes; pine, oak, and mixed forests; and extensive man-made cultivated fields.

Offshore, the Continental Shelf extends some 50 miles, to where upwellings from several deep-water canyons attract pelagic birds. The shallow inshore waters, receiving nutrients from the bordering land, are home to rich wetland and pelagic communities. Still farther offshore at about 100 miles is the Gulf Stream, which, with its warm waters, also attracts a variety of pelagic terns, shearwaters, petrels, phalaropes, and jaegers.

At the northern boundary with Maryland are the famous Chincoteague National Wildlife Refuge and Assateague Island, where birders from all over the country have spent countless rewarding hours studying the rich and varied birdlife at almost any time of the year. But peak migration times are best for seeing shorebirds (often in the many hundreds), several species of gulls and terns, waterfowl, herons, migrating hawks, and passerines. Brown-headed Nuthatches are permanent residents in the Eastern Shore's pine forests, and winter often produces Snow Buntings and Lapland Longspurs among the dunes. Also, some rare birds have been reported: Little Gull, Purple Sandpiper, Ruff, Western Kingbird, and Sage Thrasher, among others. Nearby marshes, including Saxis Marsh, are good places to look for Black Rails, Henslow's Sparrow, Sedge and Marsh Wrens, and Seaside and Saltmarsh Sharp-tailed Sparrows. From the beaches, birders are often rewarded with offshore sightings of sea ducks, alcids, loons, and gannets.

Inland and more southerly habitats have recently attracted the attention of birders and hawk-watchers, especially during fall migration. The recent establishment of Kiptopeke State Park and the Eastern Shore of Virginia National Wildlife Refuge, together with the annual Eastern Shore Birding Festival, brings large numbers of birders to these areas, where they scan the skies for raptors, the forests and shrublands for passerines, and the open fields for American Pipits, Snow Buntings, and American Golden-Plovers. Birders should also look for rare birds; Ash-throated Flycatcher, Le Conte's Sparrow, Northern Wheatear, and Black-headed Grosbeak have all appeared here in recent years, for example.

The offshore barrier islands, stretching from Assateague to Cape Charles, are accessible only by boat, and visits by birders and others are restricted by officials of the Virginia Coast Reserve. For more than a hundred years some of these islands have been renowned for their large colonies of nesting gulls, terns, and skimmers. In fact, during the 19th century wholesale slaughter of shorebirds and waterfowl on some of the islands ravaged several bird populations; most have since recovered. Along the sandy beaches and mudflats can be found Wilson's and Piping Plovers, many other shorebird species (especially during migration), Peregrine Falcons, and Merlins. Off-shore sightings have produced storm-petrels, jaegers, sea ducks, loons, gannets, and a variety of gulls and terns. The few forested and shrubby areas shelter Boat-tailed Grackles and migrating passerines. Rare birds seen from or on the islands include American White Pelican, Magnificent Frigatebird, shearwaters, and Dovekie.

One of the best birding spots in coastal Virginia is the 17-mile-long Chesapeake Bay Bridge-Tunnel. On certain islands, one can *(with prior permission)* delight in views of sea ducks (Oldsquaws, scoters), gulls, terns, mergansers, loons, gannets, and storm-petrels. The small islands with their grassy strips and rocky shores should be checked for migrating passerines and shorebirds. It is here that birders have been rewarded with views of Purple Sandpiper and a large variety of small passerines (including such surprises as a rare Rock Wren or a Le Conte's Sparrow).

MORE INFORMATION:

General Information

Chincoteague Chamber of Commerce Visitors Center
P.O. Box 258, Chincoteague, VA 23336
757/336-6161

Eastern Shore of Virginia Chamber of Commerce
P.O. Box 460, Melfa, VA 23410
757/787-2460

Wildlife Management Areas

Mockhorn Island: an island of 9,400 acres containing tidal salt-marsh and high-land habitats, 6 miles east of Cape Charles, Northampton County.

Saxis: 5,775 acres of tidal marsh interspersed with forested hammocks, 13 miles southwest of Pocomoke City, MD; Accomack County. (Details under site #1.)

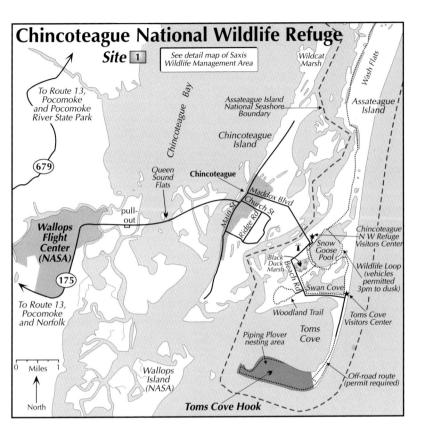

Chincoteague National Wildlife Refuge

Site 1

See detail map of Saxis Wildlife Management Area

To Route 13, Pocomoke and Pocomoke River State Park

Chincoteague Bay

Wildcat Marsh

Wash Flats

Assateague Island National Seashore Boundary

Assateague Island

Chincoteague Island

679

Queen Sound Flats

Chincoteague

pull-out

Maddox Blvd

Church St

Ridge Rd

Main St

Wallops Flight Center (NASA)

175

To Route 13, Pocomoke and Norfolk

Black Duck Marsh

Beach Rd

Snow Goose Pool

Swan Cove

Chincoteague N W Refuge Visitors Center

Wildlife Loop (vehicles permitted 3pm to dusk)

Toms Cove Visitors Center

Woodland Trail

Piping Plover nesting area

Toms Cove

Wallops Island (NASA)

Off-road route (permit required)

0 Miles 1

North

Toms Cove Hook

Site 1.
CHINCOTEAGUE NATIONAL WILDLIFE REFUGE,
Accomack County

BACKGROUND: Chincoteague National Wildlife Refuge, established in 1943, is the 13,682-acre Virginia portion of Assateague Island, which extends north into Maryland. (The entrance fee of $4 is good for multiple entry for four days; the hours are 6 am to 6 pm or 8 pm, depending on the time of year. Seniors age 62 or older can purchase a Golden Age Passport, good for admission to all National Wildlife Refuges for life, for $10.) The entire barrier island is part of Assateague Island National Seashore (757/336-6577). The nearby town of Chincoteague, once a quaint fishing-village, has adjusted to accommodate the demands of a burgeoning tourist trade. There are several comfortable motels and a number of fine seafood establishments. The unspoiled refuge beach is heavily used by tourists from late spring through the fall. For more information contact the refuge at 757/336-6122 or write Chincoteague National Wildlife Refuge, P.O. Box 62, Chincoteague, VA 23336.

ESSENTIALS: From the intersection of US-13 and Route 175, drive east on Route 175 for 10.4 miles into the town of Chincoteague. At the first traffic light after the last bridge, turn left onto Main Street. Proceed north for four blocks and then turn right onto Maddox Boulevard. The refuge is located 2.1 miles eastward.

HABITATS: Pristine Atlantic barrier beach, freshwater impoundments, tidal saltmarshes, and upland deciduous and Loblolly Pine forests are available.

BIRDS:

Spring: Numerous migrants, especially waterfowl, shorebirds, and passerines, are present. Locally breeding birds are arriving, including gulls (Herring, Great Black-backed, and Laughing), terns (Gull-billed, Common, Forster's, Royal, Sandwich, and Least), herons (Great Blue, Little Blue, Tricolored, Green, and Black-crowned and Yellow-crowned Night-), egrets (Great, Snowy, and Cattle), and Glossy Ibis. Look for Clapper Rails and American Oystercatchers and offshore flocks of Red-breasted Mergansers and scoters. Shorebird migration is best from mid- to late May.

Black Rail
Ali Wieboldt

Adrian R. Davis
Dunes typical of Assateague National Seashore.

Summer: Locally breeding gulls, terns, herons, egrets, and ibis are numerous. Breeding waterfowl, such as Gadwall, American Black Ducks, and Mallards, are present. Although peak shorebird migration occurs in August, late June and July can be excellent times for some of the rarer species, such as Ruff and Curlew Sandpiper. Hudsonian and Marbled Godwits, Wilson's Phalaropes, American Golden-Plovers, Buff-breasted Sandpipers, Baird's Sandpipers, American Avocets, and Black-necked Stilts are specialties. Look for White Ibis, an irregular late summer visitor. Black Terns often hover above the impoundments in July and August.

Fall: Passerine migration includes numerous warblers, especially along the Nature Trail and on the brush and tree edges along the west side of Snow Goose Pool. Sparrow flocks should be gleaned for Lark and Clay-colored Sparrows. Shorebird migration continues strong. Many migrant gulls and terns are present to complement post-breeding wandering herons, egrets, and ibises. The entire area is excellent for migrating diurnal raptors, especially Sharp-shinned and Cooper's Hawks. Flights of Peregrine Falcons and Merlins are strong in late September and early October. Sometimes Fulvous Whistling-Ducks, in variable numbers, stop here. By walking the Wildlife Drive in September and October, you may be rewarded with such passerine specialties as Connecticut Warbler and Philadelphia Vireo.

Winter: Many types of waterfowl, especially Snow and Canada Geese and Brant, can be expected in the impoundments. Both Red-throated and Common Loons are easily seen in Tom's Cove. A feral population of Mute Swans is present throughout the year. Wintering shorebirds, herons, and egrets should be looked for. Brown-headed Nuthatches are permanent residents in the larger pines. Snow Buntings and Lapland Longspurs may be found in the dune/beach areas. Alcids, jaegers, and white-winged gulls (Glaucous and Iceland) are possible, as are rare ducks (e.g., Eurasian Wigeon), American White Pelicans, and Peregrine Falcons. Many ducks (scoters, Oldsquaws, and Red-breasted Mergansers) and Northern Gannets can be seen from the beach.

RARE OR UNUSUAL BIRDS: Brown Booby, Little Egret, Reddish Egret, White-faced Ibis, Ross's Goose, White-cheeked Pintail, Purple Gallinule, Sandhill Crane, Bar-tailed Godwit, Ruff, Curlew Sandpiper, Mountain Plover, Sharp-tailed Sandpiper, Long-billed Curlew, Red Phalarope, Long-tailed Jaeger, Sabine's Gull, Elegant Tern, White-winged Tern, Sooty Tern, Thick-billed Murre, Gray Kingbird, Northern Wheatear, Sage Thrasher, Sprague's Pipit, Northern Shrike, Chestnut-collared Longspur, Yellow-headed Blackbird, and Snowy Owl.

SPECIAL COMMENTS: This is a principal stop-over site for many waterfowl, raptors, shorebirds, and passerines and is a very popular tourist location. The 3¼-mile Wildlife Drive loop road is available for driving after 3 pm each day. At other times it is open to bicycle and pedestrian traffic, and birds are easily viewed there. (You can rent bikes at a number of establishments in town.) This Wildlife Drive provides access to impoundments, including Swan Cove and Snow Goose Pool, which may be full of shorebirds, waders, or waterfowl, depending upon the season. Tom's Cove Hook is *closed* from March 15 to August 31 to protect nesting Piping Plovers. (Recently about 24 pairs have nested there. Sometimes, accessible individuals are observed during the nesting season on the east side of Tom's Cove or after the Hook is opened in early September.) The Wash Flats can yield excellent shorebirds and raptors in the fall. Access is by an arduous hike or via commercial tours (Assateague Island Tours: 757/336-6155). Finally, be sure to check the Bird Sightings clipboard at the visitors center (restrooms) for up-to-date reports on rarities.

Upon approaching or leaving Chincoteague on Route 175, you might consider pausing at the Wallops Flight Center (NASA). Here, behind security fences you can scan for Whimbrels and "grasspipers" in season. There may be Upland Sandpipers in mid-summer.

Stopping on either side of Queen Sound can be productive. A paved road spur and pull-out to the south offers parking and views of oyster bars good for shorebirds such as American Oystercatchers, dowitchers, and Willets. On the east side of the sound and north of the Queen Sound bridge are nearby flats favored by Dunlin, American Oystercatchers, Black-bellied Plovers, and other shorebirds. *Parking on the grassy shoulders here is not recommended, and may result in ticketing by police.*

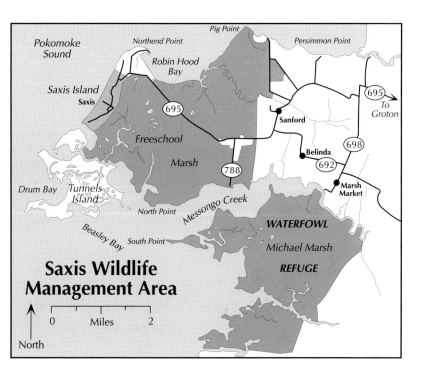

A trip to Chincoteague can often be enhanced by visiting Saxis Marsh to the west (see also map on following page). From the US-13 and Route 175 intersection, proceed south on US-13 for 3.6 miles, then turn right to follow Route 695 (Saxis Road) westward for 8.2 miles as it winds to the Saxis Wildlife Management Area. The road reaches the town of Saxis in an additional 2.7 miles (pull-offs can be hard to come by along this stretch) and ends on Pokomoke Sound 1.1 miles thereafter. In various places, in the marshes around the fishing-village of Saxis, Black Rails can be heard during May and June (*please avoid using tapes*). Less reliable but often present are, occasionally, Sedge Wren and, sparingly, Henslow's Sparrow. Virginia Rail and Marsh Wren are common. During winter Rough-legged Hawks and Short-eared Owls are often evident.

Bill Williams, Henry T. Armistead

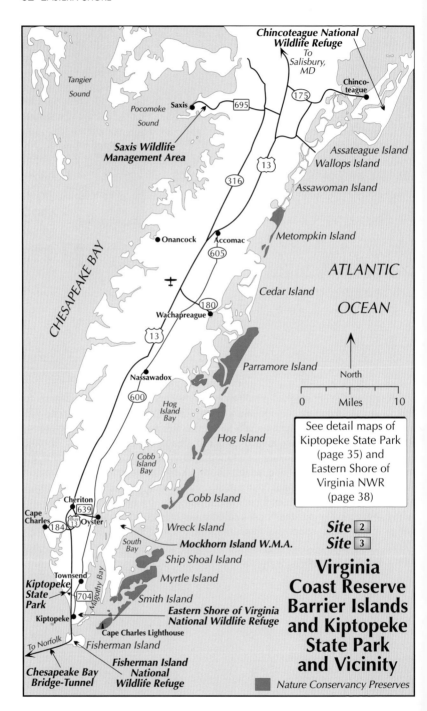

Chincoteague National
Wildlife Refuge
To Salisbury, MD

Chinco-teague

Tangier Sound

Pocomoke Sound

Saxis

695

175

Saxis Wildlife
Management Area

Assateague Island
Wallops Island

Assawoman Island

13

316

Onancock

Accomac

605

Metompkin Island

CHESAPEAKE BAY

ATLANTIC

Cedar Island

OCEAN

180

Wachapreague

13

Parramore Island

North

Nassawadox

600

Hog Island Bay

0   Miles   10

Hog Island

See detail maps of
Kiptopeke State Park
(page 35) and
Eastern Shore of
Virginia NWR
(page 38)

Cobb Island Bay

Cheriton

639

Cape Charles

184

Bus 13

Oyster

Cobb Island

Wreck Island

Mockhorn Island W.M.A.

South Bay

Ship Shoal Island

Myrtle Island

Site 2

Site 3

Townsend

704

Magothy Bay

Smith Island

Eastern Shore of Virginia
National Wildlife Refuge

Kiptopeke State Park

Kiptopeke

Cape Charles Lighthouse

To Norfolk

Fisherman Island

Chesapeake Bay
Bridge-Tunnel

Fisherman Island
National
Wildlife Refuge

Virginia
Coast Reserve
Barrier Islands
and Kiptopeke
State Park
and Vicinity

Nature Conservancy Preserves

Site 2.
THE VIRGINIA COAST RESERVE BARRIER ISLANDS,
Accomack and Northampton Counties

BACKGROUND: The Virginia Coast Reserve was formed by The Nature Conservancy in the early 1970s and subsequently was designated as an International Biosphere Reserve for the protection of shorebirds. The reserve encompasses all or part of 13 barrier islands, covers some 45,000 acres, and constitutes the least-altered barrier-island/lagoon complex along the east coast of North America. Several of the islands once had thriving human communities, but none currently does. The area's physiography is highly susceptible to storm damage.

ESSENTIALS: The barrier islands are accessible only by boat from ramps along the mainland of the Eastern Shore. Motorized vehicles, overnight camping, and pets are *not* permitted on any of the islands; a few of the islands are closed to the public altogether. Moreover, because of tricky shoals, shallow waters, and the presence of breeding endangered and threatened species of birds, those birders desiring to visit the islands are urged to contact the Virginia Coast Reserve, P. O. Box 158, Nassawadox, VA 23413 (757/442-3049) and make arrangements to join a group tour.

HABITATS: Atlantic barrier island beaches and tidal inlets stretch for more than 50 miles. Bounded on the east by open ocean and on the west by extensive tidal salt marshes, each island offers different habitats, from dunes and swales to shell-cobbled beaches to deciduous and mostly Loblolly Pine forests. Several islands have shallow freshwater impoundments. Most of the islands are sparsely to extensively covered with shrub thickets.

BIRDS:

Spring: Migrating waterfowl become plentiful over the ocean early in the period, especially loons, Double-crested Cormorants, Brant, and sea ducks. Great Cormorants have become regular, and Brown Pelicans are now common on the more southern islands. Early shorebird migration is under-way by April, when large flocks of Whimbrel, Dunlin, Black-bellied and Semipalmated Plovers, and Short-billed Dowitchers can be found on the mudflats. There will also be some Marbled Godwits. Late in the period Red Knots are often abundant on the beaches. Locally breeding gulls (Herring, Great Black-backed, Laughing) and terns (Royal, Sandwich, Caspian, Forster's, Common, Gull-billed, Least) increase throughout the period. Herons, egrets, and ibises begin to establish nesting colonies. These include Great Blue, Little Blue, Tricolored, and Green Herons; Black-crowned and Yellow-crowned Night-Herons; Great, Snowy, and Cattle Egrets; and Glossy Ibis.

Summer: Breeding activity for gulls, terns, skimmers, herons, egrets, and ibises peaks by mid-June. White Ibises are rare nesters. Wilson's and Piping Plovers nest in scattered locations. Shorebird migration begins in early July and increases through August. American Oystercatchers are widespread breeders. Wilson's Storm-Petrels are often seen in inlets or just offshore.

Fall: Shorebird migration remains strong. Raptor and passerine flights may be spectacular in late September and early October. Many gulls, terns, and herons are present. Waterfowl begin to arrive by late October. Birders may find jaegers, Little and Black-headed Gulls, and Black-legged Kittiwakes among the numerous Bonaparte's Gulls in late fall and winter.

Winter: Horned and Red-necked Grebes, all three scoters, Oldsquaws, and Red-breasted Mergansers are common off the beaches. Harlequin Ducks and both Common and King Eiders are possible. Red-throated and Common Loons frequent the inlets and the open ocean. Bonaparte's Gulls can be numerous, and Glaucous and Iceland Gulls should be looked for. In the dunes look for Snow Buntings and Lapland Longspurs as well as Short-eared Owls. Clapper Rails are common in the marshes. The extensive mudflats are excellent for Dunlins, Black-bellied Plovers, Willets, Marbled Godwits, Whimbrels, and American Oystercatchers. Merlins are often seen cruising the dunes and thickets.

RARE OR UNUSUAL BIRDS: American White Pelican, Brown Booby, Magnificent Frigatebird, Anhinga, Sooty and Greater Shearwaters, Snowy Plover, Long-billed Curlew, South Polar Skua, Sooty Tern, and Dovekie.

SPECIAL COMMENTS: Between April 1 and August 15 numerous colonial and beach-nesting species, some of which are threatened or endangered, occupy specific and fragile habitats here. *Birders must avoid visiting the islands during the nesting season.*

Bill Williams

Clapper Rail
Georges Dremeaux

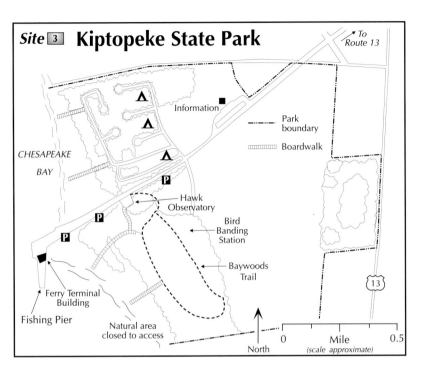

Site 3 Kiptopeke State Park

To Route 13

Information

Park boundary

Boardwalk

CHESAPEAKE BAY

Hawk Observatory

Bird Banding Station

Baywoods Trail

Ferry Terminal Building

Fishing Pier

Natural area closed to access

0   Mile   0.5

North   (scale approximate)

13

Site 3.
KIPTOPEKE STATE PARK AND VICINITY,
Northampton County

(See also the map on page 32.)

BACKGROUND: Formerly the north terminus for the ferry that traveled from Norfolk to the Eastern Shore, Kiptopeke was saved from development and dedicated as a state park (fee; 757/331-2267) in June 1992. The 375-acre site offers a full-service campground, hiking trails, a fishing pier, a boat ramp with ample parking, and a beautiful Chesapeake Bay beach. In the fall, volunteers operate songbird and hawk banding stations, and a platform is available for viewing migrating hawks and other birds. Avian studies have been conducted at this site since 1963.

The Kiptopeke area also serves as a major center for the Eastern Shore Birding Festival every October. (See the details on page 11.)

Included here are excellent birding side-trips. These are all within a nine-mile-radius circle with the lower end of Fisherman Island being on the south and Kiptopeke being the major component and center:

Eastern Shore of Virginia National Wildlife Refuge: Turn east just north of the toll plaza for the Chesapeake Bay Bridge-Tunnel. Opened in

1984 (it used to be a small military base), this refuge is an excellent location for coastal landbird migrants, provides a fine location for hawk-watching, is perhaps the most reliable place in the state for Western Kingbird, and can have large concentrations of American Woodcock in the late fall (found usually after a cold snap). In winter Saltmarsh Sharp-tailed, Nelson's Sharp-tailed, and Seaside Sparrows are found along the extensive marshes on the east side of the Peninsula, including the Eastern Shore of Virginia National Wildlife Refuge. For a selection of herons, ducks, and rails, try two ponds on the refuge. One is behind the headquarters; the other is on the southeast edge of the refuge off Ramp Road. (For details: Eastern Shore of Virginia National Wildlife Refuge, 5003 Hallett Circle, Cape Charles, VA 23310; 757/331-2760.)

Oyster: From the town of Cheriton off Business US-13 (South Bayside Road), take Sunnyside Road to the end (2.9 miles). This is a charming old waterman's town. By walking along the shell road at the northeast end of Oyster you can have views of tidal mudflats, saltmarsh, and open water. Look for shorebirds, gulls, terns, egrets, and herons here in the fall. You can also get to the north side of the Oyster harbor via Crumb Hill Road (found 2.4 miles along Sunnyside); take Crumb Hill Road 0.7 mile to the harbor. In winter around Oyster you may pick up Marbled Godwits (present from October to March), both yellowlegs, Western Sandpipers, and Willets. Wintering Saltmarsh Sharp-tailed and Seaside Sparrows are common at Oyster harbor.

Townsend: By driving Route 600, parallel to US-13 and just east of Kiptopeke, observers may be rewarded during checks for perched birds on the wires. You can also access Magothy Bay at a few spots east and south of the village of Townsend and pick up many of the same birds as those found in the Oyster area.

Fisherman Island National Wildlife Refuge: A major nesting area for terns (one of the largest colonies of Royal Terns in the state is found here), herons, Brown Pelicans (the first nesting colony in the state started here in 1987), and American Oystercatchers, this refuge is administered by the Eastern Shore of Virginia National Wildlife Refuge. The refuge is accessible *by special arrangement only* from October to January. It is reached from south of the toll plaza on the CBBT. (See the section on the Chesapeake Bay Bridge-Tunnel.)

ESSENTIALS: Kiptopeke State Park is located 3.3 miles north of the north toll plaza of the Chesapeake Bay Bridge-Tunnel. Traveling north on US-13, turn left onto Route 704, Kiptopeke Drive. (Take the SECOND break in the median—the first one is one way coming out of Route 704.) Go approximately 0.5 mile to the park entrance. The directions to other nearby birding locations are explained above.

HABITATS: The state park offers over 4,200 feet of Chesapeake Bay shoreline. Several miles of trails pass through early-stage-succession decidu-ous forest, magnificent mature primary and secondary dunes, and several hundred acres of fallow and cultivated fields. A large brush-pile is maintained

Rob Simpson
Saltmarsh Cordgrass typical of Cape Charles.

near the fields to attract birds. Near the main highway is a 2-to-3-acre ephemeral freshwater pond.

BIRDS:

Spring: Migrating waterfowl are often abundant on the Bay. The woods and fields should be searched for migrant songbirds. Along the beach look for passing shorebirds, such as Willets, Whimbrels, Sanderlings, and Dunlins. Laughing Gulls will be returning to the area along with Black Skimmers and Common, Gull-billed, Least, Royal, and Forster's Terns. Brown Pelicans will be seen fishing over open water. Overhead watch for migrant raptors, herons, egrets, and ibises. Mississippi and Swallow-tailed Kites have been seen in the area in April and May.

Summer: The Eastern Shore is home for numerous nesting gulls, terns, herons, egrets, ibises, and Brown Pelicans. These species regularly pass along the Bay shore and over the park as they travel to and from nesting sites on the Atlantic side of the peninsula. Red-headed Woodpeckers and Common Nighthawks nest near the campground. Chuck-will's-widows should be listened for in the woodland areas. Both Bald Eagles and Ospreys nest at or near the park.

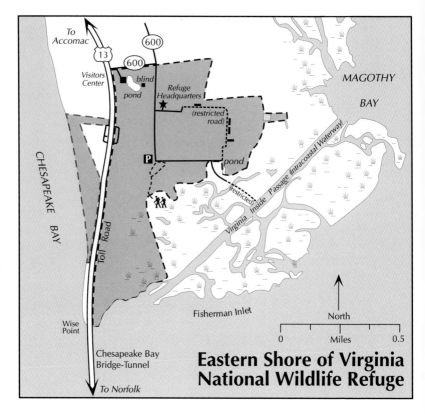

Fall: The park is perfectly situated for observing the dramatic and often overwhelming passage of migrating warblers, vireos, thrushes, swallows, woodpeckers, diurnal birds of prey, waterfowl, and shorebirds which concentrate on the lower peninsula from August through November. One may witness tens of thousands of migrant passerines in a matter of hours at this site and at the same time see several thousand raptors. Early morning flights of songbirds flying *north* may contain hundreds of Eastern Kingbirds, Northern Flickers, Blue Jays, warblers of many species, Baltimore Orioles, Cedar Waxwings, American Robins, and blackbirds. American Kestrels, Sharp-shinned and Cooper's Hawks, Ospreys, and Northern Harriers are daily migrants here by mid-September. Merlin and Peregrine Falcon flights in late September can result in 10-20 birds per hour on some afternoons. In some years Northern Saw-whet Owls are common. Nearby plowed fields should be scanned for American Golden-Plovers and Buff-breasted and Upland Sandpipers. In October, look for scarce visitors, such as Yellow-headed Blackbird, Dickcissel, Lark, Lincoln's, and Clay-colored Sparrows, and Western Kingbird. Early November may prove to be the most rewarding time of year for rarities and scarce visitors.

Winter: The fields offer numerous opportunities for wintering raptors, sparrows, juncos, American Pipits, and Snow Buntings. In the woodland areas, look for American Woodcocks, Red-headed Woodpeckers, Red-breasted Nuthatches, Hermit Thrushes, and Palm and Orange-crowned Warblers. Great Horned Owls and Eastern Screech-Owls are resident. Long-eared and Northern Saw-whet Owls are sometimes found in the dense pine stands on the east side of the Cape. The Chesapeake Bay should be searched for all three scoters, Oldsquaws, Red-breasted Mergansers, Northern Gannets, and Bonaparte's Gulls. Great Cormorants may be found on the fish-net poles. Red Crossbill is infrequently observed during winter. It is worthwhile to check the plowed fields for flocks of Horned Larks and American Pipits because these groups often include a Snow Bunting or a Lapland Longspur. Brown-headed Nuthatches, although present, are in serious decline here.

RARE OR UNUSUAL BIRDS: Pacific Loon, American White Pelican, Anhinga, Fulvous Whistling-Duck, Greater White-fronted Goose, Sandhill Crane, Northern Goshawk, Swainson's Hawk, Golden Eagle, Long-eared Owl, Northern Saw-whet Owl, Western and Gray Kingbirds, Ash-throated and Olive-sided Flycatchers, "Western" (Pacific-slope or Cordilleran) Fly-catcher, Say's Phoebe, Black-capped Chickadee, Northern Wheatear, Black-headed Grosbeak, Dickcissel, Henslow's, Le Conte's, Lark, Clay-colored, and Lincoln's Sparrows.

SPECIAL COMMENTS: During the fall bird-banding season, visitors are asked to restrain from interfering with the banding operations. Banding usually takes place from the Labor Day weekend through October. Over 250,000 birds have been banded here since 1963. Visitors to the hawk-watch are asked to keep in mind that the work being done requires much intense scanning and concentration to maintain accuracy. Check the section on hawk-watching at the end of this book, for hints on hawk-watching techniques and seasonal abundance.

Bill Williams

Site 4.
CHESAPEAKE BAY BRIDGE-TUNNEL ISLANDS,
U.S.Highway 13

BACKGROUND: Opened in 1964 and still the world's largest bridge-tunnel complex, the Chesapeake Bay Bridge-Tunnel (CBBT) crosses the mouth of the Chesapeake Bay and connects the city of Virginia Beach with Virginia's Eastern Shore. Officially named, in 1987, the "Lucius J. Kellam, Jr., Bridge-Tunnel" after a Virginia Eastern Shore businessman and civic leader, the 17.6-mile complex includes 12 miles of trestled roadway, two mile-long tunnels, bridges, and four artificial islands. These islands are located at the entrance and exit of each of the complex's two tunnels. To stop at three of these islands, you will need a permit from the CBBT's Director of Operations.

CHESAPEAKE BAY BRIDGE-TUNNEL BIRDING ACCESS

RULES: The southernmost island (#1) is usually open to the general public. This island has a restaurant and restroom facilities. *However, it is necessary to obtain prior written permission before stopping on the three northernmost islands (#2, 3, and 4).* In late 1996 the islands were closed because of construction of a parallel bridge span. Until construction is over, birding activities may be limited or reduced while the various artificial islands are periodically opened and closed. The parallel bridge span system is due to be completed sometime in 1999. To obtain a letter of permission (good for a calendar year) to visit islands #2, 3, and 4, write to: Director of Operations, Chesapeake Bay Bridge-Tunnel; P.O. Box 111; Cape Charles, VA 23310; or call 757/331-2960; www.cbbt.com/tour.html. Contact the office far enough in advance for the letter to reach your point of departure before you leave. (The letter can also be made available at the office which you designate at the toll plazas at the north or the south end of the CBBT.) Permits cannot be issued the same day that you call.

(Fisherman Island National Wildlife Refuge is at the northern end of the CBBT. It is accessible *only* through special arrangement with the Eastern Shore National Wildlife Refuge, which administers the location. See details under "Kiptopeke State Park and Vicinity" on page 36.)

The following rules *must be obeyed at all times* and are outlined in the permit letter for birding on the islands.

1) Inform the toll collector, when paying the toll (currently $10 for standard passenger cars), of your intention to stop, so that this word can be passed on to the CBBT police. A description of your vehicle, your license-plate number, and the number of persons accompanying you will be required.

2) No one is allowed to venture beyond the peripheral guardrail on each island. Do not park cars near the entrances to the islands or in front of the doors to the maintenance buildings located at the end of each island.

3) Entering and exiting the islands shall be by right turns only.

4) If more than three vehicles are traveling as a group, notify the CBBT Operations Division (Extension #40) two days prior to your arrival so that a police escort can be provided if the bridge authority deems it necessary.

Remember, your letter of permission does *not* include access to Fisherman Island or stopping on any of the roadway shoulders throughout the CBBT complex. Infractions of any of these rules will result in the loss of your privilege to stop on the islands *and may jeopardize the future visits of all birders.*

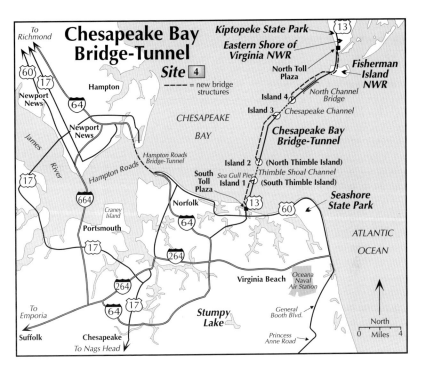

Chesapeake Bay Bridge-Tunnel

Site 4

---- = new bridge structures

To Richmond

Kiptopeke State Park

Eastern Shore of Virginia NWR

North Toll Plaza

Fisherman Island NWR

Island 4 — North Channel Bridge

Island 3 — Chesapeake Channel

Chesapeake Bay Bridge-Tunnel

Hampton

Newport News

Newport News

James River

Hampton Roads Bridge-Tunnel

Hampton Roads

Craney Island

Portsmouth

Norfolk

Island 2 (North Thimble Island)

South Toll Plaza

Sea Gull Pier — Thimble Shoal Channel

Island 1 (South Thimble Island)

Seashore State Park

ATLANTIC OCEAN

Virginia Beach

Oceana Naval Air Station

Stumpy Lake

General Booth Blvd.

North

0 Miles 4

To Emporia

Suffolk

Chesapeake

To Nags Head

Princess Anne Road

CHESAPEAKE BAY

The CBBT provides a wonderful opportunity for seeing pelagic birds and other interesting migrants "at sea." It is well known as a migrant trap for passerines during spring and especially during fall migration.

ESSENTIALS: From the Kiptopeke area, just proceed south on US-13 to the end of the peninsula until the CBBT toll plaza is reached on the right. (This is just beyond the left turn-off for the Eastern Shore of Virginia National Wildlife Refuge.)

From downtown Norfolk take the Virginia Beach-Norfolk Expressway (I-264) to I-64. Go east on I-64 until you reach Highway US-13; continue north on US-13. From Richmond or the Peninsula, take I-64 to the exit for US-13 north.

Show your letter of permission in the toll plaza office *before* reaching the toll booth.

HABITATS: This is essentially the meeting place of the open ocean with the mouth of the Chesapeake Bay. The rocky sides of the four artificial islands create a "rocky seacoast" in the open bay. Grassy strips along the interior of each side of the islands should also be thoroughly checked for migrants.

BIRDS:

Spring: Although not as spectacular as the fall migration, spring can still be a rewarding time, especially in late April and May during or immediately following high SW winds (for passerines) or high SE winds (for pelagic species). By late March most wintering species have departed. Many gulls remain; Bonaparte's is replaced by Laughing, which will stay until late fall. Also in March, flights of waterfowl may be seen winging northward. Herons, egrets, shorebirds, and passerines can occasionally be seen resting on the rocks or flying past the islands. One can get fantastic looks at exhausted landbirds (e.g., Seaside and Saltmarsh Sharp-tailed Sparrows, Marsh and Sedge Wrens, and even rails) exposed in the short grass or on open pavement. In both migration seasons, birding is largely "pot luck."

Summer: Summer is usually not as rewarding as the other seasons, but if one plans to be crossing the bay anyway, the islands should certainly be checked. Post-breeding waterbirds and early-migrating passerines constitute most of the island's summer birdlife. Summer does offer, however, a fair chance at pelagic birds. With luck and favorable winds, Wilson's Storm-Petrels can be observed. (An exceptional experience was the result of cast-offs observed after Hurricane *Bertha* in July 1996. Sightings included two Herald Petrels [not yet on the state list], 35 Black-capped Petrels, 5 Cory's Shearwaters, 6 Greater Shearwaters, 1 Audubon's Shearwater, 26 Leach's Storm-Petrels, 7 Band-rumped Storm-Petrels, 128 Wilson's Storm-Petrels, 1 Pomarine Jaeger, 1 Sooty Tern, 2 Bridled Terns, and 1 Roseate Tern.)

Fall: Fall provides the best time to observe migrating birds. Virtually any and every migrant species has been seen on or around the islands, including warblers, vireos, thrushes, orioles, tanagers, finches, kinglets, nuthatches, flycatchers, wrens, creepers, parids, and sparrows. Their appearance appears

C.J. Pennock
Looking southward from Island #1—Chesapeake Bay Bridge-Tunnel.

to follow a brisk cold front with high winds, particularly if the night wind has shifted from the N or NE to NW or W. Raptors are often seen on NE, E, and SE winds. The grassy strips sometimes host even unexpected skulking birds, such as woodcocks, rails, or bitterns.

Occasionally, Pomarine or Parasitic Jaegers are seen harassing gulls off one or more of the islands. Terns are usually most numerous in September. Late fall can produce Snow Buntings and Lapland Longspurs.

Winter: Winter provides excellent birding opportunities not readily available anywhere else in the state. Some of the regular wintering birds here are Red-throated and Common Loons, Horned and Red-necked Grebes, Northern Gannet, Double-crested and Great Cormorants, Purple Sandpiper, and Ruddy Turnstone. A wide spectrum of diving ducks is commonly present, including Surf, White-winged, and Black Scoters, Common Goldeneye, Bufflehead, Greater and Lesser Scaups, Oldsquaw, and Red-breasted Merganser. Large groups of gulls roost on the rocks, mainly Herring, Ring-billed, and Great Black-backed, and Bonaparte's Gulls will often feed along channels. Search among these gulls for Lesser Black-backed, Glaucous, and Iceland Gulls. (A Black-tailed Gull of undetermined origin appeared in the winter of 1996-1997.) Turbulent surf along the rocks provides prime habitat for Common and King Eiders and Harlequin Ducks, which winter regularly in small numbers.

RARE OR UNUSUAL BIRDS: The list is long, and, in addition to some of the birds already mentioned, includes Eared Grebe, Magnificent Frigatebird, Sooty Shearwater, Brown Booby, Barrow's Goldeneye, Atlantic Puffin and other alcids, Black-headed, Thayer's, Little, and Sabine's Gulls, Black and Yellow Rails, Purple Gallinule, Gray Kingbird, Rock Wren, Le Conte's and Henslow's Sparrows, and Yellow-headed Blackbird.

SPECIAL COMMENTS: A bulletin board for recording sightings is maintained in the lobby of the Tunnel Authority buildings at both ends of the bridge-tunnel. Sightings are included in state records maintained by the Virginia Society of Ornithology.

Teta Kain, Ned Brinkley

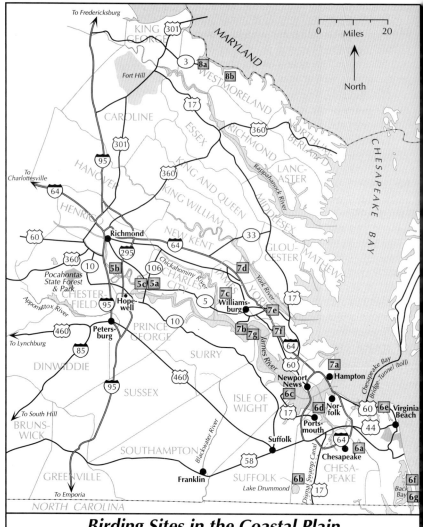

Birding Sites in the Coastal Plain

5a	Harrison Lake National Fish Hatchery	**7a**	Grandview Beach
5b	Point of Rocks Park	**7b**	Jamestown Island
5c	Presquile National Wildlife Refuge	**7c**	Jolly Pond
6a	Stumpy Lake	**7d**	York River State Park
6b	Great Dismal Swamp	**7e**	Colonial Parkway
6c	Ragged Island	**7f**	Newport News City Park
6d	Craney Island Landfill	**7g**	Hog Island
6e	First Landing/Seashore State Park	**8a**	George Washington Birthplace Nat. Mon.
6f	Back Bay National Wildlife Refuge	**8b**	Westmoreland State Park
6g	False Cape State Park		

COASTAL PLAIN

This region, also called "Tidewater Virginia," is bordered on the east by the Chesapeake Bay and on the west by the Fall Line, which stretches from Alexandria southward through Fredericksburg, Richmond, and Petersburg to the North Carolina boundary at Emporia. Because of many rapids and falls on major rivers along the Fall Line, it has long been a barrier to sea-going vessels. In the lower Coastal Plain along or near the James River are colonial sites, such as Williamsburg and Jamestown, from which many of the early historic bird sighting records originated.

Soils of the Coastal Plain are usually sandy, and, geologically speaking, this is the youngest portion of the state. The Coastal Plain is a land of low relief, sloping up westward to about 200 feet at the Fall Line. Several large rivers (Rappahannock, York, and James) provide riverine habitats and ravines in addition to their open waters. Both oak/pine and southeastern evergreen forests are characteristic, as are freshwater marshes and swamps. Because of its long occupancy by agricultural interests, starting with the early colonists, much of the land has been converted to cultivated fields.

The Chesapeake Bay, with its many miles of shorelines, tidal estuaries, and marshes, is one of the richest estuaries in the world and therefore provides habitat to a great variety of birds. From Smith Point at the mouth of the Potomac River southward, Chesapeake Bay waters are in Virginia. Shores of

Adrian R. Davis
Isolated pines along Coastal Plain.

45

the Bay and of the large tributary rivers are home to Bald Eagle, Fish Crow, Prothonotary Warbler, and Red-bellied Woodpecker. Associated marshes attract Clapper Rails, Seaside Sparrows, and Marsh Wrens.

Pine forests of the Coastal Plain hold Brown-headed Nuthatches, Pine Warblers, and Summer Tanagers. Hardwood forests have the usual complement of breeding Red-eyed Vireos, Wood Thrushes, Ovenbirds, Great Crested Flycatchers, White-breasted Nuthatches, and Carolina Chickadees, whereas in winter chickadees, nuthatches, titmice, and a variety of woodpeckers are evident.

Of special interest for many decades has been the Great Dismal Swamp. Although it was once believed to be nearly devoid of bird life, we now know that it is an area of high bird diversity at almost any season. Specialties found in the swamp include Swainson's and Black-throated Green Warblers. At times, substantial numbers of migrant landbirds and waterfowl can be seen there.

In the lower part of the Coastal Plain, special habitats attract several birds that are rare in the state. In certain pine forests one can find or hear Red-cockaded Woodpeckers, along the Meherrin River Mississippi Kites are usually found, and old or burned-over fields are home to some Bachman's Sparrows.

MORE INFORMATION:

General Information

Hampton Visitor Center
710 Settlers Landing Road, Hampton, VA 23669
800/800-2202

Hopewell Visitor Center
201-D Randolph Square, Hopewell, VA 23860
800/863-8687

Newport News Visitor Information Center
13560 Jefferson Avenue, Newport News, VA 23603
888/493-7386

Norfolk Visitor Information Center
4th View Street, Norfolk, VA 23503
800/368-3097

Portsmouth Visitor Information Center
505 Crawford Street, Portsmouth, VA 23704
800/767-8782

Potomac Gateway Visitor Center
P.O. Box 71, King George, VA 22485
540/663-3205

Virginia Beach Visitor Information Center
2100 Parks Avenue, Virginia Beach, VA 23451
800/446-8038

Williamsburg Area Convention and Visitors Bureau
201 Penniman Road, Williamsburg, VA 23185
800/368-6511

Wildlife Management Areas

Chickahominy: 5,000 acres, 12 miles southeast of Providence Forge, Charles City County.

Game Farm Marsh: 429 acres, 8 miles north of Charles City, along the Chickahominy River, featuring cypress swamp, in New Kent County.

Hog Island: a 3,900-acre peninsula jutting into the James River, near Surry, Surry and Isle of Wight counties. (See site #7g.)

Pettigrew: 933 acres of hardwood forests and wetlands along US Route 17 in Caroline County.

Princess Anne (formerly Trojan-Pocahontas/Barbours Hill): 1,546 acres of marshy shoreline, coastal freshwater bay, and marshy islands, near False Cape State Park, Virginia Beach City.

Ragged Island: 1,537 acres of brackish-water marsh and small pine islands along the James River, Hampton Roads, Isle of Wight County. (See site #6c.)

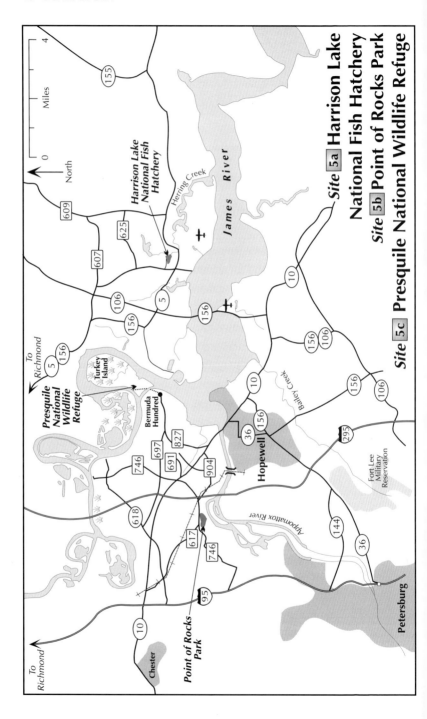

Site 5a **Harrison Lake National Fish Hatchery**

Site 5b **Point of Rocks Park**

Site 5c **Presquile National Wildlife Refuge**

Site 5a.
HARRISON LAKE NATIONAL FISH HATCHERY,
Charles City County

BACKGROUND: The fish hatchery was founded in 1934 and is now administered by the U.S. Fish and Wildlife Service. Currently only anadromous species such as striped bass and American shad are being raised.

ESSENTIALS: From Hopewell follow Route 10 east for 1.9 miles. Turn left onto Route 156 and drive 3.4 miles north to Route 5. Turn right and go east 1.5 miles to Route 658, noting hatchery signs. Turn left and go 0.4 mile to the entrance on your right. The turn-off from Route 5 is also 20.2 miles east of the Richmond city limits.

HABITATS: Mixed woodland with a few small ponds, a stream, and a nature trail. Twenty small fresh-water impoundments for raising fish occupy the principal open area. A dirt road leads from the hatchery proper along a swampy canal to a moderate-size lake. At the northeastern corner of the lake is a wooded swamp, reachable by canoe.

BIRDS:

Spring and fall: This area is best known for migrating shorebirds (both Yellowlegs, Solitary, Spotted, Least, Western, and Semipalmated Sandpipers) and post-breeding herons (Little Blue), egrets (Cattle, Great, Snowy), and the occasional White and Glossy Ibises. Wooded edges of the impoundments and lake are good places for finding migrating landbirds (warblers, vireos, thrushes). The lake attracts some migratory waterfowl.

Summer: Summer residents include Wood Ducks, Red-shouldered Hawks, and Prothonotary, Pine, and Yellow-throated Warblers, as well as Louisiana Waterthrush.

Winter: Wild Turkeys occur all year and are occasionally seen feeding on the dikes. Some waterfowl (Canada Goose, Wood Duck, Mallard, Bufflehead, Wood and Ring-necked Ducks) winter on the lake. Thickets and forest edges provide cover for wintering sparrows.

RARE OR UNUSUAL BIRDS: Ruff.

SPECIAL COMMENTS: For a number of years Least Sandpipers have wintered here occasionally in the drained fish-rearing ponds, the only inland locality in Virginia where these birds have wintered with any regularity.

Darrell Peterson, Larry Robinson, Fred Scott

Site 5b.
Point of Rocks Park,
Chesterfield County

BACKGROUND: The park was established in the early 1980s. Today it is one of Chesterfield County's best parks for birding because much of it has been left in a natural state, and the habitats are quite varied. The upland part of the park has picnic areas and a sports complex.

ESSENTIALS: From Hopewell follow Route 10 west 1.0 mile to Point of Rocks Road (Route 904). Turn left and go about 2.6 miles to the park entrance.

HABITATS: The park contains mixed woodland, small meadows or old fields delineated by hedgerows, some Appomattox River shoreline, and a tidal freshwater marsh. A nature trail includes an observation platform overlooking the marsh. Other trails have observation and photographic blinds, and one leads to a boardwalk into the marsh.

BIRDS:

Spring and fall: The hedgerows and river shore are good places for migrating landbirds, including a variety of warblers: Blue-winged, Golden-winged, Hooded, Prothonotary, Yellow, Black-throated Blue, and Black-throated Green. Yellow-throated, White-eyed, and Red-eyed Vireos can be found, as can both Summer and Scarlet Tanagers. Acadian and Great Crested Flycatchers are seen here. Tree Swallows and Gray-cheeked Thrushes have also been reported.

Summer: Among the nesting birds are Prothonotary, Hooded, and Pine Warblers, American Redstart, Northern Parula, Yellow-breasted Chat, Yellow-throated and White-eyed Vireos, Eastern Bluebird, and Summer Tanager. Wood Ducks are common most of the year.

Winter: The common birds of the Coastal Plain: White-breasted Nuthatch, Carolina Chickadee, Hermit Thrush, Cedar Waxwing, Song, Swamp, and White-throated Sparrows, Barred Owl, and Bald Eagle.

Larry Robinson, Darrell Peterson

Site 5c.
PRESQUILE NATIONAL WILDLIFE REFUGE,
Chesterfield County

BACKGROUND: This 1,329-acre man-made island in the James River is accessible only by a small cable ferry for passengers only. The island was formed in 1934 when a navigation channel was cut through the narrow base of an oxbow bend.

ESSENTIALS: From Hopewell take Route 10 west 1.0 mile to Route 827. Turn right and proceed 3.4 miles to the end of the road at Bermuda Hundred. Turn left here and follow a dirt road 0.4 mile to the ferry. Advance arrangements are required. Call 804/733-8042.

HABITATS: The NWR consists of 275 acres of upland (mostly in agricultural crops), 800 acres of hardwood swamp, and 250 acres of tidal freshwater marsh. The uplands include hedgerows, wooded river banks, and a vegetated spoil area. An additional 1,000 acres of river around the island is included in the refuge. A trail leaflet and a bird list are available.

BIRDS:

Spring and fall: Laughing Gulls are abundant in late summer and fall, with a few in spring and early summer. Bonaparte's Gulls and Caspian Terns occur somewhat irregularly at this time.

Summer: In summer Wood Ducks, Prothonotary Warblers, Northern Parulas, and American Redstarts are common in the wooded swamp, and there is usually a large Bank Swallow colony along the navigation channel. Grasshopper Sparrows are common summer residents.

Winter: The area is best known for its wintering waterfowl. About 10,000 Canada Geese and 250 Snow Geese (mostly blue morph) winter in the area from October through March. The most common wintering ducks are Mallards, American Black Ducks, Northern Pintails, and Wood Ducks, and various diving ducks, loons, and grebes are occasionally seen. Usually a group of wintering Bald Eagles use the area, and a number of nest sites are nearby. Wintering gulls include Ring-billed, Herring, and Great Black backed.

RARE OR UNUSUAL BIRDS: Short-eared Owl.

Larry Robinson, Darrell Peterson, Fred Scott

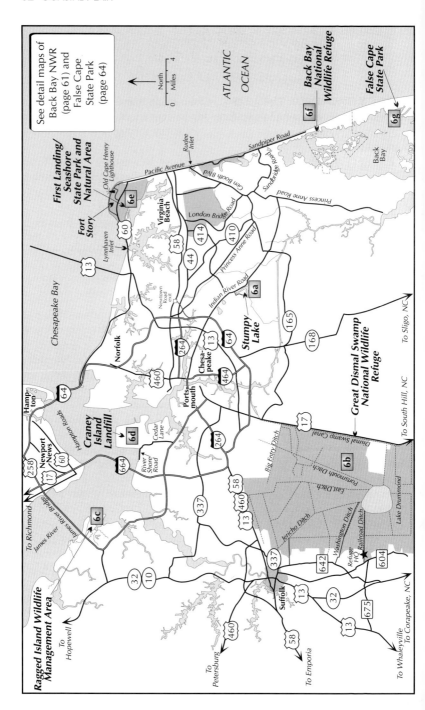

See detail maps of
Back Bay NWR
(page 61) and
False Cape
State Park
(page 64)

North
0 Miles 4

ATLANTIC
OCEAN

Back Bay
National
Wildlife Refuge

6f

False Cape
State Park

6g

Back
Bay

Sandpiper Road

Rudee
Inlet

Sandbridge Road

Gen Booth Blvd

Pacific Avenue

Princess Anne Road

First Landing/
Seashore
State Park and
Natural Area

Old Cape Henry
Lighthouse

6e

Fort
Story

60

London Bridge Road

Virginia
Beach

58

414

410

Lynnhaven
Inlet

13

44

Princess Anne Road

Chesapeake Bay

Newtown
Road
exit

Indian River Road

6a

Stumpy
Lake

165

264

13

64

168

Norfolk

460

Chesa-
peake

464

Great Dismal Swamp
National Wildlife
Refuge

To Sligo, NC

Hampton

64

Ports-
mouth

264

17

To South Hill, NC

Newport
News

258

17

60

Hampton Roads

Craney
Island
Landfill

6d

Cedar
Lane

664

River
Shore
Road

Dismal Swamp Canal

Big Entry Ditch

6b

East Ditch

Portsmouth Ditch

Lake Drummond

To Richmond

James River Bridge

6c

337

58

460

13

Jericho Ditch

Washington Ditch

Refuge
HQ

Railroad Ditch

604

Ragged Island Wildlife
Management Area

To
Hopewell

32

10

337

Suffolk

13

642

32

675

13

460

58

To
Petersburg

To Emporia

To Whaleyville

To Corapeake, NC

Site 6a.
STUMPY LAKE,
Virginia Beach

BACKGROUND: Stumpy Lake and its environs are owned by the City of Norfolk, which operates the area as a city golf course and water reservoir.

ESSENTIALS: Coming from either direction on I-64, turn off at Indian River Road (Route 165) east. Stay on Indian River Road, crossing Kempsville Road (Route 190) and Lynnhaven Parkway, and proceed less than a mile. When you see a sign for the Norfolk golf course (on your right), turn right, cross a small causeway, and continue to the club-house parking area.

HABITATS: The golf course proper provides open fairways and greens interspersed with wet mixed pine/hardwood woodlands with an understory of cane. Some swamp habitat is found around the edge of the lake. To work the area, you must be willing to walk. Birding is good at all seasons.

BIRDS:

Spring: The area attracts many northward migrants, such as Black-throated Green, Yellow-throated, and Orange-crowned Warblers and Northern and Louisiana Waterthrushes. Check for sparrows, including White-throated, White-crowned, and Swamp. Double-crested Cormorants are common, and the lake may hold a variety of migrating waterfowl. Overhead, there may be Glossy Ibises, accipiters, Red-shouldered Hawks, or Bald Eagles. Solitary Sandpiper is a common spring migrant. Bald Eagles are regularly seen throughout the year.

Summer: In the past several summers, Anhingas have been irregular visitors; sightings have included both males and females. (The Anhingas are most commonly seen from the spillway at the south end of the lake.) Great Blue Herons have a rookery on the lake's southeast finger. Many Wood Ducks are usually present. Yellow-throated and Pine Warblers breed in good numbers, along with Ovenbirds, Common Yellowthroats, and Prothonotary Warblers. Red-eyed and White-eyed Vireos are common. Summer Tanagers are regular breeders, and Scarlet Tanagers have been reported.

Fall: When water levels are low, this is an excellent place for migrant shorebirds as well as waterfowl and passerines. Shorebirds to be expected are both Greater and Lesser Yellowlegs, along with Semipalmated, Least, Spotted, and Western Sandpipers; rarer species should also be looked for. Fall is the best time for a large number of puddle ducks, such as Mallard, American Black Duck, and Blue-winged and Green-winged Teal. Black-crowned and Yellow-crowned Night-Herons are regularly found in the trees along the eastern shore of the lake and adjacent to the causeway. Feeders should be watched for sparrows and finches.

Winter: A reliable place to find Brown-headed Nuthatches, Pine Warblers, and Brown Creepers in the pine areas. The feeders in back of the club-house attract juncos and White-throated, Chipping, Fox, and Field

Sparrows. Woodpeckers, including Red-bellied, Northern Flicker, Hairy, and Downy, are regularly found. Common and Hooded Mergansers, with the latter very common, along with Ring-necked Ducks, Mallards, and American Wigeon, can all be found on the lake. Great Egret and Great Blue Heron can be noted along the shore.

RARE OR UNUSUAL BIRDS: Anhinga, Bald Eagle, Merlin, Henslow's Sparrow, and Snow Bunting.

SPECIAL COMMENTS: Birders should be careful not to park on the entrance causeway, to interfere with golfers, or to walk along the edges of the fairways or the golf course proper.

Donald Schwab, Robert Ake, Richard Peake

Prothonotary Warbler
Ali Wieboldt

Site 6b.
GREAT DISMAL SWAMP NATIONAL WILDLIFE REFUGE,
Suffolk City

BACKGROUND: Great Dismal Swamp NWR is a large, 120,000-acre wooded swamp located in the southeastern corner of the state. It has a long cultural history going back to colonial times, with such historic visitors as Lighthorse Harry Lee, Patrick Henry, and George Washington. Runaway slaves and other fugitives used it for a safe haven. Today, it is a favorite site for natural historians—especially those interested in its wide variety of butterfly and plant species.

ESSENTIALS: The refuge is reached from eastern Tidewater by following I-64 east to its junction with US-460/13/58. Follow US-460/13/58 to the Bus. 460/Bus. 58 intersection. Proceed on the Bus. Routes to Route 337 and make a left turn (traffic light; Shell Station across on right). Stay on Route 337 (E. Washington St.) to Route 642 (Whitemarsh Road). Turn (hard) left and follow Route 642 south. Coming from west of Suffolk, follow either I-460 or Route 10/32 to their junction (McDonalds on left and courthouse across on right) with Bus. 58/460, and continue south on Routes 13/32 (Main Street) to Route 337. Turn right onto Route 337 (E. Washington St.) and follow to Route 642 (Whitemarsh Road); there, make another right turn. There are two entrances to the refuge on Whitemarsh Road; both are posted with the brown-and-white information signs. The first access point is Jericho Ditch Lane (2.0 miles to parking); the second, Washington Ditch Lane, is approximately 4.5 miles south of Jericho Ditch Lane. There is a 0.5-mile-long boardwalk at the Washington Ditch Parking Area (1.0 mile from White Marsh Road). Continuing south on White Marsh Road 1.0 mile to Route 604 (Desert Road), make a left turn and continue 1.7 miles to the Refuge Headquarters. The Railroad Ditch Access (6.2 miles to lake, via Railroad, West, and Interior Ditches) is found just south of the headquarters on Route 604.

HABITATS: The refuge encompasses approximately 85,000 acres of wooded wetlands. The principal vegetation type is Black Gum/Red Maple, but stands of Atlantic White-cedar, Bald Cypress, and evergreen-shrub bogs are also found. About 40 miles of dirt roads can be hiked/biked, the roads allowing access to all of the various habitats to be found in the Virginia portion of the Great Dismal Swamp. Lake Drummond (3,000 acres), one of only two natural lakes found in Virginia, is located in the center of the swamp just north of the North Carolina line.

BIRDS:

Spring: This is the best birding season. Thrushes, Black-billed Cuckoos, and 30 species of warblers have been recorded on annual spring bird counts over the past three years. Birds seen include Blue-winged, Golden-winged, Chestnut-sided, Bay-breasted, and Mourning Warblers and Northern Waterthrush. Check the grassy strips along Route 604 in April for Upland Sandpipers.

Summer: Green Heron, Wood Duck, Red-shouldered Hawk, Barred Owl, Pileated Woodpecker, Acadian Flycatcher, White-eyed Vireo, Red-eyed Vireo, Northern Parula, Prothonotary, Hooded, Worm-eating, Swainson's, and Kentucky Warblers are all common breeders. Some of the rarer finds have included Swallow-tailed Kite, Mississippi Kite, and Anhinga.

Fall: Common Loon, Great Blue Heron, Tundra Swan, Snow Goose, Ring-necked and Wood Ducks, Broad-winged Hawk, Rusty Blackbird, and Brewer's Blackbird have occurred. Few people bird the swamp during this season, so records are scarce.

Winter: Tundra Swan, Canada Goose, Mallard, Ring-necked Duck, Common Loon, Hermit Thrush, Winter Wren, White-eyed Vireo, Solitary Vireo, and Orange-crowned Warbler regularly occur.

SPECIAL COMMENTS: Access to the interior portions of the swamp is by foot or by bike. The roads are closed to vehicle traffic but allow for easy walking. During the summer and early fall, biting insects can be bothersome; long pants and long-sleeved shirts are encouraged. A good insect repellent and a canteen of water also are good accessories. Birding by sight is best during late fall, winter, and spring. Once leaf-out occurs in late spring and summer, a good birding ear will increase your daily bird list. Mammals of interest include Black Bear, Bobcat, River Otter, and White-tailed Deer. The refuge is open from dawn to dusk.

Donald Schwab

Site 6c.
RAGGED ISLAND WILDLIFE MANAGEMENT AREA,
Isle of Wight County

BACKGROUND: Located in the shadow of the five cities that ring Hampton Roads, this small wildlife management area is typical of the many salt-marsh islands that dot the shorelines of Virginia's great rivers.

ESSENTIALS: From I-64 take the Mercury Boulevard exit (US-258 south) toward the James River Bridge. Ragged Island entrance is at the other (south) end of the James River Bridge on the left side of the road (approximately 5.5 miles from I-64).

HABITATS: Marshland, swamp, pine trees, and woodland areas.

BIRDS:

Spring: A good selection of migrant vireos, warblers, thrushes, and gnatcatchers.

Summer: Seaside Sparrow, Marsh Wren, Eastern Towhee, Indigo Bunting, Blue Grosbeak, and vireos. Ospreys usually nest on platforms erected in the marsh. Laughing Gulls, along with Royal, Common, and Least Terns, are seen over the river.

Fall: Migratory warblers, thrushes, tanagers, and vireos. Rails are common during migration and are easily seen along the boardwalk during extreme tides.

Winter: Pine and Yellow-rumped Warblers, Clapper Rails, Red-bellied and Downy Woodpeckers, Great Blue Heron, Canvasback, Common Goldeneye, and Ruddy Ducks are commonly spotted on the river. Brown-headed Nuthatches are year-round residents.

SPECIAL COMMENTS: The nature trail and elevated walkway over the marsh provide excellent opportunities for close viewing or photographing Marsh Wrens, Seaside Sparrows, and Clapper Rails during the spring, summer, and fall months. The walkway extends to the river's edge, where ducks are easily viewed in the winter.

Teta Kain, Mike and Dorothy Mitchell

Marsh Wren
Ali Wieboldt

Site 6d.
Craney Island Landfill,
Portsmouth City

BACKGROUND: This landfill island, now some 40 years old, has been created as the result of accumulated dredged material.

ESSENTIALS: Traveling from Richmond or Norfolk, take Exit 264 of I-64 onto I-664 south. Proceed 12.3 miles on I-664 to Exit 8B (135 South). Go 1.9 miles to the exit for 164 East and turn onto 164 East. Go 2.2 miles to the Cedar Lane exit. Turn left onto Cedar Lane, then left again onto River Shore Road. In about 1 mile, turn right onto Hedgerow Road and go 0.3 mile to the gate. Bear left and go to the main office of the U.S. Army Corps of Engineer for Craney Island.

HABITATS: Nearby mudflats and some marsh with rocky breakwaters.

BIRDS:

Spring: Large build-ups of migrant waterfowl and shorebirds are commonplace. These include both yellowlegs, Short-billed Dowitcher, Dunlin, Sanderling, and Semipalmated Sandpipers. Look for Eurasian Wigeon in April among the large numbers of migrant American Wigeons. During May it is not uncommon to find Gull-billed and possibly Sandwich Terns among the more common tern species.

Summer: Excellent for herons, skimmers, gulls, and terns (Least, Royal, some Caspian, Gull-billed). Least Terns and Piping Plovers nest on the island. Black-necked Stilts have been found nesting in recent years. *Care must be taken to avoid disturbance to the nesting birds. Observe the POSTED signs.* In late summer, shorebird numbers become spectacular once again.

Fall: Large flocks of shorebirds highlight the earlier weeks; waterfowl, the later weeks. Look especially for Wilson's Phalaropes and White-rumped and Stilt Sandpipers. Buff-breasted Sandpiper and American Golden-Plover can sometimes be found working the drier grassy areas. The grassy edges of the dikes provide habitat for migrant sparrows, including the uncommon Clay-colored and Lark Sparrows. Peregrine Falcons will frequent the area throughout the fall and winter.

Winter: Some shorebirds, such as Dunlins and American Avocets, can be seen year-round. A large variety of waterfowl is usually present. Rough-legged Hawk, Glaucous Gull, Short-eared Owl, Lapland Longspur, and Snow Bunting have also been seen at this season.

RARE OR UNUSUAL BIRDS: "Western" and Eared Grebes, Fulvous Whistling-Duck, Curlew Sandpiper, Franklin's and Little Gulls, Wood Stork, Le Conte's Sparrow, Rock Wren, Wilson's Plover.

SPECIAL COMMENTS: Be certain to sign the register at landfill office, and avoid disturbing the nesting birds. The landfill (757/484-1021) is open on weekdays only (no holidays either), from 7:00 am to 3:30 pm only.

Ruth Beck, Robert Ake, Richard Peake

Site 6e.
FIRST LANDING/SEASHORE STATE PARK
AND NATURAL AREA AND FORT STORY,
Virginia Beach City

BACKGROUND: In April 1607, English settlers landed here before traveling up the James River to establish Jamestown. That is why this site is now called First Landing/Seashore State Park (fee; 757/481-2131). Camping and housekeeping cabins are available, as are boat ramps and a bicycle trail. Nearby Fort Story is an active U.S. Army post; you will need to check in at the gate upon entering.

ESSENTIALS: Take I-64 to US-60 (Shore Drive) and proceed east beyond Lynnhaven Inlet for about 2 miles to a flashing light at the park's entrance. Parking is available on both sides of the main highway. To reach Fort Story, continue east on US-60 (Shore Drive) to Route 350. Turn left on Route 350. This will bring you to the west gate. Stop at the gate; if guards are present, tell them you are going to look for birds. Continue on the main road to Cape Henry Landing parking area on the left. Park in the lot and walk the trails to the beach.

HABITATS: Fort Story and the portion of Seashore State Park north of Shore Drive are predominantly open sand beach and maritime live-oak woodlands. The portion of the park/natural area south of Shore Drive is an area of mixed pine/hardwood woodlands, freshwater marshes and ponds, and a large brackish bay (Broad Bay) on the southeast side of the park. There are 15 to 20 miles of trails (with the majority restricted to foot traffic).

BIRDS:

Spring: Migration is spread over several weeks. Yellow-throated and Philadelphia Vireos can be found with a little dedicated looking. Warblers such as Black-throated Green, Cape May, Magnolia, Northern Parula, Yellow-throated, Worm-eating, and, rarely, a Kentucky, can be found, as well as Northern and Louisiana Waterthrushes and Ovenbird. The beaches present a wide range of shorebirds with Sanderling, Dunlin, Willet, and occasionally a Whimbrel. In the open water, look for both Red-throated and Common Loons, Northern Gannets, and sea ducks.

Summer: The breeding Northern Parulas make a summer walk along the boardwalk near the visitors center worth a visit. Yellow-throated Warbler, Louisiana Waterthrush, Ovenbird, Worm-eating Warbler, and Common Yellowthroat are common. Wood Thrush, Northern Cardinal, Gray Catbird, and Brown Thrasher add to the variety of species encountered. Bald Eagles that have nested in the park are now actively feeding young, and sightings over Broad Bay are common. Beaches are not very productive at this time of year, but Piping Plovers should be looked for as the summer progresses. Fort

Story's Monk Parakeets (very interesting birds, but not officially on the state list) are best viewed at this time of year (near east gate, main road).

Fall: This is the season of surprises. Warblers include, but are not limited to, Golden-winged, Blackburnian, Mourning, Connecticut, Chestnut-sided, and Bay-breasted. Vireo species are usually restricted to Red-eyed and White-eyed, but a rare Warbling should be looked for. Gray-cheeked and Swainson's Thrushes and Veery should be expected. Hawks moving south along the coast can be numerous at this time of year: Sharp-shinned, Cooper's, and Red-shouldered are frequently encountered. Broad Bay will attract many waterfowl species moving south: Blue-winged and Green-winged Teal and Northern Shoveler are early dabblers seen on the bay. Waders, such as Great and Snowy Egrets, congregate along the bay's shoreline. American Bitterns should be looked for in the grasses along Broad Bay. The beaches are at their best at this time of year, with a wide variety of shorebirds, such as Black-bellied and Semipalmated Plovers, Red Knot, Ruddy Turnstone, and Semipalmated and Least Sandpipers early, with Western Sandpipers replacing the Semipalmated later in the season. This is the time to start searching through the Bonaparte's Gulls at Fort Story for a Little Gull. Common and Red-throated Loons and Northern Gannets are back in open waters off the beaches.

Winter: You can find Hermit Thrushes, American Robins, Blue-headed Vireos, and woodpeckers such as Pileated, Hairy, and Red-bellied, as well as Yellow-bellied Sapsuckers. White-breasted and Brown-headed Nuthatches are common. Brown Creepers and Black-and-white Warblers are good finds. Eastern Screech-Owls and Rusty Blackbirds are common. Dunes should be checked for Savannah ("Ipswich" subspecies) Sparrow and Snow Buntings. Beaches are good locations for gulls (Lesser Black-backed have become fairly common), Dunlin, and Sanderlings. Look out over the ocean (actually the mouth of the Chesapeake Bay) for Bonaparte's Gulls, Northern Gannets, Great and Double-crested Cormorants, Common Goldeneye, scoters (all three species), Oldsquaw, and scaup. On Broad Bay, Gadwall, American Wigeon, Mallard, and American Black Ducks are common, with Bald Eagle possible.

RARE OR UNUSUAL BIRDS: Eurasian Wigeon, Little Gull, Black-legged Kittiwake, Razorbill, Red-necked Grebe, Lark Sparrow, Lark Bunting, Lapland Longspur, and Common Redpoll.

SPECIAL COMMENTS: The Chicken Turtle, a state endangered species and likely the rarest turtle in Virginia, is found in the ponds on Seashore State Park . *(Please do not disturb this species if encountered, but do inform park staff of any sightings.)* The woodlands are unique in many ways, including the fact that this is one of the few wooded areas in southeast Virginia which is not being over-browsed by White-tailed Deer. The ground-cover and herbaceous growth provide good cover for a wide range of wildlife.

Donald Schwab, Richard Peake

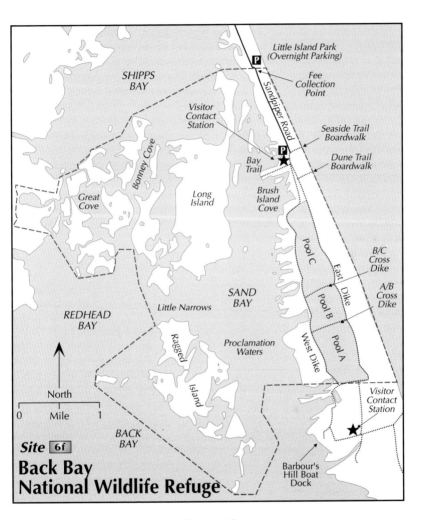

Site 6f.
BACK BAY NATIONAL WILDLIFE REFUGE,
Virginia Beach City

BACKGROUND: This is one of the oldest wildlife refuges in the state. It is located on the barrier spit separating Back Bay from the Atlantic Ocean. A visitors center in the headquarters building has displays of the various habitats and their inhabitants. Many programs on the region's natural history are presented by the staff and volunteers.

ESSENTIALS: The refuge is reachable from all exits of the Virginia Beach/Norfolk Expressway (Route 44), but the easiest way is to take the

Newtown Road exit. Turn left at the foot of the ramp onto Newtown Road; then go for one quarter of a mile and turn left onto Princess Anne Road. The other alternative is to follow the toll road (Route 44) to its end and turn right onto Pacific Avenue in the resort oceanfront area. Follow this road south to Rudee Inlet, after which Pacific Avenue becomes General Booth Boulevard. After 5.8 miles you will intersect Princess Anne Road. Make a left turn at the 7-11 store, and continue for 1 mile to Sandbridge Road (Food Lion shopping center) and turn left. Sandbridge Road will terminate in the town of Sandbridge. Turn right onto Sandpiper Road (fire house on right) and follow it to the refuge entrance. Entrance fees are required and Seasonal Closures of management areas may be in effect, so telephone ahead (757/721-2412).

HABITATS: The refuge consists of 7,732 acres of ocean beach, dunes, brackish-water impoundments and marsh, fallow agricultural fields, and wooded wetlands. The refuge has expanded in recent years and now includes properties north and west of Back Bay itself.

BIRDS:

Spring: There are many common (sometimes abundant) migrants, including loons, Brown Pelicans, Northern Gannets, scoters, Red-breasted Mergansers, Willets, Whimbrels, dowitchers, Sanderlings, Red Knots, peep (including White-rumped Sandpiper), gulls (regularly including Lesser Black-backed Gull), and terns (though rare, Roseate Terns should be looked for). Marsh and Sedge Wrens, Seaside Sparrows, and rails are back in numbers in the marshes. American Golden-Plover, Bald Eagle, and jaegers have also been recorded in spring. Look for Sooty Shearwaters off the headquarters beach in late May and early June. You may be lucky enough to encounter a rare Wilson's Plover along the headquarters beach in May.

Summer: Herons, Least Bittern, Canada Goose, American Black Duck, Mallard, Wood Duck, King Rail, Piping Plover, and Willet can be seen at this time. Other shorebirds increase in numbers as the season progresses. Ospreys, gulls, and terns are common. White Ibises may occasionally be seen flying over in small groups. June is a good time to look along the beach for visiting Roseate Terns.

Fall: Tundra Swan, Snow and Canada Geese, Blue-winged and Green-winged Teal, Northern Pintail, all three scoter species, Red-breasted Merganser, Peregrine Falcon, Merlin, Sharp-shinned Hawk, Cooper's Hawk, Osprey, Piping Plover, Semipalmated Plover, Black-bellied Plover, peeps (including White-rumped, and rarely a Baird's), Marbled Godwit, Ruff, Red Knot, Dunlin, Pectoral and Stilt Sandpipers, Black Tern, marsh birds such as Northern Harrier, Sedge and Marsh Wrens, and rails. King Rails are common. Large flights of Eastern Kingbirds and Bobolinks can be seen around the refuge headquarters in early September. Grasshopper, Lark, Seaside, and Saltmarsh Sharp-tailed Sparrows are regularly reported. Special finds have included Eared Grebe, Western Kingbird, Fork-tailed Flycatcher, Fulvous Whistling-Duck, and Clay-colored and Lark Sparrows. Check for a Clay-colored Sparrow among the flocks of Chipping Sparrows.

Winter: Waterfowl, loons, grebes, Northern Gannet, King and Virginia Rails, Sora, Common Moorhen, and landbirds, which are well represented by numbers of sparrow species, including Lark, Le Conte's, and Lincoln's. Other passerine species include Yellow-rumped, Palm, and Orange-crowned Warblers and several blackbird species. Look for Little Gulls among the vast numbers of Bonaparte's Gulls (if present) and "white-winged" gulls off the headquarters beach. Ross's Goose is becoming regular among the large flocks of Snow Geese. During winter, Snow Buntings and Lapland Longspurs are possible along the beach front.

RARE OR UNUSUAL BIRDS: Scissor-tailed, Fork-tailed, and Olive-sided Flycatchers, Western Kingbird, Fulvous Whistling-Duck, Ross's Goose, Snowy Owl, Sabine's and other rare gulls, Manx, Greater, and Cory's Shearwaters, Magnificent Frigatebird, Wood Stork, Sandhill Crane, Pacific Loon, alcids during late winter, Purple Gallinule, Eared Grebe, Western Tanager, Lark Bunting, and pelagic species.

SPECIAL COMMENTS: To work this area fully, you need a willingness to walk, a canteen of water, and binoculars. A scope will greatly increase your daily list. Portions of the dike roads are closed, so if you walk the four miles to the south boundary, you will have a four-mile hike back. Access to the beach is by a boardwalk. Low tide is best for shorebirds, but any time is good for gulls, terns, and sea ducks.

For more information contact: Refuge Manager, Back Bay NWR, P.O. Box 6286, Virginia Beach, VA 23456, 757/721-2412.

Donald Schwab, Bob Anderson

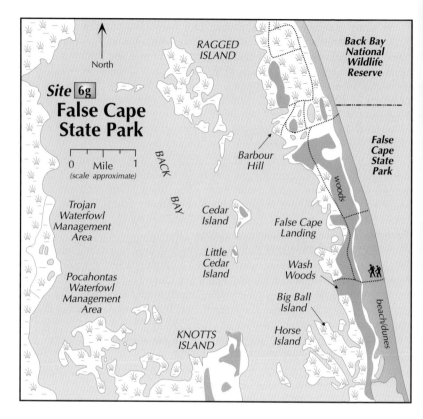

Site 6g.
FALSE CAPE STATE PARK,
Virginia Beach City

BACKGROUND: Located south of Back Bay NWR, False Cape State Park (757/426-7128) is also a barrier spit between Back Bay and the ocean. Several rare plants exist there, as do feral horses and pigs. The sand beaches are used by Loggerhead Sea Turtles for nesting. This can be a good birding site especially if you have ample time and are prepared for lots of walking. *There is no private-vehicle access to False Cape State Park.*

ESSENTIALS: The park can be reached from all exits of the Virginia Beach/Norfolk Expressway (Route 44), but the easiest way is to take the Newtown Road exit. Turn left at the foot of the ramp onto Newtown Road for one-quarter of a mile and then turn left onto Princess Anne Road. The other alternative is to follow the toll road (Route 44) to its end and turn right onto Pacific Avenue in the resort oceanfront area. Follow this road south to Rudee Inlet, after which Pacific Avenue becomes General Booth Boulevard.

After 5.8 miles you will intersect Princess Anne Road. Make a left turn at the 7-11 store, continue for 1 mile to Sandbridge Road (Food Lion shopping center) and turn left. Sandbridge Road ends in the town of Sandbridge. Turn right onto Sandpiper Road (fire house on right) and follow it to the parking area at the Virginia Beach City Park at Little Island Coast Guard Station (a parking fee is in effect during the summer). Access to the park is through Back Bay NWR and is restricted to foot or bike travel. There is parking on the Back Bay NWR at the lot near the refuge headquarters. Entrance fees to the refuge may be charged, and seasonal closures of the management areas may be in effect, so telephone ahead, (804/426-3657). When refuge management area closures are in effect, access to the park will be along the beach.

HABITATS: False Cape is a barrier spit consisting of over 4,300 acres of beach, dunes, interdunal swales, maritime forest, brackish marshes, and managed wetland impoundments (Barbour's Hill Wildlife Management Area, with 200 acres of impoundments, is encompassed within the northern portion of the park). Be prepared to travel on foot and spend the day in the area. Bring lots of water. As you enter the park from Back Bay NWR, there is a large impoundment on the east side of the road. Try the observation platform here, from which you can scope the area.

BIRDS:

Spring: Look for Brown Pelican, Willet, Whimbrel, Black-necked Stilt, both dowitchers, peeps (including White-rumped Sandpiper), and gulls (including the rarer species). The tern variety increases, and landbirding is enhanced by many species of warblers, wrens, sparrows, and other passerines moving north. Check the beach fronts in April and May for Wilson's Plover.

Summer: You will see herons (including Least Bittern), White Ibis, Canada Goose, American Black Duck, Mallard, Wood Duck, Piping Plover, and Willet. The shorebirds are present early but increase in number and species as the season progresses. Ospreys, gulls, and terns are common.

Fall: This is the season to spend time looking at the ocean and beaches with a telescope. Tundra Swan, Snow and Canada Geese, Blue-winged and Green-winged Teals, Northern Pintail, scoters, Red-breasted Merganser, Peregrine Falcon, Merlin, Sharp-shinned Hawk, Cooper's Hawk, Osprey, Piping, Semipalmated, and Black-bellied Plovers, peeps (including White-rumped Sandpiper and rarely a Baird's Sandpiper), Red Knot, Dunlin, Pectoral Sandpiper, Stilt Sandpiper, Black Tern, marsh birds such as Northern Harrier, Sedge Wren, Marsh Wren, rails, Grasshopper Sparrow, Lark Sparrow, Seaside Sparrow, and Saltmarsh Sharp-tailed Sparrow are all regularly reported. Look in the shrubs for Philadelphia Vireo, Orange-crowned and Connecticut Warblers, and rare sparrows. Special finds have included Western Kingbird, Scissor-tailed Flycatcher, and Fulvous Whistling-Duck.

Winter: This is the time to look for waterfowl (especially a variety of dabbling ducks), loons, grebes, Northern Gannet, all three species of scoters, gulls, and Forster's Tern. Bald Eagles are becoming regular during all seasons, but they are more visible now.

RARE OR UNUSUAL BIRDS: Ross's Goose, Fulvous Whistling-Duck, Wood Stork, Mississippi and Swallow-tailed Kites, Olive-sided Flycatcher.

SPECIAL COMMENTS: To work this area fully, you need a willingness to walk, a canteen of water, and binoculars. A scope will greatly increase your daily list. If you walk through the interior portion of Back Bay NWR, the hike is 4 miles to the entrance of the park. The park extends south for 6 miles to the North Carolina line. *The only drinking-water available is from a vending machine,* so it's advisable to bring your own. Camping is allowed in the park in designated areas.

For more information contact: False Cape State Park, 4001 Sandpiper Road, Virginia Beach, VA 23456, 757/426-7128

Donald Schwab, Mark Lassiter, Russ Landis

Site 7a.
GRANDVIEW BEACH,
Hampton City

BACKGROUND: Grandview Beach is part of the City of Hampton's park system. It is a popular place for walking and jogging. In the spring and summer it is frequented by beach-goers and the occasional angler.

ESSENTIALS: From I-64 at Hampton take Exit 263-B, US-258 (Mercury Boulevard) north. Go 3.0 miles (9 stoplights). At the ninth light turn left onto Route 169 (Fox Hill Road) south. Travel 3.0 miles and turn left onto Beach Road (look for a Grandview sign). Proceed 2.7 miles and turn left onto State Park Drive at Grandview Shores. Park along the street and walk to the park entrance one block ahead.

HABITATS: The beach is bounded on the east by the Chesapeake Bay. To the west is a wide expanse of brackish and freshwater marsh dominated by Needle Rush and Saltmeadow Hay, with intermittent clusters of Salt-marsh Cordgrass near a tidal pool. Several small freshwater pools are located in the marsh interior. The marsh is separated from the beach by a primary dune system and thick stands of Wax Myrtle. The northern end of the peninsula is relatively flat and sparsely vegetated with low shrubs and beach grasses.

BIRDS:

Spring: Early in the season the marsh is an excellent place for Saltmarsh and Nelson's Sharp-tailed Sparrows and Sedge Wrens. Marsh Wrens and Seaside Sparrows will be seen and heard singing over territories in the marsh as the season progresses. Clapper Rails and other rails are often very vocal. The skies will be filled with Barn Swallows and Purple Martins. Look for Least Bitterns and Common Moorhens at the pools near the park entrance.

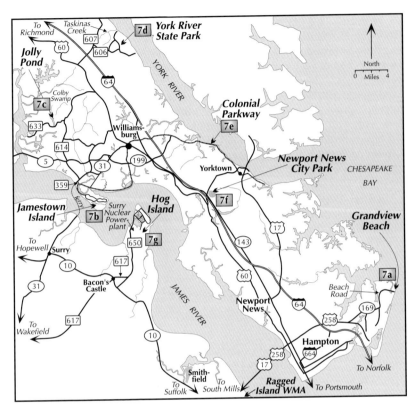

Herons, egrets, and Glossy Ibises are often present. Gray Catbirds, Common Yellowthroats, and Yellow Warblers are common along the marsh ditches. Offshore one should expect to see Brown Pelicans and Common, Royal, Caspian, and Forster's Terns. Least Terns nest at the tip of the peninsula and are usually joined by one or two pairs of Piping Plovers. *The nesting area should be avoided because both species are highly sensitive to disturbance.* On the beach one may expect Dunlins, Sanderlings, Black-bellied Plovers, Ruddy Turnstones, and possibly Red Knots.

Summer: Common birds include Osprey, Clapper Rail, Least, Common, Royal, and Forster's Terns, Laughing Gull, Willet, and Boat-tailed Grackle. Seaside Sparrows and Marsh Wrens continue to sing in the marsh. Families of Pied-billed Grebes might be seen in the pools. Over the bay look for Brown Pelicans, Black Skimmers, and terns.

Fall: The beach and marsh offer resting and feeding stops for migrant raptors, passerines, and shorebirds. Likely to be seen will be American Kestrel, Merlin, Sharp-shinned Hawk, and Northern Harrier. Common, Forster's, Royal, and Least Terns are often plentiful in September. Sea ducks arrive late in the season.

Winter: The bay waters are often covered with sea ducks, such as Common Goldeneyes, Oldsquaws, Black, Surf, and White-winged Scoters, and Red-breasted Mergansers. Common and Red-throated Loons and Horned Grebes feed near shore, and overhead are usually flocks of Bonaparte's Gulls. Check the rock foundation of the old lighthouse for Purple Sandpipers. On the beach Sanderlings and Dunlins can be abundant. In the marsh, Saltmarsh Sharp-tailed, Nelson's Sharp-tailed, and Swamp Sparrows and Sedge and Marsh Wrens are possible, as are Clapper and Virginia Rails. American Bitterns may be flushed from small pools. Snow Buntings and Lapland Longspurs are sometimes located at the tip of the peninsula. Peregrine Falcons and Merlins are occasionally seen. You can also look for "Ipswich" Savannah Sparrows at this season.

RARE OR UNUSUAL BIRDS: Great Cormorant, Harlequin Duck, King Eider, Black Rail, Yellow Rail, Glaucous Gull, Little Gull, Short-eared Owl. This is where a Black-tailed Gull was observed by many birders in the spring of 1995.

SPECIAL COMMENTS: *Do not enter the Least Tern nesting area from early May through July.* Also be sure to avoid nesting Piping Plovers.

Bill Williams, Brian Taber, Ruth Beck

Site 7b.
JAMESTOWN ISLAND,
James City County

BACKGROUND: This is the location of the first permanent English settlement in the New World, founded in 1607. It is a National Historical Park and offers a rich variety of interpretive information on local Indian culture and on the colonial way of life of the island. Twenty-two-and-a-half acres of the island are owned and maintained by the Association for the Preservation of Virginia Antiquities. Jamestown Island is a popular tourist attraction year round, yet its 5-mile wildlife drive offers quiet and enjoyable birding opportunities.

ESSENTIALS: From Williamsburg proceed west on Route 31 (Jamestown Road) for 5 miles. Turn left onto Route 359 for 0.2 mile. Turn right onto the Colonial Parkway and continue to the Park entrance. There is an entry fee. From this point drive 1.0 mile to Jamestown Island.

HABITATS: The 1,500-acre island is bounded on the south and west by the James River. The northern and eastern boundaries are marked by a strip of water called The Thoroughfare. A rich mixture of Loblolly Pine and upland deciduous forest with a thick understory combines with brackish marshes and tidal flats to offer excellent wildlife habitat. Two freshwater ponds and several tidal creeks will be encountered on the wildlife drive.

BIRDS:

Spring: The Pitch and Tar Swamp has many avian possibilities, including Yellow-throated Warbler, Common Yellowthroat, Prothonotary Warbler, Northern and Louisiana Waterthrushes, and Rusty Blackbird. Great Blue Herons feed here and nest nearby on the island. Look for migrant passerines at all of the pull-offs on the wildlife drive.

Summer: Orchard Orioles breed in the more open areas. Other nesting species include Osprey, Yellow-billed Cuckoo, Northern Flicker, Downy, Hairy, Red-headed, and Red-bellied Woodpeckers, Brown-headed Nuthatch, Gray Catbird, Ovenbird, Yellow-throated Vireo, Northern Parula, and Pine Warbler. Black Terns are possible over the river in late summer.

Fall: Bobolinks roost and feed in the Wild Rice and Tickweed marshes. Soras are often abundant in the marshes as well. Streams of swallows cruise over the river, and the forests offer resting and feeding areas for migrating flycatchers, vireos, and warblers.

Winter: Various types of waterfowl, such as Canada Goose, Mallard, American Black Duck, Gadwall, Lesser Scaup, and Bufflehead, can be expected. Brown-headed Nuthatches can be found in the Loblolly Pine forest along with Ruby-crowned and Golden-crowned Kinglets, Eastern Towhees, and numerous White-throated Sparrows. Sometimes there are large flocks of American Robins. Following snow-falls, the road margins are excellent places to find Fox Sparrows and Hermit Thrushes. Great Horned Owls and Eastern Screech-Owls are permanent residents. Bald Eagles should be looked for over the river. The Black Point area has been a reliable place to search for Red-headed Woodpeckers, especially during this season..

RARE OR UNUSUAL BIRDS: Great Cormorant, Brown Pelican, Peregrine Falcon, Yellow Rail, and Lesser Black-backed, Franklin's, and Little Gulls.

SPECIAL COMMENTS: The park opens at 8:30 am and closes at 5:00 pm. There is an $8 entrance fee. Walking on the island during spring, summer, and fall should be restricted to the paved road because ticks and chiggers are likely hazards in grassy areas

Bill Williams, William Snyder, Ruth Beck

Osprey
Gail Yovanovich

Site 7c.
JOLLY POND,
James City County

BACKGROUND: Jolly Pond is an old mill pond located at the lower reaches of Colby Swamp, just west of Williamsburg. It is privately owned.

ESSENTIALS: From Williamsburg proceed west on Route 31 (Jamestown Road) approximately one mile. Turn right onto Route 5, and travel west approximately 5 miles. Turn right onto Centerville Road (Route 614). Proceed for 3 miles to James River Baptist Church on the left. Turn left at the church onto Route 633, Jolly Pond Road. Go 2 miles to the small bridges that cross Jolly Pond.

HABITATS: This freshwater pond is surrounded by mature deciduous forest. Its banks and the swamp into which it drains are predominantly covered with Bald Cypress, Black Gum, and Red Maple.

BIRDS:

Spring: This is the best season to be at this location. Often the area's earliest Yellow-throated Warblers and Louisiana Waterthrushes are heard here in late March. From then on through May the pond road is an excellent location to see and hear virtually any migrant warbler in the entire region. Wild Turkeys are always possible.

Summer: Acadian Flycatchers, Yellow-throated Vireos, Northern Parulas, Prothonotary, Hooded, and Kentucky Warblers, and Ospreys nest here. Wood Ducks are often seen with broods on the pond. Whip-poor-wills can be heard along the road at dusk to well after dark.

Fall: As in the spring, the pond area is a trap for migrating passerines. Especially vocal are Yellow-throated Vireos and Summer Tanagers through late September.

Winter: Waterfowl, such as Mallards, American Black Ducks, Gadwalls, American Wigeons, Ring-necked Ducks, and Wood Ducks, can be expected. Pied-billed Grebes are regular visitors. The nearby roadside forest margins offer Fox Sparrows and Hermit Thrushes. Barred and Great Horned Owls are permanent residents in the area.

RARE OR UNUSUAL BIRDS: Eurasian Wigeon.

SPECIAL COMMENTS: Jolly Pond Road is a narrow twisting county road with only a few pull-off opportunities near the pond. Early morning birding from the paved road is recommended. Much of the area is heavily hunted in the winter. For maximum benefit travel the entire road, stopping at various spots to listen. The road makes a large loop back to Centerville Road. A right turn will take you back to Route 5.

Bill Williams, Ruth Beck, Brian Taber

Site 7d.
YORK RIVER STATE PARK,
James City County

BACKGROUND: The unique estuarine environment found at this 2,505-acre park serves as a nursery for marine life throughout the Chesapeake Bay. Taskinas Creek and the surrounding salt marsh within the park are designated as a Chesapeake Bay National Estuarine Research Reserve. The park is open 8 am to dusk all year. The visitors center, with its information and natural history displays, is open 10 am to 6 pm from April through mid-November, except Tuesdays (757/566-3036).

ESSENTIALS: From Richmond or Williamsburg, access to the park is via I-64. Take the Croaker exit (231-B) onto Route 607. Go northeast for about 1 mile, then turn right onto Riverview Road (Route 606) and go 1.6 miles to the park entrance.

HABITATS: Thirteen miles of trails wind past a freshwater pond and through mixed woodlands, salt marsh, and fields.

BIRDS:

Spring and fall: The woods are excellent for a wide variety of Neotropical migrant thrushes, flycatchers, vireos, tanagers, and warblers. Especially in fall, large flocks of Red-winged Blackbirds and Common Grackles can be seen.

Summer: Present are Ospreys, Great Blue Herons, Green Herons, Laughing Gulls, Northern Bobwhites, Acadian and Great Crested Flycatchers, Eastern Wood-Pewees, Red-eyed and White-eyed Vireos, Yellow-billed Cuckoos, Yellow-throated, Kentucky, Northern Parula, and Pine Warblers, Louisiana Waterthrushes, Summer and Scarlet Tanagers, Field and Chipping Sparrows, Indigo Buntings, and Blue Grosbeaks.

Winter: Many species of dabbling ducks and diving ducks, including Canvasback and Ruddy Duck, may be seen on the river. Wood Ducks are often found on the freshwater pond. Ring-billed, Herring, and Bonaparte's Gulls, Double-crested Cormorant, Pied-billed and Horned Grebes, Bald Eagle, Common Loon, Red-tailed Hawk, both kinglets, Brown Creeper, Hermit Thrush, Marsh Wren, and Swamp Sparrow can be found.

SPECIAL COMMENTS: The park invites participation in interpretive programs and guided canoe trips. The park has picnic shelters, restrooms, and an observation tower.

Brian Taber, Sue Ridd

Site 7e.
COLONIAL PARKWAY,
James City County, York County, Williamsburg City

BACKGROUND: Begun in 1931, the Colonial Parkway was completed in 1957 linking the historic Yorktown Battlefields with the Jamestown 1607 settlement. This scenic drive links some of the country's most historic sites and is owned and maintained by the National Park Service.

ESSENTIALS: This 23-mile roadway can be reached from the Colonial Williamsburg Information Center by turning left from the main parking lot to enter the Parkway. Bear right for the 11-mile Jamestown excursion or bear left for the 12-mile Yorktown journey. The Parkway may also be reached from I-64 at Williamsburg by taking Exit 242-B, Route 199 east.

HABITATS: The eastern portion of the Parkway parallels the tidal salt water of the York River. Its salt-marsh tributaries are bounded by mature deciduous and Loblolly Pine forests. The Williamsburg section is predominantly deciduous forest with intermittent suburban communities. The western end of the Parkway to Jamestown parallels the brackish James River, crossing several brackish to freshwater creeks and marshes. Deciduous hardwood and Loblolly Pine stands are scattered along the way.

BIRDS:

Spring: Ospreys nest commonly on both ends of the Parkway on duck blinds and channel markers. Because the York River is heavily used by crabbing vessels, most waterfowl leave early in the spring. At Indian Field Creek look for the small population of Boat-tailed Grackles (2-4 birds) that nest there. The nearby marshes have Clapper Rails and Green Herons. The Jamestown end of the drive will offer numerous swallows passing inland. Caspian, Royal, and Forster's Terns feed actively at the creek inlets. Any of the pull-offs along the way may produce singing migrant landbirds. Yellow-throated Warblers and Northern Parulas should be found at many stops. College Creek, on the Jamestown end, is an excellent place to see migrant raptors of 8 to 10 species crossing the river in late February to mid-May.

Summer: Both rivers continue to offer Ospreys and, in recent years, breeding Canada Geese. Laughing Gulls and Royal Terns summer throughout the area. Belted Kingfishers are regularly found near creeks, along with numerous Barn Swallows.

Fall: Ducks do not arrive until late in the season. Migrant swallows are often abundant.

Winter: On the York River end of the Parkway waterbirds are common. Species to be expected include Common Loon, Horned Grebe, Canvasback, Lesser Scaup, Bufflehead, Common Goldeneye, and Ruddy Duck. Check the far reaches of Indian Field and Flegates Creeks for Tundra Swan. Bald Eagles are frequently seen over the river. At Jones Mill Pond look for Pied-billed Grebe, Wood Duck, and Ring-necked Duck. A pair of Mute Swans will often be seen here. The James River offers Canada Goose, Mallard, American Black Duck, Northern Pintail, and Red-breasted and Hooded Mergansers. The marsh edges may produce Common Snipe. Swamp Sparrows are common, while Marsh Wrens should be looked for. During snow-falls American Pipits and Fox Sparrows are usually found along the road edge.

RARE OR UNUSUAL BIRDS: Red-necked and "Western" Grebes, Magnificent Frigatebird, Northern Gannet, Brown Pelican, Great Cormorant, Eurasian Wigeon, Glaucous Gull, Iceland Gull, Black-headed Gull, Roseate Tern, Bridled Tern, Sooty Tern, Le Conte's Sparrow, Lapland Longspur, and Snow Bunting.

Bill Williams, Ruth Beck

Site 7f.
NEWPORT NEWS CITY PARK,
Newport News City

BACKGROUND: The park covers 8,000 acres and is a popular place for hikers, joggers, golfers, and boaters. The park is open from sunrise to sunset all year. An interpretive center is open Memorial Day through September 30th, Wednesday through Sunday, from 9 am to 7 pm. From October 1 to Memorial Day, the center is open 9 am to 5 pm, weekends only.

DIRECTIONS: The park is on Route 143, in the northern end of Newport News. From I-64, take Exit 250-B. Turn left on Route 143 to the park entrance.

HABITATS: Extensive trails cross the large reservoir and wind through swamp, marsh, and mixed woodlands.

BIRDS:

Spring and fall: This is an excellent area for a great variety of migrating thrushes, flycatchers, vireos, tanagers, and warblers.

Summer: Red-shouldered Hawks, Prothonotary, Yellow-throated, and Pine Warblers, Northern Parulas, Ovenbirds, and Louisiana Waterthrushes are common. Also, this is a good place to find Summer and Scarlet Tanagers, Brown-headed Nuthatches, and Great Crested and Acadian Flycatchers.

Winter: Ring-billed Gulls, Tundra Swans, Canada Geese, American Wigeons, Pied-billed Grebes, Ring-necked Ducks, Wood Ducks, Redheads, and other waterfowl generally fill the reservoir. The swamps and woodlands host Swamp Sparrows, Rusty Blackbirds, Downy, Hairy, Red-bellied, Red-headed, and Pileated Woodpeckers, both kinglets, and many Yellow-rumped Warblers.

RARE OR UNUSUAL BIRDS: White Ibis, Eurasian Wigeon, and Glaucous Gull.

SPECIAL COMMENTS: The park includes fishing, boat rental, picnic areas, and restrooms. Eastern Bluebird nest boxes are found along trails at the golf courses.

Brian Taber, Dorothy Mitchell

Site 7g.
HOG ISLAND,
Surry County

BACKGROUND: Hog Island Waterfowl Management Area was established in 1963 by the State of Virginia after a ten-year development. It now contains three tracts of land, adding up to 3,908 acres. The most interesting tract for birds is the northernmost property, at the end of the peninsula. This area was used in colonial times to keep pigs, hence the name.

DIRECTIONS: From Williamsburg proceed west on Route 31 (Jamestown Road) to the Jamestown ferry. Take the ferry across the James River to Surry County. Continue on Route 31 four miles to the town of Surry. Turn left onto Route 10. Drive 8 miles to Route 617 at Bacon's Castle. Turn left and go to Route 650. Turn left and go 5 miles through the Surry Nuclear Power Plant property, cross the canal, and proceed to the refuge at the end of the paved road. From Smithfield take Route 10 west about 15 miles to Route 650. Turn right and proceed straight to the refuge.

HABITATS: Hog Island is a not an island at all. It is a peninsula bounded by the brackish waters of the James River on the east and west. Scattered Loblolly Pine stands and cultivated fields surround shallow freshwater impoundments; dirt roads make the area accessible to birders.

BIRDS:

Spring: American Pipits and Horned Larks may occur in the fields. Waterfowl are numerous early in the period, dwindling by late April, when Blue-winged Teal increase. Bald Eagles often congregate here to feed on carp. Spotted and Solitary Sandpipers and Greater and Lesser Yellowlegs become numerous, as do Barn, Bank, Northern Rough-winged, and Tree Swallows. Cliff Swallows should be looked for, as well as migrating raptors. Interesting shorebirds include White-rumped Sandpiper and Wilson's Phalarope.

Summer: A small breeding group of Canada Geese remains on the refuge. Blue Grosbeaks can be found in the thickets and on the wires. Eastern Bluebirds, Brown-headed Nuthatches, Eastern Kingbirds, and Orchard Orioles should be readily seen. A large Great Blue Heron colony is active near the river, and Ospreys nest in the pine stands. Late in the season, shorebirds can be numerous: both yellowlegs, both dowitchers, Black-bellied and Semipalmated Plovers, and Spotted, Western, Semipalmated, Least, Pectoral, and Stilt Sandpipers. Also be alert for Forster's, Royal, Caspian, and Least Terns and many swallows.

Fall: Tree Swallows, Bobolinks, and many heron and shorebird species predominate early. American Golden-Plovers and both Buff-breasted and Upland Sandpipers may be present. Ducks arrive by late October. Tern species include Forster's, Royal, Caspian, and Least. Bald Eagles are often visible.

Winter: Large flocks of dabbling ducks, such as Northern Pintails, Green-winged Teal, Ring-necked Ducks, Hooded Mergansers, Mallards, and American Black Ducks, are mixed with Canada Geese, American Coots, and an occasional Snow Goose. Common Mergansers should be looked for. Brown-headed Nuthatches can be found in the pine stands, and Northern Harriers and Bald Eagles cruise the fields. American Tree Sparrows have been found near the parking lot at the end of the refuge road. Sharp-shinned and Cooper's Hawks hunt the thickets.

RARE OR UNUSUAL BIRDS: American White Pelican, White Ibis, Greater White-fronted Goose, Fulvous Whistling-Duck, Eurasian Wigeon, Wood Stork, Rough-legged Hawk, Swallow-tailed Kite, Marbled Godwit, American Avocet, Ruff, Red Phalarope, Glaucous Gull, Short-eared Owl, Black-headed Grosbeak, Yellow-headed Blackbird, Dickcissel, and American Tree Sparrow.

SPECIAL COMMENTS: Controlled hunting is allowed during duck season on certain weekdays. Mosquitoes can be very bothersome, too.

Bill Williams, Ruth Beck

Site 8a. GEORGE WASHINGTON BIRTHPLACE NATIONAL MONUMENT, *Westmoreland County*

BACKGROUND: The National Monument is open year round for day use and picnicking. A visitors center with restrooms is open year round. Historical interpretation is the emphasis of the park, including optional tours of Washington's rebuilt home and restored herb garden. There are many easy paved and gravel trails through this historical colonial working farm. There are excellent views of Pope's Creek throughout the park as well as a road to access the Potomac River. Visitors can drive to beach and Pope's Creek overlooks.

ESSENTIALS: From Oak Grove go east on Route 3 for 2.9 miles to "Washington's Birthplace" sign. Turn left on Route 204 and proceed 2 miles to the entrance.

HABITATS: Includes Potomac River beach; freshwater and brackish marsh; bottomland; heavily wooded and steep ravines with large mature

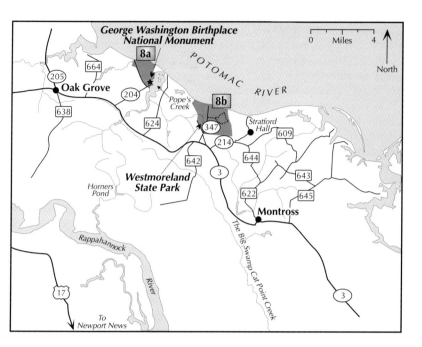

poplars, oaks, and hickories; pasture and mowed grasslands; pine forests; ponds; roads; and paths and hiking trails connecting most habitats. The trails lead through mature pine and Red-cedar forests as well as mixed deciduous hardwoods. There is also much open land under cultivation and in pasture.

BIRDS:

Spring: Large rafts of sea and bay ducks flock off the beach near the mouth of Pope's Creek in March (5,000+ scaup, Canvasback). Migrating Double-crested Cormorants often fly along the shore. Red-breasted Mergansers congregate offshore. Common Loon, Horned Grebe, Oldsquaw, Bonaparte's Gull, and Caspian Tern can be seen on the river. Migrant passerines, peaking late April to mid-May, include Canada, Black-throated Green, Kentucky, Black-and-white, and Hooded Warblers.

Summer: Nesting birds include (in addition to more common species) Least Bittern, Great Blue Heron (rookery not on property, but the species nests locally), Green Heron, Cattle Egret, Great Egret, Osprey, Bald Eagle, Wood Duck, Yellow-billed Cuckoo, Great Horned Owl, Barred Owl, Acadian Flycatcher, Eastern Wood-Pewee, Great Crested Flycatcher, Marsh Wren, Eastern Bluebird, Wood Thrush, Cedar Waxwing, White-eyed Vireo, Red-eyed Vireo, Yellow Warbler, Yellow-throated Warbler, Pine Warbler, Prairie Warbler, Prothonotary Warbler, Ovenbird, Kentucky Warbler, Common Yellowthroat, Hooded Warbler, Yellow-breasted Chat, Summer and Scarlet Tanagers, Baltimore and Orchard Orioles, Blue Grosbeak, Indigo Bunting,

Chipping and Field Sparrows, and American Goldfinch. Spotted Sandpiper, Dunlin, and Louisiana Waterthrush can be seen in late summer.

Fall: Tundra Swans, geese, and ducks return. Caspian, Royal (less common than Caspian), and Forster's Terns are usual. Migrating warblers are found in the hardwood forests.

Winter: Highlights include large rafts of ducks (including scaup, goldeneye, Canvasback, Ruddy Duck, Red-breasted Merganser, American Wigeon, and Bufflehead) on the Potomac. They can easily be observed with a spotting scope. Occasional close views of rafts in Pope's Creek are possible. Tundra Swan and Canada Goose are usual. Bald Eagles are often observed in association with waterfowl; the eagles perch in tall trees along shoreline. Surf Scoters and a few loons overwinter on this portion of the Potomac. Wood Duck, Hooded Merganser, and Gadwall are often seen on interior ponds. Seven species of woodpeckers are usually present. Winter assemblages include Carolina Chickadee, Tufted Titmouse, nuthatches (White-breasted and Red-breasted), Brown Creeper, both kinglets, Hermit Thrush, finches, Pine and Yellow-rumped Warblers, and several species of sparrows.

RARE OR UNUSUAL BIRDS: Adult and immature Bald Eagles. Shoreline has occasional unusual shorebird migrants.

SPECIAL COMMENTS: Bald Eagles nest nearby, and both adults and immatures are commonly seen year round, most often from the beach or over Pope's Creek. Visitors should take care not to disturb nesting eagles. Large rafts of bay ducks in early winter and again in late winter/early spring are spectacular.

Westmoreland State Park is nearby (Site 8b), these two sites can easily be covered together in a day, depending on how much one walks. Washington's Birthplace has more handicapped accessibility to good birding spots via trails, although both parks offer good overlooks.

Bill Portlock, J. E. Johnson

Site 8b.
WESTMORELAND STATE PARK,
Westmoreland County

BACKGROUND: Westmoreland State Park (804/493-8821) is one of the original six Virginia state parks established in the 1930s. The 1,300-acre park contains several miles of trails through diverse Coastal Plain topography. At present, it is not heavily visited except on weekends during the summer months. Camping and housekeeping cabins are available. A popular birding trail through diverse habitats is the Big Meadows Trail, which takes hikers through a mature mixed oak/hickory/pine forest to a Beaver swamp and the Potomac River. There are excellent views of the Potomac River from several vantage points in the park.

ESSENTIALS: From Montross, go west on Route 3 for 4.3 miles to the park sign. Turn right into the park entrance.

HABITATS: Includes Potomac River beach, freshwater marsh, late-successional Beaver swamp (filling in and evolving into a wet grassy meadow); bottomland, heavily wooded and steep ravines with large mature Tulip Poplars, oaks, and hickories; open and mowed grasslands; pine forest; pond; and road, paths, and hiking trails connecting most habitats. Visitors can drive to the beach and to cliffs overlooking river.

BIRDS:

Spring: Large rafts of sea and bay ducks flock in the cove beneath the cliffs in March. Migrating Double-crested Cormorants often fly close to cliffs. Common Loon, Horned Grebe, Oldsquaw, Bonaparte's Gull, and Caspian Tern are usual on the river. Migrating passerines peak in late April to mid-May.

Summer: Nesting birds include (in addition to more common species) Least Bittern, Great Blue Heron, Green Heron, Osprey, Bald Eagle, Wood Duck, Yellow-billed Cuckoo, Great Horned Owl, Barred Owl, Acadian Flycatcher, Marsh Wren, Cedar Waxwing, White-eyed Vireo, Red-eyed Vireo, Yellow Warbler, Yellow-throated Warbler, Pine Warbler, Prairie Warbler, Prothonotary Warbler, Ovenbird, Kentucky Warbler, Common Yellowthroat, Hooded Warbler, Yellow-breasted Chat, Summer Tanager, Scarlet Tanager, Blue Grosbeak, Indigo Bunting, Chipping Sparrow, Field Sparrow, Orchard Oriole, and American Goldfinch.

Fall: Tundra Swans, geese, and ducks return. Terns (Caspian, Royal, Forster's) are usual. Migrating warblers of several species are found in the hardwood forest.

Winter: Highlights include rafts of ducks, such as scaup, Common Goldeneye, Canvasback, Ruddy Duck, and Bufflehead, on the river. Tundra Swans and Canada Geese (occasionally with a few Snows and even a Greater White-fronted) are also usually present. Surf Scoters and loons can be seen along the Potomac shore. Winter assemblages of Carolina Chickadees, Tufted Titmice, and nuthatches are frequently seen, as are Brown Creeper, both kinglets, Hermit Thrush, Pine and Yellow-rumped Warblers, and several species of sparrows.

SPECIAL COMMENTS: Bald Eagles nest nearby; both adults and immatures are commonly seen year round.

Bill Portlock, J. E. Johnson

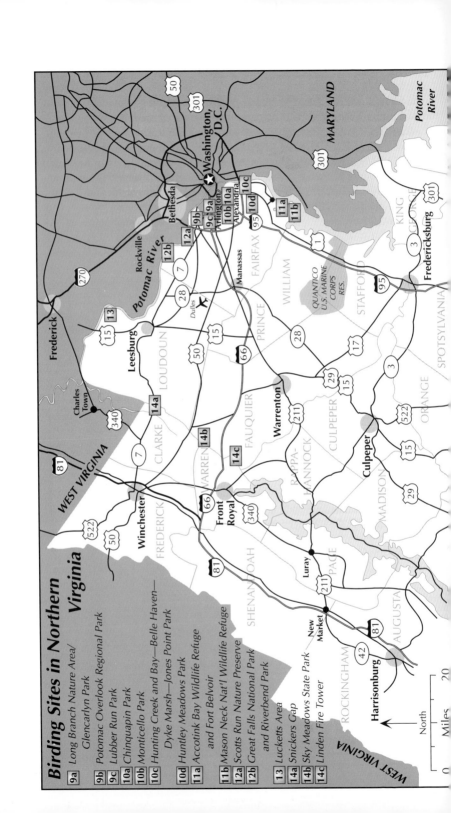

Birding Sites in Northern Virginia

- **9a** Long Branch Nature Area/ Glencarlyn Park
- **9b** Potomac Overlook Regional Park
- **9c** Lubber Run Park
- **10a** Chinquapin Park
- **10b** Monticello Park
- **10c** Hunting Creek and Bay—Belle Haven— Dyke Marsh—Jones Point Park
- **10d** Huntley Meadows Park
- **11a** Accotink Bay Wildlife Refuge and Fort Belvoir
- **11b** Mason Neck Nat'l Wildlife Refuge
- **12a** Scotts Run Nature Preserve
- **12b** Great Falls National Park and Riverbend Park
- **13** Lucketts Area
- **14a** Snickers Gap
- **14b** Sky Meadows State Park
- **14c** Linden Fire Tower

North

Miles

0   20

NORTHERN VIRGINIA

The Northern geographic division, as delineated in this book, includes the northern tier of counties, which embraces parts of classical northern Piedmont, Blue Ridge, and Ridge and Valley provinces. Separating this division was done because of birds that choose habitats here in both the breeding season and the winter. The eastern Piedmont section is noted for its crowded metropolitan and suburban areas, its rolling hills, and its farmlands. The Blue Ridge mountains attain elevations up to about 2,500 ft. The Skyline Drive into Shenandoah National Park begins at Front Royal. The westernmost section includes portions of the northern Shenandoah Valley, at Winchester for example, and the northernmost extension of North Mountain along the Appalachians.

Even in some of the metropolitan areas of northern Virginia, birds may be both abundant and diverse. Backyard birders easily record breeding House Finches, House Wrens, White-breasted Nuthatches, Tufted Titmice, Carolina Chickadees, and even Pileated Woodpeckers and (rarely) Pine Siskins. Some years ago when Evening Grosbeaks invaded the state, good numbers of them were recorded at feeders throughout the area.

Because of the broad transect taken by this division, habitats are highly variable, as are some of the birds inhabiting them at different seasons. In the northern Piedmont, for example, grassy fields or their edges attract American Kestrels, Grasshopper Sparrows, Eastern Meadowlarks, and the occasional Dickcissel, while Prothonotary Warblers, Warbling Vireos, and Baltimore Orioles may be seen along the Potomac River. One special site near Lucketts is probably the most reliable place in the state to see breeding Upland Sandpipers. Shrubland birds include Indigo Bunting, Prairie Warbler, and Brown Thrasher. Along this northern portion of the Blue Ridge Mountains, including the Skyline Drive, the hardwood forests yield breeding Scarlet Tanagers, Cerulean, Kentucky, and Hooded Warblers, Great Crested and Acadian Flycatchers, and Red-tailed Hawks. At almost any season, Common Ravens' croaks can be heard as the birds pass high overhead. In the open grassland and cultivated fields of the Shenandoah Valley one can find breeding Blue Grosbeaks, Grasshopper Sparrows, Vesper Sparrows, and, perhaps, Savannah Sparrows and Bobolinks. On the west, in the northernmost part of the Appalachian Mountains in Virginia, look for breeding Rose-breasted Grosbeaks, Worm-eating Warblers, and Cedar Waxwings.

This section of the Blue Ridge is well known for its hawk-watching sites. It is here that fall has yielded hundreds of raptors migrating through the state. These include Broad-winged Hawks and other buteos, all three accipiter species, a Gyrfalcon, and the occasional Golden Eagle.

Winter is an exciting time to look for birds in this northern section of the state. It is then that one is likely to find Northern Shrikes, Rough-legged

Hawks, Snowy Owls, Lapland Longspurs, Snow Buntings, and White-crowned and American Tree Sparrows.

MORE INFORMATION:

General Information

Alexandria Visitor Center
221 King Street, Alexandria, VA 22314
703/838-4200

Arlington County Visitor Center
735 18th Street South, Arlington, VA 22202
800/677-6267

Fairfax County Convention and Visitors Bureau
Tysons Corner, 8300 Boone Boulevard (Suite 450), Vienna, VA 22182
703/790-3329

Fredericksburg Visitor Center
706 Caroline Street, Fredericksburg, VA 22401
800/678-4748

Loudoun County Tourism Council
108-D South Street SE, Leesburg, VA 20175
800/752-6118

Warrenton-Fauquier County Visitor Center
183A Keith Street, Warrenton, VA 20186
540/347-4414

Winchester-Frederick County Visitor Center
1360 South Pleasant Valley Road, Winchester, VA 22601
800/662-1360

Wildlife Management Areas

Phelps: 4,500 acres of rolling Piedmont country, some forested and some in an open, grassy-shrubby habitat, along the Rappahannock River, near Kellys Ford, Fauquier and Culpeper counties.

G. Richard Thompson: 4,000 acres of forested Blue Ridge Mountains, 4 miles north of Linden; Warren, Fauquier, and Clark counties. (See more details under sites #14b and #14c.)

Site 9a.
LONG BRANCH NATURE AREA/GLENCARLYN PARK,
Arlington County

BACKGROUND: This 18-acre nature center was established in 1972 on previously owned residential property. It is surrounded by urban homesites in the middle of Arlington County. Long Branch (stream) connects to Four Mile Run and the W & OD trail (Washington and Old Dominion Railroad) on its east end. Glencarlyn Park also connects with the W & OD trail but at a point a little farther north. (In conjunction with Long Branch and Glencarlyn Parks, Four Mile Run and the W & OD trail can be comfortably birded in between and south to Columbia Pike, Route 244, and north beyond Carlin Springs Road.) The Nature Center is closed on Mondays. Glencarlyn has picnic and other outdoor facilities.

ESSENTIALS: From the Beltway (I-495) take Exit 8 to US-50 Arlington. Drive east 4.8 miles on US-50 to the Carlin Springs Road exit on the right. Turn right onto Carlin Springs Road and go south 0.5 mile. Turn left into the Long Branch Park entrance road shared with Northern Virginia Doctors' Medical Center. Continue straight to the parking lot and Nature Center.

Glencarlyn Park can be reached from Carlin Springs Road east to the 3rd and Harrison Streets junction. The W & OD trail can be accessed at many crossing points, but the relevant places with nearby parking are at Leesburg Pike, Columbia Pike, Arlington Boulevard, Carlin Springs Road and Wilson Boulevard.

HABITATS: Within Long Branch Park, the narrow stream (Long Branch), bounded on both sides by hillsides of mixed hardwoods and deciduous understory, flows east and rather steeply downhill into Four Mile Run. Upland areas nearby have mixed conifers and hardwoods. Two small ponds and one small artificially controlled meadow are connected by nature trails. Trails also connect to mixed woodlands in Glencarlyn north through the hills and along Four Mile Run. The W & OD trail, generally paralleling Four Mile Run, is on the elevated, old Washington and Old Dominion Railroad bed and draws a variety of nonbirding recreation users. Sparrow Swamp, an attractive wet area hosting a variety of wildlife, is along the W & OD trail a little south of the Long Branch stream mouth.

BIRDS:

Spring: Most eastern species of migrant warblers can be found (Blue-winged, Golden-winged, Black-throated Blue, Blackpoll, both waterthrushes), along with Yellow-billed Cuckoo, flycatchers, vireos, thrushes, Scarlet Tanager, Rose-breasted Grosbeak, Indigo Bunting, and Baltimore Oriole. Black-crowned Night-Heron and Solitary Sandpiper have been seen at Sparrow Swamp.

Summer: Especially obvious at this season are Red-eyed Vireos, a few nesting warbler species, Pileated Woodpeckers, Eastern Phoebes, Wood Thrushes. Scarlet Tanagers, and Baltimore Orioles. Over 40 breeding species have been recorded.

Fall: From mid-August into October most eastern species of warblers (including Golden-winged, Orange-crowned, and even Connecticut) have been found. Flycatchers, both kinglets, thrushes, vireos, sparrows, and hawks are also seen at this time.

Winter: Woodpeckers (Pileated, Hairy), sparrows (Song, White-throated), Eastern Towhee, Dark-eyed Junco, Carolina Chickadee, Brown Creeper, Carolina Wren, Winter Wren, and raptors have been recorded.

RARE OR UNUSUAL BIRDS: Yellow-crowned Night-Heron, Glossy Ibis, Connecticut Warbler, Lincoln's Sparrow, Common Redpoll.

Charlotte Friend, Paul G. DuMont, Terry Boykie

Site 9b.
POTOMAC OVERLOOK REGIONAL PARK,
Arlington County

BACKGROUND: This was the former site of the Donaldson farm, circa 1870. The 95-acre park, established in 1971, is a preserve amid the suburbs and urban sprawl of Arlington. The Nature Center and trails provide an ideal setting for studying birds and other aspects of the region's rich cultural and natural history. About 140 species of birds have been recorded over the years.

ESSENTIALS: From I-66 eastbound, take Exit 72 (Lee Highway, US-29). At the bottom of the exit ramp, turn left onto Lee Highway and proceed about 1 mile to Military Road. Turn right and continue on Military Road to Marcey Road; turn right again and follow this road to the park. From I-66 westbound take Exit 71 (Glebe Road); turn right onto Glebe Road and follow it to Lee Highway (US-29). Turn right again, follow Lee Highway to Military

Rose-breasted Grosbeak
Gail Diane Yovanovich

Road, turn left, and follow it to Marcey Road. Another right will take you to the park entrance.

HABITATS: The park contains mostly heavily forested hills and valleys with oaks, beech, and Tulip Poplar, also brushy areas and fields in various successional stages; all of these provide cover, food, and water for a large variety of birds. The Donaldson Run Trail leads to the Potomac River.

BIRDS:

Spring: Many species of migrant warblers can be found (Blue-winged, Black-throated Blue, Blackburnian, Blackpoll), as well as thrushes (Hermit, Veery, Swainson's, Gray-cheeked), Scarlet Tanager, Indigo Bunting, Rose-breasted Grosbeak, Baltimore Oriole, and hawks. Along the river can be seen Great Blue and Green Herons, Wood Duck, and Herring and Ring-billed Gulls.

Summer: Breeding birds include woodpeckers (including Pileated), Chimney Swift, Great Crested Flycatcher, Acadian Flycatcher, House and Carolina Wrens, Blue-gray Gnatcatcher, Red-eyed and White-eyed Vireos, Northern Cardinal, Wood Thrush, Scarlet Tanager, and Eastern Towhee. Especially over the distant river, Ospreys and Bald Eagles can be seen at this time of year.

Fall: Beginning in mid-August many species of warblers pass through the park. Abundant berry crops attract migrant thrushes, Gray Catbird, American Robin, and Blue Jay. Flycatchers, both kinglets, and several vireos are also seen.

Winter: Woodpeckers (Hairy, Pileated), sparrows (Song, White-throated, possibly Fox), Dark-eyed Junco, Carolina Chickadee, Brown Creeper, Carolina Wren, Cedar Waxwings, and raptors, such as Red-tailed and Red-shouldered Hawks, will winter in the park.

RARE OR UNUSUAL BIRDS: Red-breasted Nuthatch (in some years), Wild Turkey, Whip-poor-will, Nashville Warbler, Pine Siskin.

Charlotte Friend, Toni Pepin

Site 9c.
LUBBER RUN PARK,
Arlington County

BACKGROUND: Lubber Run Park is a small county park adjacent to Lubber Run Center. There is no nature center, but restrooms are available in the Center during working hours. Call Long Branch Nature Center at 703/358-6535 for information. This park is a favorite of local birders for spring and fall migrants, especially warblers.

ESSENTIALS: From the Beltway (I-495) take Exit 8 to US-50 (Arlington). Go 5.6 miles east on US-50 to Park Drive. Turn left on North Park Drive and continue 1.0 mile to the parking lot at Lubber Run Center.

HABITATS: The park is about one mile long with paths following the stream. Hillsides are covered with upland deciduous mixed hardwoods.

BIRDS: The woodland birds here are the same as those at nearby Long Branch Nature Center. There are no ponds, but the stream attracts bathing birds.

Spring: A very good place to visit during May for warblers, thrushes, and other spring migrants. Most species of eastern migrant warblers (Blue-winged, Golden-winged, Cape May, Black-throated Blue, Palm, Blackpoll, Wilson's, Canada, both waterthrushes), Yellow-billed Cuckoo, flycatchers, thrushes (Hermit, Veery, Swainson's, Wood), vireos, Scarlet Tanager, Rose-breasted Grosbeak, Lincoln's Sparrow, and Baltimore Oriole are regularly found in the park.

Fall: From mid-August through September many eastern species of warblers (including Golden-winged) are found. Flycatchers, both kinglets, thrushes, and vireos are regularly seen. Look for Philadelphia Vireo in low vegetation near the creeks.

Charlotte Friend

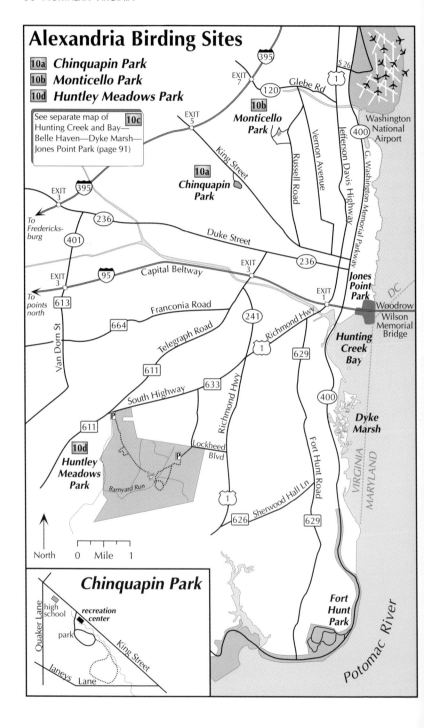

Alexandria Birding Sites

10a *Chinquapin Park*
10b *Monticello Park*
10d *Huntley Meadows Park*

See separate map of
Hunting Creek and Bay—
Belle Haven—Dyke Marsh—
Jones Point Park (page 91) **10c**

395

EXIT 7

120

Glebe Rd

S 26

1

10b
Monticello Park

EXIT 5

Washington
National
Airport

400

King Street

10a
Chinquapin Park

Russell Road

Vernon Avenue

Jefferson Davis Highway

G. Washington Memorial Parkway

EXIT 3 395

236

To Fredericks-
burg

401

Duke Street

236

EXIT 3

95 Capital Beltway

EXIT 3

To points north 613

Franconia Road

241

Richmond Hwy

Jones Point Park

EXIT 1

Woodrow Wilson Memorial Bridge

DC

664

Telegraph Road

1

629

Hunting Creek Bay

Van Dorn St

611

633

Richmond Hwy

South Highway

611

P

Lockheed Blvd

P

400

Dyke Marsh

10d
Huntley Meadows Park

Barnyard Run

1

626 Sherwood Hall Ln

629

Fort Hunt Road

VIRGINIA
MARYLAND

North 0 Mile 1

Fort Hunt Park

Potomac River

Chinquapin Park

Quaker Lane

high school

recreation center

park

King Street

Janeys Lane

Site 10a.
CHINQUAPIN PARK,
Alexandria City

BACKGROUND: Chinquapin Park comprises an indoor swimming-pool and updated recreation center. But behind the developed area is one of the largest forested tracts in Alexandria. The park sits atop a small ridge, one of the highest points in the city.

ESSENTIALS: From I-395 take King Street (Route 7) toward Alexandria. Turn right on Chinquapin Drive, just past T. C. Williams High School. Park at the recreation center lot or on the loop a little farther up. (*Note:* on weekends, it is best to be there early, before all of the community activity of soccer games and gardening starts up.)

HABITATS: The park has a mixture of open ball fields, pine and deciduous woods, two woodland streams, a small marshy, boglike area, and flower and vegetable gardens cultivated by neighbors. The open grassy area with large deciduous trees contained within the loop drive is a good place for birds, as is the entire perimeter of trees surrounding this part of the park. Because of all the human activity that takes place in and around the park, Chinquapin Park is best during migration seasons.

BIRDS:

Spring and fall: Migrants stop in the trees on the loop drive. Baltimore and Orchard Orioles, Scarlet Tanagers (occasional Summer Tanager), and Rose-breasted Grosbeaks are common spring migrants, along with Palm, Blackpoll, Magnolia, and Chestnut-sided Warblers. Cedar Waxwings in spring flocks are common, and American Redstarts and Least Flycatchers can be found along the tree line. Check the grassy areas for migrant sparrows, in particular Savannah, Field, and White-crowned. The gardens in the southeast corner can be a very productive birding area, particularly in the early spring and fall. Common Yellowthroat, House Wren, Chipping Sparrow, and Song Sparrow can all turn up here. At the corner of the gardens, work the tree line left and right for Black-throated Green, Black-throated Blue, and other migrating warblers. In spring and fall take the path that bears to the right at the corner where the tree line meets, checking the pines for Cape May, Magnolia, and Black-and-white Warblers, both kinglets, and Red-breasted Nuthatches. Golden-winged and Mourning Warblers have been reported here irregularly. As you explore the trails, several species of thrushes (Hermit, Wood, Swainson's, and Gray-cheeked) are seen regularly during migration; Ovenbirds are also common migrants. Both Louisiana and Northern Waterthrushes are common spring migrants and occasional fall migrants; they will pop up out of the Skunk Cabbage if alarmed. Follow the trail and the stream all the way to the end, watching for bathing birds on both sides of the trail, until you come back out at the lower parking lot next to the recreation center. In winter a Long-eared Owl has been seen in the pines behind the baseball diamond.

Summer: Eastern Kingbirds nest here, as do Pine Warblers despite the decreasing number of pines. Wood Thrushes also breed in the park.

Winter: Red-shouldered, Sharp-shinned, and Cooper's Hawks are regular winter residents, and American Crows will often alert you to their presence. American Kestrels have been regular winter visitors as well, usually in the trees overlooking the gardens. Keep an eye out also for year-round Downy, Hairy, and Red-bellied Woodpeckers, along with Yellow-bellied Sapsuckers in the winter. This park is also a good place to check in winter for Hermit Thrush, Brown Creeper, kinglets, Winter Wren, finches (Common Redpoll has occurred), and sparrows.

Mark Farmer, Jackson Abbott

Site 10b.
MONTICELLO PARK,
Alexandria City

BACKGROUND: This small, 15-acre park is located in the City of Alexandria, and is essentially an island in the midst of an urban setting. Because of its steep-sided slopes, the park offers one of the best places in northern Virginia to get eye-level, close-up views of migratory birds.

ESSENTIALS: To reach Monticello Park from King Street, take Russell Road for 2.9 miles to Beverley Drive. Turn left on Beverley. The park is 200 yards up Beverley on the left, just before the road bears right.

HABITATS: Monticello Park is a creek valley whose slopes are heavily forested with tall oaks, maples, Tulip Poplar, beech, and other deciduous trees. The understory on both sides of a small, intermittent stream is a dense vegetation of Mountain Laurel, honeysuckle, and other plants.

BIRDS:

Spring and fall: By far, it is best here in spring when migrants stop off to bathe and drink along the stream. Most of the eastern warblers—Blackburnian, Bay-breasted, Tennessee, Chestnut-sided, Magnolia, American Redstart, Hooded, and Kentucky, to name but a few—are seen here every year. It is one of the more reliable spots in the region for Wilson's Warblers. Other regular migrants include Winter Wren, Rose-breasted Grosbeak, Indigo Bunting, and Great Crested Flycatcher. The middle of the park, where there is a slight S-curve in the creek that is overgrown with shrubbery, provides an excellent viewing angle to watch the birds bathing at very close range. Many local birders use their weekday lunch hour to bring a sandwich and watch the birds at this spot. Keep an eye on the laurel growing on the hillsides for Ovenbird and for all the thrushes, including Gray-cheeked. They can all be in good numbers in the spring and at that season are practically underfoot. The hillsides are also good for Worm-eating and Black-throated Blue Warblers. Be aware that unusual migrants can also be found, that any of the migrating hawks could appear, and that even Red-headed Woodpeckers have been sighted here.

SPECIAL CONCERNS: There is minimal warbler activity in the park before 10:00 a.m. The park's hillside are steep, so the sun does not strike the bathing areas until then. However, waterthrushes and *Catharus* thrushes are best seen early in the morning before the day's activities scatter them elsewhere, or toward evening, when the park is relatively quiet once again.

The hotter, the dryer and more sunny the weather, the better the bird activity. If the leaves of the trees are wet, there is less need for the birds to come all the way down to the creek in search of water.

Mark Farmer, Joe Stephens

Site 10c.
HUNTING CREEK AND BAY, BELLE HAVEN, DYKE MARSH, AND JONES POINT PARK,
Alexandria City and Fairfax County

BACKGROUND: The Hunting Creek and Bay/Belle Haven/Dyke Marsh area along the Potomac River is unusual for this region because it provides a freshwater tidal area, mudflats, and marsh, therefore acting as a magnet to migrants and nesters alike. These three areas form a narrow, continuous waterfront area just south of Alexandria along the George Washington Parkway, and the Belle Haven Picnic Area provides a convenient parking location and access to all three areas.

Dyke Marsh is maintained under the jurisdiction of the National Park Service, which also oversees the nearby Mount Vernon Trail. Since the 1940s, over 290 species of birds have been seen at Dyke Marsh or nearby.

Jones Point Park , at the foot of the Woodrow Wilson Bridge, is north of these three areas.

ESSENTIALS: Follow the George Washington Memorial Parkway south from I-95, below the Woodrow Wilson Bridge. On the parkway about one mile south of the Hunting Towers Apartments is a well-marked left turn into the Belle Haven Picnic Area and parking lots. The paved road to the right ends at the Belle Haven Marina, but before you go that far, a dirt trail (with a chain preventing vehicular entrance) goes off to the right.

Jones Point Park, just north of these areas, is at the foot of the Virginia end of the Woodrow Wilson Bridge, and is accessed via South Street or South Royal Street.

HABITATS: The Hunting Creek area combines some fine tidal mud-flats, open river, and edge. The Belle Haven site constitutes trees and brush along the river. The Dyke Marsh trail wends through a bottomland deciduous

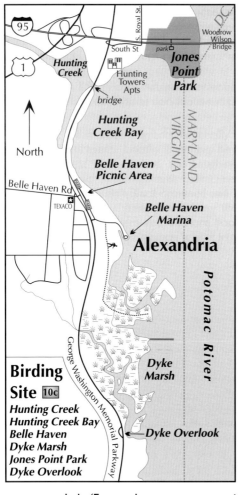

Birding Site 10c

Hunting Creek
Hunting Creek Bay
Belle Haven
Dyke Marsh
Jones Point Park
Dyke Overlook

woods with a small swamp. The trail then turns out into the marsh on a fill, overgrown with weeds, saplings, and patches of cattail, and edged with a rocky shoreline. The marsh supports cattails, Wild Rice, Pickerel Weed, and Phragmites.

HUNTING CREEK: The Hunting Creek/Dyke Marsh area is a unique location because of its habitats and because it lies on a particularly rich flyway. This flyway is part of the Chesapeake drainage which many migrant birds follow. During migration many birds stop to rest on the Hunting Creek flats or to pass along the edges of Dyke Marsh. Shorebirds are particularly noticeable from July to October; in winter ducks and gulls are common.

Automobile traffic on the George Washington Parkway does not allow for easy parking, so walking north along the bike path from the Belle Haven Picnic Area parking lot is a good way to reach the creek bridge, from which viewing is recommended. (For an alternate vantage point, see Jones Point Park below.) Low tide is the most rewarding time for shorebird study, when the mudflats are largest and the bird populations at their peak. The distances from the bridge to the flats are long, so a scope is needed. Lucky birders sometimes find Red Knot, Buff-breasted Sandpiper, Ruff, and American Avocet among the commoner species. Willet, Sanderling, and to a lesser degree, American Golden-Plover are regular migrants during August and September. Otherwise, Semipalmated Sandpipers are the most common peep; they can be found among the yellowlegs (Greater and Lesser), Killdeer, Short-billed Dowitchers, and Spotted and Solitary Sandpipers. In the late fall and early winter, look for Lesser Black-backed Gull among the commoner gull species. Black Terns are irregular visitors in late summer, followed by Forster's and Caspian Terns.

Bonaparte's Gulls are also irregulars which can sometimes be found among the usual gulls (Ring-billed, Herring, Laughing, and Great Black-backed). Herons are also well represented, with Great Blue Herons, Great Egrets, and Black-crowned Night-Herons being the most common, and Little Blue Herons (mostly immatures) and Snowy Egrets appearing in the late summer and fall. On the upper river side can be found Wood Ducks and wintering Hooded Mergansers and Bufflehead, along with possible Green-winged Teal. To the east look for Bald Eagles on the mudflats with the gulls, especially in winter, and nesting Osprey in the summer. A tip: the Hunting Creek Bridge is best on cloudy days, or mid-day, when you are not looking directly at the sun's glare.

BELLE HAVEN: Although the river is an obvious highlight of the site, the picnic areas should also be explored carefully for birdlife. The sycamores are the trees to watch in the spring and summer for nesting Warbling Vireos and Baltimore and Orchard Orioles. Annual surveys turn up several pairs of each, as well as Eastern Kingbirds, Blue-gray Gnatcatchers, American Gold-finches, American Robins, and Northern Mockingbirds. Fish Crows, Com-mon Grackles, Brown-headed Cowbirds, Mallards, and Canada Geese are also common. The Potomac River attracts Osprey, Double-crested Cormo-rants, Bald Eagles, and Forster's and Caspian Terns; Black Terns appear irregularly in the late spring and again in early fall. Wintering waterbirds include Northern Pintail, American Black Duck, Northern Shoveler, Ruddy Duck, Lesser Scaup, Common and Hooded Mergansers, and the occasional Common Loon, Red-breasted Merganser, and Red-necked Grebe. From Belle Haven you have the choice of going north to the stone bridge at Hunting Creek or going south to enter the Dyke Marsh area.

DYKE MARSH: The Dyke Marsh trail is the centerpiece of the area. It can be reached from the Belle Haven south parking lot by following (on foot) the bike path south about 100 yards to the road that leads to the Belle Haven Marina. Turn east toward the river/marina on this road, and look for the wood-chip trail and Dyke Marsh sign on your right. This is known as the "Haul Road." The young, deciduous woodland borders the bays and marshes of the Potomac. The first part of the road is excellent for spring and summer migrants: Northern Parula, Black-throated Green and Blackburnian Warblers, American Redstart, Magnolia Warbler, and Ovenbird, among other warblers, along with Blue-headed and Red-eyed Vireos, Great Crested and Acadian Flycatchers, Gray Catbirds, and Cedar Waxwings. Baltimore Orioles are common in the tops of the poplars; Ruby-throated Hummingbirds can be found in the open, vine-covered areas. Be sure to keep an eye on the path ahead for Song Sparrows, wintering White-throated and Fox Sparrows, and annual movements of Field and White-crowned Sparrows. Year-round residents include five species of woodpeckers, Carolina Chickadees, Tufted Titmice, White-breasted Nuthatches, Northern Cardinals, and Carolina Wrens. Barred and Great Horned Owls make occasional appearances. During the fall lucky observers may see Philadelphia Vireos and Connecticut and Mourning Warblers. In winter the careful, patient observer can sometimes find a Northern Saw-whet Owl by systematically checking dense honeysuckle and ivy tangles.

The path makes a distinct left turn, and the birdlife changes with it. Nesting Yellow Warblers are now in abundance, along with Baltimore and Orchard Orioles. Resident Eastern Towhees and summering Brown Thrashers scratch for food on the sides of the path. Red-winged Blackbirds and Marsh Wrens call from the marsh. Be sure to take advantage of all the little "windows" through the foliage to scan the marsh and the channels for Killdeer, Common Snipe, and American and nesting Least Bitterns, these last two being most easily seen as the incoming tide flushes them to higher ground. High tide can bring in Blue-winged and Green-winged Teal, Wood Ducks, Lesser Scaup, and Ruddy Ducks. Although the trail can be muddy, it is worth taking to the end, for the marsh at the point can produce Marsh Wrens at very close range and the occasional Willow Flycatcher in the summer. Large, mixed-species swallow flights, including Cliff, are not uncommon during May. Northern Goshawks and Rough-legged Hawks have wintered along the Haul Road.

JONES POINT PARK: This park is sometimes worth a quick visit to get another view of waterbirds on the northern side of Hunting Creek Bay. It's a good place in winter to check for ducks and gulls, and for Bald Eagles and cormorants (with an occasional Great Cormorant) on nearby pilings. The woods can be good for migrating songbirds, and in summer the swampy areas have held nesting Willow Flycatchers in the past. (Strict state-listers should note that the Maryland and District of Columbia lines meet up with the Virginia line at Jones Point, sometimes creating confusing jurisdictional disputes as to on which state lists some waterbirds actually belong!)

The roads down to Jones Point (especially South Street) can also provide nearby parking for those interested in visiting the bridge at Hunting Creek (see above.)

RARE OR UNUSUAL BIRDS: Eared Grebe, Great Cormorant, Greater Shearwater, Anhinga, White Ibis, American Avocet, Hudsonian and Marbled Godwits, Sharp-tailed and Curlew Sandpipers, all three phalaropes, Parasitic Jaeger, Little, Black-headed, and Lesser Black-backed Gulls, Black-legged Kittiwake, Sooty Tern, Black Skimmer, Swainson's Warbler, Western Tanager, Dickcissel, and Boat-tailed Grackle have all appeared in this area.

SPECIAL COMMENTS: As an afterthought to any of the above birding sites, the George Washington Parkway south to Mount Vernon runs parallel with the Potomac River and has several pull-outs that are worth exploring on your own. In the winter, these pull-outs offer waterbird-watching opportunities, with possible sightings of Common Loon, all three mergansers, Pied-billed, Horned, and Red-necked Grebes, Canvasbacks, Redheads, scoters, and Oldsquaws. In the spring, the larger picnic and recreation areas of Riverside and Fort Hunt Park can be explored for migrating and breeding birds. Recently, Bald Eagles have nested across the cove at the Riverside pull-out.

A bike path runs the length of the Parkway, making the river views readily accessible for bicycling birders and birders willing to make short walks from the series of pull-outs. Along the way look for Eastern Bluebirds, Indigo Buntings, and Blue Grosbeaks. Be aware that vehicles on both the Parkway and the bike path move at a very brisk pace on the Parkway during commuter hours and on the bike path on weekends.

Mark Farmer, Jackson Abbott

Site 10d.
HUNTLEY MEADOWS PARK,
Fairfax County

BACKGROUND: The land on which Huntley Meadows rests was farmed from the 1750s to the 1930s. Several federal agencies used the land as a research area from the 1940s to the 1970s; during the latter period Beavers dammed Barnyard Run, creating a freshwater marsh. When the land was declared excess to federal needs in 1975, it was deeded to the Fairfax County Park Authority for use as a park. A boardwalk through the park's major wetland was built in the late 1970s. The boardwalk and nearby tower were completely rebuilt in 1992-1994. The National Park Service retained review rights over proposed land-use changes; this right was exercised in the late 1980s to stop a four-lane commuter road from being built through the park.

ESSENTIALS: From I-95 take Exit 1 (US-1) south, toward Fort Belvoir. Go south 3.1 miles to Lockheed Boulevard; turn right (west), and drive 0.6 mile to the park entrance on the left. (This is the end of Lockheed Boulevard, although the road continues to the right as Harrison Lane.) The parking lot is 0.2 mile inside the gate, at the visitors center and trail head.

The park is open all year from dawn to dusk. The visitors center is closed on Tuesdays, Thanksgiving, Christmas, and New Year's Day. Otherwise, it is open 9 am to 5 pm weekdays and noon to 5 pm on weekends and other holidays, but hours vary seasonally. Bird lists, restrooms, a trail map, a log of recent sightings, informative displays, and several feeders make a stop at the visitors center worthwhile.

Access to the Hike-Bike Trail is from the other side of the park, at the intersection of South Kings Highway and Telegraph Road. There is a small parking lot on South Kings Highway. The gate is for park maintenance vehicles only, and it is locked on an irregular schedule. Access for the handicapped can be arranged at the visitors center.

HABITATS: Mixed mature and secondary deciduous/coniferous bottomland woods with interspersed brushy fields, grading to flooded woodland, freshwater marsh, and open water. The pond and marsh are maintained by Beaver, with several lodges visible from the boardwalk and the two-story observation tower. The 1,424-acre park harbors the largest non-tidal fresh-water marsh in the region. There are four miles of paved, gravel, or wooden trails.

BIRDS: Huntley Meadows has a bird list of 200 species. It is known regionally for its summering Yellow-crowned Night-Herons, King Rails, and Red-headed Woodpeckers. The latter are often easy to see, even allowing photographers to approach them on the Heron Trail Boardwalk for close portraits. Fluctuating water levels affect the populations of these species, with not all of them breeding every year. Sixty-five species breed in the park, including Acadian Flycatcher, Wood Thrush, Prothonotary Warbler, and Orchard Oriole. The Hike-Bike Trail is excellent for viewing displaying American Woodcock in season, as well as breeding Blue Grosbeak. In some years Barred Owls will roost close to the trails; wintering birds include Winter Wren, American Tree Sparrow, and Swamp Sparrow. Birding is good here all year round, but especially so during migration.

RARE OR UNUSUAL BIRDS: Spring migration brings in Pied-billed Grebe, American Bittern, Virginia Rail, Sora, Olive-sided Flycatcher, and Mourning Warbler. Summer birders come for the breeding King Rails. Late summer has yielded Glossy Ibis and Little Blue Heron. Fall migration reports include Merlin, Peregrine Falcon, Connecticut Warbler, Gray-cheeked Thrush, and Lincoln's Sparrow.

SPECIAL COMMENTS: Huntley Meadows Park is a favored breeding site for several species rare in Virginia, especially the waterbirds noted above. It is a popular stop for Big Day birders because the park's varied habitats create good conditions for the surprisingly large bird list of 200 species in an urban setting. Concern that the Beaver will eventually deplete their food resources within the park is the current management problem facing the staff. Ongoing problems are water pollution due to run-off from housing develop-ments and roads upstream, as well as the continual threat of road building near or through the park. Habitat damage from a large deer population is another management concern.

Erika Wilson, Jackson Abbott

Site 11a.
ACCOTINK BAY WILDLIFE REFUGE, FORT BELVOIR,
Fairfax County

BACKGROUND: This area, more than 1,300 acres in size, is administered by the Department of the Army (703/806-4007). At the mouth of
Accotink Creek, it contains nine hiking trails and two self-guided interpretive
trails. The checklist of birds for Fort Belvoir is based on the records of the
late Jackson Abbott, who found over 200 species on the post.

ESSENTIALS: Take the Fort Belvoir/Newington exit (Exit 166A) from
I-95 and go southeast on Backlick Road 3.0 miles to US-1 (also known as
Jefferson Davis Highway and Richmond Highway). Go straight through the
intersection of Backlick Road and US-1 and enter Fort Belvoir. (The proposed
Fairfax County Parkway extension between I-95 and US-1 may change this
approach to Fort Belvoir in the future.) Note also that Backlick Road changes
to Pohick Road once you enter the post.

Pohick Road traffic is one-way inbound to the post from about 6:55 to
8:05 am and one-way outbound from 2:50 to 5:40 pm. Follow Pohick Road
through Tulley Gate and continue south past the first possible right (Poe Road
at 0.1 mile). At 0.4 mile you will see a small parking lot on the right and a sign
saying "Pohick Loop Trail." This is a circular trail with handicap access. The
main entrance to the refuge is 0.2 mile (0.6 mile from US-1) farther along
Pohick Road. Turn right into the large parking lot at the refuge and head to
the far right corner, where there is a glass-enclosed map and a box which
usually contains a brochure describing the refuge and a bird checklist.

You may also want to visit Accotink Bay, Pohick Bay, and Gunston Cove.
To get to them, continue on Pohick Road another 0.7 mile to the stoplight
at the intersection of Pohick and Gunston. (Pohick changes to 12th Street
after this intersection). Turn right on Gunston and drive 0.6 mile to Warren.
Turn right again on Warren and drive 0.9 mile to the shoreline. You will be
looking across Gunston Cove towards Pohick Bay Regional Park. If you follow
the road to your right, you will see where Accotink Bay joins Pohick Bay to
create Gunston Cove. There are several points in this area where you can
park and get a good view of the water.

If you want to visit Accotink Bay Wildlife Refuge in the afternoon when
Pohick Road is one-way outbound, turn left at the intersection of Backlick
Road and US-1 and go 0.9 mile to Belvoir Road. Turn right on Belvoir Road,
go through the gate which marks the main entrance to the post, and drive 1.1
miles to a stoplight. Turn right at the stoplight onto 12th Street. After 0.2
mile you will be at the stoplight for the intersection of Gunston Road and
12th Street/Pohick Road described above.

HABITATS: The refuge encompasses about 1,200 acres of varied
habitats, including wetlands, marshes, grasslands, free-flowing streams, beaver
ponds, and mature deciduous woods. The north end has a stand of Loblolly

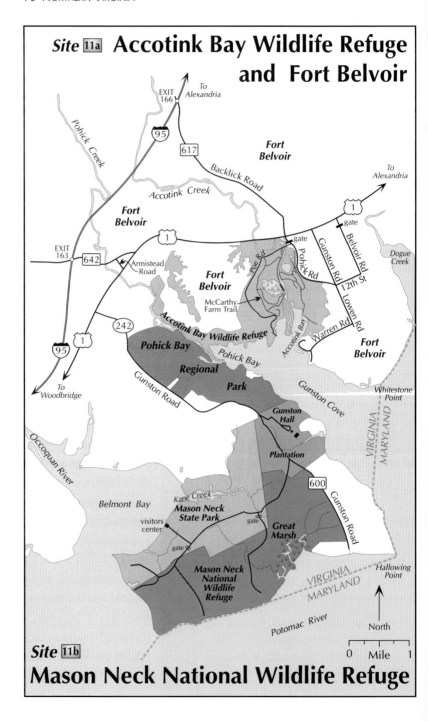

Site 11a Accotink Bay Wildlife Refuge and Fort Belvoir

Site 11b Mason Neck National Wildlife Refuge

Pines and a grassy meadow. The south end opens into Accotink Bay. In addition, the refuge benefits from adjoining areas of the post that are closed to the public but open to wildlife.

BIRDS: During the spring it is possible to record over 100 species in a single day. Look for wintering sparrows in the grasslands and weedy marshes, and migrating warblers on the trails along Accotink Creek. Four of our "P" warblers (Northern Parula, Pine, Prairie, and Prothonotary) breed here, and a fifth, Palm, can be found during migration.

Great Horned Owls, Barred Owls, and Eastern Screech-Owls are resident. Look for *Empidonax* and Olive-sided Flycatchers during August and Connecticut Warbler and Philadelphia Vireo during September. Red-headed Woodpeckers are an irregular treat year round, but you have to be keen to pick up their soft call. Wood Ducks nest near the water edges, and migrant Blue-winged Teal rest in the more-open water areas. In late winter the forest edges often harbor migrant Fox Sparrows and Eastern Bluebirds. In the marshy areas look for Common Snipe, Green-winged Teal, American Black Duck, and Swamp Sparrow.

In addition, Accotink Bay to the south is an excellent place to view herons, waterfowl, gulls, a few shorebirds, and Bald Eagles year round. The bay is best for Bald Eagles and shorebirds at low tide, but during the winter you always have a chance of finding unusual waterfowl or gulls if you scan the open water of Gunston Cove and Pohick Bay with a scope.

SPECIAL COMMENTS: The refuge is open to the public from dawn to dusk all year. This location has been largely overlooked by local birders, so most likely you will have it all to yourself if you visit during a weekday. On weekends you may encounter a few hikers. Several of the trails that were built in the flood plain when this was an engineer training area are now overgrown, and the old boardwalk is no longer usable. Other trails are in excellent condition, including an interpretive trail (Pohick Loop Trail) built in 1994; it is handicapped accessible. (Historical note: the only "recent" sightings for Bachman's Warbler in Virginia were nearby in the Lebanon area across Dogue Creek from Accotink Bay Wildlife Refuge: May 8 to June 2, 1954, and May 10 to 31,1958. Both times the bird was a singing male; no females could be found. The first sighting, in 1954, attracted national attention. News of the 1958 sighting was kept quiet for 25 years.)

Carter Whatley, Ken Hollinga, Paul G. DuMont

Site 11b.
MASON NECK STATE PARK AND
NATIONAL WILDLIFE REFUGE,
Fairfax County

BACKGROUND: The shores of Mason Neck were used by native American Indians as fishing and clamming sites. Europeans first settled here in the 1750s, with George Mason establishing Gunston Hall in 1755. The land was heavily logged and farmed, although poor drainage kept the human population low. In the 1960s residential development posed a threat to the only remaining Bald Eagle nest in the area, as well as putting pressure on a small Great Blue Heron colony. In 1967 The Nature Conservancy purchased parcels which it transferred to the US Fish & Wildlife Service, thus leading to the establishment of Mason Neck National Wildlife Refuge in 1969. Further purchases and transfers led to the establishment of Mason Neck State Park (703/550-0960), opened to the public in 1985, and Pohick Bay Regional Park

American Woodcock
Ali Wieboldt

on the northeast side of Mason Neck. During the 1980s four governmental agencies and Gunston Hall Plantation met to cooperate in managing their joint properties to protect their natural resources while providing environmental education and a wide variety of recreational opportunities. These range from Pohick Bay Park's golf course, campground, and boat-ramp facilities to Gunston Hall's historic exhibits, Mason Neck State Park's canoe trips, and Mason Neck NWR's environmental education program for school groups.

ESSENTIALS: From I-95 take Exit 163 (Route 642) east, toward Gunston Hall. Drive east 0.7 mile, follow the sign for US-1 by turning right on Armistead Road for 0.2 mile, and then right again onto US-1 south. Go south 0.8 mile to Route 242 (Gunston Hall Road); this left turn is well marked, with signs for Gunston Hall, Pohick Bay Park, and Mason Neck Management Area. Take Route 242 east for 4.5 miles, passing Pohick Bay Park and Gunston Hall (where Route 242 becomes Route 600), to a large sign for Mason Neck Management Area at High Point Road on your right. High Point Road passes through both the NWR and the state park, ending at the latter's visitors center.

Mason Neck State Park and Mason Neck National Wildlife Refuge are adjacent areas; they are both open all year, although there is a deer-hunting season between mid-November and mid-December, when you need to check on access. Portions of the refuge may also be closed when eagles are nesting and roosting. Mason Neck State Park is open from 8 am to dusk; a nominal fee is charged. The visitors center is staffed during the summer only. Mason Neck National Wildlife Refuge is open from dawn to dusk; there are no fees.

HABITATS: The Mason Neck Management Area consist of 5,000+ acres, most of it in mature hardwood forest, consisting of White and Chestnut Oaks, Red Maple, American Beech, and Tulip Poplar. There are smaller areas of mixed deciduous/coniferous woodland, grasslands, bushy areas, and several marshes, both tidal and non-tidal. The largest of these is the 285-acre tidal Great Marsh in Mason Neck NWR. Most of the marshes host Wild Rice, a favorite wildlife forage food. The refuge and park are bounded on three sides by the tidal Potomac River, Occoquan Bay, and Belmont Bay, providing waterfowl foraging areas, as well as fishing grounds for Double-crested Cormorants, Ospreys, and Bald Eagles.

Five trails provide access to all the major habitat types except the grasslands. Trails in Mason Neck State Park are: the Bayside Trail, which starts at the visitors center, edges Belmont Bay, crosses a tidal marsh via a boardwalk, and returns through woodland. The Wilson Spring Trail branches off the Bayside Trail, winding through woodlands hosting the local breeding birds, and ends at the entrance road near the parking lots. The Kanes Creek Trail starts opposite the visitors center and passes through woodlands to a blind overlooking Kanes Creek. Trails in Mason Neck NWR include the Woodmarsh Trail, a loop which begins at the parking lot on High Point Road, winds through woodland, skirts the Great Marsh, and returns through more woodlands. The Great Marsh Trail begins at a small parking lot on the west side of Gunston Hall Road, 1.5 miles south of High Point Road. This short trail leads to a broad platform overlooking the Great Marsh; it is best in the morning when the sun is behind the trees. The Great Marsh Trail and the area around the state park's visitors center are the best birding spots, especially in winter, when Belmont Bay and the Potomac River may be full of waterfowl.

BIRDS: The Mason Neck area has a bird list of 226 species. It is known for its Bald Eagles, a large Great Blue Heron colony, and wintering waterfowl. Although the Bald Eagle nesting and roosting sites are strictly off-limits, Bald Eagle sightings are common throughout the year. During the winter it is hard to miss seeing several of the 50+ birds that feed and roost in the area, especially when the Potomac River and adjacent shallow waters are frozen. The Great Blue Heron colony hosts an impressive 2,000 to 3,000 birds, and a small group of Great Egrets has recently established itself at the same site. Again, the breeding site is off-limits, but the size of the colony means that you will see Great Blue Herons aplenty all year, although their numbers drop during hard winters. Waterfowl numbers and variety are greatest during migration, but good numbers of Canada Goose, Mallard, American Black Duck, Lesser Scaup, Bufflehead, Common Merganser, and Ruddy Duck remain during the winter months, with lesser numbers of Tundra Swan, Wood Duck (in mild winters), American Wigeon, Canvasback, Greater Scaup, Ring-necked Duck, Common Goldeneye, and Hooded Merganser. Summer breeders include Osprey, American Woodcock, Acadian Flycatcher, Wood Thrush, Yellow-throated Vireo, Northern Parula, Ovenbird, and Scarlet Tanager.

RARE OR UNUSUAL BIRDS: Look for Red-headed Woodpecker and Yellow-throated Warbler during spring and summer and a Golden Eagle among the wintering Bald Eagles.

SPECIAL COMMENTS: Bald Eagles are the main attraction at Mason Neck; the land was protected, and is managed, with their interests in mind. They can be seen in all months, although they are most visible in hard winters when the Potomac River and adjacent waters freeze. Even though Mason Neck extends out into the Potomac River, it is not particularly favored by landbird migrants, unlike Great Falls National Park (site 12b) to the north. A suggested birding trip would be to walk the Great Marsh Trail in the morning, when the light is right, and then backtrack to Mason Neck State Park after it opens. In the winter concentrate on waterfowl visible from the visitors center area on Belmont Bay (a spotting scope will be helpful). At other seasons, walk the Bayside Trail; add the Wilson Spring Trail during the spring and early summer for migrants and local breeders. Local birders can volunteer for the weekly Bald Eagle census, the annual Great Blue Heron census, and the Fort Belvoir Christmas Bird Count; these activities give birders access to areas normally closed to the public.

Erika Wilson, Jackson Abbott

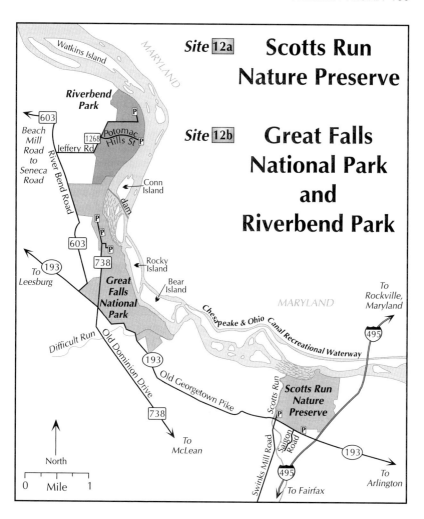

Site 12a Scotts Run Nature Preserve

Site 12b Great Falls National Park and Riverbend Park

Site 12a.
SCOTTS RUN NATURE PRESERVE,
Fairfax County

BACKGROUND: Acquired by Fairfax County in 1970, the preserve is now leased to the Fairfax County Park Authority. It was formerly known successively as Burling Park and Dranesville District Park, and is a popular area with hikers and bicyclists. There are no buildings or other facilities, but trails are convenient and well maintained.

ESSENTIALS: From Washington Beltway (I-495) take Exit 13 west (Route 193, Old Georgetown Pike). The Preserve is the wooded area on the right. The main parking area is at the bottom of the hill, 0.6 mile from I-495; a smaller area is 0.2 mile down the hill. From either parking area trails lead through the park to the Potomac River.

HABITATS: A park of 385 acres, it is basically deciduous woodland with several cleared areas, now returning to forest. It is intersected by several small streams. The mouth of Scotts Run, which forms the western boundary of the park, is an attractive rocky gorge with a hemlock grove.

BIRDS:

Spring: Probably because of its heavily timbered slopes and proximity to the Potomac River, this is a good area to observe migrating thrushes, vireos, and warblers (Black-throated Blue, Black-throated Green, Blackpoll, Bay-breasted). Look for Lincoln's Sparrow in the brushier sections, as well as cuckoos, tanagers, Indigo Buntings, and Blue Grosbeaks. Louisiana Water-thrushes begin to arrive in early April.

Summer: Look for both tanagers, Wood Thrush, vireos (Yellow-throated and Red-eyed), Broad-winged and Red-shouldered Hawks, Worm-eating, Cerulean, Kentucky, and Yellow-throated Warblers, Louisiana Waterthrush, Eastern Phoebe, and Acadian Flycatcher. (In the 1980s there was a small breeding population of Brown Creepers, but they seem to have disappeared in recent years.)

Common breeding birds include White-breasted Nuthatch, House Wren, Downy and Hairy Woodpeckers, Eastern Wood-Pewee, Eastern Kingbird, Blue-gray Gnatcatcher, and Baltimore and Orchard Orioles.

Fall: In August expect flycatchers, including Olive-sided, and Blue-winged Warblers. Warblers such as Canada, Bay-breasted, Blackpoll, Tennessee, Cape May, Magnolia, and Wilson's are expected during September. Also look for migrating Osprey and Broad-winged Hawks. During October, Winter Wren, both kinglets, Swamp and White-throated Sparrows, and juncos are common. Always keep an eye toward the sky, because Tundra Swans, flocks of Canada Geese, and the occasional Double-crested Cormorant can fly over at any time.

Winter: Residents include woodpeckers, three owls (Barred, Great Horned, and Eastern Screech-), Red-tailed and Red-shouldered Hawks, and some ducks on the river, mostly Buffleheads and Common Mergansers.

RARE OR UNUSUAL BIRDS: Common Moorhen, Lincoln's Sparrow.

SPECIAL COMMENTS: Beginning in 1973, breeding bird censuses were taken here for about 16 years. During that time, the number of breeding species dropped from 25 to 19, and the total number of pairs decreased from 327/100 acres to 261/100 acres. The percentage of breeding Neotropical migrants remained essentially unchanged.

Robert Watson, C. W. Per-lee, Jr.

Site 12b.
GREAT FALLS NATIONAL PARK
AND RIVERBEND PARK,
Fairfax County

BACKGROUND: Great Falls Park has 800 acres along the west bank of the Potomac River, administered by the National Park Service. It is 9 miles upriver from Washington, D.C. The large visitors center has restrooms, a staff office, parking, picnic areas, and trails. Fishing, rock-climbing, and kayaking are very popular in the park. *CAUTION: Dangerous undertows beneath both the Falls and the spillway have resulted in many drownings.* Riverbend Park, about half the size of Great Falls Park, has 12 miles of trails, with good access to songbird and duck habitats.

ESSENTIALS: From the Capital Beltway (I-495) take Route 193 (Georgetown Pike) west 4.3 miles to the first traffic light (at Old Dominion Drive). Turn right onto the entrance road into Great Falls Park. Riverbend Park can be found 2 miles farther upriver off River Bend Road.

HABITATS: Potomac bedrock terrace, riparian floodplain, swamps, and upland deciduous forest.

BIRDS:

Spring and fall migration: The river corridor is an outstanding migration route. Many birds can be found, from Eastern Bluebirds to Wild Turkeys to day-roosting Common Nighthawks. Thirty-five warbler species have been recorded here; 15 or 20 can be seen on a good day in May. Blackburnian, Bay-breasted, Kentucky, and Hooded Warblers are reliable. Olive-sided Flycatcher, Summer Tanager, and numerous thrushes can be seen in migration. Over the river all 5 eastern swallows have been seen together. Raptors use the river: good flights of Broad-winged Hawks can be seen, plus seven other hawk species. In early spring northbound ducks include Northern Pintail, American Wigeon, Ring-necked Duck, Bufflehead, and Hooded Merganser.

Summer: Along the river are Cerulean and Yellow-throated Warblers, Yellow-throated and Warbling Vireos, and both of our orioles. Scarlet Tanager, Wood Thrush, Worm-eating, Hooded, and Kentucky Warblers, Ovenbird, and Louisiana Waterthrush nest in the woods.

Winter: This is a good place to find Ring-necked Ducks, American Black Ducks, Buffleheads, and Common Mergansers. In the woods are kinglets, Winter Wren, Purple Finch, and Pileated Woodpecker.

RARE OR UNUSUAL BIRDS: Swainson's Warbler is a very rare spring and summer visitor. Sandhill Crane, Fulvous Whistling-Duck.

SPECIAL COMMENTS: This is one of the best places in the area for migrant warblers. Try the scenic trail along the rim of Mathers Gorge with views of the Potomac below. In April and May there is an extensive wildflower display.

Kerrie Kirkpatrick, Benjamin Warfield

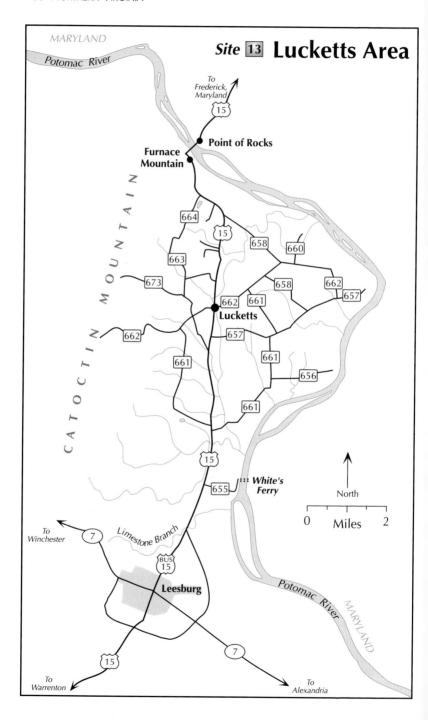

Site 13 Lucketts Area

Site 13.
LUCKETTS AREA,
Loudoun County

BACKGROUND: The historic rural village of Lucketts is located on US-15, the old "Carolina Road" and the original north/south artery of early colonial times. However, the Lucketts birding area stretches downriver from the Point of Rocks bridge over the Potomac River south for 10 miles to White's Ferry (originally General Jubal Early's ferry), the oldest operating ferry in the mid-Atlantic states. Much of the rich farmland in the area has been owned by the same families for generations. Many log cabins built by Quakers and German immigrants are located here, as are a wealth of Native American and Civil War artifacts.

ESSENTIALS: From I-495 (Capital Beltway) take Route 7 west 22 miles to US-15. Drive north about 8 miles on US-15 to the center of Lucketts. Turn right on Route 662; immediately on your right will be the Lucketts Community Center. A former school which is usually open on weekdays and Saturday mornings, the center has restrooms downstairs. In a wet spring you can park at the center and walk about a block up Route 662 (east) to a marshy area on the left where shorebirds are often found. To cover the Lucketts area, explore the roads on the east side of US-15 between Routes 661 and 658 (south to north). Alternatively, you could start your exploration of the area at Route 661, 3.2 miles south of Route 662, or at Route 658, 2.4 miles north of Route 662.

HABITATS: Lucketts is an area of open farmland, small streams, and mixed deciduous woodlots, but the number of houses in the area is increasing each year. A few farm ponds are visible from the roads, and a small lake can be found just north and west of the area (off Wilt Store Road). In addition, Lucketts is noted for its limestone conglomerate formations which appear as large rock outcroppings, most notably along Route 658. From northeast to southeast, the Potomac River forms the boundary of the area; although it is seldom visible from public roads, it is used by many birds as a migration route, most notably by swallows in fall.

BIRDS: About 170 species of birds have been recorded in the Lucketts area in the last 10 years. It is known for its Upland Sandpipers, which here are at the southern edge of their breeding range. Other field birds, including Northern Bobwhite and Eastern Meadowlark, are permanent residents, and Bobolinks pass through in spring. In the spring Grasshopper Sparrows and Indigo Buntings are common. During the summer check wet swales and fields with scattered trees for Willow Flycatchers. Yellow-throated Vireos are common breeders. Ring-necked Pheasants are found occasionally. A large colony of Purple Martins and smaller numbers of Tree and Barn Swallows nest in Lucketts. Northern Rough-winged, Bank, and Cliff Swallows have been found on the wires here in late summer and fall. Raptors, swallows, and sparrows are other attractions. Osprey, Bald Eagle, Northern Harrier, Rough-legged Hawk, American Kestrel, and Merlin have all been recorded, chiefly in migration and winter. Look for Vesper Sparrows in spring and summer and White-crowned and American Tree Sparrows in fall and winter. Common Snipe, Black-billed Cuckoo, Loggerhead Shrike, and Warbling Vireo have all been found in the area. During fall migration and winter Horned Larks and American Pipits are erratic; among them may be a rare Lapland Longspur.

RARE OR UNUSUAL BIRDS: For many years, Lucketts has been one of the best places in Virginia to find Upland Sandpipers in spring and summer, but this species is becoming increasingly hard to find. These birds may disappear from the area within the next few years. The state's only recorded Lewis's Woodpecker was found in Lucketts. Fall migrants and winter visitors have included Snow Goose, Northern Goshawk, Bald Eagle, Rough-legged Hawk, Merlin, Dunlin, Short-eared Owl, Common Raven, Northern Shrike, Lapland Longspur, Snow Bunting, and Common Redpoll. Spring and summer reports include Cattle Egret, Summer Tanager, Dickcissel, and Pine Siskin.

SPECIAL COMMENTS: Lucketts is a good birding area at all seasons. It is located less than an hour by car from Dulles International Airport, and many species of birds which are no longer seen in the more heavily developed inner suburbs of northern Virginia can be found here. However, each year more development is creeping up US-15 from Leesburg toward Lucketts, and only time will tell the effect on bird populations here. *As indicated above, most of the area is in private ownership, and visiting birders should not enter private land without permission.*

Valerie B. Kitchens

Upland Sandpiper
Ali Wieboldt

Site 14a.
SNICKERS GAP,
Clarke County

BACKGROUND: Snickers Gap is the location of a long-vanished resort hotel. Guests traveled the W & OD Railroad to Purcellville, then went by wagon up the mountain to the gap. The commuter lot serves as a hawk-watching site. It had been a maintenance site for the Virginia Department of Transportation, which still owns the land. The wooded area south of the site belongs to the National Park Service. Formerly, the Appalachian Trail came through the site, but it is now located 0.3 mile to the west. A walk of less than a mile in either direction on the Trail leads to dramatic rock outcrops with scenic views. Snickers Gap was developed as a hawk-watch site in 1990.

ESSENTIALS: From I-495 (Capital Beltway) take Route 7 west for about 41 miles to Route 601 at the crest of the gap. This is 5.4 miles past the

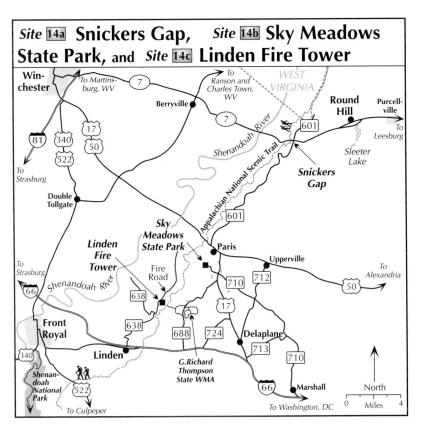

Site **14a** Snickers Gap, Site **14b** Sky Meadows State Park, and Site **14c** Linden Fire Tower

turn-off for the town of Round Hill and at the Loudoun/Clarke Counties line. Park in the commuter lot at the southwest corner, and watch from there.

HABITATS: Forested rocky outcrops, with homes and farmland interspersed. The altitude is 1,100 feet.

BIRDS: This is an excellent site for fall hawk migration. A very steady flight of raptors downridge results in hawks being seen every day from early September through late November (with the exception of full days of heavy rain). East winds before an approaching cold front seem to bring the birds closest. Northwest winds after passage of a cold front are the classic conditions of good hawk flights, but they can send birds very high over this site. High numbers of Broad-winged Hawks are seen during their peak flights, occurring September 14 through 24. Sharp-shinned Hawks, Merlins, and Peregrine Falcons peak the first ten days of October. Northern Goshawks and Golden Eagles can be expected after October 15.

Other migrants to be expected are warblers, Ruby-throated Hummingbirds, Blue Jays, sparrows, cormorants, gulls, geese, swans, loons, and an occasional heron. Passerines sometimes fall out along the ridge top, filling the trees with warblers (15 species possible), vireos, tanagers, grosbeaks, and kinglets. Monarch Butterflies and dragonflies (a favorite food of Broad-winged Hawks, American Kestrels, and Merlins) also stage heavy migrations down the ridge.

Resident birds include Common Raven, Pileated and Red-headed Woodpeckers, Cedar Waxwing, Wild Turkey, and Ruffed Grouse.

RARE OR UNUSUAL BIRDS: Swainson's Hawk sighted October 1993 and 1996.

SPECIAL COMMENTS: Seasons outside the fall are not monitored. Also check the section on hawk-watching at the end of this book for hints on techniques and seasonal abundance.

Kerrie Kirkpatrick

Site 14b.
SKY MEADOWS STATE PARK,
Fauquier County

BACKGROUND: Sky Meadows State Park (540/592-3556) originated as a bequest from Paul Mellon of a 1,132-acre farm dating back to the 1700s. It opened as a State Park in 1983, and now includes a 248-acre corridor north along the Appalachian Trail to US-50, and a 462-acre section east of the original park which opened to the public in 1991. The park has several trails and 12 primitive hike-in campsites that are available on a first-come, first-served basis. The Ashby Inn (703/367-3900) in nearby Paris is within walking distance of the park.

ESSENTIALS: From I-66 take Exit 23 at US-17 north (Delaplane/Paris exit). Go north 6.5 miles on US-17 to Route 710; turn left (west) and go 1.2

miles to the visitors center and parking area. Return to US-17 and go north 0.65 mile to the entrance road and thence to the bridle trail which is on your right opposite the entrance road to the fishing pond.

Alternatively, from US-50 take US-17 at Paris southward 0.4 mile to the lower pond and the bridle trail and an additional 0.6 mile to Route 710. Turn right to reach the visitors center.

HABITATS: Sky Meadows is a 1,842-acre park on the eastern slope of the Blue Ridge stretching eastward across the valley to Lost Mountain, with elevations ranging from 600 feet to over 1,800 feet. Lower elevations contain open woodlands, pastures, and brushy areas along Gap Run. A large pond along US-17, regularly used by anglers, and a smaller one west of the entrance road provide some areas for migrant waterfowl. Other farm ponds are within a half mile of the park.

BIRDS:

Spring: You can find both vultures, 6 species of woodpeckers (including Pileated Woodpecker and Yellow-bellied Sapsucker), and Common Snipe (marshy area at south edge of cattails and north of the pond which is along US-17). Flocks of migratory sparrows (including Chipping, White-crowned, and Savannah) are best seen along the beginning of the bridle trail.

Summer: Among interesting birds are Red-tailed Hawk (a pair consistently present on Lost Mountain), Belted Kingfisher and Louisiana Waterthrush (breeding along Gap Run south of the bridle trail), Willow Flycatcher, Warbling Vireo and Yellow Warbler (in willows east of US-17 and west of the bridle-trail barn), Blue Grosbeak (currently, pairs at the beginning to the entrance road and at the beginning of the bridle trail), Vesper Sparrow (just south of the park on Route 710, 0.2 mile east to white silo, where a pair has bred in the field to the north), Grasshopper Sparrow (abundant in fields to both east and west—singing birds can often be approached closely on fence posts along the bridle trail), and Eastern Meadowlark.

Fall: Look for migrating hawks, including Osprey, Bald Eagle, Northern Harrier, accipiters, and buteos. Warblers of several species are often concentrated along brushy streams.

Winter: Ruffed Grouse, Wild Turkey, Red-tailed Hawk, and Dark-eyed Junco can be found.

RARE OR UNUSUAL BIRDS: Recent rarities include singing Henslow's Sparrow (summer 1993, in the wet field beyond the bridle-trail barn) and Savannah Sparrow (summer 1994 in the field west of the north bridge under US-17). Cliff Swallows and Horned Larks have both bred at the park.

SPECIAL COMMENTS: A resident population of Red-headed Woodpeckers in the open cattle-grazed woods north of the entrance road provides the most reliable spot for this species in the northern Piedmont. The woodpeckers are present all year.

A Bluebird Trail has increased populations of both Eastern Bluebirds and Tree Swallows. The bridle-trail area, only recently established, includes a good part of Lost Mountain and affords a particularly lovely view facing the Blue Ridge.

The area adjacent to and south of the park is the 4,160-acre G. Richard Thompson Wildlife Management Area, which extends south along the Blue Ridge to I-66. It contains several trails from the Blue Ridge to the valley below and traverses a variety of second-growth habitats. The area includes a large pond near the northernmost parking lot and is well worth visiting during any visit to Sky Meadows. The wet bushy area by the northern parking lot is reliable for both Yellow-breasted Chat and White-eyed Vireo, both species being of spotty occurrence during summer in the western northern Piedmont. This brushy area may be reached by proceeding south on US-17 from the park entrance road 0.6 mile to Route 688, turning right, and proceeding southwest for 1.2 miles to the first parking lot (Parking Area 3 on the entrance sign).

The small pond along the entrance road to the park is often good for the few species of shorebirds that regularly occur in this area (Killdeer, Spotted, Solitary, and Least Sandpipers and Lesser Yellowlegs) as well as both Great Blue and Green Herons. It is also attracts migratory waterfowl, such as Green-winged Teal.

A park checklist of 161 species, prepared in 1987, is available, but some of the status codes are overly optimistic. Since the list was prepared, Snow Goose, Willow Flycatcher, Marsh Wren, Warbling Vireo, Mourning Warbler, and Henslow's Sparrow have been reported at the park.

Roger Clapp, J. A. Klakowicz

Site 14c.
LINDEN FIRE TOWER,
Fauquier County

BACKGROUND: The first large Broad-winged Hawk flight seen in the southeast (20,000 hawks on September 21, 1981) was monitored at this site. The fire tower was maintained until 1995 by the Virginia Forest Service and the Department of Game and Inland Fisheries for access to their radio antennas. It is currently in disrepair. With decreasing maintenance, there is no vista over the trees. (Most other fire-watch towers were dismantled during the 1970s when air surveillance took precedence.) The Appalachian Trail comes through the site, which is part of the state's G. Richard Thompson Wildlife Area. The AT and various fire roads are available for hiking and birding. The site has recently been recognized as having one of the largest displays of White Trilliums in the country. Many other wildflowers bloom profusely as well, enhanced by extra sunlight resulting from Gypsy Moth defoliation during the late 1980s. While the site is no longer an official hawk-counting location (local counters moved to Snickers Gap in 1990), it is still a fine site to visit.

ESSENTIALS: From I-66 take the Linden exit. Drive east on Route 55 to the Linden crossroads. Turn left (north) on Route 638 and drive 5.5 miles to the Virginia Forestry Fire Tower. (Do not follow 638 down the west ridge; instead, continue straight on the Fire Road.) The fire tower site is located among microwave towers.

HABITATS: Forested rocky outcrops, with homes and farmland interspersed. Altitude 2,100 ft.

BIRDS: This is a good site for hawk migration. East winds bring hawks very close to the tower, giving spectacular views. However, the west slope of the mountain is very gradual, creating poor lift and keeping hawks far away from the ridge crest on west winds. High numbers of Broad-winged Hawks are seen from September 14 to 24. Sharp-shinned Hawks, Merlins, and Peregrine Falcons will peak during the first ten days of October. Northern Goshawks and Golden Eagles can be expected after mid-October.

Other migrants to be expected include Ruby-throated Hummingbirds, Blue Jays, sparrows, cormorants, gulls, geese, swans, loons, and an occasional heron. Passerines sometimes fall out along the ridge top, filling the trees with warblers, vireos, tanagers, grosbeaks, and kinglets.

Resident birds include Common Raven, Pileated and Red-headed Woodpeckers, Cedar Waxwing, Wild Turkey, and Ruffed Grouse. Interesting breeding warblers at the Linden Fire Tower area include Cerulean, Worm-eating, Kentucky, and Hooded, as well as American Redstart and Ovenbird.

SPECIAL COMMENTS: Seasons outside the fall are usually not monitored here. Also check the section on hawk-watching at the end of this book for hints on hawk-watching techniques and seasonal abundance.

Kerrie Kirkpatrick

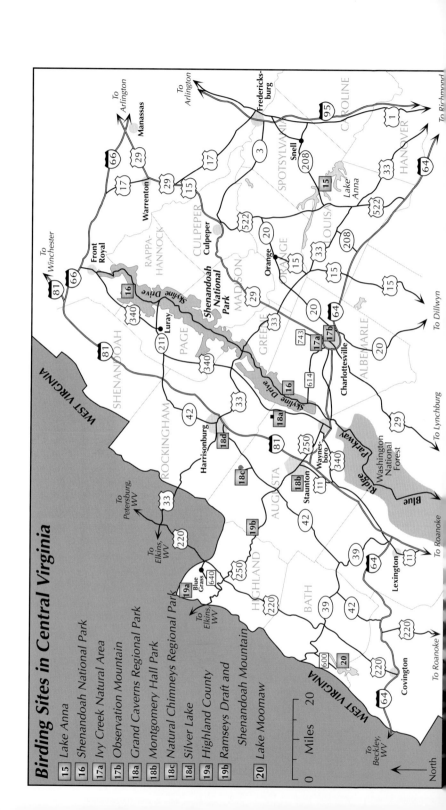

Birding Sites in Central Virginia

15 Lake Anna
16 Shenandoah National Park
17a Ivy Creek Natural Area
17b Observation Mountain
18a Grand Caverns Regional Park
18b Montgomery Hall Park
18c Natural Chimneys Regional Park
18d Silver Lake
19a Highland County
19b Ramseys Draft and Shenandoah Mountain
20 Lake Moomaw

CENTRAL VIRGINIA

From east to west the Central section cuts across the central Piedmont, Blue Ridge Mountains, Shenandoah Valley, and Appalachian Mountains. Its habitats differ little from those of the northern section, but here the mountains are higher, reaching elevations of 3,000 feet or more. With few exceptions, the birdlife of the Central section is similar to that of the Northern section.

Some of the large man-made lakes in the Piedmont have yielded interesting birds, especially those associated with passing hurricanes, such as Bridled, Sooty, and Caspian Terns. At other times these lakes attract waterfowl, such as Hooded Mergansers, Blue-winged and Green-winged Teals, scoters, goldeneyes, and Wood Ducks. Look for shorebirds around their edges; you can find both yellowlegs, Semipalmated Plovers, and Solitary and Spotted Sandpipers.

One of the last strongholds of the Loggerhead Shrike in Virginia is the central portion of the Shenandoah Valley, an area also renowned for its scenery and its history.

Along the Skyline Drive and the Blue Ridge Parkway are high-mountain hardwood forests which attract breeding Wild Turkeys, Ruffed Grouse, Black-and-white Warblers, Blue-headed Vireos, Whip-poor-wills, Broad-winged Hawks, and American Redstarts. Along the roadsides look for the familiar (Carolina) Dark-eyed Junco and Chestnut-sided Warblers.

Exciting birding sites in this central division are the western counties of Augusta, Bath, and Highland. It is here that extensive mountains ranging up to 4,400 feet dominate the landscape and thus provide breeding sites for several Canadian-zone birds such as Red-breasted Nuthatch, Canada Warbler, Golden-crowned Kinglet, and Hermit Thrush. A journey in early summer on Forest Service roads through high-elevation hardwood forests will produce Black-throated Green, Magnolia, and Blackburnian Warblers. Lowlands and their extensive cultivated fields will probably yield Savannah and Vesper Sparrows, Bobolinks, and Horned Larks.

The northwestern mountains of Highland County can claim breeding or probable breeding records of several birds which are unusual in the state. These include Mourning Warbler, Northern Waterthrush, Purple Finch, and Swamp Sparrow.

Although winters may be uncomfortably cold in Highland County, at that season birders have observed Golden Eagles, Rough-legged Hawks, Evening Grosbeaks, Common Redpolls, and Pine Siskins. Also, when heavy snows blanket the landscape, Red Crossbills often come to cleared roadsides, presumably in search of grit.

MORE INFORMATION:

General Information

Charlottesville-Albemarle County Visitors Center
P.O. Box 161, Charlottesville, VA 22902
804/293-6789

Front Royal-Warren County Visitors Center
414 East Main Street, Front Royal, VA 22630
800/338-2576

Harrisonburg-Rockingham County Convention and Visitors Bureau
10 East Gray Street, Harrisonburg, VA 22801
540/434-2319

Shenandoah Valley Travel Association
P.O. Box 1040, New Market, VA 22844
540/740-3132

Staunton-Augusta County Travel Information Center
1250 Richmond Avenue, Staunton, VA 24401
800/332-5219

Waynesboro-Augusta County Visitor Center
301 West Main Street, Waynesboro, VA 22980
540/949-8203

Western Highlands Travel Council
241 West Main Street, Covington, VA 24426
540/962-2178

Wildlife Management Areas:

Gathright: two tracts, situated on both sides of Lake Moomaw, containing 13,428 acres of bottomland, 7 miles west of Warm Springs, Bath County. (See site #20.)

Goshen: a large area of montane forests and streams, 12 miles south of Lexington, Rockbridge County.

Little North Mountain: 17,538 acres of montane forests, south of Goshen, western Augusta and Rockbridge Counties.

Hardware River: 880 acres of low ridges and gently rolling farmland, 20 miles southeast of Charlottesville, Fluvanna County.

Highland: 13,978 acres of high-elevation forests, south of Monterey and west of McDowell, Highland County.

Rapidan: 8,000 acres broken into 10 tracts, chiefly mature hardwood forest, 25 miles southwest of Culpeper, Madison and Greene Counties.

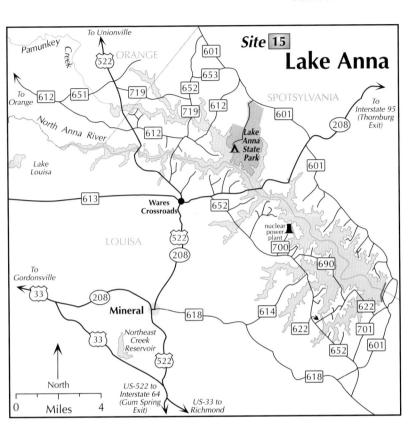

Site 15.
LAKE ANNA,
Louisa, Spotsylvania, and Orange Counties

BACKGROUND: Lake Anna is a long, many-armed, 7,000-acre impoundment formed by Virginia Electric and Power Company to cool the nuclear reactors at its North Anna Power Station. It was filled in 1972. The cooling function is performed by several drowned creek mouths (called lagoons) south of the eastern part of the lake that are joined by large canals and separated from the main lake by dikes. Birders discovered the lake in late 1977; it has since provided many remarkable records of waterbirds, shorebirds, and a few other specialties.

ESSENTIALS: From the north take the Thornburg (Route 606) exit west from I-95 for 5.2 miles to Route 208. Continue west on Route 208 for 14.2 miles to the North Anna River, 16.0 miles to Route 652, and 17.5 miles to US-522 at Wares Crossroads. From the south take the Mineral (US-522) exit north from I-64 for 23.4 miles to Wares Crossroads, being careful to watch for turns in the town of Mineral. The chief accesses to the Lake from Wares Crossroads are north on US-522 to the North Anna River and Pamunkey Creek, east on Route 208 to the North Anna River, and east on Route 652 from Route 208 to the east end of the lake. Route 652 offers only a few lake crossings, but the roads that run northeast from it have many vantage points. Particularly notable is the Route 622 causeway (called Dike 3) across the mouth of Rock Creek, which you can reach by taking Route 652 east for 7.8 miles from Route 208, turning left on Route 622, and proceeding 2.2 miles to the causeway. However, there are many dozens of road accesses to all parts of the lake, and any access to the lake can be productive, so you may want to buy a map locally and explore on your own.

HABITATS: The broadest (about 1.5 mile wide) and deepest (up to 70 feet) waters in the lake are at its east end, most readily observed from Dike 3. Marshes have been steadily increasing in extent in a number of areas, most notably at the heads of the western arms of the lake and in the Route 1201 area (Duerson Point). The dikes are rock-covered and in the water, a unique habitat on most of the Virginia Piedmont. During drought years the lake may fall as much as three feet, leaving gravelly and muddy areas all around it. In severe winters the western half or more of the lake freezes completely, but there is almost always appreciable open water in the eastern end of the lake. The cooling lagoons rarely freeze. Within a few miles of the lake is almost every type of terrestrial habitat that occurs on the central Virginia Piedmont.

BIRDS:

Landbirds are generally those normally to be expected on the Virginia Piedmont; the accounts below concentrate on waterbirds, shorebirds, and other Lake Anna specialties. Species that can be expected year round (though eagles are not easy to find) are Great Blue Heron, Canada Goose, Mallard, American Black Duck, and Bald Eagle.

Spring: As migration progresses, the wintering birds diminish in number, being mostly gone by mid-April. However, Common Loon numbers may surge in April, and new species pass through steadily. Among the latter may be Double-crested Cormorant, Great Egret, Blue-winged Teal, Osprey, several shorebirds (Spotted, Solitary, Pectoral, Least, and Semipalmated Sandpipers; both yellowlegs; Dunlin), Laughing Gull, several terns (Forster's, Common, Caspian, and Black), and Marsh Wrens. Ring-billed Gull numbers often remain high until late spring.

Summer: Early summer is slow at Lake Anna, although Canada Geese, Wood Ducks, Mallards, and American Black Ducks nest there. Common Loons and Ospreys may summer, and a few late-migrating terns may pass through. Cliff Swallows nest under some of the bridges over the western arms of the lake. Late summer brings the beginning of fall migration and sometimes (with luck) a hurricane. Migrants may include Double-crested Cormorants, Great Egrets, Blue-winged Teal, the same shorebirds as in spring, and Forster's and Caspian Terns.

Fall: Migration progresses with Common Loon and Osprey numbers up and waterfowl variety and numbers steadily increasing. Other wintering birds arrive, including Horned and Pied-billed Grebes, several gull species, and Snow Buntings. A few additional shorebird species (e.g., Black-bellied Plover, Common Snipe, dowitchers, and White-rumped Sandpiper) may pass through, as may a few more terns.

Winter: Likely are Common Loon, Pied-billed Grebe, a wide variety of ducks, American Coot, and Bonaparte's, Ring-billed, and Herring Gulls. Other species seen at this time of year are Red-throated Loon, Horned and Red-necked Grebes, Double-crested Cormorant, Tundra Swan, Snow Goose, Oldsquaw, scoters, Rough-legged Hawk, Great Black-backed Gull, Short-eared Owl, and Snow Bunting. Waterfowl numbers and variety may surge as their migration gets underway in late winter.

RARE OR UNUSUAL BIRDS: Eared Grebe, Brown Pelican, Least Bittern, Harlequin Duck, Ruddy Turnstone, American Golden-Plover, American Avocet, Sanderling, Lesser Black-backed Gull, Sandwich, Sooty and Bridled Terns, and Lark Sparrow.

SPECIAL COMMENTS: Boat traffic and fishing on Lake Anna have increased substantially through the years, so most water-surface birds do not reach the numbers that they once did, nor do they linger as long. However, the lake attracts a wide variety of migrants and harbors waterbirds forced down by storms. The marshes are poorly known and may host breeding rarities. They are best worked by boat, as is most of the rest of the lake. *Most properties are private, and their owners see too much of the public; do not trespass.* Marinas may let you look for birds at their establishments if you ask first. A public boat landing is available along US-522, and Lake Anna State Park (540/854-5503) is located north of the lake and west of Route 208. A visitors center is located at the power station (at the north end of Route 700, along the south edge of the lake). To bird this large lake efficiently, a telescope is almost essential.

John B. Bazuin, Jr.

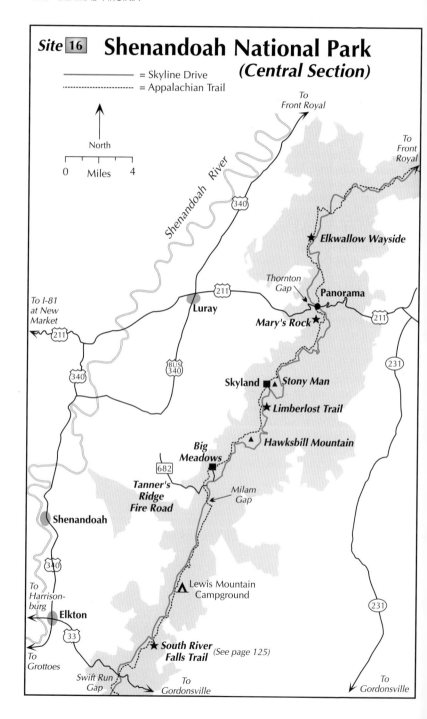

Site 16 **Shenandoah National Park**
(Central Section)

———————— = Skyline Drive
•••••••••••••••••••• = Appalachian Trail

North

0   Miles   4

Shenandoah River

To
Front Royal

To
Front
Royal

340

★ *Elkwallow Wayside*

Thornton
Gap

211

To I-81
at New
Market

Luray

Panorama

Mary's Rock ★

211

211

231

BUS
340

340

211

Skyland ■▲ *Stony Man*

★ *Limberlost Trail*

▲ *Hawksbill Mountain*

*Big
Meadows*

682

*Tanner's
Ridge
Fire Road*

Milam
Gap

● Shenandoah

340

To
Harrison-
burg

● **Elkton**

▲ Lewis Mountain
Campground

231

33

★ **South River** *(See page 125)*
Falls Trail

To
Grottoes

*Swift Run
Gap*

To
Gordonsville

To
Gordonsville

Site 16.
SHENANDOAH NATIONAL PARK
A Special Section by David W. Johnston

Shenandoah National Park, established in 1926 and opened to the public in 1939, may be entered from the north at Front Royal, on US-340 south of I-66. It straddles a section of the beautiful Blue Ridge Mountains of the Appalachian Mountains. To the west lies the Great Valley of Virginia (Shenandoah Valley), while to the east is the rolling Virginia Piedmont country. Through the length of the park runs the 105-mile-long Skyline Drive which follows the ridge tops from Front Royal on the north to Rockfish Gap, where the road continues south as the Blue Ridge Parkway. (For details on the Blue Ridge Parkway, see the Special Section by Marcus B. Simpson, Jr, under the Southern Mountains and Valleys region [p. 165].)

Skyline Drive is well known for its many parking overlooks, these offering spectacular panoramic views of valleys and the Piedmont. Along the Drive are picnic grounds, campgrounds, visitors centers, and trailheads for hikes into the surrounding forests or to unique rock formations or waterfalls. The highest point on the Drive is Skyland (3,680 feet); three miles south of Skyland is Hawksbill Gap Parking Area, from which a trail leads to the highest peak in the park, Hawksbill Mountain (4,051 feet).

The 195,000-acre park is a hiker's paradise, the many trails leading through dense hardwood forests of oaks and Tulip Poplar, along hemlock glens, and beside rippling mountain streams. The Appalachian Trail is part of the park's system of trails. The off-road trails offer some of the best opportunities for birding in the park.

Even before the park officially opened its doors, lists of birds and other wildlife were being generated. In 1935 Charles J. Spiker, a wildlife technician, prepared a check-list of birds of the park, therein recording 70 species. (A partial list in 1934 by Maurice Sullivan included the interesting report of a "resident pair [of Duck Hawks=Peregrine Falcons] on Old Rag Mountain.") In 1950, the famous ornithologist Alexander Wetmore listed 175 species for the park. Today, because of numerous recent observations by park personnel and visiting birders, Christmas bird counts, and breeding bird censuses, the number of species of birds recorded in the park has reached approximately 205.

As a place of changing scenes, seasons, and weather conditions, the park offers a plethora of flowering plants. In early spring appear the blooming Red Maples, Serviceberry, and Hepatica, followed by later-blooming Trillium, Pink Azaleas, Columbine, and Mountain Laurel. Fall is the season of asters, goldenrods, and spectacular leaf-colors covering entire mountainsides, from the burgundy dogwoods to the yellow hickories to the deep-red oaks.

Accompanying these dramatic seasons of plant changes are parades of birdlife. (Many birders enter Shenandoah National Park via Front Royal and therefore will drive southward. The birding sites in the park are described below by season and roughly from north to south.)

Spring heralds the passage of migrants: brilliant warblers, vireos, thrushes, grosbeaks, finches, sparrows, and even some waterbirds (geese, ducks). It is also the time when the breeding birds arrive to set up territories, find mates, and raise their families. Ruffed Grouse are drumming, Wild Turkeys gobbling, various owls hooting, and Whip-poor-wills stirring the night air. Birders especially interested in birds of prey can look for Great Horned and Barred Owls and Red-tailed, Red-shouldered, and Broad-winged Hawks. Spring birding sites are aplenty in the Park. Check overlooks, picnic areas, and especially the inviting trails. The stretch extending 1.3 miles from **Tanner's Ridge Overlook to Milam Gap** can be excellent for migrants. This site is accessible along the Appalachian Trail and is parallel to the Skyline Drive.

Summer is a time of much activity in the bird world: male songbirds continue to sing their territorial songs, and pairs are busy feeding hungry youngsters. Hardwood forests boast a host of breeding Neotropical migrants, such as American Redstart, Ovenbird, Black-throated Blue Warbler, Hooded Warbler, Acadian Flycatcher, Rose-breasted Grosbeak, Scarlet Tanager, and Wood Thrush. The cut-back vegetation below the many overlooks along Skyline Drive will often be inhabited by Indigo Buntings, Chestnut-sided Warblers, and Eastern Towhees. At this season, a good spot to try is the **Limberlost Trail**. Following the trail from the parking lot at mile-marker 43, this 1.5-mile (round trip) hike will take you to a stand of hemlocks. Among interesting species that you may see along the loop trail are Blue-headed Vireo, Blackburnian Warbler, and Veery. The **South River Falls Trail** (at mile-marker 62.8) is particularly popular. (It is special enough that it is treated separately by Leonard Teuber immediately after this Special Section on Shenandoah National Park.) In the summer, also look for Peregrine Falcons, which were recently re-introduced into the park. By late summer, though, many family groups have already moved out of the mountains, and southbound migrants begin to be seen.

As in the spring, fall brings large numbers of migrant landbirds, most of them this time dressed in drab plumages and usually not singing. Often the treetop migrants move through in waves and may be accompanied, at least temporarily, by resident species such as chickadees, titmice, and small woodpeckers. The **Skyland** area is usually productive at this season for migrating birds. The Tanner's Ridge to Milam Gap stretch is even better at this season than in spring. Also try the **Tanner's Ridge Fire Road** for migrant passerines. You will be rewarded at the overlooks by the progression of migrating buteos, accipiters, falcons, Northern Harriers, and perhaps Bald and Golden Eagles. A productive hawk-watching spot in the park is **Hawksbill Mountain**. Found at mile-marker 46.7, there is a mildly strenuous 1.7-mile-long trail to the top. At the summit you will find Balsam Fir and Red

Rob Simpson
Tulip Poplar grove in Shenandoah National Park.

Spruce. **Mary's Rock** and **Stony Man** are possible hawk-watching alterna-
tives. (The Stony Man Nature Trail, found at mile-marker 41.7, is 1.6 miles
long, following a portion of the Appalachian Trail)

In winter, when most park facilities are closed in the face of inclement
weather, some birds remain: the Carolina race of Dark-eyed Junco, Common
Raven, most woodpeckers, titmice, chickadees, nuthatches, and White-
throated Sparrows. In winter you might also come across a Golden Eagle.

Among the larger resident birds frequently observed along the Drive even
by casual tourists are Wild Turkey, Ruffed Grouse, Common Raven, and
soaring vultures and Red-tailed Hawks.

General wildlife-viewing along the Skyline Drive, from the overlooks, and
in picnic grounds is usually rewarding, especially in summer. Often seen are
White-tailed Deer and smaller mammals such as Eastern Chipmunks, Gray
Squirrels, and Groundhogs (Woodchucks), as well as the occasional Bobcat,
Opossum, Raccoon, and Striped Skunk. Black Bears are usually seen mostly
in the back country, but are occasionally spotted elsewhere.

Visitors centers (Dickey Ridge, Big Meadows) offer a wide variety of interpretive activities, including educational programs, bird hikes, natural history displays, bird lists, books on the park and its wildlife, and a special birds-of-prey program. A particularly favorite spot for easy wildlife observing is at the **Big Meadows** visitors center. Here, in season, the expansive, treeless meadow supports a host of low-growing plants, such as Spirea, Red-panicled Dogwood, Blueberry, ferns, Queen Anne's Lace, and various goldenrods, grasses, sedges, and composites (daisies, asters). In turn, this grassland/shrubland habitat attracts White-tailed Deer, Woodchucks, rabbits, American Woodcocks, Barn Swallows, Eastern Bluebirds, Eastern Towhees, Common Yellowthroats, Eastern Meadowlarks, Song and Field Sparrows, and Northern Bobwhites.

Some rare birds have been recorded at various times in this montane park. These include Horned Grebe, Mississippi Kite, Rough-legged Hawk, Virginia Rail, Upland Sandpiper, Short-eared Owl, Bewick's Wren, Northern Shrike, Connecticut Warbler, Bachman's Sparrow, Brewer's Blackbird, Pine Grosbeak, and White-winged Crossbill.

Campgrounds, Restaurants, and Accommodations.

Four campgrounds are found in the park, all suitable for both tents and trailers (no trailer hook-ups):

Mile-marker 22.2—Mathews Arm (186 sites)
Mile-marker 51.2—Big Meadows (227 sites)
Mile-marker 57.5—Lewis Mountain (32 sites)
Mile-marker 79.5—Loft Mountain (221 sites)

Most are open only in the summer, May through October, and are usually crowded in summer. Reservations are usually required—especially in peak seasons. Call or write ARA Virginia Skyline Co., Inc., P.O. Box 727, Luray, VA 22835 (800/999-4714).

Seven picnic areas along the Drive have tables, fireplaces, drinking-water fountains, and comfort stations: Dickey Ridge (Mile 4.7), Elkwallow (24.1), Pinnacles (36.7), Big Meadows (51.2), Lewis Mountain (57.5), South River (62.8), and Loft Mountain (79.5).

Lodging is available in motel-type units and rustic cabins at two lodges: **Skyland**, (Mile 41.7) and **Big Meadows**, (Mile 51.2). Housekeeping cabins can be rented at **Lewis Mountain** (Mile 57.5). These limited facilities are in high demand and need to be reserved far in advance of a planned trip.

Food is available in the park at several facilities: Panorama Restaurant (Mile 31.6), Dining Halls (Skyland, Mile 41.7; Big Meadows, Mile 51.2), Cafeterias (Elkwallow Wayside, Mile 24.0; Loft Mountain Wayside, Mile 79.5), Grill Room (Big Meadows Wayside, Mile 51.2), and groceries at Elkwallow Wayside, Big Meadows Wayside, Lewis Mountain Campstore, and Loft Mountain Campstore. Restaurants and dining halls are often crowded, so allow plenty of time for eating.

Gas stations along the Skyline Drive are limited to Elkwallow Wayside, Big Meadows, and Loft Mountain. Only gasoline, oil, air, and water are available; the stations do not make repairs or change tires.

Although the park permits backcountry camping in many areas, strict rules have been imposed on campers, and some areas are off limits. If you want to enjoy the backcountry, be sure to check with a Park Ranger about required permits before setting off.

Although bicycling has been encouraged as an adjunct to birding along certain paths and trails elsewhere in this book, *no mountain bicycling is allowed along the trails at Shenandoah National Park*. Bicycling is allowed on the Skyline Drive, however. Please plan accordingly.

The park is often closed in mid-winter (December through March) because of severe weather. Even when it is open, food and accommodations are limited. Plan ahead and call or write ARA Virginia Skyline (800/999-4714).

For further information about the park, write or call: Shenandoah National Park, Route 4, Box 348, Luray, VA 22835 (540/999-3500).

SOUTH RIVER FALLS TRAIL, SHENANDOAH NATIONAL PARK, *Greene County*

BACKGROUND: Although Shenandoah National Park offers many fine sites for observing birds, South River Falls Trail (at mile 62.8) may very well be the best location for observing breeding birds. The trail begins at South River picnic area and is 2.5 miles (round trip) to the upper falls viewing-area.

ESSENTIALS: From Elkton drive east 6 miles on US-33 to Skyline Drive, then north 2.8 miles to South River picnic area. From Luray drive 9 miles east on US-211 to Skyline Drive, then south 21.4 miles to South River picnic area.

HABITATS: Mixed deciduous forest near the picnic area, and mostly hemlocks near the stream. Take South River Fire Road back (slightly longer but more gradual) for different birds through mature hardwoods with some second growth and scrub near the top.

BIRDS:

Spring: Excellent after May 1 for arriving migrant and resident landbirds.

Summer: The trail is best in June for seeing the greatest numbers and diversity of nesting species: Barred Owl, Winter Wren, Black-throated Blue, Black-and-white, Cerulean, Hooded, Blackburnian, Kentucky, and Worm-eating Warblers, Louisiana Waterthrush, Northern Parula, Yellow-throated Vireo, Rose-breasted Grosbeak, and Scarlet Tanager.

Fall: Not recommended for fall migration.

Winter: Not recommended because of snow and inclement weather.

Leonard Teuber

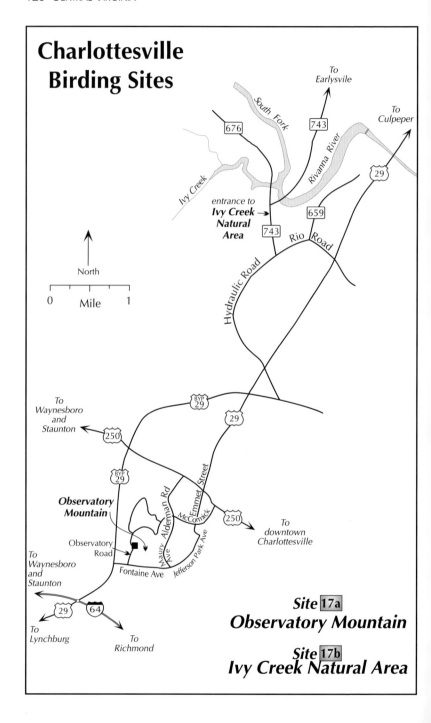

Charlottesville Birding Sites

To Earlysvile

To Culpeper

South Fork

676

743

Rivanna River

Ivy Creek

29

entrance to
**Ivy Creek
Natural
Area**

659

743

Rio Road

North

0   Mile   1

Hydraulic Road

To
Waynesboro
and
Staunton

BYP
29

29

250

BYP
29

**Observatory
Mountain**

Maury Ave

Alderman Rd

Emmet Street

McCormick

250

To
downtown
Charlottesville

Observatory
Road

Jefferson Park Ave

To
Waynesboro
and
Staunton

Fontaine Ave

29

64

To
Lynchburg

To
Richmond

Site 17a
Observatory Mountain

Site 17b
Ivy Creek Natural Area

Site 17a.
IVY CREEK NATURAL AREA,
Albemarle County

BACKGROUND: The Ivy Creek Natural Area (ICNA) was acquired in increments between 1975 and 1981 by Albemarle County and the City of Charlottesville with the assistance of The Nature Conservancy and state, county, city, and private contributions. The Ivy Creek Foundation, a volunteer organization, provides free educational programs for the public and ecological monitoring and maintenance supervision for the City and County. The area is traversed by more than six miles of walking trails, all open to the public during daylight hours.

ESSENTIALS: ICNA is located on the northern outskirts of Charlottesville and is bounded by the South Rivanna Reservoir, Ivy Creek, and Hydraulic Road. From US-29, proceed north on Route 743 (Hydraulic Road); continue approximately 0.5 mile past the intersection with Route 631 (Rio Road). The entrance is marked on the left "Ivy Creek Natural Area." The paved entrance road leads to a parking lot, from which a marked paved path (handicapped accessible) leads to an information kiosk, restrooms, and a barn converted into a nature-study headquarters, staffed part-time. A short trail for the handicapped leads through a birding area and on to a viewpoint.

HABITATS: ICNA encompasses approximately 215 acres of exceptionally varied habitat: woodlands (coniferous and deciduous trees), streams and marshes, overgrown farm fields, thickets and second growth, and shoreline along the reservoir. This broad range of habitats provides a diversity of flora and of birdlife.

BIRDS: At ICNA, 186 species of birds have been found in the varied habitats as described above. Especially prominent are those birds common to coniferous and deciduous trees, thickets and second-growth woodlands, overgrown fields, and lakes and streams. Permanent residents include Wild Turkeys, Pileated and Red-bellied Woodpeckers, and American Kestrels.

Spring: As is true of other sites in Virginia's Piedmont, migrant thrushes, warblers (31 species), vireos, and raptors are common at ICNA. Some 8 species of sandpipers have also been seen.

Summer: Among the breeding summer residents are Scarlet and Summer Tanagers, Baltimore and Orchard Orioles, Carolina Chickadees, and Red-tailed and Red-shouldered Hawks.

Fall: This season, like the spring, attracts migrating warblers and other passerines. At this site in the Blue Ridge foothills, hawks of several species have been recorded as they migrate southward.

Winter: In addition to the permanent residents identified above, at least 17 species of waterfowl are found in winter on the reservoir.

SPECIAL COMMENTS: Along the trails White-tailed Deer, Bobcat, and other mammals have been seen. ICNA is also noted for its variety of flowering plants, including water plantains, arums, sedges, yams, irises, lilies, orchids, grasses, bluebells, honeysuckles, heaths, geraniums, mints, roses, nightshades, and violets.

Paul Saunier, Jr.

Site 17b.
OBSERVATORY MOUNTAIN,
Charlottesville City

BACKGROUND: Formerly called "Observatory Hill," Observatory Mountain is easily accessible from Charlottesville. It is a distinct promontory and is the site of the McCormick astronomical observatory.

ESSENTIALS: From I-64, exit at 22-B (University of Virginia exit) onto US-29 north. Go 0.6 mile and exit onto US-29 (north, business). Turn right and go 0.7 mile to the first traffic light and make a left turn; at the next light make another left turn. Go 0.2 mile past dormitories on the left; bear left and follow the road up a hill past the green water-tower to McCormick Observatory. Parking may be difficult to find here. Recently, the area has become popular with mountain-bikers.

HABITATS: Upland oak and mixed hardwoods, with scattered pines. The summit has stunted White Oaks and pines which fill with warblers on good flight days during migration. Migrants tend to land on the summit and forage down the slopes as the morning progresses. Trails are numerous, though not marked. If you become lost at any time, simply head uphill and meet the summit road.

BIRDS:

Spring and fall: Fairly good for migrant warblers (a total of 37 species have been listed here), thrushes (7 species), tanagers, Baltimore Oriole, Rose-breasted Grosbeak, Yellow-billed Cuckoo, Ruby-throated Humming-bird, woodpeckers (7 species). In the second week of May, it is easy to list 20 species of warblers within two hours of dawn.

Summer: Breeding birds include Red-bellied Woodpeckers, Red-eyed Vireos, and Hooded and Black-and-white Warblers.

Winter: Look for Wild Turkey, White-breasted Nuthatch, and Carolina Chickadee.

RARE OR UNUSUAL BIRDS: Black-headed Grosbeak, "Lawrence's" Warbler.

Charles Stevens, Brian W. Keelan

Site 18a.
GRAND CAVERNS REGIONAL PARK,
Augusta County

BACKGROUND: This park is noted regionally for its large and beautiful caverns. In summer it is very popular because of its swimming-pool, tennis courts, and fishing opportunities. Well-kept trails are good for hiking and birding—especially during migration.

ESSENTIALS: From I-81 in Augusta County exit on Route 256 going east toward Grottoes. In Grottoes turn right onto Route 825 and proceed 0.5 mile to the park entrance. A small entrance fee might be charged.

HABITATS: The park is located on South River and includes a wooded ridge of mature hardwood forest, edges, and open areas. A steep path leads to the top of the ridge. Trails wander through the woods as well as along the river. There have been 114 species of birds recorded here.

BIRDS:

Spring: The best birding here is at this season. During spring migration 25 species of warblers (e.g., Black-throated Green), vireos, thrushes, and flycatchers have passed through.

Summer: Some of the nesting birds include several species of woodpeckers, Baltimore Oriole, and warblers (Black-and-white Warbler, Ovenbird, Louisiana Waterthrush).

Fall: At times migrant warblers are plentiful, including Cape May and Black-throated Green. Rose-breasted Grosbeaks and Cedar Waxwings have also been recorded. This is also a good time for hawk-watching.

Winter: Woodpeckers, chickadees, and titmice are present and, in sheltered places, Purple Finches and the occasional Evening Grosbeak.

SPECIAL COMMENTS: Since about 1985 some migrants, such as Warbling and Yellow-throated Vireos, have greatly decreased in numbers. In recent years Gypsy Moth damage has killed many hardwood trees, and Cerulean and Hooded Warblers seem to have been eliminated.

Leonard Teuber

Site 18b.
MONTGOMERY HALL PARK,
Augusta County

BACKGROUND: In the early 1820s, John Howe Peyton, the Commonwealth Attorney for Augusta County for 32 years, built a large mansion on several hundred acres southwest of Staunton. The estate was called Montgomery Hall. In 1946 the land was purchased by the City of Staunton and is now a city park of some 150 acres.

Site 18a Grand Caverns Regional Park
Site 18b Montgomery Hall Park
Site 18c Natural Chimneys Regional Park
Site 18d Silver Lake

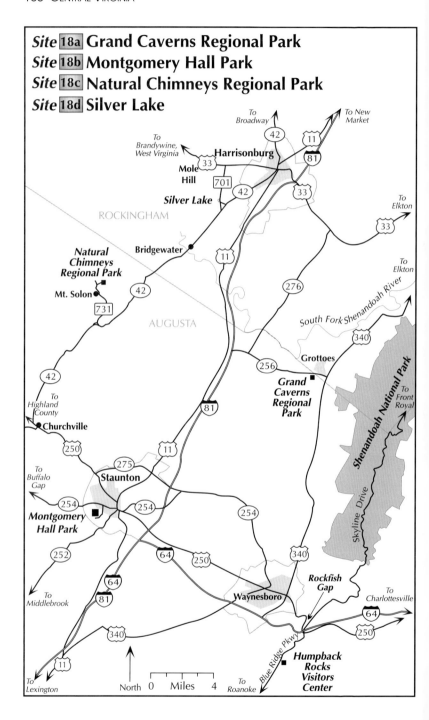

ESSENTIALS: Exit I-81 at US-250 and follow it into Staunton to its junction with Route 254. Follow Route 254 west to Beverley Street, then proceed west to the intersection with Montgomery Avenue, which leads to Montgomery Hall Park.

HABITATS: Mixed deciduous woods with a few pines. The park has a nature trail through wooded areas, an old orchard, and weedy fields.

BIRDS:

Spring: An excellent time for migrating warblers, including Black-and-white, Magnolia, Cape May, Black-throated Green, Cerulean, Blackburnian, Kentucky, Mourning, Wilson's, and American Redstarts. Also migrating through are several species of thrushes, Baltimore Orioles, and Scarlet Tanagers.

Summer: Common breeding birds include Gray Catbirds, Brown Thrashers, and Eastern Towhees. Less common but also found are White-eyed Vireos and Yellow-breasted Chats.

Fall: This city park is one of the best local sites for fall migrants, including Philadelphia Vireo, Nashville and Connecticut Warblers, and nine species of sparrows, including Lincoln's.

Winter: Many White-throated Sparrows, Northern Cardinals, and Dark-eyed Juncos winter here, plus American Robins, Eastern Bluebirds, Cedar Waxwings, and an occasional Hermit Thrush.

RARE OR UNUSUAL BIRDS: Orange-crowned Warbler (fall), Black-billed Cuckoo (summer).

YuLee Larner

Site 18c.
NATURAL CHIMNEYS REGIONAL PARK,
Augusta County

BACKGROUND: Natural Chimneys is a prime tourist attraction because of the tall rocky chimneys which have resulted from erosion of softer soil and rocks. Camping, a picnic area, trails, and a swimming-pool are open in the summer. An entrance fee is charged. The park, originally under private ownership, is now managed by a Regional Park Authority, representing Augusta and Rockingham counties and the cities of Staunton and Harrisonburg. A popular annual jousting tournament is held each summer.

ESSENTIALS: From Staunton take US-250 west to Churchville, then Route 42 north to the intersection with Route 731 at Moscow. Or from Harrisonburg take Route 42 south to the intersection with Route 731 at Moscow. Then drive 2.5 miles to the park.

HABITATS: Trails lead through mixed deciduous woods and a stand of pines along the ridge and along North River through sycamores and bushy areas. Open fields and evergreen areas are accessible along campground roads. On one fine day in early May 1971, 99 species were observed in the park.

BIRDS:

Spring: Eastern Phoebes and Pine Warblers return very early in spring. It is also a good place for Ruffed Grouse, Northern Bobwhite, American Woodcock, and migrating warblers.

Summer: A large number of species nest here. These include Gray Catbirds, Baltimore Orioles, and Pine Warblers.

Fall: As in the spring, this is a good location for finding migrating thrushes, vireos, warblers, and sparrows.

Winter: This is a good location for seeing American Robins, Eastern Bluebirds, Eastern Towhees, Winter Wrens, Carolina Wrens, and a variety of woodpeckers and sparrows.

RARE OR UNUSUAL BIRDS: Merlin (spring), Long-eared Owl (summer).

YuLee Larner, Leonard Teuber

Site 18d.
SILVER LAKE,
Rockingham County

BACKGROUND: Silver Lake is a small, spring-fed lake. It never completely freezes over even in the coldest winters. Because of its isolated position in the northern Shenandoah Valley, it attracts a large variety of waterbirds.

ESSENTIALS: From Harrisonburg take Route 42 south to Dayton. In Dayton turn right onto Route 732. After about 0.2 mile, turn right onto Route 701. Silver Lake will appear to the left of the highway.

HABITATS: The lake is surrounded by cultivated fields and residences. Mole Hill, a unique geological feature of the valley, overlooks the lake and can be reached easily by scenic back roads.

BIRDS:

Spring: Migrating waterfowl are often found (see *Winter*). Several species of swallows visit the lake, and Barn and Northern Rough-winged Swallows begin nesting. Unusual birds at this time include Caspian, Common, Forster's, and Black Terns, Great Egrets, and, at least formerly, the occasional Cattle Egret.

Nearby Mole Hill is an excellent spot to see migrating warblers. This monadnock is a forested "island" in the sea of farms and suburban developments that now make up the Shenandoah Valley. Migrating landbirds seem to congregate on this "island." Mole Hill is privately owned, so prior permission to hike into the woods should be obtained. On part of the hill birds can be seen from the road.

Summer: Of special interest in this area are the Red-headed Wood-peckers breeding in the Mole Hill area. They can usually be found somewhere along the roads that border Mole Hill, often in the area around Smith's Greenhouse. Silver Lake appears to be a minor staging area for Northern Rough-winged and Tree Swallows in late summer.

Fall: The American Wigeons and other winter residents begin arriving around the second week in October.

Winter: A small population of ducks are winter residents. The most common species are a mixed lot of local and migratory Mallards. Usually you can also expect to find American Wigeons, Ring-necked Ducks, Gadwalls, Northern Shovelers, and a Pied-billed Grebe or two. Canada Geese are regular visitors, some with neck collars indicating their origin as Ohio and Pennsylvania but also local non-migratory individuals. American Coots have disappeared from this lake in the last several years, and most of the Ring-necks have moved to another lake in the area. At least once during each winter or spring, one can expect to see Blue-winged and Green-winged Teals, Redhead, Greater and Lesser Scaups, American Black Duck, Bufflehead, Hooded Merganser, Common Goldeneye, Ruddy Duck, and Northern Pintail. Much less expected but possible are Horned and Red-necked Grebes, Common Loon, Canvasback, Snow Goose, Tundra Swan, and Common Moorhen. All of the waterfowl are found before April 1 or the opening of trout season, whichever comes first. Great Blue Herons, Killdeer, and a resident pair of Belted Kingfishers are often found. White-crowned and White-throated Sparrows often winter in the fields around the lake.

RARE OR UNUSUAL BIRDS: Eurasian Wigeon.

SPECIAL COMMENTS: This lake provides one of the best opportunities in the Valley to observe waterfowl close up. However, the recent decision to allow year-round trout fishing here has probably decreased the availability of this lake to waterfowl.

Clair Mellinger, Randall Shank, Richard Peake

Site 19a
Highland County

BP = Beaver Ponds

North

0   Miles   4

Site 19b
Ramseys Draft and Shenandoah Mountain

Site 19a.
HIGHLAND COUNTY

BACKGROUND: Sometimes called "Virginia's Little Switzerland," this county is a high-elevation, remote, and sparsely populated region. It has the highest mean elevation of any county in the state, and some of its birdlife is characteristic of more northern regions. Spring comes late to the county, and in winter many roads are open only to four-wheel-drive vehicles. This area is one of the most exciting birding spots in the state, especially in summer.

ESSENTIALS: The only accommodations are in Monterey, the county seat and its principal town, at the junction of US-220 and US-250. The best birding areas are found in the northwestern part of the county and include Bear Mountain Road (Route 601), Locust Springs, Forest Road 55, and Route 642 to Bluegrass.

1. Bear Mountain Road, Co. Route 601, is a sharp left turn off US-250, 6.5 miles west of Hightown. Although state-maintained for the first 1.5 miles, this is a dirt road which is very steep and is best avoided in poor weather.

2. Locust Springs, at the extreme northwest tip of the county, and in the George Washington National Forest, is reached by taking US-250 west 7.1 miles past the state line, then right on WV-28 for 6.7 miles. Look for the Locust Springs Picnic Area sign and make a sharp right turn onto the forest service road (FR-55, also called Allegheny Road). At 0.45 mile turn left, then bear right at 0.7 mile back into Virginia and to the picnic area.

3. Allegheny Road continues along the state line for 7.4 miles to Route 642, which winds along Laurel Fork and over Middle Mountain, Straight Fork, and Lantz Mountain for another 10.4 miles to Route 643 in the Blue Grass Valley.

4. The lowlands and pastures around the Blue Grass area can be covered via the loop of Routes 642, 640, 644, and 643, then back to 642 and east along the North Fork of the Potomac River to US-220.

HABITATS: Mountaintops are mostly covered with a rich growth of mature northern hardwoods, such as Northern Red Oak, Yellow Birch, and Sugar Maple. Some stands of Red Spruce are found at the highest elevations. The fertile valleys are planted in various grain crops, and the steeper slopes are mostly sheep pastures.

BIRDS:

Spring: Because of the high elevation, spring arrives late in Highland County. Many breeders do not arrive until mid-May. Brewer's Blackbirds are sometimes found around feedlots in mid-March, during the time of the Maple Festival. If you are coming from Staunton, be alert for Red Crossbills along US-250 on Shenandoah Mountain, at the Highland/Augusta County line. They are most often seen collecting grit along the roadside early on spring mornings, but they may also be seen at other times or seasons. You may wish to stop at the parking area at the crest (or *carefully* at one of the hairpin curves just west of the crest) and listen for their distinctive call notes. If you are especially venturesome, listen for Long-eared and Northern Saw-whet Owls at the higher elevations in late winter or early spring. (Generally, the first week in June is considered best for birding: the Mourning Warblers will be starting to sing, but the Golden-winged Warblers will stop by mid-June.)

Summer: Common summer breeding birds include Black-capped Chickadee, Ruffed Grouse, Common Raven, Cedar Waxwing, Chestnut-sided Warbler, and Dark-eyed Junco. Check brushy clear-cuts, especially the Beaver ponds at the US-250 crossing of Back Creek west of Hightown, or sometimes in Back Creek Valley (Route 600), for Golden-winged Warblers. Another spot for Golden-winged Warblers has recently been the first mile or so along Route 631, off US-250, just east of Monterey.

The high meadow along Bear Mountain Road (Route 601) is a good place for Horned Lark and Vesper and Savannah Sparrows, and check the spruce stand on the right for Yellow-bellied Sapsucker, Magnolia Warbler, and Purple Finch. Although there are no recent records, be alert for Bewick's Wren in any high meadows with brush piles and stunted trees and shrubs.

The area around Locust Springs Picnic Ground, especially downstream at the Beaver ponds along Buck Run and Locust Springs Run, can be one of the most rewarding birding spots during the summer. Nesting birds recorded in this area include Alder and Least Flycatchers, Hermit Thrush, Veery, and Magnolia, Black-throated Blue, Black-throated Green, Canada, Blackburnian, and Mourning Warblers. Also look for Red-breasted Nuthatch, Brown Creeper, Golden-crowned Kinglet, Blue-headed Vireo, Rose-breasted Grosbeak, and Purple Finch.

An early morning start on Allegheny Road almost assures a Ruffed Grouse and many of the other Locust Springs species. Another place to try for Alder Flycatcher is at the Beaver ponds above the Route 642 crossing of Straight Fork, 6.6 miles east of the intersection with Allegheny Road. Ascending the next ridge, look for Golden-winged Warbler, and for Cerulean, Worm-eating, Kentucky, and Hooded Warblers as you descend into Blue Grass Valley.

Emerging from the woods into the high meadows, look for Vesper and Savannah Sparrows. Cliff Swallow, Horned Lark, and Bobolink are regularly seen in Blue Grass Valley.

Winter: Birdlife is sparse during the winter. However, quality sometimes makes up for quantity, and the Blue Grass area of Highland County is famous among birders for its wintering population of Golden Eagles. Check along Routes 642, 640, 643, and especially Route 644, all the way to the state line. Also look for Rough-legged Hawks in this area and down the valley toward Hightown. American Tree Sparrows are usually present. Common Redpolls, Pine Siskins, and Evening Grosbeaks are a possibility if it is a good "winter finch" year. They are often found at residential feeders in Monterey.

RARE OR UNUSUAL BIRDS: Northern Goshawk, Northern Saw-whet Owl, Bewick's Wren (formerly common), Varied Thrush, Say's Phoebe, Nashville Warbler, Northern Waterthrush, Brewer's Blackbird, Swamp Sparrow, Common and Hoary Redpolls.

SPECIAL COMMENTS: At the southwest edge of Highland County (and for that matter at the very edge of Virginia) there are some interesting breeding birds to pursue. Among those are Ruffed Grouse, Wild Turkey, and especially Mourning Warbler at Paddy's Knob. (If you missed the Mourning Warblers at the Buck Run Beaver ponds below Locust Spring, this might be another reason for this Paddy's Knob side-trip.) Take US-220 some 4 miles south of Monterey to Route 84. Take 84 westward for 15 miles through part of the George Washington National Forest and into West Virginia. Turn left (south) on Forest Road 55 for 2.8 miles. On the right is West Virginia; on the left just a short distance away is Virginia. Into Virginia you will see an abandoned road and trail which you can walk and try there for the Mourning Warblers.

John and Thelma Dalmas

Site 19b.
RAMSEYS DRAFT AND SHENANDOAH MOUNTAIN,
Augusta County

BACKGROUND: Although Ramseys Draft is technically a beautiful mountain stream, the name also refers locally to a large Wilderness Area in the George Washington National Forest in the watershed of the stream. The west side of the watershed is Shenandoah Mountain, straddling the boundary between Augusta and Highland Counties. A trail alongside Ramseys Draft, damaged a few years ago by a flood, leads upward to several peaks of 3,500 feet. The Confederate breastworks on Shenandoah Mountain are also important among the Civil War battlefields preserved in Virginia.

ESSENTIALS: From Staunton take US-250 west for 24.9 miles to Ramseys Draft Picnic Area. At this point you can hike the trail beside the stream. From the picnic area drive 2 miles to the crest of the mountain at the Confederate breastworks at the Highland County line.

HABITATS: Forest records indicate that much of the Ramseys Draft watershed is virgin hardwood forest with scattered pines. Immediately beside the stream are large hemlocks.

BIRDS:

Spring and summer: Especially in summer at Ramseys Draft, breeding birds include high-elevation species in the state: Winter Wrens, Least Flycatchers, Black-capped Chickadees, Louisiana Waterthrushes, Northern Parula, Blackburnian, Black-throated Green, and Canada Warblers, American Redstarts, Ovenbirds, Wood Thrushes, Wild Turkeys, and Ruffed Grouse. On Shenandoah Mountain other species include Red Crossbills, Pine Warblers, Dark-eyed Juncos, and Scarlet Tanagers.

Fall: Look for Gray-cheeked Thrushes along the Shenandoah Mountain trail.

Winter: White-throated Sparrows, Golden-crowned Kinglets, Dark-eyed Juncos, Black-capped Chickadees, Ruffed Grouse, Red-breasted Nuthatches, and Red Crossbills are among the winter birds to be expected.

YuLee Larner

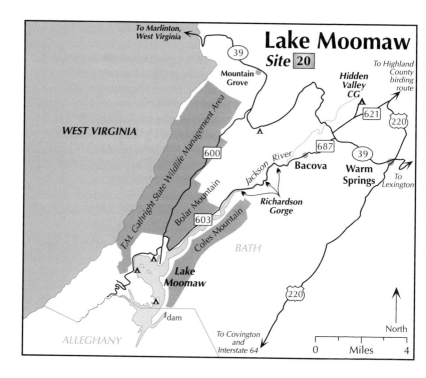

Site 20.
LAKE MOOMAW,
Bath County

BACKGROUND: This mountain lake is 12 miles long and has a shoreline of some 40 miles. In 1981 the U.S. Army Corps of Engineers completed the dam, and a recreation level of the lake was reached the next year. The Corps maintains a visitors center above the dam, a picnic area, and a bank-fishing area below the dam. In addition to the lake, the area includes over 13,000 acres in the T. M. Gathright Wildlife Management Area. The lake attracts anglers and boaters on weekends, so birding is more successful on weekdays.

ESSENTIALS: From Warm Springs follow Route 39 west for about 12 miles to Route 600. Take Route 600 south to Lake Moomaw, about eight miles. You can return to Warm Springs via Route 603 through Richardson Gorge, then Route 687 through Bacova back to Route 39.

HABITATS: A wide variety of fruit-producing shrubs and vines are found along the lake shore. Mixed deciduous trees and a few pines cover the steep mountain sides, and hemlocks and rhododendrons are found along the Jackson River in Richardson Gorge.

BIRDS:

Spring: This is an excellent mountain site for finding migrating warblers and swallows, a variety of gulls and terns, and Double-crested Cormorants. Late migrants may include Common Loon and Cattle Egret.

Summer: Nesting species at the lake and nearby areas include a variety of warblers (Golden-winged, Worm-eating, Yellow-throated), vireos (Blue-headed, Red-eyed), Ruffed Grouse, and Willow Flycatcher. Wild Turkeys are very common.

Fall: Fishing continues into the fall, and widespread hunting in surrounding mountains in late fall and early winter is discouraging to birders. Little information on birds is available at this time of year.

Winter: White-throated Sparrows, Northern Cardinals, Dark-eyed Juncos, both kinglets, Brown Creepers, and nuthatches winter, as do occasional Eastern Bluebirds, American Robins, and Cedar Waxwings. Evening Grosbeaks have been found in large numbers but only irregularly. Bald Eagles winter along the shore of Lake Moomaw, and Golden Eagles are occasionally seen. Many species of ducks and grebes arrive when the ice melts in late February and into March and April; these include American Black Duck, Mallard, Northern Pintail, Redhead, Ring-necked Duck, Greater and Lesser Scaups, Bufflehead, and all three species of mergansers.

RARE OR UNUSUAL BIRDS: Red-necked Grebe.

SPECIAL COMMENTS: For a productive side-trip, try the nearby Hidden Valley campground and trail in the George Washington National Forest. Located off Route 621, the site is good in the fall (October) for sparrows and field birds, and in late spring (June) for a variety of flycatchers, vireos, and warblers in the woodlands.

YuLee Larner

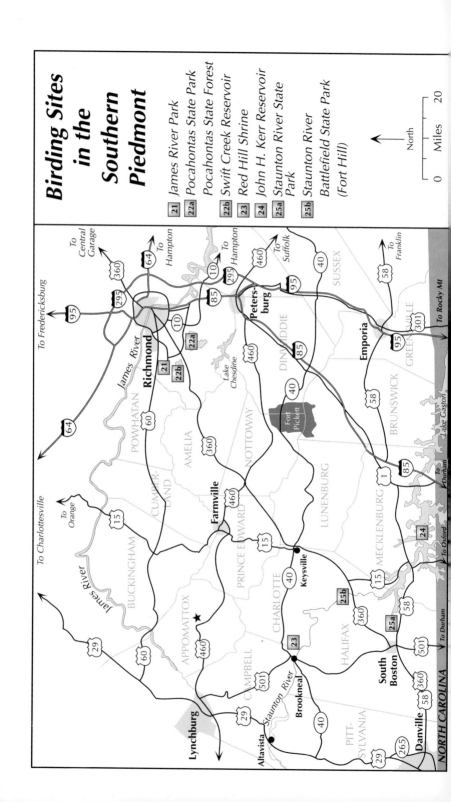

Birding Sites in the Southern Piedmont

- **21** James River Park
- **22a** Pocahontas State Park
- **22b** Pocahontas State Forest
- **22b** Swift Creek Reservoir
- **23** Red Hill Shrine
- **24** John H. Kerr Reservoir
- **25a** Staunton River State Park
- **25a** Staunton River
- **25b** Battlefield State Park (Fort Hill)

North

0   Miles   20

SOUTHERN PIEDMONT

Compared with other regions of the state, the Southern Piedmont is probably the least known ornithologically. Even so, recent forays by the VSO and results of Virginia's Breeding Bird Atlas Project have greatly improved our knowledge of birds there.

Much of the Southern Piedmont is a mosaic of rolling farm land, small woodlots, and some extensive forested tracts, which are classified as pine, oak/pine, or mixtures of other deciduous types (oaks, hickories, Tulip Poplar). Mature deciduous forest tracts attract both Whip-poor-wills and Chuck-will's-widows, Scarlet Tanagers, and Yellow-throated Warblers, whereas pine forests are home to Pine Warblers, Summer Tanagers, and, especially along the North Carolina boundary, Brown-headed Nuthatches.

Cultivated or grassy fields are home to Eastern Meadowlarks, Grasshopper Sparrows, Horned Larks, and the occasional Dickcissel. In fields overgrown with shrubs and other brush, birders are rewarded with nesting Indigo Buntings, Blue Grosbeaks, White-eyed Vireos, Common Yellowthroats, and also Yellow-breasted Chats. Searching the overgrown fields neighboring mature pine forests may produce the rare Bachman's Sparrow. Wet fields may contain a small colony of breeding Henslow's Sparrows.

Winter birding in this region will be rewarding, partly

Adrian R. Davis
Typical Piedmont farmland.

because of the mild winters when compared with those at more northern sites in the Piedmont. Extensive overgrown fields often have a complement of Savannah and Vesper Sparrows, Northern Harriers, and an occasional Short-eared Owl. The bare-leaved deciduous forests contain White-breasted Nuthatches, Downy and Red-bellied Woodpeckers, Carolina Chickadees, and perhaps Wild Turkeys. Extensive thickets of blackberry bushes and other tangled vegetation often contain White-throated and White-crowned Sparrows, and perhaps Common Yellowthroats and Fox Sparrows as well.

Large water impounds, such as Kerr Reservoir, often are rewarding birding sites, especially during migration. Look for loons, grebes, terns, shorebirds, and waterfowl such as Red-breasted Mergansers, Oldsquaws, and scoters.

MORE INFORMATION:

General Information

Lynchburg Visitor Center
216 12th Street, Lynchburg, VA 24504
800/732-5821

Petersburg Visitor Center
425 Cockade Alley, Petersburg, VA 23803
800/368-3595

Richmond Metro Visitor Center
1710 Robin Hood Road, Richmond, VA 23220
800/365-7272

South Hill Tourist Information Center
201 South Mecklenburg Avenue, South Hill, VA 23970
800/524-4347

Wildlife Management Areas

Amelia: 2,217 acres, 10 miles north of Amelia Courthouse, Amelia County.

Briery Creek: 845 acres, 7 miles south of Farmville, Prince Edward County.

Dick Cross (formerly Elm Hill): 1,400 acres, east of Castle Heights, Mecklenburg County. (See site #24)

Horsepen Lake: 2,910 acres of rolling hills, near Buckingham Courthouse, Buckingham County.

Powhatan: 4,117 acres in gently rolling Piedmont country, 35 miles southwest of Richmond, Powhatan County.

Site 21.
JAMES RIVER PARK,
Richmond City

BACKGROUND: James River Park is an island of wilderness in the heart of Richmond; it is also the best birding site in the area. The park is largely a fragmented greenways corridor along the river's south side. Its numerous trails go along the river's edge and through a variety of habitats.

The two largest and most productive park sections are a two-mile strip called the "Main Section" and, several miles west, a mile-long section called the "Pony Pasture." Both generally have similar birds, except that the "Pony Pasture" has a wetland and is best for observing resident owls.

ESSENTIALS: The park is on the south side of the James River in the west end of the city. Both park sections lie off Forest Hill Avenue (Route 417). Coming from the north, Forest Hill is the first toll exit off Route 76 south of the river.

To reach the Main Section, drive left (east) on Forest Hill for 2.1 miles, turn left onto 42nd Street, go 0.4 mile until it ends at Riverside Drive, then left to the parking lot entrance. If the gate is locked, park on the street. At the parking lot start looking for birds, walk over the bridge across the railroad tracks, continue to the visitors center, and then go toward Boulevard Bridge.

To reach the Pony Pasture Section, drive right (west) on Forest Hill Avenue for 0.6 mile to the stoplight, and turn right onto Hathaway. As the road turns to the left, Hathaway becomes Longview. Take Longview for 0.7 mile until it ends. Turn right and go 100 yards, turning left onto Riverside Drive. The parking lot is another 100 yards off Riverside. If the lot is locked, go another 200 yards to the west and park at the turn-off by the river and walk back to the parking lot. The river overlook is a good place to see eagles, ducks, cormorants, and Ospreys. This area has many trails which lead into different habitats.

HABITATS: A fairly narrow strip of river bottomland (plus islands) adjoins the James River for nearly 2 miles with much mature hardwood forest, scrub, open areas, and a small marsh.

BIRDS:

Spring: At the height of migration, some 20 species of warblers can be observed in one day. These include Blue-winged, Black-throated Green, Blackpoll, Canada, Magnolia, and Ovenbird. Other transients are Rose-breasted Grosbeak, Gray-cheeked and Swainson's Thrushes, Veery, Spotted Sandpiper, and the occasional Marsh Wren and American Bittern.

Summer: Breeding warblers include Prothonotary, Yellow-throated, and Yellow Warblers, American Redstart, Yellow-breasted Chat, and Northern Parula. Summer residents also include Mallard, Osprey, American Black and Wood Ducks, Acadian and Great Crested Flycatchers, Scarlet Tanager,

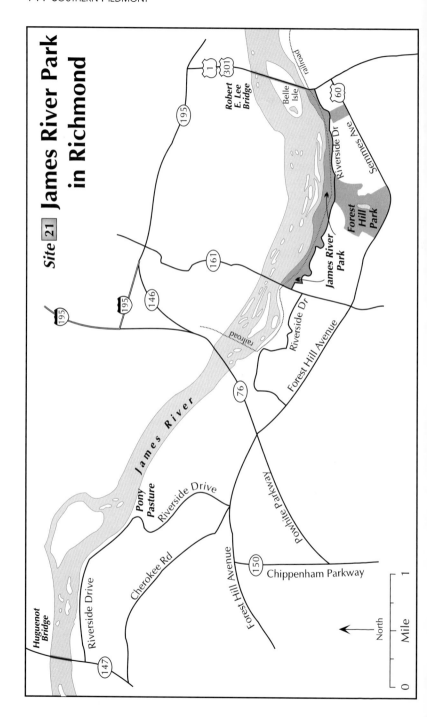

Site 21 **James River Park in Richmond**

Wood Thrush, Blue Grosbeak, and Red-tailed and Red-shouldered Hawks. Post-breeding dispersal brings several swallow species and Black Terns.

Fall: This park is one of the best places in the Richmond area to observe migrating warblers. After nesting in the park, Ospreys and Bald Eagles continue to be sighted along the river.

Winter: The river is a good winter birding site. Here one can see mixed flocks of ducks (American Black, Mallard, Bufflehead, Common Merganser), Pied-billed Grebes, Double-crested Cormorants, and many gulls (Herring, Ring-billed, Great Black-backed). Common landbirds include Hermit Thrush, Swamp Sparrow, Cedar Waxwing, Yellow-bellied Sapsucker, and the other usual eastern woodpeckers. Blue-gray Gnatcatcher, Baltimore Oriole, and Glaucous Gull have been seen recently on winter bird counts. Common in some winters have been the irruptive Pine Siskins, Evening Grosbeaks, and Red-breasted Nuthatches.

RARE OR UNUSUAL BIRDS: White-winged Scoter, Olive-sided Flycatcher, Sora, and "Brewster's" Warbler.

SPECIAL COMMENTS: Although best known for migrant landbirds, this area is productive year round. Its wildflowers are abundant and varied, also.

Darrell Peterson, Mary Arginteanu, Fred Scott

Great Crested Flycatcher
Georges Dremeaux

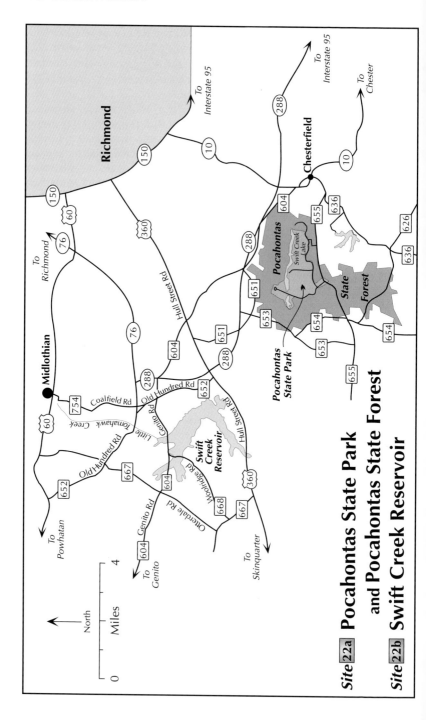

Site 22a Pocahontas State Park
and Pocahontas State Forest
Site 22b Swift Creek Reservoir

Site 22a.
POCAHONTAS STATE PARK
AND POCAHONTAS STATE FOREST,
Chesterfield County

BACKGROUND: First developed by the National Park Service in the 1930s and then known as the Swift Creek Recreational Demonstration Area, Pocahontas State Park (804/796-4255) is the largest state park in Virginia, with over 7,600 acres and three small lakes. Camping is available. The park is named after Pocahontas, the famed daughter of Chief Powahatan, who ruled the tribes in the Powahatan Confederacy. Legend has it that Pocahontas saved Captain John Smith's life. She later married an Englishman and moved to London.

ESSENTIALS: The park is located approximately 20 miles south of Richmond. Take Exit 62 off I-95 and go north on Route 288 for 6.1 miles to Ironbridge Road (Route 10). To reach the park entrance, go east on Route 10 for 1.5 miles to Beach Road (Route 655), turn right, and go 4 miles to the park entrance road. The visitors center is 1.8 miles from the park entrance; Beaver Lake parking area is located at 1.9 miles.

HABITAT: The park is mostly mature and second-growth upland hardwood, pine, and mixed forests. Swift Creek Lake forms the nucleus of the park. Facilities include many miles of trails, camping and picnic areas, a nature center, a swimming-pool, and a boating area. The surrounding state forest is managed for timber production and has many clear-cuts of various ages; it can be reached by surrounding country roads as well as by internal trails. A map is available at the visitors center.

BIRDS:

Spring: Migrants begin arriving from the south: Yellow-billed Cuckoo, Eastern Kingbird, Purple Martin, Gray Catbird, Yellow-throated and White-eyed Vireos, Yellow-throated, Hooded, and Prairie Warblers, and Scarlet and Summer Tanagers.

Summer: This area is best known for its good populations of Piedmont forest breeding birds. Typical species include Worm-eating, Pine, and Hooded Warblers, American Redstarts, Northern Parula, Ovenbird, Yellow-breasted Chats, and Whip-poor-wills, while the clear-cuts have species that prefer more open areas. The lakes have many nesting Wood Ducks, the occasional Pied-billed Grebe, and Green and Great Blue Herons.

Fall: Typical migrants include Spotted and Solitary Sandpipers, Common Nighthawks, and Blue-winged, Magnolia, Blackburnian, and Chestnut-sided Warblers. Although the park is not a premier locale for migrating waterfowl, Lesser Scaup, Hooded Merganser, and Pied-billed Grebe have been seen on Beaver Lake.

Winter: Among the more common residents are Northern Cardinal, Carolina Wren, Red-tailed and Red-shouldered Hawks, Wild Turkey, and Song Sparrow. Brown-headed Nuthatches are present but uncommon. Other woodland birds include Yellow-bellied Sapsucker, Winter Wren, and Brown Creeper. Bufflehead and Hooded Mergansers may winter on the park lakes.

RARE OR UNUSUAL BIRDS: At least formerly, Henslow's and Bachman's Sparrows.

SPECIAL COMMENTS: There are good spring wildflowers on the Beaver Lake Trail.

Mary Arginteanu, Darrell Peterson, Larry Robinson, Fred Scott

Site 22b.
SWIFT CREEK RESERVOIR,
Chesterfield County

BACKGROUND: This is the largest body of water in the Greater Richmond area and is potentially one of its best places to see waterfowl.

ESSENTIALS: From Midlothian on US-60 drive south on Coalfield Road (Route 754) 4.4 miles to Genito Road (Route 604). Turn right and drive 2 miles west to the lake parking overlook on the causeway. Other observation points are reached by going 0.3 mile west on Genito Road and turning left on Woolridge Road (Route 668) or by going 1 mile west on Genito to another causeway. There are observation points in Brandermill, especially at the boat-launching ramp area at Sunday Park, and along a walking/jogging trail accessible from the cul-de-sac at the end of Riverbirch Trace. (Follow signs on Brandermill Parkway from Genito Road).

HABITATS: This large Piedmont lake has a wooded shoreline and small islands. Brandermill and other subdivisions are slowly surrounding the lake, but at present the main deterrent to birding is heavy vehicular traffic. (It is not a place to bring a large group.)

BIRDS:

Spring, fall, and winter: The lake is heavily used by transient and wintering waterbirds. Species occurring in migration include Common Loon, Horned Grebe, Tundra Swan, Common and Red-breasted Mergansers, Osprey, and Herring and Bonaparte's Gulls. The most common wintering waterbirds are American Coot, Pied-billed Grebe, American Wigeon, Ring-necked Duck, Lesser Scaup, Bufflehead, Hooded Merganser, and Ruddy Duck. Bald Eagles are fairly regular in fall and winter.

Summer: Except for Wood Duck, summer waterbirds are few in number. Landbirds are generally those typical of the southeastern Piedmont (Whip-poor-will, Red-headed Woodpecker, Summer Tanager, Eastern Bluebird, Carolina Wren, and Yellow-throated Vireo).

RARE OR UNUSUAL BIRDS: Red-necked Grebe, Surf Scoter, and Oldsquaw.

SPECIAL COMMENTS: Increasing development of the area and especially along the shoreline is a potential problem for waterfowl visiting the lake and for birding opportunities.

Darrell Peterson, Larry Robinson, Fred Scott

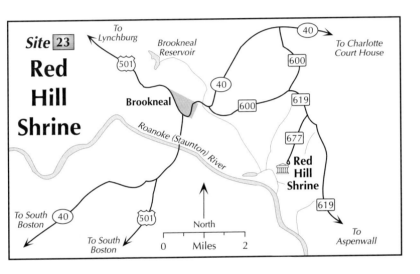

Site 23.
RED HILL SHRINE,
Charlotte County

BACKGROUND: Red Hill Shrine, the last home and burial place of Patrick Henry, is located in the southwest corner of Charlotte County. It is a pleasant place for birding in the beautiful southern Piedmont countryside near the Roanoke River. Nearby are other points of interest, including Appomattox Court House (26 miles), Peaks of Otter (65 miles), and Natural Bridge (70 miles).

ESSENTIALS: The Shrine can be approached on Route 40 from Brookneal. It is 5 miles from Brookneal on Road 677 and is 18 miles from Charlotte Courthouse.

HABITATS: Forested areas, open fields, and bushy edges provide good habitat for a variety of species. The focal point of the grounds is the largest Osage Orange tree in North America.

BIRDS:

Spring: This is the best season (late April through mid-May) for birding at Red Hill. Migrating warblers are abundant in the large sycamores and river birches. Possible species include Cape May, Yellow, Northern Parula, Black-throated Blue, and Yellow-throated Warblers. Shorebirds are occasionally seen along the swales in the open fields. Also, migrating Bobolinks have been seen.

Summer: Nesting species are those usually associated with the southern Piedmont: Blue Grosbeak, Grasshopper Sparrow, Indigo Bunting, Yellow-throated Warbler, Prairie Warbler, Yellow-throated Vireo, and Summer Tanager.

Fall: Bushy edges are good for migrating thrushes, vireos, warblers, and sparrows.

Winter: White-throated and Field Sparrows, Northern Cardinals, Dark-eyed Juncos, Eastern Towhees, and Eastern Bluebirds winter here.

SPECIAL COMMENTS: Red Hill Shrine is owned and operated by the Patrick Henry Memorial Foundation. Expect a small entrance fee.

John and Thelma Dalmas

Turkey Vulture
Ali Wieboldt

Site 24.
JOHN H. KERR RESERVOIR,
Mecklenburg County

BACKGROUND: Kerr Dam was completed in 1953 to provide hydro-electric power to the region and to help control floods. The 50,000-acre Kerr Reservoir is 300 feet above sea level and is the largest inland body of water in Virginia. The reservoir, also called Buggs Island Lake, extends 39 miles up the Roanoke River and has over 800 miles of shoreline. The U.S. Army Corps of Engineers manages a number of wildlife management areas and camping sites around the lake. Two state parks—Occoneechee (camping; 804/374-2210) and Staunton River (camping; see site #25a)—are found on the north shore of the reservoir. North Bend Park, also on the north shore, is managed by the Corps.

ESSENTIALS: Because of its large size, the reservoir can be reached by different routes. From I-85 going south, exit at either US-1 or U-58 and follow either route through South Hill.

Because of the reservoir's many arms, we have identified a "loop route" to maximize birding over the reservoir. About 5 miles south of South Hill, continue on US-58 and drive 4.4 miles to Buggs Island Road (Route 4); turn left to go to the dam. At 4.7 miles you will reach Dick Cross (Elm Hill) Wildlife Management Area on the left just across the road from Brames Amoco gas station and country store. Staying on the main dirt road and keeping a small utility building and the dog kennels to your left, follow the road to a parking lot on the left just before the barricade. Just in front of you will be the observation platform overlooking Clyde's Pond. Here during winter and early spring you should be able to find a variety of ducks. Tundra Swans have been seen here, and when the water level is low you can find a few shorebirds in season. You can follow the dirt road on foot to the bottom on the hill and to the right and over the dike of Clyde's Pond. As you cross the dike, you will be looking straight toward the river below the dam. By continuing to follow the old dirt road toward the river and to the left, you will come upon another new pond that was made by Ducks Unlimited and the Army Corps of Engineers. Nearby fields have yielded Grasshopper Sparrows in summer and White-crowned Sparrows and various hawks in winter.

After birding the Dick Cross WMA, return to Buggs Island Road. Turn left; in 0.9 mile you will reach the turn to the dam. Turn left at the sign to the powerhouse and proceed to Tailrace Park below the dam. From this park one should to be able to see Bald Eagles at any time of the year, with better luck from fall to spring. Scan the trees on Buggs Island and check the rocks in the river when the water is low—while being sure to keep a watch overhead as well. Look for Palm Warblers around the play area and the restrooms and along the river bank. Spotted Sandpipers are found here during some winters. This is a good place to find River Otters playing on the rocks.

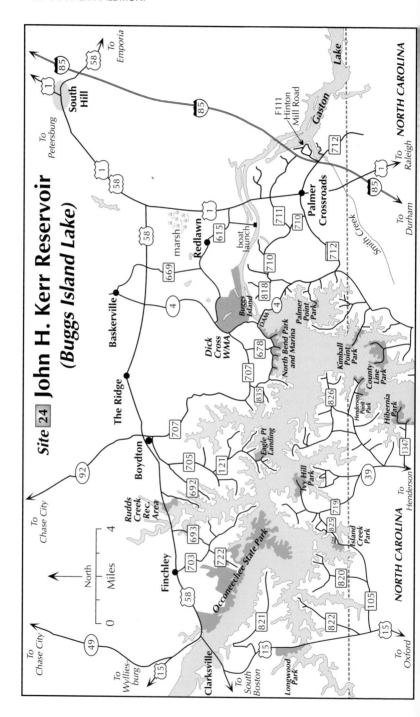

Site 24 John H. Kerr Reservoir
(Buggs Island Lake)

Return to Buggs Island Road (Route 4), turning left to go to the top of the dam. At the "Y" intersection take the fork to the right onto May Chapel Road (678) to the pull-off on the left. Scan the lake for waterfowl, gulls, terns, and eagles. Park in front of the Management Center Office and go to the office to pick up a map of John H. Kerr Reservoir. This map shows in detail the location of the two Virginia state parks and the Corps' day-use areas around the lake in both Virginia and North Carolina. With this map one can explore any of the other areas not covered in this loop. You can also pick up a new Wildlife Management Guide that shows the location and details of the 26 wildlife management areas around the reservoir and also pick up a bird list for the reservoir and the surrounding area. The office also has an attractive overlook of the lake (U.S. Army Corps of Engineers, Route #1, Box 76, Boydton, VA 23917; 804/738-6143). From the overlook you can usually find Common Loons and some ducks in winter and during migration. Brown-headed Nuthatches are also in the area pine trees.

Leaving the Management Center, turn left onto May Chapel Road and turn left at the next drive immediately on the left, which is the entrance to North Bend Park (fee from April to October). Explore North Bend Park by following the roads. Park at your leisure and walk around the shoreline where possible, looking for gulls, loons, grebes, and ducks from late fall to early spring. Warblers, thrushes vireos, and other songbirds migrate through from late March to early June. *Avoid walking in these woods after the weather warms up, and always check yourself for ticks.*

After you have explored this side of the lake, you can now return to May Chapel Road, which will take you back to Buggs Island Lake Road. Go to the right at the "Y" intersection to cross over the dam. There is a good pull-off on the right 1.4 miles from the Powerhouse exit and another pull-off 0.8 mile farther (at the end of the earthen dam on the left) in which you can park and look out over the lake. From either one of these two pull-offs you can walk along the shoulder of the road along the lake.

From the last pull-off on the left, get back on Buggs Island Lake Road and go to the left 1.4 miles to Palmer Point Road, turn right, and go 0.9 mile to Palmer Point Park day-use area. After passing the toll booth (fee during the summer), turn to the left and park near the boat ramp. You can walk along the shoreline to the left of the boat ramp to the next point; and from there you will able to see a large cove. Do not walk past this point because you will soon run into private property. This cove in winter will sometimes have large rafts of ducks taking shelter from the high winds that can rip over the lake. Returning to the parking lot, you can see the dam. You can walk along the shoreline from the right of the boat ramp all the way around to the swimming area. The park also extends past the swimming area, but one can see almost everything from the swimming area. Brown-headed Nuthatches can be found year round within the park.

Return to Buggs Island Lake Road, turn right, and drive 1.2 miles to Palmer Springs Road (712). Drive 4.0 miles to US-1. *Quickly* go straight across, and in 1.5 miles you will reach I-85 (no entrance to the highway here). Proceed to the bridge over Smith Creek and park at the small pull-off on the right. From this spot, turn around and drive back across the bridge over Smith Creek and turn right on Hinton Mill Road (F111). This is private property with very little traffic, and you can pull to the side of the road and look for waterfowl.

Return to Palmer Springs Road and turn right to return to US-1. At US-1 turn right. In 2.5 miles you will reach the bridge over part of Lake Gaston. Just past the bridge is a turn to the left which dead-ends at a parking lot and a boat ramp; there is a small marsh area on your right before you reach the parking lot. Here you can park and follow a foot trail under the bridge to a small point from which you can look downstream. Return to the parking lot and then explore the marsh. Here you will find ducks, geese, and gulls during the winter, and herons and egrets in the summer.

From the parking lot at the steel bridge turning left on US-1, you can either walk or drive the short distance until you see a marsh area on your left. Pull well off the road and scope the area. The Wood Stork was once seen here and in the marsh area off Hinton Mill Road.

This is the end of the "loop route." If you wish to return to South Hill, you can go straight north on US-1.

If you want to find birds of the open fields during winter, go north on US-1 and turn left onto Redlawn Road (615). Proceed to Baskerville Road and turn right. During the winter you might find American Pipits, Horned Larks, and other birds of the open fields along this road. It is all private property, so stay along the road or be sure to get permission to bird on anyone's property.

HABITATS: Lake Gaston downstream has many open marshes, and Dick Cross WMA has weedy fields, woods, cultivated fields, and two large ponds that attract a variety of wading-birds and waterfowl.

BIRDS:

Spring: Cliff Swallows nest on the dam and under nearly every bridge in the area. At Dick Cross WMA one can find Blue Grosbeak, Indigo Bunting, Orchard Oriole, Summer and Scarlet Tanagers, Yellow-breasted Chat, and Pine, Prairie, and Yellow-throated Warblers. On the lake above the dam in April you can find Caspian Terns, American Coots, and sometimes large rafts of Red-breasted Mergansers. The ponds at Dick Cross and the marshes around Lake Gaston might turn up a Marsh Wren, a King Rail, or a Least Bittern. The woods in North Bend State Park provide an excellent place to look for migrant warblers, vireos, tanagers, and thrushes.

Summer: Birds are scarce because of the large crowds of people and the heavy use of boats on the lake; however, you might see a Bald Eagle. Unusual summer records include Horned Grebe, Glossy Ibis, Tricolored Heron, and Wood Stork. This is the time to check for Mississippi Kites and, where the right habitat prevails, to listen for Henslow's and Bachman's Sparrows. Black Terns migrate through in August and September.

Fall: Migrating shorebirds might be found if the water level is low below the dam. Shorebirds along the lake shore will be hard to find because of the varying water levels. Gulls and terns begin to arrive in late September and early October, and ducks begin to arrive late in the season. Also, in October and November look for loons, grebes, Oldsquaws, scoters, and other bay ducks which stop regularly as they move through the area.

Winter: Large numbers of Bonaparte's and Ring-billed Gulls and wintering ducks, loons, and grebes (Pied-billed and Horned are regular, and Red-necked and a "Western" have been found) can be seen out on the lake. Bald Eagles can be found with ease during the winter. Other raptors to look for include Red-tailed, Red-shouldered, Sharp-shinned, and Cooper's Hawks, Northern Harrier, and maybe even a Rough-legged Hawk. Owls of the area include Great Horned, Barred, and Eastern Screech- or an occasional Short-eared Owl. Check the many field edges and hedgerows for sparrows. Also seen during the winter are American Pipits and White-crowned Sparrows, and Virginia Rails in the marshes.

RARE OR UNUSUAL BIRDS: Kirtland's Warbler (1974), Red Crossbill, Snow Bunting, Greater White-fronted Goose, Glaucous Gull, Clay-colored, Henslow's, and Harris's Sparrows, American Avocet, Ruddy Turnstone, Wood Stork, Black-legged Kittiwake, Western Kingbird, Mississippi Kite, Sooty Tern, jaegers, and Western Grebe.

There were also a number of surprising birds in September 1996, waifs from Hurricane *Fran.* Some sightings were still under consideration by the state records committee at press time, but they include reports of: Black-capped Petrel, Cape Verde Petrel, Herald Petrel, Cory's Shearwater, Red-necked Phalarope, Red Phalarope, Pomarine and Parasitic Jaegers, Sabine's Gull, Sandwich Tern, Sooty Tern, and Black Skimmer.

SPECIAL COMMENTS: Loggerhead Shrikes still breed here. Check areas along US-58 west from where US-58 and US-1 separate along to where Route 4 crosses US-58. Also look for them along Baskerville Road between US-58 and Redlawn Road. They might also be found by driving around any of the country roads. They are easier to find in winter than in summer. *If you find them in summer, remember that the species is an endangered breeder in Virginia. Please remain as far back as possible and do not disturb the birds.*

Jeffrey Blalock, John Dalmas

Site 25a.
STAUNTON RIVER STATE PARK,
Halifax County

BACKGROUND: Staunton River State Park (804/572-4623) is located where the Staunton and Dan Rivers meet and flow into the Kerr Reservoir (also known as Buggs Island Lake). Camping facilities and housekeeping cabins are available. The park was once part of the homeland of the Occoneechee Indians.

ESSENTIALS: From Richmond take US-360 west, turn east onto State Route 344, go 2 miles to Scottsburg, and then follow Route 344 for 10 miles to the park entrance. If you are traveling east or west near the North Carolina boundary on US-58, turn east on US-360 to Route 344. (*Note* that US-360 to Road 344 is the best route for cars which are towing boats or campers; all of the county roads off Route 360 that can be taken to Route 344 are narrow and have many curves.)

A map of the park and its trails is available at the park entrance. The park has a loop trail that follows the banks of the two rivers. It should be used only from late fall to early spring because of chiggers and ticks in warm weather. This trail offers a nice walk through some thick woods with possible views of waterfowl, eagles, herons, and some shorebirds. Another trail, Captain Staunton's Trail, has its head located to the left of the parking lot at the park manager's office. It is also a loop trail, one that leads you to a high bluff on the Staunton River with excellent views upstream, where you can see ducks, grebes, or Bald Eagles.

If you are pressed for time, drive to the boat ramp on the Staunton River at the turn-off to the left of the boat houses. When the water level is low, you can walk along the shoreline to the point of the two rivers—even though you may have to climb over fallen trees. Otherwise, walk back up the road and turn left to go to the cabins. In the winter walk around the barricade and continue along the paved road to the last cabin, where you will find a trail through the woods to the point where the two rivers meet. As you drive past the boat houses, you will cross over the River Bank Trail on both sides of the road. At the boat ramp you can park and walk along the trail. The River Bank Trail leads to the Dan River.

HABITATS: Chiefly riverine forests with tall hardwood trees and a well-developed understory.

BIRDS:

Spring: Most migrating warblers can be found at this time: Worm-eating, Chestnut-sided, Cerulean, Black-and-white, Pine, Palm, Blackburnian, Black-poll, Prothonotary, Ovenbird, and both waterthrushes. Vireos include Red-eyed, White-eyed, Yellow-throated, and Blue-headed, with the occasional Warbling. Four species of thrushes can also be found. Bald Eagles may be seen flying overhead or perched on a snag over the water or resting on a sandbar if the water level is low. A few shorebirds use the mudflats along the Staunton River. In early spring some lingering ducks may be seen, as well as Caspian Terns and American Coots.

Summer: In the riverine forests are breeding Red-eyed and Yellow-throated Vireos, Northern Cardinals, and several types of woodpeckers, including Downy, Hairy, Red-bellied, Red-headed, Pileated, and Northern Flicker. Bald Eagles may be seen because they breed near the park. Late summer brings in Double-crested Cormorants, herons, and egrets, and, when water levels are low, the river mudflats attract yellowlegs, dowitchers, Sanderlings, Dunlins, Common Snipes, Least, Pectoral, Solitary, Spotted, and Semipalmated Sandpipers, American Golden-Plovers, and Black-bellied Plovers. In August early migrating Caspian, Common, Forster's, and Black Terns have been seen.

Fall: Shorebird numbers increase, and some species remain until mid-November. Ducks of several species start to arrive, including Mallard, Gadwall, Canvasback, Ring-necked, Lesser Scaup, and Hooded and Common Mergansers. The occasional Tundra Swan has been seen at this time of year. The River Bank Trail offers good encounters with migrating warblers, vireos, thrushes, and tanagers. Wild Turkeys can also be found in large flocks or individually. *Note:* if the weather is still warm, chiggers and ticks can be problems.

Winter: In some winters Red-headed Woodpeckers are found here in large numbers. Bald Eagles, ducks, gulls (Ring-billed, Herring, and even Bonaparte's), Pied-billed and Horned Grebes, and an occasional Common Loon may be seen on either of the two rivers. Wintering hawks include Sharp-shinned, Red-tailed, Red-shouldered, Cooper's, and, rarely, Rough-legged. Birds found in the woodlands or nearby include the three species of eastern nuthatches, Pine Warblers, and Fox, White-throated, White-crowned, and Song Sparrows.

Jeffrey Blalock

Site 25b.
STAUNTON RIVER BATTLEFIELD STATE PARK
(FORT HILL),
Halifax and Charlotte Counties

BACKGROUND: Formerly known as Fort Hill, this new state park (804/454-4312) was opened in 1995. It is the site of the only battle of the Civil War fought in Halifax County. Defending the old railroad bridge over the Staunton River on June 25, 1864, the Confederates were outnumbered by five to one but turned away four Union assaults.

ESSENTIALS: Coming from the east on US-360, turn right on Route 92 toward Clover and go 4.5 miles to county Route 600. From South Boston go east on US 360 for about 12 miles, turn left on Route 92, and then go 2 miles through Clover to county Route 600. From the intersection of Route 92 and Route 600, go 2.5 miles north on Route 600 and turn right onto county Route 855 into the park. After exploring this area, you may wish to loop back to US-360 by continuing north for 4.5 miles on Route 600, then right on Route 746 for 1.8 miles, crossing the river into Charlotte County, and then turn right on Route 607. From this point it is 3 miles to Randolph and 9.5 miles back to US-360.

HABITATS: The park is made up of 88 acres of deciduous riverbottom woods along the Staunton River. The area along the road into Fort Hill is made up of brushy areas, vital habitats for sparrows. The open fields surrounding the area are great for Northern Harriers and Red-tailed and Red-shouldered Hawks.

BIRDS:

Spring: Warblers, tanagers, vireos, and thrushes should be found in the woods along the river. Sparrows are frequent along the road leading up to the fort and along the trail to Randolph.

Summer: Glossy Ibises have been seen here, along with Great Blue Herons and other large wading-birds. The bridge over the river makes a great place from which to watch for warblers. Blue Grosbeak, Eastern Towhee, Indigo Bunting, and Field Sparrows can also be found. Listen for Henslow's Sparrows in any weedy fields, but especially those along Route 607.

Fall: This is a good place to check for warblers in the early fall, as well as for tanagers, vireos, and thrushes. Sparrows and shorebirds may be found in the fields from the road or from the railroad trail to Randolph.

Winter: You should be able to find plenty of sparrows: White-throated, Fox, Swamp, Field, Chipping, Song, and maybe even some White-crowneds. Palm Warblers have been seen, and woodpeckers, including Red-headed, can be found in the trees along the river banks. Raptors should be looked for as you drive to the park from Clover: Cooper's, Sharp-shinned, Red-tailed, and Red-shouldered Hawks and Northern Harriers.

RARE OR UNUSUAL BIRDS: Rough-legged Hawk.

SPECIAL COMMENTS: Old Dominion Electric Co-operative and Virginia Electric and Power Company have opened a new science and history center which features exhibits on the role of electricity and on the effects of the Battle of Staunton River Bridge and of the Civil War in southside Virginia. Behind the center is the start of a trail to some newly created wetlands where there is an observation platform.

There is also a new trail following an old railroad bed from the railroad bridge to Randolph. This trail is above the fields and is great for finding shorebirds in spring and fall and for hawks during the winter.

Jeffrey Blalock

Chestnut-sided
Warbler
Georges Dremeaux

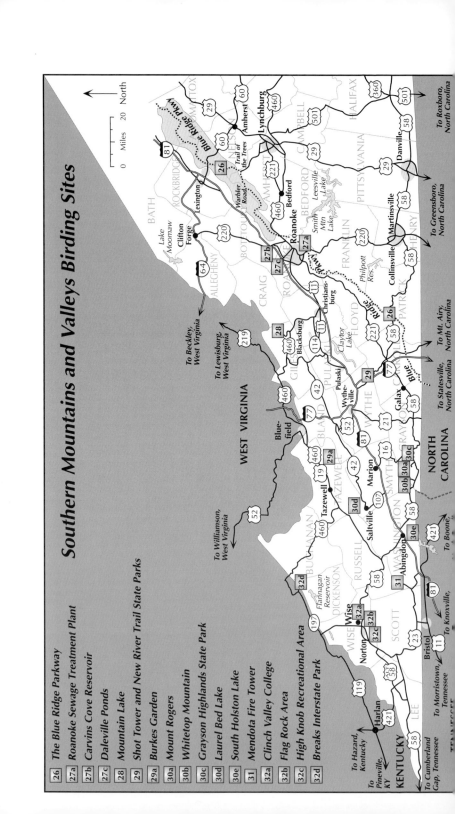

Southern Mountains and Valleys Birding Sites

26 The Blue Ridge Parkway
27a Roanoke Sewage Treatment Plant
27b Carvins Cove Reservoir
27c Daleville Ponds
28 Mountain Lake
29 Shot Tower and New River Trail State Parks
29a Burkes Garden
30a Mount Rogers
30b Whitetop Mountain
30c Grayson Highlands State Park
30d Laurel Bed Lake
30e South Holston Lake
31 Mendota Fire Tower
32a Clinch Valley College
32b Flag Rock Area
32c High Knob Recreational Area
32d Breaks Interstate Park

SOUTHERN MOUNTAINS AND VALLEYS

This large region embraces southern portions of the Blue Ridge (Blue Ridge Parkway), as well as the Ridge and Valley and Appalachian provinces of other authors. It contains many of Virginia's highest mountains, including Mount Rogers (5,238 ft) and Whitetop Mountain (5,046 ft). Long parallel ridges are separated by intervening valleys. Characteristic forests of the mountains are complex mixtures of deciduous trees (formerly oak/chestnut) at lower elevations, hemlocks in ravines, northern hardwoods at higher elevations, and remnants of spruce and fir on the highest mountain-tops. Valleys have some agricultural fields, woodlots, and stream bottomlands.

Wintertime weather conditions are often severe in the mountains, so the best birding times are during migration and summer. In summer this region attracts a large variety of exciting birds—Willow and Least Flycatchers, several warblers (Blue-winged, Blackburnian, Black-throated Blue, Worm-eating), Ruffed Grouse, Black-billed Cuckoo, Red-breasted Nuthatch, Veery, and Dark-eyed Junco. Birders should also look for the erratic Red Crossbills, Golden Eagle, and Northern Goshawk. Croaks of Common Ravens are frequently heard in the mountains and valleys.

An interesting distributional pattern in Virginia is found in both Swainson's and Black-throated Green Warbler populations. Both species have small

W. Juergen Schrenk
A view from the Blue Ridge Parkway.

161

breeding populations in the Dismal Swamp, as well as here in the Southern Mountains and Valleys.

Highlighted among Virginia's rarest breeding birds are several found in the high mountains, at least formerly if not at present. One should look for Nashville and Magnolia Warblers, Yellow-bellied Flycatchers, Swainson's Thrush, Golden-crowned Kinglet, Pine Siskin, and Purple Finch. Bewick's Wren was formerly a breeding bird of the region. Discovery of nests of any of these species would be a major contribution to Virginia's ornithology.

MORE INFORMATION:

General Information

Appalachian Mountain Region Visitor Center
17507 Lee Highway (Suite 2), Abingdon, VA 24210
888/827-6867

Big Stone Gap-Wise County Tourist Information Center
P.O. Box 236, Big Stone Gap, VA 24219
540/523-2060

Danville Area Chamber of Commerce
P.O. Box 1538, Danville, VA 24543
804/793-5422

Lexington Visitor Center
106 East Washington Street, Lexington, VA 24450
540/463-3777

Roanoke Valley Visitor Information Center
114 Market Street, Roanoke, VA 24011
800/635-5535

Salem Visitor Center
P.O. Box 886, Salem, VA 24153
888/827-2536

Southwest Highlands Gateway Visitor Center
Drawer B-12, Max Meadows, VA 24360
800/446-9670

Wildlife Management Areas

Clinch Mountain: the largest management area (includes 300-acre Laurel Bed Lake), extending into Russell, Washington, Tazewell, and Smyth Counties, chiefly north of Saltville. (See details under site #30d.)

Crooked Creek: 1,750 acres, 4 miles south of Galax, Carroll County.

Fairystone Farms: 5,286 acres, 15 miles northwest of Martinsville, Patrick and Henry counties.

Havens: 7,158 acres of parcels in the Appalachian Highlands, 10 miles northwest of Roanoke, Roanoke County.

Hidden Valley: a high-elevation area about halfway between Abingdon and Lebanon, Washington County.

James River: 1,213 acres of hilly woodlands to flatlands in the Piedmont, 15 miles southwest of Lovingston, Nelson County.

Stewart's Creek: 1,100 acres of steep, wooded hillsides and streams along the Blue Ridge Mountains, 7 miles southeast of Galax, Carroll County.

Turkeycock Mountain: 1,790 acres of rugged, forested mountain terrain, north of Martinsville, Franklin County.

White Oak Mountain: 2,700 acres of rolling, hilly forests, 5 miles southeast of Chatham, Pittsylvania County.

Yellow-breasted Chat
Ali Wieboldt

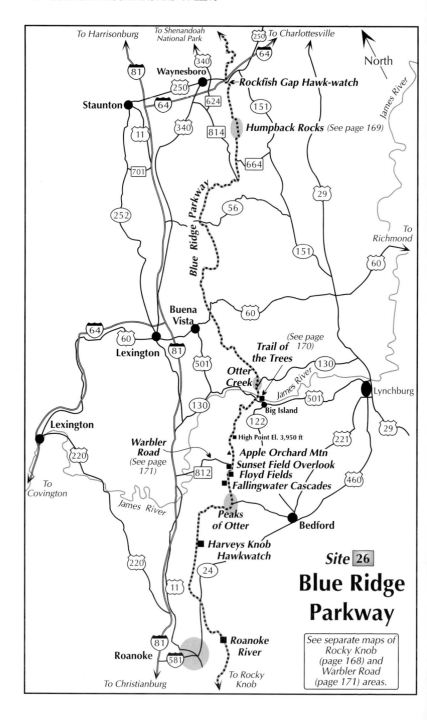

To Harrisonburg

To Shenandoah National Park

To Charlottesville

250

64

North

340

81

Waynesboro

250

← Rockfish Gap Hawk-watch

Staunton

64

624

151

James River

11

340

814

Humpback Rocks (See page 169)

701

664

252

Blue Ridge Parkway

56

29

To Richmond

151

60

Buena Vista

60

64

60

Trail of the Trees

(See page 170)

Lexington

81

501

Otter Creek

130

James River

Lynchburg

130

Big Island

501

29

Lexington

122

220

High Point El. 3,950 ft

221

Warbler Road (See page 171)

Apple Orchard Mtn

812

Sunset Field Overlook

460

To Covington

James River

Floyd Fields

Fallingwater Cascades

220

Peaks of Otter

Bedford

Harveys Knob Hawkwatch

24

Site 26

Blue Ridge Parkway

11

81

Roanoke River

See separate maps of Rocky Knob (page 168) and Warbler Road (page 171) areas.

Roanoke

581

To Christianburg

To Rocky Knob

Site 26.
THE BLUE RIDGE PARKWAY

A Special Section by Marcus B. Simpson, Jr.

The Blue Ridge Parkway provides easy access to some of the best scenery and birding sites in Virginia. The parkway also begins the Southern Mountain and Valleys region as identified in this book, starting at Rockfish Gap. The Parkway (administered by the National Park Service) winds generally along the main crest of the Blue Ridge Mountains for 217 miles to the North Carolina state line. From Rockfish Gap to the Roanoke River, the range consists mostly of a steep mountain ridge line, with occasional outliers and parallel ridges that extend onto the Piedmont to the east or onto the Great Valley to the west. South of the Roanoke River Gap, the topography changes to a broad, undulating plateau with scattered knobs, ridges, and a steep, eroded eastern escarpment that descends abruptly to the Piedmont. Most of the area is cloaked in medium to mature deciduous forests, with local stands of hemlocks and pines. Spruce and fir apparently do not occur naturally in the region.

Elevations on the Parkway range from a low of 646 feet near the James River to a high of 3,950 feet on the shoulder of Apple Orchard Mountain. Vegetation and birdlife vary predictably from biota typical of the Piedmont to that of middle and high elevations of the southern Appalachian mountains. The cool, moist climate of the high country forms an ecologic island of "northern" plants and birds that are generally more typically found in Canada and the northern United States. In an easy drive along the Parkway, birders can move quickly from riparian woodlands with Baltimore Orioles and Prothonotary and Yellow-throated Warblers up to a high oak-and-cove forest with Veeries, Winter Wrens, Rose-breasted Grosbeaks, and Canada and Cerulean Warblers. Such compressed avian diversity combines with beautiful mountain scenes, rhododendrons, azaleas, wildflowers, numerous trails, accommodations, and campgrounds to provide a fine birding experience. A number of major birding sites are found along or near the Parkway, including several premier hawk-watching localities. Mile markers are placed along the shoulder of the Parkway, thus making it easy to locate spots mentioned in this and other guide books. The birdlife described below is to be expected during the late spring through the late summer months. *Segments of the Parkway are often closed during the winter because of ice and snow.*

For the **Rockfish Gap Hawk-watch** exit I-64 at Rockfish Gap to begin the Parkway drive. Right at milepost 0 is the hawk-watch, at the deck of the "Inn at Afton" (formerly a Holiday Inn). The site, at an elevation of 1,100 feet, is manned by hawk-watchers from September into November. (See the section on "Hawk-watching in Virginia" for more details.)

To reach **Humpback Rocks** area, continue to the visitors center at mile 5.8 (el. 2,320 ft.). The Pioneer Farm Exhibit area is a good spot for some species, and the Humpback Rocks parking area (el. 2,360 ft.) provides access to "Big Rocks" (el. 3,210 ft.) via the Appalachian Trail. This parking lot area and the trail are particularly good for spring migrants and summer forest-resident birds. (For more details on this site, see the separate treatment following the description of the Blue Ridge Parkway.)

Many Parkway overlooks south of Humpback Rocks provide excellent birding, but the next major spot is where the **James River** carves through the Blue Ridge en route to the Atlantic Ocean. Local access is from US-501, whose interchange with the Parkway is at mile 63.7. At this low elevation, the bird life is more typically Piedmont and coastal than montane. From the James River visitors center (el. 668 ft.) at mile 63.6, a short trail descends to a footbridge spanning the river beneath the Parkway. Yellow-throated Vireo and Yellow-throated Warbler may be seen in the sycamores along the river banks; Barn and Cliff Swallows nest under the Parkway bridge. In summer Yellow-breasted Chat, and Yellow and Prothonotary Warblers may be noted on the opposite shore after you cross the footbridge; this is also a good spot from which to watch migrating nighthawks during the last week of September. Migratory shorebirds, waterfowl, coastal waders, and hawks may be occasionally seen from the footbridge. The moderately steep "Trail of the Trees" begins adjacent to the north base of the footbridge and forms a 0.4-mile loop, providing good chances for observing Barred Owl, Wood Thrush, White-breasted Nuthatch, and Warbling Vireo. (For details on this site, see the separate treatment following the description of the Blue Ridge Parkway.) For a more extended hike, consider the "Otter Creek Trail," which runs close by noisy Otter Creek for 3.8 miles from the visitors center to the Otter Creek campground (el. 777 ft.). Belted Kingfisher, Blue-headed Vireo, Northern Parula, Pine Warbler, and Louisiana Waterthrush are among the regular possibilities along this fairly gentle route.

Heading south from the James River, the Parkway climbs steeply over 14 miles to its highest elevation in Virginia on the shoulder of **Apple Orchard Mountain**, one of the best birding spots in the Blue Ridge. Park at Sunset Field Overlook (el. 4,225 ft.) at mile 78.4, walk 150 feet along FR-812 from the north end of the lot, and take a dirt road that splits right and heads 1.6 miles up through the forest of oaks and rhododendrons toward the mountain summit. The Veery chorus at dawn and dusk is particularly fine here. Other expected birds include Barred Owl, Ruffed Grouse, Common Raven, Winter Wren, Blue-headed Vireo, Chestnut-sided, Black-throated Blue, Cerulean, and Canada Warblers, Scarlet Tanager, Rose-breasted Grosbeak, and Dark-eyed Junco.

For premier roadside birding, return to your car and drive down FSR 812, which forms the upper segment of what has been affectionately called "Warbler Road." (For details on this site, see the separate treatment following the description of the Blue Ridge Parkway.) This site is interesting enough that birders will sometimes want to spend most of a day birding its length.

Continuing southward on the Parkway, pull off into "Floyd Fields" (el. 3,200 ft.) at mile 80.4, which is a good spot for Wild Turkey in early morning or late afternoon. Excellent views can be had of many species noted previously at Apple Orchard Mountain by walking along the Parkway shoulder for about 0.5 mile either north or south from Floyd Fields. The woods here consist of beautiful hemlocks, oaks, mountain laurels, and rhododendrons.

Eight miles farther south on the Parkway, the **Peaks of Otter Recreation Area** provides more prime birding spots, complete with campground, motel, restaurant, a network of five easy-to-strenuous trails, and, unfortunately, a great many people during the summer months. Pick up a trail map from the visitors center at mile 86 to obtain details of the various hiking routes. Easy birding can be had in the campground, in the picnic grounds, around Abbot Lake, and along portions of the Parkway. A particularly attractive bird walk is on the Parkway shoulder between the Fallingwater Cascades parking area (mile 83.1) and the Flat Top parking lot (mile 83.5). Here, the Parkway cuts through the head of a cove hardwood forest, where you may find Black-throated Blue, Cerulean, Blackburnian, and Kentucky Warblers. The Elk Run Trail and Johnson Farm Loop Trail are fairly easy routes through a variety of habitats, but the strenuous Flat Top Mountain Trail provides the best birding at the Peaks.

The Flat Top Mountain Trail can be accessed from the picnic grounds via a steep 1.8-mile climb to the summit (el. 4,004 ft.), or from the Flat Top parking

W. Juergen Schrenk
Vista from the Blue Ridge Parkway.

lot at mile 83.5 for a somewhat more gentle 2.8-mile ascent. By either route, watch and listen for Winter Wren, Veery, Blue-headed Vireo, Scarlet Tanager, Rose-breasted Grosbeak, Dark-eyed Junco, and a variety of warblers, including Black-throated Blue, Cerulean, Blackburnian, Worm-eating, and Canada. Many of the same species can be seen on nearby Sharp Top (el. 3,875 ft.). To avoid climbing the extremely steep trail, wait until the shuttle-bus service to the summit begins in mid-morning.

At mile 95.2 you will encounter **Harvey's Knob**, a fall hawk-watch site. Located at 2,524 feet, the hawk-watch takes place at the overlook parking lot. From the first of September to the end of November the site is manned by volunteers from the Lynchburg and Roanoke Valley Bird Clubs. (See the section on "Hawk-watching in Virginia", page 192, for more details.)

Rocky Knob Recreation Area
Blue Ridge Parkway

North

To Roanoke

Rocky Knob Campground

166

Saddle Overlook

Picnic Loop Trail

Visitor Center

Rocky Knob

Black Ridge Trail

8

To US 221 at Shelors Mill

605

Grassy Knoll

Rock Castle Creek

Rock Castle Gorge National Recreation Trail

726

To North Carolina

Rocky Knob Cabins

166 = Mileage Post

Adapted from *Birds of the Blue Ridge Mountains* by Marcus B. Simpson, Jr., 1992, The University of North Carolina Press.

More than 80 miles south of the Peaks of Otter, the last major birding spot on the Parkway in Virginia is the 4,500-acre **Rocky Knob Recreation Area**, where a campground, rental cabins, picnic area, and network of trails offer a spectrum of activities from roadside birding to strenuous backcountry hikes. An early morning stroll through the picnic grounds (el. 3,150 ft.) at mile 169 may yield Cedar Waxwing, Blue-headed Vireo, Scarlet Tanager, and Chestnut-sided, Black-throated Blue, and Worm-eating Warblers. Wild Turkeys are occasionally seen at the forest edge between mile 168.5 and 170.5 and around mile 173. Park on the shoulder at mile 170.2, near the trail crossing, and listen for Grasshopper Sparrows in the fields on the right; Horned Larks are sometimes noted in the pastures along the trail on the opposite side of the Parkway. Or try the moderately strenuous 1.1-mile loop hike around the summit of Rocky Knob; the trail begins at the Saddle Overlook (el. 3,380 ft.) at mile 167.9 and heads south toward the visitors center. In addition to the species noted at the picnic grounds, you may observe Great Crested Flycatcher, Yellow-throated Vireo, Ovenbird, American Redstart, and Cerulean, Kentucky, and Hooded Warblers. The Saddle Overlook is also a little-known but sometimes excellent spot for studying the autumn hawk migration.

For a strenuous 10.8-mile loop hike, the Rock Castle Gorge National Recreation Trail passes through an array of habitats, ranging from open pasture on the gorge escarpment to magnificent cove hardwood forests along Rock Castle Creek, where one may see, in addition to many of the species mentioned above, both species of cuckoos, Black-throated Green Warbler, Louisiana Waterthrush, Scarlet Tanager, and Rose-breasted Grosbeak. Access to the trail is marked at numerous spots along the Parkway, including the visitors center and campground, but you will need a detailed map, proper hiking gear, and prime physical conditioning if you intend to undertake this entire circuit.

For additional information on birding in the region, see *Birds of the Blue Ridge Mountains*. (See References section, page 264.) For up-to-date information regarding the Parkway, contact the Blue Ridge Parkway offices in Asheville, NC (704/298-0398). Also note that the Parkway is often closed in bad weather.

HUMPBACK ROCKS VISITORS CENTER AND PIONEER FARM EXHIBIT, *Augusta County*

BACKGROUND: The site is a typical mountain farm of the 1890s. The visitors center is a mini-museum of tools and kitchenware typically used by mountain farmers; it also provides an excellent collection of books and field guides for sale. Nearby are a one-room log cabin, log barn, root cellar, and spring house.

ESSENTIALS: Rockfish Gap is located where I-64 crosses the Blue Ridge and the Blue Ridge Parkway (to the south) begins. The Visitors Center/Museum and Pioneer Farm are at mile post 5.8 (el. 2,320). Facilities are open from about May 1 through October.

HABITATS: Typical clearings are associated with the authentic farm buildings. Trees include oak, hickory, Tulip Poplar, hemlock, and dogwood. At the end of the self-guiding trail through the farm, there is a large hillside pasture with a spring-fed stream and a swampy area extending into a woods.

Drive 0.2 mile south to the Humpback Rocks parking area (el. 2,360 ft.), where a connector trail ascends steeply for about a mile to the "Big Rocks" (el. 3,210 ft.) via the Appalachian Trail.

BIRDS:

Spring: Courtship flights of the American Woodcock may be seen in late March to early April in the open (garden) area of the farm. Along the rail fence look for Wild Turkeys and Grasshopper Sparrows. Also, listen for Ruffed Grouse drumming. Migration is easily observed from the parking lot and the trail down the road. Look for warblers, including Chestnut-sided, Black-throated Blue, and Cerulean, as well as other mountain forest species, such as Veery, Scarlet Tanager, and Dark-eyed Junco.

Summer: Although the farm area has many tourist visitors in summer, Eastern Phoebes nest in the barn, Blue-gray Gnatcatchers and Yellow-throated Vireos in the tall trees, and Gray Catbirds along the stream. The parking lot and trail have many of the more common forest species, lingering into the summer.

Fall: Migrating hawks can be seen from various overlooks along the Blue Ridge Parkway, as can Common Ravens, both vultures, and migrant warblers, thrushes, and tanagers.

Winter: The Parkway may be closed during periods of snow and ice. Otherwise, look for small groups of Dark-eyed Juncos and chickadees, as well as woodpeckers and, sometimes, Eastern Bluebirds. Examine the hemlocks for crossbills.

SPECIAL COMMENT: At times, migrating warblers, vireos, and thrushes can be plentiful.

Ruth Snyder

TRAIL OF THE TREES, BLUE RIDGE PARKWAY, *Bedford and Amherst Counties*

BACKGROUND: This trail has proven to be an excellent place to observe birds along the Blue Ridge Parkway. The visitors center, with a nice exhibit featuring information about the James River Canal, is open from spring through autumn.

ESSENTIALS: From Lynchburg, take US-501 north and drive 10 miles to Big Island. From Big Island continue on US-501 for 1 mile to the Blue Ridge Parkway. Turn right onto the Parkway, cross the James River, and pull into the parking lot at James River visitors center.

HABITATS: River bottomland in field and forest together with upland hardwood-hemlock forest on bluffs overlooking the river. The Trail of the Trees, a loop trail, is just past the visitors center on the right at the beginning of the bridge. It is an easy walk and be sure to continue on across the bridge over the James River to the canal and bird that side of the river.

BIRDS:

Spring: Migrant waterfowl including Blue-winged Teal, swallows (5 species), Warbling Vireo, warblers (Yellow-throated, Black-throated Green, Prothonotary), and Rose-breasted Grosbeaks.

Summer: Nesting birds include Baltimore Oriole, Warbling Vireo, Scarlet Tanager, and Barn, Cliff, and Tree Swallows. Following a walkway under the highway bridge, you can see many Cliff Swallow nests above you as you cross the James River.

Fall: In late August and early September, large flocks of Common Nighthawks and Broad-winged Hawks can usually be seen.

Winter: The Blue Ridge Parkway will be closed during inclement weather. Still, waterfowl of several species have been seen on the river, including American Black and Wood Ducks. Crossbills are occasionally seen in the hemlocks.

Dan Puckette

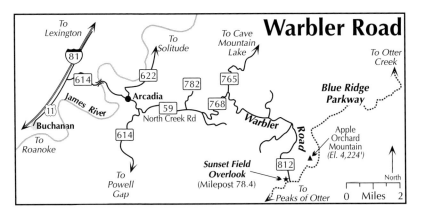

"WARBLER ROAD,"
Botetourt County

BACKGROUND: The variation in altitude and habitats combine to make this one of the best spring birding areas along the Blue Ridge. This road off the Blue Ridge Parkway has been dubbed "Warbler Road" by local birders because of the many species of warblers seen here in migration.

ESSENTIALS: From Sunset Field Overlook at Blue Ridge Parkway Milepost 78.4 (3,480 feet), turn left onto Parkers Gap Road (FR-812) from a short connector off the north end of the overlook. Proceed on FR-812 for 5.8 miles, making frequent stops, and make a sharp left turn onto FR-768. Continue down for another 2.7 miles and turn right onto North Creek Road (FR-59). In another 2.9 miles, turn right onto Route 614. From here it is 1.6 miles to the James River (775 feet) and 3.1 miles to I-81. The total distance from Sunset Field Overlook to the James River is about 13 miles, with a descent of 2,700 feet.

There are several dead-end roads from the main route which can also be explored. Parker's Gap Road (FR 812) also ascends from Sunset Field and parallels the Parkway for 1.5 miles to a gate (3,950 feet) near the summit of Apple Orchard Mountain. At Parker's Gap, 2.6 miles down from Sunset Field, there is a 1.9-mile spur down to Apple Orchard Falls Branch of North Creek. North Creek Road (FR-59) continues upstream 1.1 miles from its junction with FR-768. From 614 at Arcadia, Route 622 (Solitude Road) parallels the James River for 2.7 miles. (*Note:* Parker's Gap Road is sometimes blocked during timber harvesting.)

HABITATS: Some of the most diverse habitats are found along this 13-mile transect. The highest elevations are relatively undisturbed northern hardwood forest, mostly Northern Red Oak. Tulip Poplars dominate the moist north-facing slopes down to Parker's Gap, while the dry ridges from Parker's Gap to North Creek are typical oak/hickory forests. Timber harvesting is carried out on a large scale, and it is necessary to look for clearings at the right stage of succession to find certain birds. Some clear-cuts are planted in pines. There are miles of trout streams lined with hemlock at the lower elevations, as well as good open-field and riparian habitats along the James River.

BIRDS:

Spring: In early May, with most of the breeding birds on territories, migrants such as Tennessee, Cape May, Bay-breasted, Blackpoll, and Yellow-rumped Warblers can easily push your daily list of warblers to over 25 species. The best places to find warbler waves are in the middle elevation oak/hickory forests where the leaves have just emerged and the catkins are fully developed. The most reliable places have been along FR-768.

Summer: Breeding birds at the higher elevations include Canada, Chestnut-sided, Blackburnian, and Black-throated Blue Warblers, Veery, Blue-headed Vireo, Dark-eyed Junco, Ruffed Grouse, Rose-breasted Grosbeak, and sometimes Winter Wren, Black-billed Cuckoo, and Least Flycatcher. Middle elevation woodlands are excellent for Wild Turkey, Scarlet Tanager, Ovenbird, American Redstart, and Black-and-white, Cerulean, and Worm-eating Warblers. Recent clear-cuts often attract Common Yellowthroats and Prairie Warblers, while old clear-cuts are ideal for Yellow-breasted Chat, Kentucky and Hooded Warblers, and sometimes Golden-winged and Blue-winged Warblers. The hemlock ravines are good for Louisiana Waterthrush, Northern Parula, and Black-throated Green Warbler. Check mature pine stands for Pine Warblers. Check the Route 614 crossing of Jennings Creek for Warbling Vireo, Yellow Warbler, Blue Grosbeak, and both of our orioles. Along the James River look for Yellow-throated Warblers, especially at the swamp forest along Route 622 (Solitude Road), where Prothonotary Warblers have also been found.

Fall: Not as productive as the other seasons, but areas with a dense understory are good for fall warblers.

Winter: This trip is not recommended during winter months because of poor road conditions and relative scarcity of birdlife.

SPECIAL COMMENTS: Although this trip is less than 20 miles in length, it is wise to set aside the better part of a day to bird this area. The birdlife is so interesting and varied here that virtually every stop takes longer than originally planned. It can be decidedly cold in the early morning at the top of the mountain, so bring warm clothes, even in summer. Also be sure to bring adequate food and drinks because there is nowhere to stop for refreshments between the Peaks of Otter and Arcadia.

John and Thelma Dalmas, Jeffrey Blalock

Broad-winged Hawk
Gail Diane Yovanovich

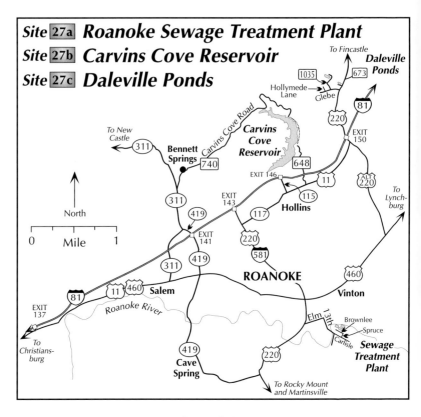

Site 27a.
ROANOKE SEWAGE TREATMENT PLANT,
Roanoke City

BACKGROUND: This 60-acre facility is an advanced waste-treatment plant for Vinton, Salem, Roanoke County, Roanoke City, and Botetourt County. *This is a working facility, but we are allowed to bird the major part of this site. Please be respectful of the management's requests. Also, do not block any roads.*

ESSENTIALS: From I-581 (east) take the Elm Ave Exit and go 0.8 mile via Elm Avenue (which becomes Bullitt Avenue) to 13th Street and turn right onto 13th Street (watch for the "Water Pollution Control Plant" sign). Go another 0.8 mile to Carlisle Ave (first street after the bridge over the Roanoke River) and turn left. Go one block to Spruce Street and turn left. Cross past Brownlee Avenue and watch for the open gate (chain link) on your left. Enter on your right. Park on your right, or take the first cross-dike past the 30-million-gallon concrete basin. On the left you will see a white metal box on a railing with the Roanoke Valley Bird Club logo on it. Inside is a clipboard containing notations on recent sightings at the sewage treatment plant. *On your first visit during regular working hours, go to the office and register.* (The office is located on Brownlee Avenue. Go to the left end of building, upstairs.) Use extreme caution when driving the narrow roads, and *under no circumstances* should you walk out on the sludge ponds, even if they appear dry; the sludge is 10 to 15 feet deep.

HABITATS: Concrete impoundments, sludge ponds with pools and extensive mudflats (sludge-flats), river with wooded edge and fields, and nearby gravel storage lots. Beyond the sewage treatment plant's eastern edge are riparian woods extending to the Niagara Dam.

BIRDS: Since 1976 the total number of species of birds has accumulated to 242, a commendable number for the Mountains and Valley region. Approximately 47 species of birds have nested on the treatment plant property.

Spring: Pectoral, Spotted, Solitary, Least, Semipalmated, and White-rumped Sandpipers, Lesser and Greater Yellowlegs, Semipalmated and Black-bellied Plovers, Red-necked and Wilson's Phalaropes, Dunlin, Barn, Tree, Bank, Cliff, and Northern Rough-winged Swallows, White-eyed Vireo, and Blue Grosbeak.

Summer: The previous list of shorebirds as well as Black-necked Stilt, Western and Baird's Sandpipers, Sanderling, Short-billed Dowitcher, Green Heron, and Yellow-crowned Night-Heron.

Fall: The spring shorebirds may occur, as well as Buff-breasted Sandpiper, American Golden-Plover, Broad-winged Hawk, American Pipit, Nashville Warbler, Rose-breasted Grosbeak, and Fox Sparrow.

Winter: Killdeer, Common Snipe, Hooded Merganser, Great Blue Heron, Belted Kingfisher, Cooper's and Sharp-shinned Hawks, American Kestrel, and Ring-billed Gull.

RARE OR UNUSUAL BIRDS: Snowy Egret, White Ibis, Fulvous Whistling-Duck, Peregrine Falcon, Piping Plover, American Avocet, Whimbrel, Baird's Sandpiper, Long-billed Dowitcher, Wilson's, Red-necked, and Red Phalaropes, Lesser Black-backed Gull, Western Kingbird, Henslow's and Le Conte's Sparrows, Bobolink, and Yellow-headed Blackbird.

SPECIAL COMMENTS: As a principal stop-over site for migrating shorebirds, the sewage treatment plant has on record 32 species of shorebirds. In the past few years the local birders have noticed a decline in the number and diversity of shorebirds visiting this area. We feel that several factors may have caused this unfortunate change: on-site habitat disturbance, fluctuations in the water levels, more human activities, and insect-control measures, to name a few. We hope that this situation will be a short-term one.

Mike Purdy

Site 27b.
CARVINS COVE RESERVOIR,
Botetourt and Roanoke Counties

BACKGROUND: Carvins Cove Reservoir is Roanoke's primary water supply, a 630-acre lake with a 25-mile shoreline. The lake and its 12,000-acre watershed offer birding, hiking, fishing, picnicking, limited boating, and horseback trails. Hunting, trapping, and swimming are strictly prohibited.

ESSENTIALS: To reach the boat landing from I-81, take Exit 146 (Hollins), then follow Route 115 south for 1 mile. Turn left (north) at the traffic light onto US-11 for 1.2 miles; turn left (north) on Route 648 (curvy), and then drive 2.6 miles to the boat landing. An easy, short trail leads left from a wooden fishing pier. The best walk starts at the picnic area on the knoll across from the parking lot for the Watershed Patrol Office; take the fire road at the iron-pipe gate.

To reach the North Cove Recreation Area (via Bennett Springs) from I-81, take Exit 141 (Salem/New Castle), then Route 419 north for 0.5 mile to the traffic light. Turn right (north) onto Route 311 for 2.4 miles; turn right (northeast) on Route 740 (Carvins Cove Road), and drive 4.5 miles to the end of the hard-surface road. Drive or walk 1.9 miles to the picnic area (closed to vehicles October 1 to April 1).

HABITATS: The watershed includes deciduous and coniferous trees and a marshy swamp near the North Cove Recreation Area. Surrounding mountains rise among slopes and hollows to 2,980 feet.

BIRDS:

Spring: A variety of ducks, Common Loon, Ruffed Grouse, Wild Turkey, Ring-billed, Bonaparte's, and Herring Gulls, migrating warblers, vireos, and swallows.

Summer: Wandering herons, egrets; Double-crested Cormorant; Wood Duck; Ruffed Grouse, Wild Turkey; Eastern Screech-, Great Horned, and Barred Owls; Whip-poor-will; Black-and-white, Pine, Worm-eating, and Hooded Warblers, Ovenbird, Louisiana Waterthrush, and Scarlet Tanager.

Fall: Migrating warblers in September; Common Loon, Horned and Pied-billed Grebes, ducks by late October, Ruffed Grouse, Wild Turkey; Red-breasted Nuthatch, and Pileated, Downy, and Hairy Woodpeckers.

Winter: A good variety of ducks and other waterfowl, Ruffed Grouse and Wild Turkey, Eastern Screech-, Great Horned, and Barred Owls, a variety of woodpeckers, Common Raven, occasional Pine Warbler, Blue-headed Vireo, and Purple Finch.

RARE OR UNUSUAL BIRDS: Scattered records of White-winged Scoter, White Ibis, Tundra Swan, Common Merganser, Snow Bunting, and a wintering Bald Eagle.

SPECIAL COMMENTS: Boating and canoeing are rigidly restricted. Only locally owned, fee-paid boats and canoes may enter the reservoir—and then only under tight inspection at the boat landing.

The best birding is from the bank and by foot. Low water levels in the fall sometimes attract migrating shorebirds. A six-mile-long fire trail links the boat landing picnic area and the North Cove Recreation Area. There are several narrow lake-edge trails, including one from the boat landing to the dam; some are interrupted by small streams feeding the lake. A high-elevation trail ascends a mountain from a point near the North Cove Recreation Area entrance.

Food and lodging are available at (1) Exit 146, I-81, starting-point above, and (2) Exit 150, I-81, via US-11, about 3 miles north of its intersection with Route 648, above. There is a seasonal snack bar at the boat landing and restrooms at the boat landing and at North Cove Recreation Area.

Norwood Middleton

Site 27c.
DALEVILLE PONDS,
Botetourt County

BACKGROUND: Ponds of 12 and 1.5 acres, respectively, are in developing residential areas but have good vantage points. Full accommodations are available near Exit 150 of I-81 (below).

ESSENTIALS: On I-81 at Exit 150 10 miles north of Roanoke, proceed to nearby traffic light at US-11 and US-220. Turn north (toward Fincastle) on US-220 and continue for 2.4 miles. Turn left (west) onto Glebe Road (Route 675) for 0.4 mile, then right (north) onto Orchard Lake Drive (Route 1035) for 0.6 mile to the larger of the two ponds. The smaller pond may be reached by returning to US-220. Turn left (north) and proceed 0.5 mile, make a U-turn at Route 673 onto the southbound lane, go 0.3 mile, and turn right (west) at a private lane (across a cattle-guard). Layman's Pond is closed to the public.

HABITATS: A small stream which connects the shallow ponds; a few marshy areas, small mudflats, limited borders of cattails, marsh grasses, willow, Multiflora Rose.

BIRDS:

Spring: By mid-April, Sora, American Bittern, shorebirds, swallows, Common Loon, Osprey, and Marsh Wren are all possible.

Summer: Nesting species arrive by mid-May and include Green Heron, White-eyed Vireo, Baltimore and Orchard Orioles, and Eastern Kingbird. Wandering herons and egrets, migrating shorebirds, and swallows feed here in July and August.

Fall: Migrating warblers and sparrows, including Lincoln's, can be seen. Waterfowl arrive in good numbers by late October. Sora, American Bittern, Merlin, Loggerhead Shrike, Osprey, and Marsh Wren can sometimes be seen.

Winter: Up to five species of ducks, Belted Kingfisher, Common Snipe, Killdeer, Great Blue Heron, and White-crowned and Swamp Sparrows winter here.

RARE OR UNUSUAL BIRDS: The first Virginia record of the white morph ("Great White Heron") of the Great Blue Heron, Least Bittern, Purple Gallinule, Saltmarsh Sharp-tailed Sparrow.

SPECIAL COMMENTS: Visitors to the larger pond above may wish also to check nearby sparrow fields by returning to Glebe Road (Route 675), turning right at 0.1 mile, then taking the next right on Hollymeade Lane (dead end). Depending on progress of residential development, visitors may also wish to walk the stream side between the two ponds.

Norwood Middleton, Barry Kinzie

Site 28.
MOUNTAIN LAKE,
Giles County

BACKGROUND: Mountain Lake (3,800 ft.) is the highest natural lake in the state. Known for its old stone hotel, the Biological Station of the University of Virginia, high-elevation forests (3,000-4,400 ft.), and scenic beauty, the region has attracted ornithologists and naturalists for over a century. Since the first bird records were obtained in 1885, 166 species of birds have been found in this area. Several accessible peaks exceed 4,000 ft. In addition to the year-round hotel, more-modest accommodations are available in nearby towns along US-460 (Blacksburg, Pembroke).

ESSENTIALS: Exit I-81 at Christiansburg, follow US-460 westward bypassing Blacksburg, continue 15 miles to Route 700, and follow it 9 miles up to Mountain Lake and the hotel. The gravel road, formerly called Salt Sulphur Springs Turnpike and now Route 613, continues to the Biological Station (1 mile), War Spur overlook, and the entrance to the Mountain Lake Scenic Area, the Appalachian Trail, and Wind Rock.

HABITATS: Extensive mountain hardwood forests, virgin hemlock stands, spruce bogs, rocky cliffs, trout streams, rhododendron and mountain laurel thickets, one large (deep) and several small lakes. At the lower end of Mountain Lake, a private road to White Pine Lodge leads through a deep ravine with virgin hemlocks and mountain laurel thickets. Winter Wrens and Black-throated Green Warblers may be seen along this ravine.

BIRDS:

Spring: Migratory thrushes (5 species), vireos, warblers, and finches pass through the mountain forests, and waterfowl occasionally visit the lakes. Many summer residents are arriving to establish territories.

Summer: At the hotel and the Biological Station are nesting Least Flycatchers, Cedar Waxwings, Rose-breasted Grosbeaks, Scarlet Tanagers, and Red-eyed and Blue-headed Vireos. Nearby hardwood forests also have Veeries, Ovenbirds, Barred Owls, and several warblers (Blackburnian, Chestnut-sided, Worm-eating). In old-growth hemlock stands, look for Golden-crowned Kinglets, Black-throated Green Warblers, and, in the understory, Winter Wrens and Black-throated Blue and Canada Warblers. Overhead can be seen or heard Red Crossbills and Common Ravens. Brown Creepers, Pine Siskins, and Golden-winged Warblers have bred near the Biological Station.

Fall: Mixed-species flocks of warblers, vireos, thrushes, and finches are common but scattered in the forests. From mountaintops or rocky pinnacles, such as Wind Rock and Bald Knob, hawk-watchers have reported many

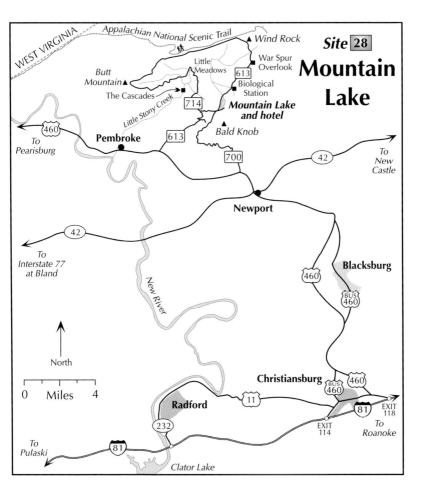

migrating raptors, including the occasional Merlin, Peregrine Falcon, and Golden Eagle.

Winter: Flocks of resident (the Carolina race) and migratory Dark-eyed Juncos are commonly found along roadsides and clearings. Hardwood forests harbor chickadees, titmice, nuthatches, Ruffed Grouse, and Wild Turkeys. Common Ravens and Golden Eagles might also be seen.

RARE OR UNUSUAL BIRDS: Winter Wren, Golden-crowned Kinglet, Red Crossbill, Least Flycatcher, hybrid chickadees, Brown Creeper, Pine Siskin, Golden Eagle, and Mourning and Magnolia Warblers. Except for the eagle and the two warblers, these rarities have been found breeding or probably have bred in the area in recent years.

SPECIAL COMMENTS: The Mountain Lake region has been intensively studied by ornithologists investigating junco behavior, hybridizing chickadees, and effects of Brown-headed Cowbird parasitism on passerines. Ornithology and natural history courses are regularly taught in summer at the Biological Station. Chickadees should be studied carefully because both the Black-capped and the Carolina species and their hybrids have been found in the high-elevation forests.

Barney's Wall, just above Little Stony Creek and the Cascades, was a former (1940s) nesting site of the Peregrine Falcon.

David W. Johnston

Site 29.
SHOT TOWER AND NEW RIVER TRAIL STATE PARKS,
Wythe County

BACKGROUND: The New River Trail State Park (540/699-6778) was formerly the route of the Cripple Creek Branch of the Norfolk and Western Railroad. The track was removed in the mid-1980s, and the result is a 57-mile linear park. The Shot Tower is a historical landmark located near the lead mines at Austinsville. Lead was produced here from colonial times, and this was an important source of lead shot for the Confederacy during the Civil War. Several types of accommodations are available in Wytheville and at Fort Chiswell.

ESSENTIALS: Take I-77 south from I-81 (Exit 81) for 7.8 miles to Exit 24 on I-77 at Poplar Camp, Wythe County. Drive north on US-52 for about 2 miles to Shot Tower and New River Trail State Parks. The area can also be reached via US-52 south from Fort Chiswell or north from Hillsville.

The New River Trail State Park headquarters have been relocated downriver to the old railroad community of Forster's Falls.

HABITATS: Hardwood ridge, open former railway bridges (swallows), open river (ducks), steep rocky cliffs (nesting Red-tailed Hawks), and open meadow areas south of Shot Tower and north of New River.

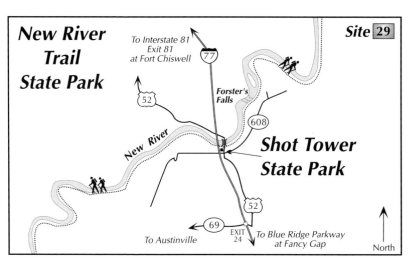

BIRDS:

Spring and fall: Some 24 warbler species have been seen here, including Wilson's, Orange-crowned, Yellow-throated, Blackpoll, Cerulean, Cape May, Magnolia, Black-and-white, Chestnut-sided, Black-throated Green, Northern Parula, Ovenbird, Worm-eating, Yellow-rumped, Blackburnian, Palm, Louisiana Waterthrush, Common Yellowthroat, Yellow-breasted Chat, Kentucky, Hooded, and Canada. A number of flycatchers are seen in May, even Yellow-bellied Flycatcher. Spotted Sandpipers are often seen along the river. Raptors include an occasional Osprey and Bald Eagle. Thrush species found here include Swainson's, Gray-cheeked, and Veery. Spring always yields a few Blue-winged Teal and some Wood Ducks.

Summer: Nesting birds include American Redstart, Red-eyed, White-eyed, and Warbling Vireos, Baltimore Oriole, Scarlet Tanager, Red-winged Blackbird, Wood Thrush, and Yellow Warbler.

Winter: Winter ducks include Common Goldeneye, Hooded Merganser, Mallard, Bufflehead, and a few American Black Ducks.

SPECIAL COMMENTS: The area of the trail west from the Shot Tower for about 1 mile is a fantastic spring wildflower walk. Because most of the observations from this site are made during spring migration, early May would be considered the best time to see the birds mentioned. However, with this area now being part of the 57-mile linear New River Trail State Park, many opportunities have been opened up for the naturalist. The parks cater to hiking, bicycling, and horseback riding. The gentle slope of the trail makes birding by bike a real pleasure here.

Stan Bentley

Site 29a.
BURKES GARDEN,
Tazewell County

BACKGROUND: Burkes Garden is in the New River drainage. It is a fairly flat, elliptical, high mountain valley about eight miles long and four miles wide. It's walled in on all sides by mountain ridges and with a single narrow drainage. The anticline valley has a floor elevation which varies from 3,050 to 3,200 feet. Mountain elevations around the valley include 3,800 to 3,950 feet on the north at Garden and Round Mountains; 4,000 feet on the east and south at Garden Mountain; and 4,400 to 4,700 feet on the west at Chestnut Ridge and Beartown Mountain. The valley was discovered by James Burke in the 1740s and he settled the area in 1754, only to be driven out a few year later by threats of the Shawnees.

ESSENTIALS: Exit US-460 on to Route 61 north of Tazewell. Continue just over 8 miles to Route 623. Turn right onto 623 and continue approximately 8 miles to Gose Mill Pond where you enter the Burkes Garden valley floor. Route 623 is the main road across the valley floor. You can enjoy two good loop drives for seeking Golden Eagles and Rough-legged Hawks in winter. Route 666 turns left at Gose Mill Pond and travels 6 miles, becoming Route 625. Route 625 continues another 6 miles back to 623. The southeast loop turns off at the Post Office on Route 623. This is Route 727, which is 3 miles distance to Route 667. Turn left onto 667 and continue 4 miles back to Route 623. The Appalachian National Scenic Trail runs along Garden Mountain on the southeast side of the valley.

HABITATS: As a natural refrigerator, the valley provides excellent habitat for northern species, both during the breeding season and in winter. Most of the valley floor is farm land. Mature stands of White Oaks with little to no understory create great hunting perches for raptors as well as habitat for Red-headed Woodpeckers, which regularly winter in the valley. The many streams, mill ponds, and beaver ponds provide habitat for migrant waterfowl and a few wintering species. The mountain ridges support northern conifers. The high-elevation valley floor provides habitat for many higher elevation species, as do the surrounding mountains.

BIRDS:

Spring: Migratory thrushes, vireos, warblers, and finches pass through the valley and surrounding mountain forest, and waterfowl frequent the pond at Gose Mill.

Summer: Breeding species of interest include Wood Duck, Red-headed Woodpecker, Willow Flycatcher, Least Flycatcher, Horned Lark, Tree Swallow, Common Raven, Black-capped Chickadee (Tazewell Beartown Mountain), Veery (in the valley), Hermit Thrush (Tazewell Beartown Mountain), Cedar Waxwing, Warbling Vireo, Blue-winged Warbler, Canada Warbler

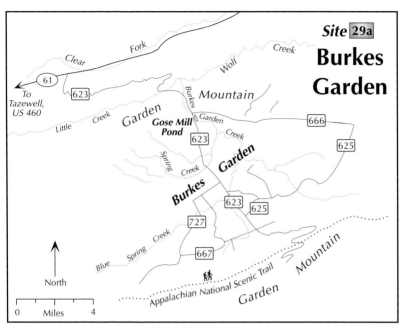

(valley floor), Vesper Sparrow, Savannah Sparrow, Dark-eyed Junco, Bobolink, and Baltimore Oriole.

Fall: Migratory thrushes, vireos, warblers, and finches pass through the valley and surrounding mountain forest, and waterfowl frequent the pond at Gose Mill.

Winter: Rough-legged Hawk, Bald Eagle, Golden Eagle, Common Snipe, Long-eared Owl, Short-eared Owl, Horned Lark, and Red-headed Woodpecker are found here.

RARE OR UNUSUAL BIRDS: This is one of Virginia's most dependable areas to see wintering Golden Eagles and Rough-legged Hawks during January until mid-February. Bald Eagle has also been found here In winter. A dead Long-eared Owl was found along the road in 1997, and Short-eared Owl has been found near the Gose Mill Pond.

SPECIAL COMMENTS: A country store on Route 623 is open dally and provides a warm stove in winter, some prepared food, and a clean rest room.

Wallace Coffey

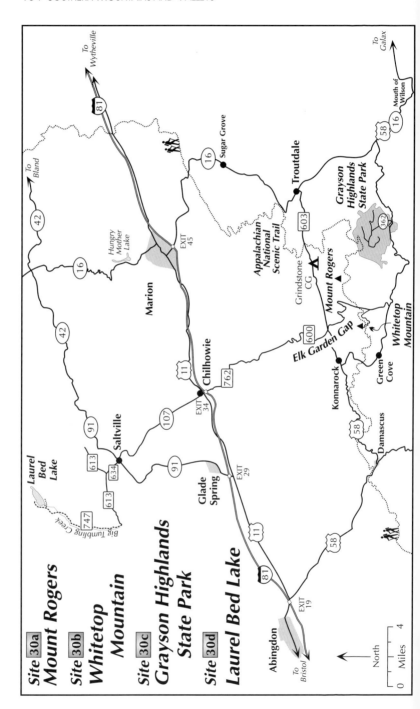

Site 30a
Mount Rogers

Site 30b
Whitetop Mountain

Site 30c
Grayson Highlands State Park

Site 30d
Laurel Bed Lake

Site 30a.
MOUNT ROGERS,
Grayson and Smyth Counties

BACKGROUND: Mount Rogers, in the Mount Rogers National Recreation Area, the highest peak in Virginia, attracts large numbers of hikers, students of natural history, and sightseers. For birders, the summit of Mount Rogers offers an opportunity to see many species of birds that occur in few other places in Virginia as breeding species, although most of these species can be found as easily at nearby Grayson Highlands State Park (site #30c) and at Whitetop Mountain. The closest camping is at Grindstone Campground; motels are available in Abingdon and Chilhowie.

ESSENTIALS: From Marion or points north on I-81, exit on Route 16 and go southeast to Troutdale. There turn right on Route 603 and proceed toward Konnarock; take a left at Route 600 and proceed to Elk Garden Gap (2.5 miles). There you can park (it is unwise to park overnight) and hike one of the trails to the top of Mount Rogers (about 3 miles). From Abingdon take US-58 to Route 603 to Route 600. An easier route to the summit is the longer trail from Grayson Highlands State Park.

HABITATS: Northern hardwood forest and open grassland on the lower slopes give way to a forest of Red Spruce, Fraser Fir, and Yellow Birch (unique in Virginia) on the upper slopes and summit.

BIRDS:

Early spring, late fall, and winter: Common Raven, Red-breasted Nuthatch, Golden-crowned Kinglet, and Dark-eyed Junco are fairly common. Look also for Golden Eagles, Horned Larks, Black-capped Chickadees, Brown Creepers, and both species of crossbills.

Late spring: Look for the species listed above, migrants, and early nesters. Grindstone Campground (about 4 miles from Route 600 on Route 603 to Troutdale) is the best spot for seeing Least Flycatchers in late spring and summer.

Summer: Besides an abundance of birds typical of northern hardwood forest, Mount Rogers offers many species of the northern coniferous forest, including Northern Saw-whet Owl, Hermit Thrush, Magnolia Warbler, and Purple Finch. In the bushy areas below the summit, Alder Flycatcher can be found. Yellow-bellied Flycatcher once bred here but has not been seen in recent years.

Early fall: Excellent for migrant passerines as well as many of the residents. Look for Olive-sided Flycatchers.

RARE OR UNUSUAL BIRDS: Hermit Thrush, Swainson's Thrush, Magnolia Warbler, and Purple Finch probably reach the southern limit of their breeding ranges on Mount Rogers or nearby ridges.

SPECIAL COMMENTS: The summit of Mount Rogers is Virginia's highest point, 5,729 feet (1,746 m). Breeding populations of birds listed for the summit forest are generally rather small (often fewer than 10 individuals). *Taped songs or owl calls may disrupt normal behavior patterns and interfere with ongoing research.* Please remember and care for the fragility of this "island in the sky."

Richard Peake, Philip Shelton

Site 30b.
WHITETOP MOUNTAIN,
Grayson, Smyth, and Washington Counties

BACKGROUND: Part of the Mount Rogers National Recreation Area, Whitetop Mountain, the second highest summit in Virginia, allows easy access to a forest of northern hardwoods and some spruce. The meadows that comprise the open eastern face of the summit are reminders of the resort hotel that stood near the summit of the mountain in the first half of this century. The spectacular views available from these open areas draw many sightseers to Whitetop, but the mountain is rarely so crowded that birding is hampered. The closest camping is at Grindstone Campground or at Grayson Highlands State Park; motels are available in Abingdon and Chilhowie.

ESSENTIALS: From Marion and points north on I-81, exit on Route 16 and go southeast to Troutdale. There turn right on Route 603 and proceed toward Konnarock; take a left on Route 600 and proceed to Elk Garden Gap. From Abingdon take US-58 to Route 603 and Route 600 to the Gap (2.5 miles); about 0.4 farther is the entrance to a gravel road; turn right here and proceed to the summit. This trip gives easy access to spruce-forest birds.

HABITATS: The road up Whitetop passes through mature northern hardwoods mixed with stands of Red Spruce. The eastern face of the summit is open, being covered with grass and brush. Except for a radar installation, the summit is covered with spruce. There is a path through the woods below the summit (at the first horseshoe turn); it offers excellent birding in the birch/spruce forest.

BIRDS:

Early spring, late fall, and winter: Often the summit is inaccessible, but watch for Common Raven, Red-breasted Nuthatch, Golden-crowned Kinglet, and Dark-eyed Junco. Golden Eagles, Brown Creepers, and crossbills are possible.

Late spring, summer, and early fall: Many of the "northern" species found on Mount Rogers can be found on Whitetop with less effort. Brown Creeper, Winter Wren, Golden-crowned Kinglet, Red-breasted Nuthatch, Blue-headed Vireo, Veery, Hermit Thrush, and Black-throated Green and Blackburnian Warblers are more common on Whitetop than on Mount

Rogers. Northern Saw-whet Owls have occurred, and Magnolia Warblers have recently established themselves on the summit.

Richard Peake

Site 30c.
GRAYSON HIGHLANDS STATE PARK,
Grayson County

BACKGROUND: Located adjoining the Mount Rogers National Recreation Area, Grayson Highlands State Park (540/579-7092) has become a popular recreation spot during its two decades of existence. The park itself offers high altitudes (3,400 feet and above), and trails from Massey Gap in the park provide the least strenuous access to the summit of Mount Rogers. A visitors center, accessible by car, tops the ridge above Massey Gap. Camping is available in the park or in campgrounds in the Mount Rogers Recreation Area. The nearest motels are at Chilhowie and Abingdon.

ESSENTIALS: From Marion and farther north on I-81, exit at Route 16 and continue through Troutdale to US-58. Turn right and proceed 3 miles to the park entrance (Route 362) on your right. From Abingdon take US-58 through Damascus and Green Cove; continue 15 miles to the park entrance on your left.

HABITATS: The variety of habitats includes fields with rock walls, pastures, rhododendron thickets, northern hardwoods, Red Spruce, and Fraser Fir. Sullivan's Swamp, a rhododendron bog, is a short hike from Massey Gap across the pasture. In June trails leading from Massey Gap to Mount Rogers provide probably the most spectacular bloom of rhododendrons to be seen anywhere in Virginia.

BIRDS:

Late spring, summer, early fall: Both Alder and Willow Flycatchers have been found at Sullivan's Swamp. Look for Brown Creeper, Golden-crowned Kinglet, vireos, Chestnut-sided Warbler, Scarlet Tanager, and Rose-breasted Grosbeak, as well as migrant Cape May and Tennessee Warblers. Northern Saw-whet Owls have been reported. Northern Goshawks and Pine Siskins have been observed in June. Although not seen here since the 1980s, Bewick's Wren should be watched for.

Late fall, winter, early spring: Look for Common Raven, Brown Creeper, Golden-crowned Kinglet, and Dark-eyed Junco. Golden Eagles and Red Crossbills are possible.

SPECIAL COMMENTS: Camping is available here as well as at Grindstone Campground in the Mount Rogers National Recreation area (4 miles from Route 600 on Route 603).

Richard Peake

Site 30d.
LAUREL BED LAKE,
Russell County

BACKGROUND: Located in the Jefferson National Forest, Laurel Bed Lake is a man-made lake created by damming Big Tumbling Creek, thereby flooding what had previously been a spruce bog. The lake thus created sustains a put-and-take trout fishery maintained by the Virginia Department of Game and Inland Fisheries in Big Tumbling Creek below the lake. The road leading up to the lake is steep and rather rough in places, but it can be traversed in cars without four-wheel drive. The nearest motels are in Abingdon, Saltville, and Chilhowie.

ESSENTIALS: From I-81 take Exit 39, go north on Route 107 for 8.6 miles to Route 91 at Saltville, and then west (left) on Route 91 for 0.2 mile to the first stop light. Turn right at the light, then go 0.1 mile, and turn right again on Route 634. (There is no route marker for the first mile on Alison Gap Road.) At a First Christian Church on the right, go 1.4 miles on Alison Gap Road, then left (west) at a Church of Prophecy onto Route 613. Proceed on Route 613 for 3.9 miles and turn right (north) on Route 747, a gravel road. At 2.2 miles pass Clinch Mountain Wildlife Area headquarters, tell the person at the snack bar that you will not be fishing, or buy a permit if you will be. Continue on the same road, now an unnumbered Virginia Game Commission road, for 3 miles. At this point a primitive campground is 2.8 miles straight ahead. Turn left here over a wooden bridge and reach the road to the dam on the right at 2.2 miles (the dam is 0.3 mile). Continue ahead and at .05 mile reach the upper boat ramp and the end of the road. Total distance from Exit 39 to the upper boat ramp is 25 miles.

HABITATS: Man-made lake 3,600 feet above sea level surrounded with climax oak/hickory forest. The lake covers what was once spruce bog; a remnant survives.

BIRDS:

Spring: Migrant hawks, waterfowl, shorebirds, and warblers.

Summer: A large variety of warblers (Black-throated Blue, Black-throated Green, Chestnut-sided, Magnolia) can be found in the woods around the lake. Magnolia Warbler is best found in the woods south of the upper boat ramp. Pied-billed Grebes, Wood Ducks, and Tree Swallows have nested. Also look for Common Raven, Blue-headed Vireo, Veery, and Rose-breasted Grosbeak. Black-capped Chickadee has been found here in recent years.

Fall: Waterfowl, shorebirds, swallows, and warblers are common migrants.

Winter: Usually inaccessible.

RARE OR UNUSUAL BIRDS: Baird's Sandpiper.

SPECIAL COMMENTS: Shorebirds occur in spring, summer, and fall when the water level allows open mudflats.

Richard Peake, Anton M. Decker

Site 30e.
SOUTH HOLSTON LAKE,
Washington County

BACKGROUND: South Holston Lake is a Tennessee Valley Authority reservoir astride the Virginia-Tennessee border in Southwest Virginia. The lake was impounded in November 1950, is 24 miles in length, and covers 7,580 acres. About nine miles of the lake's shoreline are in Washington County, Virginia. The remainder is in Sullivan County, Tennessee. It is the most upstream reservoir in the Tennessee Valley system and the only one in Virginia. The western shoreline in Virginia is agricultural, although fast developing with luxury homes, recreational facilities, and a county park. The eastern shoreline is on the edge of the Jefferson National Forest and the Cherokee National Forest in Tennessee. The lake is adjacent to more than 35,000 acres of national forest. Most of the water in Virginia is in the former narrow riverbed and is rather shallow. The lake is fed by the Middle Fork Holston River and South Fork Holston River as well as Wolf Creek and Spring Creek in Virginia.

ESSENTIALS: To reach the best birding areas of the lake at Spring Creek, drive south from Abingdon and Interstate 81. Take Route 75 south about 8 miles to the Spring Creek Bridge near the Tennessee state line.

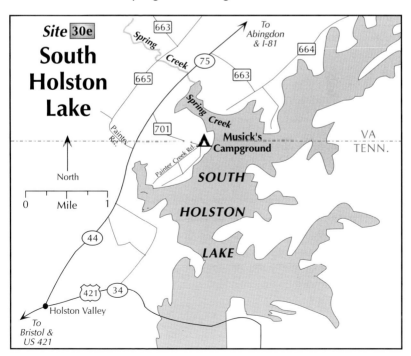

Alternatively, from Bristol, Virginia, travel south on US-421 from Exit 1 of I-81. Continue through Bristol in Sullivan County, Tennessee, until reaching Tennessee Route 44. Then turn north (left) onto Route 44. After crossing the Virginia state line you will come to Spring Creek. One of the best sites for birding is Musick's Campground, a private commercial facility located on Painter Creek Road along the Virginia border. Access to the shoreline is free for birding. To reach the campground, turn off Route 76 onto Route 701 near the state line. The road takes you back into Tennessee. When the road makes a curve to the right, go straight into Musick's Campground. You must stop and sign in at the registration box located on a post next to the driveway near the top of the hill in the campground. *This registration is operated by the Bristol Bird Club and is a requirement for using the access.* This site not only has excellent water birding with a high percentage of rarities, but it offers you the chance to record a bird in both Tennessee and Virginia. Motels and food are located in both Abingdon and Bristol.

HABITAT: The area at Spring Creek and the mouth of Spring Creek rear Musick's Campground is one of the hottest birding spots between Roanoke and Knoxville. This is a wide, shallow area of the impoundment. It's the best waterbird and shorebird habitat at South Holston Lake. Abundant food is provided by the flow from Spring Creek and the under-current from the rivers flowing into the impoundment. The mudflats along Route 75 are the best shorebird habitat at South Holston Lake.

BIRDS:

Spring and fall: The area is outstanding for migrant waterfowl, shorebirds, eagles, and a variety of herons, hawks, swallows, and gulls and terns. In fall the "Great White Heron" (*Ardea herodius*, white morph) has been found here in two separate years.

Summer is not very productive for water-related species.

Late fall and winter is the best season of the year, supporting the state's largest population of wintering Pied-billed Grebes and Eared Grebes. State-record numbers of Eared Grebes have been recorded here, and up to 200 Pied-billed Grebes have been recorded. Red-necked and Horned Grebes can also be found here and have been seen at the same time. It is also a good place to find Bald Eagles in winter.

RARE OR UNUSUAL BIRDS: Species of interest found at the mouth of Spring Creek include Eared Grebe, Red-necked Grebe, Double-crested Cormorant, night-herons, White Ibis, Oldsquaw, Surf Scoter, Bald Eagle, Merlin, Peregrine Falcon, Sandhill Crane, Black-bellied Plover, American Golden-Plover, Ruddy Turnstone, Sanderling, Western Sandpiper, dowitcher, Laughing Gull, Caspian Tern, Common Tern, Forester's Tern, Black Tern, and American Pipit.

Wallace Coffey

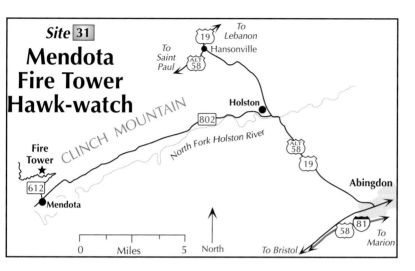

Site 31.
MENDOTA FIRE TOWER,
Washington County

BACKGROUND: Clinch Mountain runs roughly northeast to south-west along the southwestern part of the state; and it is one of the last big mountains before reaching the Cumberland Plateau. The highest point of the Clinch Mountain is 4,724 feet. At 3,100 feet, Mendota Fire Tower sits a little lower and above the community of Mendota, founded in 1794. This hawk migration route and observation spot is one of the oldest in the state, having been discovered by Dr. Stephen M. Russell in the early 1950s. Among the official counters were Holmes Rolston, E. E. "Scotty" Scott, and Tom Finucane; George Larkins and his mother Violet currently keep the official records. Mendota Fire Tower is on private land, but the owners have not objected to having birders at the tower. The site is visited not only by birders for raptor migrations, but also by locals because of the spectacular views in fall when the leaves change. Its relative inaccessibility and its distance from heavily populated areas mean that hawk-counters are most likely to be present on weekends during the month of September. Coverage during the week is spotty.

Hawk-watchers whose attention wanders during the "noon lull" can often find interesting warblers and vireos in the surrounding forests. This is also a good spot from which to watch migrating Red-headed Woodpeckers.

ESSENTIALS: From Abington take US-19 north 7.7 miles to Route 802. Take 802 southwest for 14.7 miles to Route 612. Drive 612 north about 3.1 miles up Clinch Mountain. Park on 612 and walk 0.3 mile up a steep, unmarked access road to the tower.

HABITATS: Oak hardwood forest predominates along the ridge line, with valleys consisting of riverbottom farmland.

BIRDS: The raptors migrating past this tower display the typical ridge pattern: an upsurge in Broad-winged Hawk, Osprey, and American Kestrel numbers peaking around 19 or 20 September, followed by a small but steady migration of accipiters, larger buteos, and eagles (both Golden and Bald).

RARE OR UNUSUAL BIRDS: Northern Goshawk, Peregrine Falcon, Rough-legged Hawk, and Golden Eagle.

SPECIAL COMMENTS: Other seasons are not monitored. Migrating vultures are counted only later in the season. Numbers have been declining at this spot from the highs reported in the 1970s and 1980s. Check the section on hawk-watching at the end of this book for hints on techniques and more details on seasonal abundance.

George Larkins, Alice Kirby

Site 32a.
CLINCH VALLEY COLLEGE CAMPUS,
Wise County

BACKGROUND: A four-year branch of the University of Virginia, Clinch Valley College was founded in 1954 on land in the town of Wise that had been part of the county poor farm. The college land has several times undergone surface mining for coal, and much of the nearly 400-acre campus consists of reclaimed strip mines that offer a variety of habitats.

ESSENTIALS: Following US-23 from Norton to Wise, watch for signs to Clinch Valley College. Go through Wise past the Courthouse to the third traffic light. Turn right on Route 646 and proceed 0.4 mile to the second entrance to the College. Entering, drive past the dormitories and proceed to the picnic area. Park at the picnic area and follow the cross-country trail to the football field and the ponds.

HABITATS: Fields, lawns, brush, ponds, mixed woodland of various ages, as well as reclaimed and unreclaimed stripmines, offer a variety of habitats.

BIRDS:

Spring: A good place to see American Woodcock and excellent for migrant thrushes, vireos, warblers, and sparrows (including Lincoln's). The wooded ridge above the faculty housing sometimes produces Bay-breasted, Tennessee, and Chestnut-sided Warblers. Nashville Warblers have been recorded. Wilson's Warblers are regular. Red-necked Grebe has occurred.

Summer: Golden-winged Warblers have occurred regularly in the young Black Locust stands on open unreclaimed stripmine areas. In the woods Hooded and Kentucky Warblers are common. "Brewster's" Warbler has occurred on more than one occasion, and Willow Flycatcher is regular.

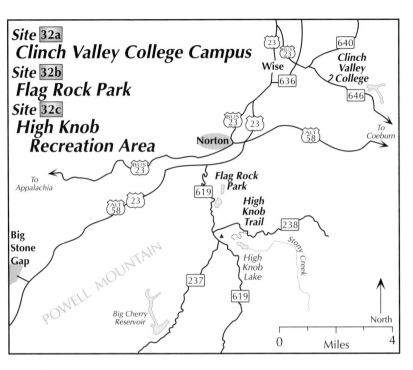

Site 32a
Clinch Valley College Campus
Site 32b
Flag Rock Park
Site 32c
High Knob Recreation Area

Fall: Excellent for migrant thrushes, vireos (including Philadelphia), warblers, tanagers, Rose-breasted Grosbeaks, and sparrows. Northern Goshawk has occurred. From mid-September to early October, Bay-breasted, Cape May, and Tennessee Warblers are common.

Winter: Ruffed Grouse and Red-shouldered Hawks are often found, and Common Redpolls have occurred. Pileated Woodpecker is regular. In some years a blackbird roost has been present in the pines behind the faculty housing.

Richard Peake

Site 32b.
FLAG ROCK PARK,
Wise County

BACKGROUND: A well-known local landmark, the rock formation known as Flag Rock provides the focal point of Flag Rock Park, a city park that has for many years been a popular recreation spot for local residents. The park is part of the watershed of the City of Norton, which owns and maintains it. Camping is available nearby at High Knob, and motels are located in Norton.

ESSENTIALS: After reaching Norton via Alternate US-58 coming from Coeburn, take the first left turn after passing Norton High School. Then take Route 619 to the left and begin a rapid climb. Halfway up the mountain, you will see an entrance to the park on the left. If the gate is open, drive to the parking area; if the gate is closed, park out of the way at the gate and hike in. The park is generally open around Memorial Day and closes in late September or early October with hours from 10 a.m. to 9 p.m.

HABITATS: Deciduous woods of various ages with a mixture of hemlock and a considerable understory of laurel and rhododendron. Many "mountain" bird species can be found here at a fairly low elevation.

BIRDS:

Spring: The rocks that give the park its name are a good place to look for migrating hawks, and migrant passerines can be seen along the entrance road, especially summer-resident warblers such as Hooded and Kentucky.

Summer: Many of the mountain species can be located here with ease, including Black-throated Blue and Black-throated Green Warblers, Blue-headed Vireo, and Dark-eyed Junco.

Fall: A good spot for migrant passerines, especially the slope below the entrance road. From mid-September to early October look for Bay-breasted, Cape May, and Tennessee Warblers.

Winter: Great Horned Owls and Wild Turkeys have been seen.

Richard Peake

Site 32c.
HIGH KNOB RECREATION AREA,
Wise County

BACKGROUND: Located on Powell Mountain, High Knob Recreation Area is part of the Clinch Ranger District of the Jefferson National Forest. The observation tower at the summit is a popular sight-seeing spot which, on clear days, offers excellent views of the surrounding mountain ridges in Kentucky, North Carolina, Tennessee, and Virginia. Camping is available at High Knob and elsewhere nearby in the National Forest. Motels are located in Norton.

ESSENTIALS: After reaching Norton via Alternate US-58 coming from Coeburn, take the first left turn after passing Norton High School. Then take Route 619 to the left and begin a rapid climb. At the top of the mountain you will encounter an intersection. Take the Forest Service road to the left. After 0.2 mile you will find a road on the right leading to the summit and observation tower. In summer this is one of the better spots in the Virginia Cumberlands for Chestnut-sided Warbler, and there is a winter record for Snow Bunting. About 2 miles farther down the main road, you will see a gate on your right.

Along this road stop to listen for a Least Flycatcher. From May through October you can drive in and continue to the parking area (the rest of the year you must walk in). From the parking area walk left down the well-marked trail and hike around the lake. At the lower end of the lake, below the dam, are some additional trails along Little Stony Creek.

HABITATS: Mature northern hardwoods (beech, hickory, oak, maple) on the ridges and slopes above 3,300 feet and stands of hemlock around the lake.

BIRDS:

Spring: Excellent for Blue-headed Vireos, resident warblers, and Dark-eyed Juncos. (Note: *Be sure to wear colorful clothing during spring gobbler-hunting season.*)

Summer: The only place in Wise County for summering Winter Wren and the best spot locally to find Blackburnian, Black-throated Blue, and Canada Warblers, Rose-breasted Grosbeak, Blue-headed Vireo, and Veery. Magnolia Warbler, Least Flycatcher, and Red-breasted Nuthatch have been present in rec*ent years.*

Fall: Warbler flocks containing Ceruleans, Black-throated Greens, and Chestnut-sideds become common as early as late June. From mid-September to early October, Bay-breasted, Cape May, and Tennessee Warblers are common.

Winter: Common Ravens and Wild Turkeys occur; Barred and Great Horned Owls are fairly common.

SPECIAL COMMENTS: It is best not to bird the area on weekends from June to September. If you have no choice, plan to bird in the early morning.

Richard Peake

Site 32d.
BREAKS INTERSTATE PARK
Dickinson County
(and adjacent areas of
Buchanan County, Virginia,
and Pike County, Kentucky)

BACKGROUND: Breaks Interstate Park lies at the northern end of the Cumberland overthrust block, which extends southwest into Tennessee, forming the last true mountains until one reaches the Rocky Mountains. The park was created in 1954 through joint action of the Virginia and Kentucky legislatures, and now comprises 2,500 acres of varied mountain habitats. Facilities include a modern concession building, a conference building, cabins, a motor lodge with 24 units, a campground, a pool and playground facilities, a man-made lake, picnic areas, and foot trails. The concessions and lodges are closed from November to mid-April, but the best time for birding is during the breeding season, when all facilities are open.

ESSENTIALS: From the west, approach from Elkhorn City, Kentucky, on Route 80 and proceed into Virginia to the park entrance on the right (about 2 miles from the state line). From the northeast, proceed past Grundy on Route 460 to Harmon, and make a left onto Route 609; continue to Breaks. From there turn left onto Route 80 (100 yards); take another left and proceed to the park entrance (1/4-mile) on the right. From the southeast, go to Haysi and follow Route 80 to the park entrance (8.5 miles on the left).

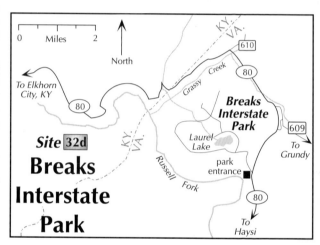

HABITATS: With the disappearance of the American chestnut, oaks and hickories now form the climax of the hardwood forest in the Breaks, but in the cool, wet ravines, hemlock and rhododendron are common. The park is bisected by the Russell Fork of the Big Sandy River, which follows the fault at the eastern end of the Cumberland overthrust block and then cuts across Pine Mountain (el. 2,800 feet) and down to Elkhorn City, KY (el. 820 feet). Russell Fork has created a steep, narrow gorge through Pine Mountain, creating the spectacular scenery that is the main feature of Breaks Interstate Park as well as the varied bird habitats. Species generally associated with higher altitudes (Blue-headed Vireo, Canada Warbler, and Black-throated Blue Warbler) are found side-by-side with low-altitude species (Swainson's Warbler).

BIRDS:

Early spring, late fall, and winter: Common Raven, Wild Turkey, and woodland passerines such as nuthatches, chickadees, titmice, and kinglets are common. Waterfowl may be found on the lake.

Late spring: Look for early arriving Neotropical migrants such as warblers (including Swainson's) and thrushes by the last week of April.

Summer: The park offers one of the best places in Virginia to find the mountain population of Swainson's Warbler. The rhododendron growth around the rim of the park above the Russell Fork and the Garden Hole section are the best spots to find this bird. In addition the park offers a large number of other warbler species, including Black-throated Green, Black-throated Blue, Worm-eating, and Yellow-throated.

Early fall: Excellent for migrant passerines and migrating hawks.

RARE OR UNUSUAL BIRDS: The park affords fairly easy opportunities for finding Swainson's Warblers during May, June, and early July, although they can be difficult to see if they are not singing. Golden Eagles have also been sighted in the park during breeding season, although they are more easily found in nearby Burkes Garden during the winter.

SPECIAL COMMENTS: Although the park does not offer any species that could not be found elsewhere in Virginia, the abundance and ease of viewing of many species are better here than in other areas. Moreover, the park offer insight into how much of Southwest Virginia must have looked before it was heavily settled. Even if a visitor fails to see many birds, the beauty of the area — in early summer, for example, a visitor might see the endemic Cumberland Flame Azalea — will amply reward anyone.

Richard Peake

Typical Virginia Hawk Migration Along the Mountain Ridges

Thicker lines indicate higher relative abundance.

	AUGUST	SEPTEMBER	OCTOBER	NOVEMBER
Black Vulture				
Turkey Vulture				
Osprey				
Bald Eagle				
Northern Harrier				
Sharp-shinned Hawk				
Cooper's Hawk				
Northern Goshawk				
Red-shouldered Hawk				
Broad-winged Hawk				
Red-tailed Hawk				
Rough-legged Hawk				
Golden Eagle				
American Kestrel				
Merlin				
Peregrine Falcon				

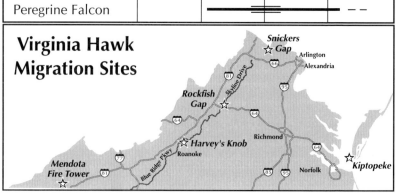

Virginia Hawk Migration Sites

Snickers Gap
Arlington
Alexandria
Rockfish Gap
Skyline Drive
Harvey's Knob
Roanoke
Richmond
Mendota Fire Tower
Blue Ridge Pkwy
Norfolk
Kiptopeke

HAWK-WATCHING IN VIRGINIA

by Kerrie Kirkpatrick and Myriam Moore

In Virginia, hawk-watching opportunities are focused primarily on the fall migration. From August through early December thousands of hawks that breed in the Northeastern forests and the Canadian maritime provinces move across New England into a relatively narrow corridor that brings them to Virginia, down the Blue Ridge and Appalachian Mountains, and along the coast. Within this corridor are excellent opportunities to see a great number and variety of diurnal raptors.

In the mountains fall migration commences in August with the first southward movements of Osprey, American Kestrel, Bald Eagle, and Broad-winged Hawk. Major flights are underway by the second week of September. Highest concentrations of hawks occur early in the migration season as a result of the very narrow "window" of migration time for one species of hawk, Broad-winged Hawk, which moves through our area in a three-week period. In addition, this hawk is the most numerous migrant. During only ten days, September 12 to 22, huge numbers are possible, with hundreds expected on good flight days. Most of these will be Broadwings, but other hawks (Northern Harrier, Osprey, Sharp-shinned Hawk, American Kestrel, and Bald Eagle) use the same thermals as the Broadwings to gain the lift that they need. These thermals, or columns of rising warm air, enable the hawks to "float" upwards and then glide long distances gradually downward until another thermal is found. Ideally, hawks can move long distances without flapping their wings at all.

As Broadwing migration declines, accipiter numbers increase. By the first week in October, Sharp-shinned and Cooper's Hawks are at their peak with dozens—sometimes hundreds—being seen in a day at mountain lookout sites. Merlins and Peregrine Falcons, both increasing in numbers enough to be expected at one or two a day, are most likely to be seen at this time.

After mid-October, hawk-watchers look for the "Big Birds": Red-tailed and Red-shouldered Hawks in increasing numbers, and the first Northern Goshawks, Rough-legged Hawks, and Golden Eagles. Buteo numbers peak during the first week in November, when counts can be a hundred birds per day. Delaying weather patterns, however, can produce flights of several hundred, with hawks gliding through in impressive squadron formations. Golden Eagles, Rough-legged Hawks, and Northern Goshawks are sought out one bird at a time. Eagerly awaited through cold and windy days, each one is a prize. Northern Harriers and Bald Eagles are much appreciated as they come through, still in migration during November. Most hawk-watches close by the end of that month. By then numbers of birds are low, and mountain

sites have become extremely cold. Watchers who brave December conditions find occasional birds of the North—eagles and Northern Goshawks—still on the move.

Along the coast, flights have a different seasonal pattern and species
composition. Broadwings and the other buteos are not as common, but
numbers of falcons and accipiters are much higher. American Kestrels and
Sharp-shinned Hawks are plentiful through September and early October,
with the highest numbers occurring during the first two weeks of October.
Peregrine Falcons and Merlins are also seen in higher numbers at the coast;
both are seen in double digits per day in early October. When Broadwings
are seen along the coast, they move through at this time, nearly two weeks
later than those seen in the mountains. Coastal flights produce mostly
immature hawks of all species. The initially easier travel along the coast leads
to the Gulf of Mexico, a difficult crossing for falcons, and a long detour through
Mexico for accipiters and buteos, which avoid water crossings.

Kiptopeke, Virginia's coastal hawk-watch site, has always produced high
numbers of falcons and accipiters. In 1995 a full-time hawk-counter was
stationed there, and the results were astounding. Dawn to dusk counts
throughout the season produced records for almost every species. Thousands of Sharp-shinned Hawks and American Kestrels and hundreds of
Cooper's Hawks and Peregrine Falcons—numbers that observers at mountain sites can only dream of—were tallied.

Other migrants move along the ridges in autumn. High-flying flocks of
loons, geese, and swans can be spectacular as they cross the mountains
heading southeast (the hawks' path is southwest) from the Great Lakes to
the Chesapeake Bay. Flocks of gulls and cormorants are also seen on this
path, as well as occasional Great Blue Herons. Songbirds sometimes fall out
along the ridge-tops, filling the trees with warblers, vireos, tanagers, grosbeaks, and kinglets. Dragonflies (favorite prey of American Kestrels and
Broadwings) and Monarch Butterflies also stage heavy migrations down the
ridges. Resident birds include Wild Turkey and Ruffed Grouse, Pileated and
Red-headed Woodpeckers, Cedar Waxwing, and Common Raven. Rarities,
including a Brown Pelican and three Sandhill Cranes, have also been seen in
the mountains. Unusual hawks have been observed at several sites: Swainson's Hawks, Mississippi Kites, Swallow-tailed Kites, and a Gyrfalcon.

The other fall migrants along the coastal hawk-watching route are also
impressive. Warblers, flycatchers, vireos, swallows, sparrows, woodpeckers,
waterfowl, and other groups of birds will pour along the coast for a
noteworthy migrational event.

For almost thirty years hawk-watching has increased in interest and
geographic coverage in the state. Beginning in 1964, at a fire tower in Botetort
County, Myriam Moore encouraged regular hawk-watches in the state. By
the 1970s, many permanent sites had become established in New England and
along the Appalachians, and observers were reporting their statistics to the
USF&WS. Realizing that much of the total picture was still missing, enthusiasts

formed their own national group, the Hawk Migration Association of North America. HMANA's goals were to exchange information and to identify the full range of hawk migration routes. Hawk-watchers were urged to explore all sites where hawk migration might be detected, using standard reporting forms and procedures.

Virginia's watchers responded with nearly forty sites monitored for hawk-watching potential. Many proved productive and very interesting. It was determined that migration through Virginia is on a broad front, as well as along ridges, so it can be witnessed from many unexpected locations.

Virginia's wealth of mountain ranges, ridges, gaps, foothills, and coastline offers migrating hawks many choices of suitable flight paths and a tremendous challenge to Virginia birders to gain insight into the migration movements across the state. With the flights so widely dispersed, our watchers must be content with very few of those exciting moments when the sky is filled with hawks. Often the birds are quite high or at a great distance, disappointing those watchers who would like to shake hands with every passing hawk. Many days offer little high drama other than the panoramic views that many of our lookouts provide. Waiting for the hawks is part of hawk-watching. Empty skies come to every hawk-watch site, just as big days can and do occur unexpectedly at any location.

Five major sites (four on mountain ridges, one on the coast) are currently staffed for full-season coverage. They are, roughly from north to south, as follows:

Snickers Gap Located just past Round Hill on Route 7 at the intersection with 601, this site is manned daily September into November. See the listing for Snickers Gap under "Northern" (site #14a). (Contacts: Jesse Fulton 703/671-0752 and Kerrie Kirkpatrick 703/560-4950.)

Rockfish Gap This site, at Afton Mountain by milepost 0 of the Blue Ridge Parkway near Waynesboro, is manned daily from September into November. It is sponsored by the Augusta Bird Club. See the listing for the Blue Ridge Parkway under "Southern Mountains and Valleys" (site #26). (Contact: John Irvine 540/432-2335.)

Harvey's Knob On the crest of the Blue Ridge, 15 miles northeast of Roanoke, this hawk-watch is at the overlook parking lot. It is manned from the beginning of September to the end of November by volunteers from the Lynchburg and Roanoke Valley Bird Clubs. See the listing for the Blue Ridge Parkway under "Southern Mountains and Valleys" (site #26). (Contacts: Gary Carter 540/563-2128 and David Holt 540/384-6674.)

Mendota Fire Tower This fire tower, on the crest of Clinch Mountain near Route 802 in Washington County, is a 15-minute walk from the road. See the listing for Mendota Fire Tower under "Southern Mountains and Valleys" (site #31). (Contact: George Larkin 423/247-9007)

Kiptopeke State Park This site, at the southern tip of the Delmarva Peninsula, has a 30-year history as a volunteer hawk-watch and banding station. It is now managed by KESTREL. (the new Eastern-shore bird observatory) and is planned to be the first Virginia hawk-watch to have a team of full-time counters. Good from late August through November. See the listing for Kiptopeke under "Eastern Shore" (site #3). (Contacts: Kiptopeke State Park 757/331-1040 and Bill Williams 757/229-6095.)

Participation at these and other hawk-watching stations in the state is encouraged. If you would like to help count hawks, call the listed contacts for further information on dates, locations, directions, and leaders.

Other stations are identified and updated in current issues of the *The Raven*. Moreover, there are also other locations for general hawk-watching in the fall that are mentioned in this book. Some are former monitoring posts (such as Linden Fire Tower); others are just productive sites (such as Hawksbill Mountain, Mary's Rock, and Stony Man, all in Shenandoah National Park).

Related Organizations

Kiptopeke Environmental Station Research and Education Laboratory
KESTREL
P.O. Box 111, Franktown, VA 23354

Raptorians: David Holt
3094 Forest Acre Trail, Salem, VA 24153
540/384-6674

Raptor Society of Metropolitan Washington
Paul Napier, President
P.O. Box 482, Annandale, VA 22003
703/742-9462 or (o) 703/620-8277

Hawk Migration Association of North America
William J. Gallagher, Secretary
P.O. Box 822, Boonton, NJ 07005-0822
201/335-2488

PELAGIC BIRDING IN VIRGINIA

by Brian Patteson

Pelagic birding off Virginia remains largely unexplored when compared to the activity in the neighboring states of Maryland and North Carolina. Nevertheless, good numbers of pelagic seabirds are often seen off the Virginia coast, and the underwater topography offshore—with three submarine canyons: Poor Man's, Washington, and Norfolk (north to south)—is configured so that good birding areas can be reached from any coastal departure point. At present most pelagic trips to Virginia waters depart from Virginia Beach, Virginia, or Ocean City, Maryland. Small fishing fleets also exist at Chincoteague and Wachapreague, Virginia. The canyons along with other irregularities along the continental shelf are productive areas where nutrient upwellings from the ocean floor attract considerable numbers of bait-fish, which in turn attract larger predatory fish, pelagic birds, and cetaceans.

Although the western edge of the Gulf Stream is often 20 miles or less from Cape Hatteras, North Carolina, it is usually located well over 100 miles east of Virginia Beach, which is beyond the range of all licensed charter boats used for birding in Virginia waters. This means that some Gulf Stream specialties which are regularly encountered off Cape Hatteras are great rarities on Virginia pelagic trips. The influence of the Gulf Stream on pelagic birding is limited to drifting bodies of warm water ("warm-water eddies") that break off from the main current and drift westward over the edge of the shelf. However, because Virginia is located farther north and the water is colder, certain northern birds, particularly the alcids, are more likely to be seen on Virginia trips than on North Carolina trips.

The list of pelagic bird species that regularly occur off the Virginia coast is substantial. This list includes representatives from the Arctic, Antarctic, West Indies, and eastern Atlantic Ocean. To see the fullest spectrum of pelagic birds possible in Virginia waters, it is necessary to take several trips at different seasons. Although pelagic birds can be encountered off Virginia at almost any time of the year, some times are better than others for seeing large numbers of birds.

PELAGIC BIRDING BY SEASON

WINTER (December-March) Winter is the season for some of the most exciting pelagic trips in Virginia. Alcids are the main attraction, and three species (Razorbill, Dovekie, and Atlantic Puffin) occur regularly off the Virginia coast, although puffins often do not arrive until February. Both

SEASONAL DISTRIBUTION OF PELAGIC SEABIRDS IN VIRGINIA

SPECIES	WINTER	SPRING	SUMMER	FALL
Northern Fulmar	O	R		R
Black-capped Petrel		X (May)	R	X
Cory's Shearwater		U (May)	C	C
Greater Shearwater		C/U (May)	C	U
Sooty Shearwater		C	X	
Manx Shearwater	R	U/R	R	U/R
Audubon's Shearwater			C/U	C/U
Wilson's Storm-Petrel		C	C	C/U
Leach's Storm-Petrel		U (May)	U/O	O/R
Band-rumped Storm-Petrel			R	
White-faced Storm-Petrel			X	X (Sep)
Brown Booby			X	X
White-tailed Tropicbird			X	X
Red-necked Phalarope		U	O	U
Red Phalarope	U/O	O		O
Great Skua	O/R			
South Polar Skua		R		
Pomarine Jaeger	W/O	U	O	U
Parasitic Jaeger	W/O	U	R	U
Long-tailed Jaeger		R (May)		O
Sabine's Gull		X		R
Black-legged Kittiwake	C/U	R		O
Arctic Tern		R		X
Bridled Tern		X	U	U
Sooty Tern			X	X
Dovekie	C			
Razorbill	C	X		R (Nov)
Thick-billed Murre	X			
Common Murre	X			
Atlantic Puffin	U	R		

Winter = Dec-Mar; **Spring** = Apr-15 Jun; **Summer** = 15 Jun-15 Aug; **Fall** = 15 Aug-Nov

Common = Likely to be seen on all trips   **R**are = Only 1-2 seen each season
Uncommon = Usually present; may not be seen on all trips **X** = Vagrant; not expected to occur
Occasional = Seen only a few times each season   regularly (less than 5 state records)

Common and Thick-billed Murres have also been found on winter Virginia trips, but they are not to be expected on most trips. Black-legged Kittiwakes are usually fairly common for most of the winter, although they may start to disappear by early March. The kittiwakes, however, are greatly outnumbered by large flocks of Herring Gulls and Northern Gannets that attend the fishing trawlers many miles offshore. By chumming these flocks close to the boat, a keen-eyed birder can often spot a Lesser Black-backed Gull and, occasionally, a Glaucous or an Iceland Gull, or even a Northern Fulmar. Fulmars are usually rare on these trips, but their occurrence, like that of so many other pelagic species, is sporadic. Some days they may be common, but on most days they are scarce or absent.

The real prize in winter, however, is the elusive Great Skua. Birders travel from all across the country to Virginia to try their luck with this hard-to-come-by North American "life bird." For those who find it, the skua is worth the trip. Nothing can match the raw power of a skua tearing through a flock of gulls in its quest to pirate a meal. Although skuas were virtually guaranteed on pelagic trips off the mid-Atlantic coast during the 1970s, they are now much harder to find as the foreign fishing fleets and their attendant gull flocks have been forced out of U.S. territorial waters (which range to 200 miles offshore). Still, about one-half of the winter trips off Virginia succeed in finding at least one Great Skua. Other birds of interest in winter include Manx Shearwater and Red Phalarope. Both of these species are more likely to be seen on early winter trips, but they may linger later during mild winters. Early December pelagic trips might also produce lingering Greater Shearwaters and Pomarine and Parasitic Jaegers, but few birding trips are scheduled until at least January, in order to maximize the chances of seeing the most alcids.

SPRING (April-early June) The first pelagic spring migrants off Virginia are those that nest in the North Atlantic regions. Manx Shearwaters, Northern Fulmars, Red Phalaropes, and Pomarine Jaegers are all heading north in April, but few birding trips are scheduled at this time because overall numbers of birds are so low.

A more productive time for birding offshore is usually in late May or early June. Manx Shearwaters, Leach's Storm-Petrels, jaegers (all three species), Red-necked Phalaropes, and Arctic Terns are all possible in late May, and these species are often joined by South Atlantic breeders on their way to rich feeding (wintering) grounds in the North Atlantic. Wilson's Storm-Petrel is usually the most abundant of the southern-hemisphere species, followed by Greater and Sooty Shearwaters. A few Cory's Shearwaters from the eastern Atlantic begin to appear in late May as well. The shearwater numbers usually reach a peak in early June. If good foraging opportunities occur off Virginia, these birds may linger and form large flocks. When this happens, it is a good time to look for South Polar Skuas harassing the shearwaters. These skuas, like the shearwaters which they accompany, are usually bound for waters north of Virginia and are seldom seen after June.

SUMMER (late June-August) Summer typically begins with large numbers of Greater Shearwaters and Wilson's Storm-Petrels off the Virginia coast. Most Sooty Shearwaters have already left Virginia waters by mid-June. The Greater Shearwaters appear to be very hungry at this time of year and may dive after bait, much to the consternation of offshore fishermen. Usually the Greater Shearwaters start to leave Virginia waters some time in July. After that, a few can sometimes be found, usually among larger flocks of Cory's Shearwaters, which may be very common through August. Summer also offers the best chances for seeing Gulf Stream specialties. Bridled Terns and Audubon's Shearwaters are regularly seen in late summer, particularly in the vicinity of the Gulf Stream eddies with large amounts of Sargasso-weed. Wilson's Storm-Petrels are still common in summer, although they are found mostly over deeper waters (500+ fathoms) than in spring. By carefully searching through flocks of Wilson's Storm-Petrels in deep-water areas, one may find a few summering Leach's Storm-Petrels, and, if the sea surface temperature is near 80° F, there may be a few Band-rumped Storm-Petrels in these flocks as well. Also worth thinking about is White-faced Storm-Petrel. This eastern Atlantic species has been seen off Virginia at least four or five times, usually over deep water and usually in August. When seen well, White-faced Storm-Petrels are unmistakable: they move about by bounding across the waves with their long legs and gliding on bowed wings, flapping only when absolutely necessary.

Other species to be looked for on summer trips include Black-capped Petrel, White-tailed Tropicbird, and Sooty Tern. These three species occur regularly off the North Carolina coast and may be found off Virginia on occasions when the Gulf Stream edges westward.

FALL (September-November) Early-fall pelagic trips offer a chance to see many of the same species as seen on August trips with the exception of Band-rumped Storm-Petrel. Cory's, Greater, and Audubon's Shearwaters, Wilson's Storm-Petrels, and Bridled Terns are all frequently seen on September trips, and there is a better chance of seeing jaegers off the Virginia coast in fall than at any other season. Pomarine Jaeger is typically the common jaeger encountered offshore, but early to mid-September offers a good chance to see Long-tailed Jaegers in Virginia waters. Parasitic Jaegers are sometimes seen on pelagic trips, but they are just as likely to be seen harassing flocks of terns near the beach, especially in late fall. Red-necked Phalaropes are often seen on September trips, and a few Red Phalaropes may be among them. Red Phalaropes, however, usually do not become common until later in the fall. In early fall the offshore waters are usually still warm, so virtually any rarity possible in August is of equal likelihood in September. A rare migrant that is more likely in September or October is Sabine's Gull.

Few pelagic birding trips are scheduled after September because at that time, as in early spring, the diversity of species and numbers of individuals are low enough that few birders are willing to gamble on a later fall trip. We do know, however, that the first Northern Fulmars, Red Phalaropes, and Black-legged Kittiwakes may show up by late September, and Greater and Manx Shearwaters are sometimes found in good numbers in late fall. Both Pomarine and Parasitic Jaegers occur regularly from September to late November.

SEEING PELAGIC BIRDS FROM THE SHORE

Because the edge of the continental shelf is so far (50-65 miles) from the Virginia coast, and that is where most pelagic seabirds occur, the possibilities for seeing pelagic birds from shore in Virginia are rather limited. They are usually best seen during or immediately after periods of strong easterly winds. Accessible vantage points for ocean-watching include the beach at Chincoteague NWR (site #1), the Chesapeake Bay Bridge-Tunnel (site #4), Fort Story (site #6e), Back Bay NWR (site #6f), the Virginia Beach ocean front, and Sandbridge Beach. (Access to some of these sites is periodically limited.) Pelagic species seen occasionally from shore during strong onshore winds include Sooty Shearwater (often in late May), Wilson's Storm-Petrel (May-August; summers in Chesapeake Bay), Red-necked and, rarely, Red Phalaropes (May and September), Pomarine and Parasitic Jaegers (spring, fall, and early winter), Black-legged Kittiwake (late fall-winter), and Razorbill (winter).

During the strongest storms many other pelagic species are possible. In fact, nearly all of Virginia's pelagic birds have been seen from shore at one time or another, but one could spend a lifetime looking unsuccessfully for most of them from shore. Some of the most interesting records of pelagic birds on shore have been found during or following hurricanes and other tropical storms. In some cases, seabirds are carried hundreds of miles inland by such systems. Hence, it may be possible to find Sooty Terns or Black-capped Petrels or tropicbirds on an inland lake under such conditions. (For example, in 1996 alone hurricanes *Bertha* and *Fran* and tropical storm *Josephine* in July, September, and October, respectively, produced some wonderful sightings at the the Chesapeake Bay Bridge-Tunnel and Kerr Reservoir. See sites #4 and #24 for details.) Experience has shown, however, that hurricanes which brush the coast and veer offshore usually do not displace pelagic birds inland or even onshore. The most interesting storms for Virginia birders are those that come ashore south of the state and travel inland, because most of the displaced birds are typically found east of the eye of the storm.

HOW TO GET OFFSHORE

At present the birder looking for an opportunity to get offshore in Virginia waters has three options: sign up for an organized pelagic birding trip, hitch a ride on an offshore fishing trip, or charter a boat with a few friends. Unlike the situation in some other states, whale-watching trips are not viable options for pelagic birding in Virginia because the target species of these trips, the Humpback Whale, occurs very close to shore in Virginia waters.

The best arrangement for pelagic birding in the state is to sign up for an organized trip devoted strictly to that purpose. The price is reasonable, and you have the advantage of having other birders on the boat to spot birds and the experience of the leaders to find and to identify birds. A good deal of the day will be spent in productive offshore waters where pelagic birds are known to occur, and a special effort may be made to bird over deep water in order to find certain specialties. Chumming, if productive in that season, will be undertaken to attract birds to the boat.

A less satisfactory alternative is to go offshore on a party fishing boat (headboat). Because organized pelagic birding excursions are limited to a few times of the year, this may be your only affordable alternative. The best trips are those that go far offshore in search of Yellowfin Tuna (*not Bluefin Tuna*—those trips stay inshore) in late summer and fall. Because the usual method of fishing is to chum the tuna close to the boat, you may get some close looks at birds coming to sample the chum.

Another possibility for offshore birding is to go on bottom-fishing trips. During most of the year these trips stay too close to shore to see many pelagic birds, but during the late fall, winter, and early spring you may be able to find a boat going out 30-50 miles, where there is a better opportunity for seeing pelagic birds. The disadvantage of both tuna trips and bottom-fishing trips is that they do not move around much, so if you are prone to motion sickness, you may be in for a long day. Some boats welcome birders, whereas others may prefer not to have birders along. Some may even offer a discount for non-fishing passengers.

The third alternative—to charter a boat with a few friends and organize your own pelagic trip—is better than taking a fishing trip, that is, if you can afford it. Such trips are not cheap, about $150 to $200/person or more depending on the size of the boat, plus a tip for the mate. You will, however, be able to go offshore when and wherever you want (weather permitting). Keep in mind, however, that such a trip requires careful planning. Your charter boat captain is your best resource. He will know where the most productive areas are from his recent fishing trips. Often, where you find good fishing offshore is where you will find good birding as well. Underwater hills and ridges and submarine canyons tend to be good because of their upwellings of nutrients from the ocean bottom, but surface features like temperature breaks and areas of Sargasso-weed are also very important. In late summer and fall feeding schools of tuna may attract large numbers of shearwaters and a few jaegers. Your boat captain will be able to keep abreast of such conditions by monitoring his two-way radio. By using LORAN or GPS it is then possible to find hotspots quickly and accurately. But remember that it is up to you to tell him what you want. Remember to be calm and courteous. If you can afford it and if you can communicate well with your captain and with others in your party, a small-party do-it-yourself pelagic birding trip is an experience that cannot be beaten.

Lastly, if you do get offshore on your own, do not forget that your records are valuable for increasing our understanding of pelagic bird distribution off Virginia. Please submit trip results and field notes to *The Raven* and *North American Birds* (formerly *Field Notes*). Records of rarities and high counts should also be sent with appropriate documentation to VARCOM, the Virginia Rare Bird Records Committee. Remember that your contributions are important; most of what is known about pelagic birds off the Virginia coast is the result of research by bird students like yourself.

Organized pelagic birding trips

Because organizers, their phone numbers, and their addresses may change over time, it is a good idea to consult the American Birding Association newsletter, *Winging It*, for current information. Each January ABA publishes an issue that lists all pelagic trips scheduled for the upcoming year in North America. News about Virginia trips may also be found at times in the *VSO Newsletter*. At present, organizers offering pelagic birding trips to Virginia waters include:

Brian Patteson
   P.O. Box 772, Hatteras, NC 27943
   252/986-1363
   www.patteson.com
   Trips last about 12 hours; cost: $75-$150

Party fishing boats

Ocean City, Maryland The *OC Princess* now offers weekly tuna charter trips from August to October. They also tend to fish farther offshore than other Ocean City headboats on their bottom trips. Call and check ahead (1-800-457-6650) because at certain times of the year they may operate close to shore. (Dedicated Virginia state-listers will also wish to inquire which of these boats go into Virginia waters.)

Charter boats

A large charter-boat fleet can be found at several marinas in Ocean City, Maryland, which is a good departure point for trips to Poor Man's and Washington Canyons (about 55 and 60 miles offshore, respectively). Another major base for charter boats is Virginia Beach, Virginia, from which boats can travel some 65 nautical miles to Norfolk Canyon. Smaller fleets can be found at the Eastern Shore communities of Chincoteague and Wachapreague.

AN ANNOTATED CHECKLIST OF BIRDS FOUND IN VIRGINIA

Virginia's avifauna presently consists of about 431 species: approximately 390 occurring regularly, 2 extinct, and 21 hypothetical. Of the 390-odd regular species, approximately 217 are known to breed in the state, and others are likely to do so. These numbers increase periodically as birders find more new species for the state list (especially pelagics) and new breeding records are found. The following annotated list has as its basis the 1987 "Blue Book". This basic source has been updated to include comments and observations of birders all over the state, as well as records accepted by the state's Rare Birds Committee (VARCOM) through 1998.

Species followed by a star (★) are those which are also covered (or mentioned) in the "Specialties" section immediately following this annotated listing of Virginia birds.

Red-throated Loon (*Gavia stellata*) Common to abundant transient and uncommon to common winter resident in rivers, bays, and lakes of the Coastal Plain, in the Chesapeake Bay, and especially in the ocean off the Eastern Shore. Both spring and fall migrations are often spectacular, with thousands of birds seen migrating just offshore. Occasional birds have been found in summer, mostly at coastal locations. It is much less common in the Piedmont (12 records, mostly from Lake Anna, Oct-Apr) and in the Mountains and Valleys (Nov-Dec).

Pacific Loon (*Gavia pacifica*) Four state records: a specimen found at Back Bay National Wildlife Refuge (30 April 1987) and single birds seen at Back Bay (25 December 1995 and 1996) and near Kiptopeke (6 December 1994).

Common Loon (*Gavia immer*) Common transient and winter resident in rivers, bays, lakes, and the open ocean of coastal Virginia. Farther inland, most birds have been reported as fly-overs in migration or wintering in small numbers on large reservoirs such as Lake Anna and Kerr Reservoir. In winter Common Loons may outnumber Red-throateds by a 4:1 ratio and are more widely distributed than Red-throateds. Occasionally, summering individuals have been found in the state.

Pied-billed Grebe (*Podilymbus podiceps*) Statewide, an uncommon to common transient and winter resident on ponds, lakes, and bays, usually in small numbers. Occasionally, this bird breeds on impoundments with dense emergent vegetation at widely scattered sites, from the Coastal Plain to the Mountains and Valleys.

Horned Grebe (*Podiceps auritus*) Overall, an uncommon to common transient and winter resident, and rare summer visitor on bays, inlets, and open water of the Coastal Plain. Farther inland, it is less common in winter and migration, often being found on large bodies of water (e.g., Kerr Reservoir).

Red-necked Grebe (*Podiceps grisegena*) Rare and irregular winter visitor on coastal waters and the lower Chesapeake Bay. Rare spring transient statewide. From February to April 1994, an unprecedented invasion was reported from several parts of the state.

Eared Grebe (*Podiceps nigricollis*) Rare fall migrant and winter visitor to estuaries, inlets, and bays of the Eastern Shore. Elsewhere in the state, a casual transient which should be looked for on any large body of water.

Western Grebe (*Aechmophorus occidentalis*) A rare transient and winter visitor with about a dozen records from the state, most of them on Chesapeake Bay waters. Occasionally, it has been found farther inland, with scattered records on lakes and reservoirs in winter. The specific identity of birds seen prior to 1985 is now uncertain because sufficient details were not provided to distinguish between Western Grebe and the recently described Clark's Grebe (*Aechmophorus clarkii*). A Western Grebe was definitely seen at Portsmouth on 1 January 1995.

Yellow-nosed Albatross (*Diomedea chlororhynchos*) A vagrant, seen twice in the state: 55 miles east of Chincoteague, 3 December 1979, and at Back Bay, 28 November 1981.

Northern Fulmar (*Fulmarus glacialis*) This highly pelagic species is an uncommon winter visitor and a rare spring and summer visitor over deep Atlantic Ocean waters. Although birds are usually seen in small numbers, 23 were seen on 9 May 1982 off Virginia Beach. Occasionally, birds are washed up dead on beaches.

Black-capped Petrel (*Pterodroma hasitata*) This usually pelagic species is a rare and irregular wanderer to deep offshore Virginia waters in late summer or early autumn. Probably as a result of strong hurricane winds, four autumn records have been documented for the Mountains and Valleys.

Cory's Shearwater (*Calonectris diomedea*) Another pelagic species, this shearwater is an uncommon to common transient and summer visitor well offshore. Usually, single-day trips have reported 30-100, but in late summer and autumn hundreds may be seen. Occasionally, it has been seen from shore during strong easterly winds.

Greater Shearwater (*Puffinus gravis*) Uncommon to common spring, summer, and fall transient in offshore Atlantic waters. Most common in June and July. It, too, has been occasionally seen from shore during stiff easterly gales.

Sooty Shearwater (*Puffinus griseus*)n Common spring transient (May, Jun) in offshore waters. More than the other shearwaters found in Virginia, it can be seen from the shore during this time. Occasionally, it has been recorded at other times (Nov, Dec, Mar) along the coast.

Manx Shearwater (*Puffinus puffinus*)n An uncommon winter visitor well offshore, found chiefly from November to June. Twenty-two were seen near Norfolk Canyon, 30 May 1988. Occasionally, a dead bird has been washed onshore (e.g., 2 Nov 1985, Back Bay NWR).

Audubon's Shearwater (*Puffinus lherminieri*) This highly pelagic tropical species is usually an uncommon but regular visitor from June to October. It is usually seen in small numbers, but some offshore daily counts have been in the hundreds. One sighting from the Chesapeake Bay Bridge-Tunnel (21 Aug 1974). Rarely has it been seen at other times of the year.

Wilson's Storm-Petrel (*Oceanites oceanicus*)n Common to abundant visitor (May-Sep) to nearshore and offshore Atlantic waters with daily counts of several hundred at Norfolk and Washington Canyons in May. A regular summer visitor in the lower Chesapeake Bay, its large tributaries, and near the Chesapeake Bay Bridge-Tunnel.

White-faced Storm-Petrel (*Pelagodroma marina*) This rare visitor has been recorded three times in August (photographed) and September over deep Atlantic canyon waters.

Leach's Storm-Petrel (*Oceanodroma leucorhoa*) This uncommon, irregular, and local visitor can be found well offshore from May to September. Although usually found over deep waters, it has also been seen in bays and along the immediate coast.

Band-rumped Storm-Petrel (*Oceanodroma castro*)✴ This species is rare over deep offshore waters, with only a couple of records in late summer. There were 12 birds seen at Washington Canyon, 17 August 1991 (photographed).

White-tailed Tropicbird (*Phaethon lepturus*) Following Hurricane Hazel, a dying bird was picked up at Staunton on 15 October 1954. Otherwise, the species is a very rare late-summer visitor in offshore waters, mostly over 100 miles offshore in the Gulf Stream.

Brown Booby (*Sula leucogaster*) Recorded four times along the coast (Virginia Beach and Northampton and Accomack Counties.) from June to late September. Most of the birds seen were immatures.

Northern Gannet (*Morus bassanus*) This is a common to abundant transient and winter resident offshore and in the lower Chesapeake Bay, with a peak period from December to April. In winter it is often seen in the thousands off Cape Henry, the Chesapeake Bay Bridge-Tunnel, and at Cape Charles.

American White Pelican (*Pelecanus erythrorhynchos*)✴ Irregular and uncommon (usually one to three birds) in autumn and winter and a rare summer visitor along the coast. The numbers of sightings have increased in recent years. A few scattered inland and Chesapeake Bay sightings have been reported.

Brown Pelican (*Pelecanus occidentalis*)n Fairly common summer and fall resident on beaches, bays, and inlets of the Eastern Shore region, the lower

Chesapeake Bay, and its major tributaries. It breeds locally on Fisherman Island, where it has recently shown a remarkable annual increase, and on a small island in the Chesapeake Bay. It is an uncommon to rare winter visitor along the Atlantic coast. There are several inland records from the western Coastal Plain and Piedmont.

Great Cormorant (*Phalacrocorax carbo*)n Uncommon, local, and increasing migrant and winter resident (Oct-Apr) on jetty and inlet locations along the Atlantic coast. It is most consistently recorded along the Chesapeake Bay Bridge-Tunnel and southern Northampton County, where daily mid-winter counts are often over 30. Rare in fall and winter in the lower Chesapeake Bay and major tributaries, with several records as far upstream as Alexandria. A few summer records along or near the coast.

Double-crested Cormorant (*Phalacrocorax auritus*) Abundant transient and uncommon winter and summer visitor in coastal and lower Chesapeake Bay waters, breeding in Hopewell, Newport News, and Fairfax Counties, and probably in Prince William County. The breeding population has increased dramatically in the last decade. Farther inland, it is an uncommon transient and rare summer visitor. Flocks along the Atlantic coast may number in the hundreds in autumn.

Anhinga (*Anhinga anhinga*)✶ Rare in spring, summer, and fall, mostly seen on rivers and lakes in the extreme southeastern part of the state, especially at Stumpy Lake and Lake Drummond. Three records from the Piedmont and one from the Mountains and Valleys.

Magnificent Frigatebird (*Fregata magnificens*) Very rare spring and summer wanderer, chiefly along the coast; at least some occurrences have been associated with hurricanes. One autumn record for the Mountains and Valleys.

American Bittern (*Botaurus lentiginosus*) Uncommon transient and winter visitor in freshwater or salt marshes on the Coastal Plain, decreasing in numbers since the 1960s. Farther inland, uncommon and local transient. Very rare throughout the state in summer but has bred recently in Fairfax County.

Least Bittern (*Ixobrychus exilis*) Uncommon transient and summer resident in freshwater and salt marshes, breeding locally from the Coastal Plain to the Mountains and Valleys. Very rare in winter in Coastal Plain marshes.

Great Blue Heron (*Ardea herodias*) Uncommon to common permanent resident of marshes and the edges of ponds, lakes, and rivers statewide. Breeding colonies, increasing over the last decade, are common on the Coastal Plain; it breeds at widely scattered locations farther inland.

Great Egret (*Ardea alba*) Common transient and breeding summer resident of the Eastern Shore and Coastal Plain. Its habitats include impoundments, ponds, and marsh edges. Farther inland, it is a scarce spring and fall migrant, with scattered late summer records. It is rare along the Eastern Shore and other Coastal Plain sites in winter.

Little Egret (*Egretta garzetta*) Two records for Chincoteague: one bird was first seen on 17 May 1992 (photographed) and remained on the refuge until 28 September, and another (or the same?) bird appeared on 18 August 1993.

Snowy Egret (*Egretta thula*) Common transient and breeding summer resident on the Barrier Islands, where numbers of breeding birds have been decreasing in recent years. It is found on Coastal Plain lakes, marshes, and bays. In winter it is rare at scattered coastal sites. Farther inland, it is a rare migrant.

Little Blue Heron (*Egretta caerulea*) Uncommon to common transient and breeding summer resident on the Barrier Islands. It, too, is found on Coastal Plain marshes, lakes, and other bodies of water. Farther inland, it is a rare to uncommon transient and late summer visitor. Late summer to winter sightings are usually the all-white immatures.

Tricolored Heron (*Egretta tricolor*) Uncommon to common transient, breeding summer and uncommon winter resident on the Coastal Plain, where its habitats include mudflats and salt marshes. It is also decreasing as a breeding bird on the Barrier Islands. Rare transient and late summer visitor farther inland.

Reddish Egret (*Egretta rufescens*) This accidental visitor has been reported (but poorly documented) three times in the state: 2-26 June 1942 and 27 April 1957 at Norfolk, and 21 September 1978 at Chincoteague.

Cattle Egret (*Bubulcus ibis*) Common to abundant transient (small flocks of 15 to 35 birds) and common breeding summer resident, chiefly in coastal areas. It prefers cattle pastures and other short-grass areas, including roadsides. On the Barrier Islands fewer nests were found in 1993 than in previous years. It is rare in winter and as a transient farther inland.

Green Heron (*Butorides virescens*) Common transient and breeding summer resident statewide, usually near or in freshwater swamps, salt marshes, streamside thickets, and residential areas. It is a rare bird anywhere in the state in winter.

Black-crowned Night-Heron (*Nycticorax nycticorax*) Common coastal and uncommon inland transient, summer resident near the coast especially in marshes and lake edges. Formerly it bred at widespread sites in the state from the Eastern Shore to Danville to Rockingham County, but currently its breeding colonies are chiefly on the Eastern Shore and some Chesapeake Bay islands, and at an isolated colony in Rockingham County. It is much less common in winter.

Yellow-crowned Night-Heron (*Nyctanassa violacea*) Uncommon and irregular transient and summer resident in coastal thickets, swamps, and lakeside habitats. Current breeding sites are concentrated on the Barrier Islands and at residential sites in the Norfolk/Hampton/Newport News area. Isolated breeding sites farther inland include Fairfax, Loudoun, Roanoke, and Giles Counties. It is a rare winter visitor near the coast.

White Ibis (*Eudocimus albus*)✳ Uncommon and irregular summer visitor to the Eastern Shore area. Rare to uncommon breeder (one nest in 1994) on Fisherman Island. Farther inland, it is a rare and irregular post-breeding wanderer.

Glossy Ibis (*Plegadis falcinellus*) Common transient and summer resident of coastal shallow ponds, marshes, and estuaries. It breeds on the Barrier Islands and on one Chesapeake Bay island. Farther inland, it is a rare transient and summer visitor. At coastal locations it is rare in winter.

White-faced Ibis (*Plegadis chihi*) One record: an adult was photographed at Chincoteague 8 July 1979. Apparently the same bird was seen there on 2 August 1979.

Wood Stork (*Mycteria americana*) Rare and irregular late summer, autumn, and winter visitor, chiefly in the extreme southeastern part of the state. Farther inland, late summer records are widely scattered. This stork frequents ponds, lakes, and rivers.

Greater Flamingo (*Phoenicopterus ruber*) Flamingoes have been seen in Virginia about ten times, in summer or as fall visitors. Most records have been from the Coastal Plain. The origins of all birds are suspect, and specific identification in all instances might be questioned.

Fulvous Whistling-Duck (*Dendrocygna bicolor*) Rare and irregular visitor throughout the year on the Coastal Plain, mostly in the extreme southeastern part of the state. Occasionally, irruptions have been reported along the Eastern Shore, where it may occur in small flocks in wildlife refuges. In the remainder of the state it is only an irregular and casual visitor.

Tundra Swan (*Cygnus columbianus*)n *Common transient and winter resident, mostly in coastal waters (Chesapeake Bay, major rivers, Back Bay NWR). It is also found feeding and resting in large fields, where flocks often include 25 or more birds. Farther inland, where migrating flocks have been seen or heard at night, it is less common. In recent years, the state's wintering population has been estimated as 5,000 to 7,000 birds.*

Mute Swan (*Cygnus olor*)✳ Locally established (chiefly domesticated) as a resident and occasional breeder on the Coastal Plain. Farther inland, it is an uncommon and widespread breeder, apparently increasing in numbers.

Greater White-fronted Goose (*Anser albifrons*)✳ Rare and irregular fall, winter, and spring visitor to the Coastal Plain and the eastern Piedmont. It has been found with Canada Geese resting on lakes and ponds or grazing in grassy fields. Rarely has it been found in the Mountains and Valleys.

Snow Goose (*Chen caerulescens*) Abundant transient and irregular winter resident in coastal areas. Farther inland, it is a rare transient and winter visitor. The white morph greatly outnumbers the blue morph.

Ross's Goose (*Chen rossii*)✳ Rare transient and winter visitor; five records chiefly from coastal locations.

Brant (*Branta bernicla*) Common to abundant but irregular transient and winter resident in coastal locations and the lower Chesapeake Bay. Many wintering birds are found on Eastern Shore lagoons. Scattered fall and winter records farther inland.

Barnacle Goose (*Branta leucopsis*) One record, perhaps an escaped bird, Arlington, 10 November 1956.

Canada Goose (*Branta canadensis*) Common transient, winter resident, and breeder over much of the state, with the largest breeding populations in northern and central Virginia. Greatly increasing as a breeding bird in recent years as feral birds apparently become permanent residents on freshwater ponds, lakes, and tributaries.

Wood Duck (*Aix sponsa*) Uncommon to common transient or resident and breeding over much of the state, especially the southcentral part. Prefers bottomland swamps and flooded sites. Uncommon to rare in winter.

Green-winged Teal (*Anas crecca*) Uncommon to common transient and winter resident statewide, with migrating flocks sometimes numbering in the hundreds along the coast but much rarer farther inland. It has bred at Chincoteague (1955) and in Washington County (1984).

American Black Duck (*Anas rubripes*) Uncommon to common transient and winter and summer resident over much of the state but more common in tidewater regions. It breeds commonly along the Eastern Shore, the lower Chesapeake Bay, and at other Coastal Plain sites. Widely scattered breeding sites are also known from the Piedmont and Mountains and Valleys.

Mallard (*Anas platyrhynchos*) The most abundant and widespread duck over most of the state. Apparently, feral birds become domesticated and often hybridize with other ducks.

White-cheeked Pintail (*Anas bahamensis*) Only two records, both specimens: 17 December 1937 at Back Bay and 14 November 1966 near Chincoteague.

Northern Pintail (*Anas acuta*) Common to uncommon transient and winter resident over much of the state, breeding rarely at Chincoteague and on certain Barrier and Chesapeake Bay islands. Along the coast, wintering flocks may number in the hundreds, but typically contain 10 to 20 birds.

Blue-winged Teal (*Anas discors*) Common to uncommon transient, scarce winter resident (coastal), and uncommon local breeder chiefly at coastal sites and in far southeastern Virginia (rarely in the Piedmont and Mountains and Valleys). Spring flocks often consist of 50 to 60 birds, but flocks may include several hundred birds in fall.

Northern Shoveler (*Anas clypeata*) Locally uncommon transient and winter resident along the coast, uncommon to rare farther inland, but has been increasing since the 1970s. Not known to breed in recent years. Along the coast, flocks of several hundred have been seen in late winter.

Gadwall (*Anas strepera*) Common to abundant transient and winter resident mainly near the coast, occasionally breeding on the Eastern Shore and on some Bay islands. Flocks up to several hundred individuals have been seen in late November along the coast. Uncommon transient and winter resident farther inland.

Eurasian Wigeon (*Anas penelope*)n Rare transient and winter visitor (Oct-May) on the Coastal Plain, primarily on the Eastern Shore and Tidewater area. A few fall and winter records (Oct-Mar) from the Piedmont and Mountains and Valleys.

American Wigeon (*Anas americana*) Uncommon to common transient and winter resident throughout much of the state. The largest wintering populations are found along the Chesapeake Bay and its major tributaries, where flocks numbering up to 50 birds may occur.

Canvasback (*Aythya valisineria*) Locally common transient and winter resident chiefly on the Chesapeake Bay, its major tributaries, and (formerly) in Back Bay; rare in summer. Farther inland, an irregular and uncommon or rare transient and winter visitor.

Redhead (*Aythya americana*) Fairly common transient and winter resident, chiefly in coastal locations. Farther inland, rare transient and winter visitor. Greatly decreasing in numbers in recent years.

Ring-necked Duck (*Aythya collaris*) Fairly common transient and winter resident, rare in summer, on freshwater lakes and ponds throughout much of the state.

Greater Scaup (*Aythya marila*) Common to uncommon transient and winter resident, mostly along the coast and the Chesapeake Bay; rare in summer. Farther inland, a rare transient and winter visitor. Scaups of this and/or the following species often occur in rafts of hundreds of individuals.

Lesser Scaup (*Aythya affinis*) Fairly common transient and winter resident over much of the state, more numerous at coastal sites. Rare summer visitor.

Common Eider (*Somateria mollissima*)n Rare and irregular transient and winter resident, and very rare summer visitor along the coast and in the lower Chesapeake Bay, especially along jetties. No inland records.

King Eider (*Somateria spectabilis*)n Rare and irregular transient, winter resident, and very rare summer visitor along the coast and in the lower Chesapeake Bay, especially along jetties. No inland records.

Harlequin Duck (*Histrionicus histrionicus*)n Rare and irregular local winter resident and summer visitor in coastal locations, recorded mostly from the Chesapeake Bay Bridge-Tunnel artificial islands. Usually in small numbers, 1 to 6. One winter record from the Piedmont and two from the Mountains and Valleys.

Oldsquaw (*Clangula hyemalis*) Common transient and winter resident along coast and the Chesapeake Bay and its major tributaries; rare in summer. Commonly 50 to 60 birds may be seen in a loose flock. Farther inland, a rare transient and winter visitor on large impoundments.

Black Scoter (*Melanitta nigra*)n Fairly common transient and uncommon to locally abundant winter resident on the coast and in the Chesapeake Bay;

rare in summer. Farther inland, a few scattered spring, fall, and winter records.

Surf Scoter (*Melanitta perspicillata*)n The most common wintering scoter on the coast, in the Chesapeake Bay, and on its lower major tributaries; rare in summer. Farther inland, a few scattered fall, winter, and spring records. Flocks often number in the hundreds.

White-winged Scoter (*Melanitta fusca*)n Less common than the other scoters, this species is an uncommon to common transient and winter resident on the coast and in the Chesapeake Bay; rare in summer. Farther inland, a rare transient and winter visitor on rivers and large lakes.

Common Goldeneye (*Bucephala clangula*) Uncommon to common transient and winter resident, and rare summer visitor near the coast and Chesapeake Bay. Farther inland, an uncommon transient and winter resident, especially on larger impoundments and rivers.

Barrow's Goldeneye (*Bucephala islandica*) Two accepted records, both from the Chesapeake Bay Bridge-Tunnel: 27 February to mid-March 1982 and 5 March 1994.

Bufflehead (*Bucephala albeola*) Uncommon to common transient and winter resident near the coast, less common but regular farther inland, especially on larger bodies of water.

Hooded Merganser (*Lophodytes cucullatus*) Common to uncommon transient and winter resident over much of the state. A few breeding records near the coast and in Fairfax County.

Common Merganser (*Mergus merganser*) Uncommon transient and winter resident in freshwater coastal locations; usually less common farther inland (large lakes and rivers). One breeding record for Fairfax County (1965) and two for the Mountains and Valleys (1953-54).

Red-breasted Merganser (*Mergus serrator*) Common transient and winter resident and uncommon summer visitor on the eastern shore and the lower Chesapeake Bay. Usually a scarce migrant and rare winter visitor to the western Coastal Plain, Piedmont, and Mountains and Valleys.

Ruddy Duck (*Oxyura jamaicensis*) Uncommon to common transient and winter resident over much of the state, but much more common in coastal areas. Rare in summer.

Black Vulture (*Coragyps atratus*) Fairly common and increasing breeding resident throughout the western Coastal Plain, Piedmont, and Mountains and Valleys. Uncommon on the Eastern Shore. Its numbers have steadily increased over the past decades.

Turkey Vulture (*Cathartes aura*) Common breeding resident throughout the state, outnumbering Black Vultures about 3 to 1. Apparently, more northern populations move into the state and farther south in winter.

Osprey (*Pandion haliaetus*) Common transient and breeding summer resident on Coastal Plain bays and estuaries; very rare in winter. The breeding population has greatly increased over the past 20 years and has expanded up major rivers. Elsewhere, an uncommon transient, summer visitor, and rare breeder in the southern Piedmont.

Swallow-tailed Kite (*Elanoides forficatus*)n Rare spring and summer visitor at widely scattered sites over the state, especially at Tidewater sites, Back Bay NWR, and the Great Dismal Swamp.

White-tailed Kite (*Elanus leucurus*) One record: Charles City County, 5 June 1988.

Mississippi Kite (*Ictinia mississippiensis*)n Uncommon and scarce summer visitor to wooded areas in extreme southern portions of the state, regular in varying numbers along the Meherrin River, Greensville County. Breeding has been confirmed at Woodbridge (adults and young in 1995, nest with young in 1996). Elsewhere in the state it is a regular vagrant in late spring and summer.

Bald Eagle (*Haliaeetus leucocephalus*)n Uncommon permanent resident and transient of bays, rivers, and estuaries, breeding chiefly on the Coastal Plain. Numbers increasing in recent years. Farther inland, a rare transient and local permanent resident or winter visitor, sometimes breeding on the Piedmont near large lakes and rivers.

Northern Harrier (*Circus cyaneus*) Common transient and winter resident of grassy fields and marshes statewide; uncommon breeder on Coastal Plain marshes. Farther inland, rare in summer.

Marsh Harrier (*Circus aeroginosus*) One record: a bird seen by several observers at Chincoteague NWR, 4 December 1994.

Sharp-shinned Hawk (*Accipiter striatus*) Common transient (especially in the fall) and less-common winter resident or permanent resident in a wide variety of forests and forest edges throughout the state. Recent breeding records are known from the lower Piedmont and at high elevations in the Mountains and Valleys.

Cooper's Hawk (*Accipiter cooperii*) Common transient (especially in autumn migration) or permanent resident in a wide variety of forests and forest edges throughout the state. Occasionally, it breeds, mostly in northern Virginia and west of the Blue Ridge. Usually less common than Sharp-shins.

Northern Goshawk (*Accipiter gentilis*) Uncommon to scarce and irregular late fall migrant and winter visitor to forests and their edges in northern regions of the Mountains and Valleys, Piedmont, and western Coastal Plain. A few summer records in the Mountains and Valleys (Mount Rogers, Mountain Lake), but breeding has not been confirmed.

Red-shouldered Hawk (*Buteo lineatus*) Common to uncommon breeding resident of bottomland forests and swamps, statewide but much more common east of the Blue Ridge.

Broad-winged Hawk (*Buteo platypterus*) Common to abundant transient (uncommon on Coastal Plain), especially in autumn migration, and uncommon to common breeding summer resident in hardwood forests, especially in the Piedmont and Mountains and Valleys. Reports of this bird in winter are mostly questionable.

Swainson's Hawk (*Buteo swainsoni*) Four records: Chincoteague (Aug, photographed), Snickers Gap (Oct), Beaverdam (Loudon County, Oct), and Fisherman Island (Oct).

Red-tailed Hawk (*Buteo jamaicensis*) Common transient and breeding resident statewide. It prefers to forage over fields and along forest edges. This is the most commonly seen hawk in the state at all seasons, perching along roadsides or soaring overhead. Apparently, there is an influx of northern birds in winter.

Ferruginous Hawk (*Buteo regalis*) Rare. Two records: a bird seen and photographed at the Eastern Shore of Virginia National Wildlife Refuge between 11 January and 4 March 1995; a sight record from Washington County, 14 January 1973.

Rough-legged Hawk (*Buteo lagopus*)n Uncommon and irregular winter visitor over open country and marshes in northern Virginia, the central Piedmont, and Accomack County (Dec-Mar). Much less common to the south. Dark morphs seem to predominate.

Golden Eagle (*Aquila chrysaetos*)n Rare to uncommon in extensive open country chiefly in winter but with records for every month. It is widely scattered over the state but is more common in autumn migration and winter, especially in the Mountains and Valleys. Although birds, perhaps pairs, have sometimes been seen in summer, breeding in the state has never been confirmed.

American Kestrel (*Falco sparverius*) Uncommon to common breeding resident in open country, along roadsides, and near woodland margins, statewide. Most breeding sites are in the northern Piedmont and in the Shenandoah Valley. Along the Eastern Shore it is an abundant fall transient and is one of the most common hawks seen on Christmas counts over the state.

Merlin (*Falco columbarius*) Uncommon to common transient and rare winter resident or visitor, widely scattered over the state but most numerous over Coastal Plain shrubby fields, marshes, and mudflats.

Peregrine Falcon (*Falco peregrinus*)n This endangered species is a fairly common and increasing fall migrant on the Eastern Shore, where it is also an uncommon spring migrant and winter visitor. Rare migrant on the western Coastal Plain, Piedmont, and the Mountains and Valleys. Very rare in winter away from the Eastern Shore. Introduced birds are now breeding at scattered locations in the state.

Gyrfalcon (*Falco rusticolus*) Two records for the Mountains and Valleys: 29 January 1984, Rockingham County (died 14 February 1996 at the Wildlife Center of Virginia at Weyer's Cave), and an immature banded and photographed at Short Hill Mountain (Loudoun County), 27 November 1991.

Ring-necked Pheasant (*Phasianus colchicus*) Rare to uncommon introduced breeding resident at widely scattered locations in the state, preferring fields and croplands. Numbers have sharply decreased in the past decade.

Ruffed Grouse (*Bonasa umbellus*) Common resident in the mountainous regions of the Mountains and Valleys and western Piedmont, preferring dense hardwood forests. Rare to uncommon localized populations in the northern Piedmont and Coastal Plain.

Wild Turkey (*Meleagris gallopavo*) Once nearly extirpated, but introductions have helped to increase its numbers. Currently, it is a locally common to uncommon resident in a variety of forests statewide.

Northern Bobwhite (*Colinus virginianus*) Common or uncommon breeding resident of abandoned fields, hedgerows, and forest borders statewide, but decreasing in many locations of the state.

Yellow Rail (*Coturnicops noveboracensis*) Near the coast, presumably an uncommon migrant and winter resident in marshes and wet grassy areas. Farther inland, only a few records during autumn migration. This secretive bird, along with some other rails, is difficult to locate and might be more numerous than the records indicate.

Black Rail (*Laterallus jamaicensis*)n Rare to uncommon, local breeder and transient in extensive salt marshes of Accomack and Northampton Counties, and the Tidewater area, where it is also a rare and local winter resident. Rare transient or (formerly?) summer visitor in remainder of the state,with records from Sweet Briar, Blacksburg, and Roanoke. As with the other secretive rails, it may be more common than the records indicate.

Clapper Rail (*Rallus longirostris*)n Common migrant, summer and uncommon winter resident in salt and brackish marshes near the coast, the Chesapeake Bay, and its major tributaries. Several old records of migrants in the Piedmont and Mountains and Valleys. Apparently decreasing in recent years.

King Rail (*Rallus elegans*)✳ Locally common transient, breeding summer resident, and rare winter resident chiefly in freshwater and brackish marshes of the Coastal Plain. There are scattered, mostly old, breeding records in marshy, freshwater habitats of the Piedmont and Mountains and Valleys. Hybrids with the Clapper Rail have been found.

Virginia Rail (*Rallus limicola*) Uncommon and local transient, breeding summer resident, and winter resident of marshes and wet grassy areas of the Coastal Plain. Also breeds in the Mountains and Valleys, but is generally much less common away from the coast.

Sora (*Porzana carolina*) Common to abundant transient and rare to locally uncommon winter visitor on the Coastal Plain. Rarely, it has been found breeding on the Coastal Plain and Mountains and Valleys. It prefers marshes (freshwater or salt) and wet grassy areas over much of the state.

Paint-billed Crake (*Neocrex erythrops*) One record: a specimen on 15 December 1978, Henrico County.

Purple Gallinule (*Porphyrula martinica*) Rare migrant and summer visitor on freshwater ponds and marshes with open water, chiefly on the Eastern Shore and Tidewater area. Farther inland, it has been seen at widely scattered sites. Two winter records are known, one each from the Piedmont and the Mountains and Valleys.

Common Moorhen (*Gallinula chloropus*) Uncommon to rare transient, breeding summer resident, and winter resident on freshwater marshes and pond edges, chiefly on the Coastal Plain and lower Piedmont. A rare breeder or transient farther inland.

American Coot (*Fulica americana*) Uncommon to common transient and local winter resident on lakes, ponds, and marshes statewide, occasionally breeding, chiefly on the Coastal Plain and Piedmont. Apparently decreasing in recent years.

Limpkin (*Aramus guarauna*) One record: 20 April to 9 June 1971, a bird photographed at Lynchburg.

Sandhill Crane (*Grus canadensis*) Rare transient and winter visitor with about a dozen records scattered over the state, chiefly in fall or winter and on the Coastal Plain. In far southwestern Virginia, it is probably a rare but regular transient.

Black-bellied Plover (*Pluvialis squatarola*) Common to abundant transient, common to uncommon winter resident, and uncommon summer visitor on the Chesapeake Bay and coastal tidal mudflats, beaches, and plowed fields. Rare transient farther inland.

American Golden-Plover (*Pluvialis dominica*)✷ Uncommon fall and scarce spring migrant to wet grassy areas in coastal areas, often appearing in sizable flocks. Very rare in summer. Generally uncommon and irregular fall migrant on the Coastal Plain and Piedmont. Rare fall migrant in the Mountains and Valleys.

Snowy Plover (*Charadrius alexandrinus*) One record. A bird was seen 19 to 21 June 1995, Cedar Island, Accomack County (photographed).

Wilson's Plover (*Charadrius wilsonia*)n Uncommon summer resident on Barrier Island beaches, where a small number of breeding pairs seems to be stable; summer visitor along the lower Chesapeake Bay. Very rare transient inland.

Semipalmated Plover (*Charadrius semipalmatus*) Common to abundant transient and uncommon or rare winter visitor along the coast; uncommon but regular transient farther inland.

Piping Plover (*Charadrius melodus*)n This endangered plover is an uncommon transient and summer resident on the coast and the lower Chesapeake Bay. It breeds on Barrier Island beaches, where populations seem to be stable. A rare winter visitor. Very rare transient farther inland.

Killdeer (*Charadrius vociferus*) Widespread summer resident throughout the state, nesting on bare ground, large flat roofs, or short-grass fields. In winter it is uncommon to common along the coast, less common inland.

Mountain Plover (*Charadrius montanus*) One record: a bird photographed at Chincoteague, 16 and 17 October 1976.

American Oystercatcher (*Haematopus palliatus*) Common breeding resident along the coast, especially on the Barrier Islands, where numbers have declined in recent years. Along the lower Chesapeake Bay, it is a less common breeder and transient and rare winter resident. Only one record (11 Jan 1924) away from the Coastal Plain (Brunswick County).

Black-necked Stilt (*Himantopus mexicanus*)n Uncommon transient and summer resident near the coast, breeding in small numbers at Chincoteague NWR and Craney Island. Recently increasing in numbers. One record for the Piedmont: 28 April 1986, Kerr Reservoir.

American Avocet (*Recurvirostra americana*)n Locally fairly common spring and fall transient and winter resident along the coast and at Craney Island, where it bed in 1991. Much less common as a transient farther inland (about a dozen records).

Greater Yellowlegs (*Tringa melanoleuca*) Common transient, chiefly in the spring, uncommon and local winter resident on the Coastal Plain. Farther inland, a fairly common transient and winter visitor. Less common than the Lesser Yellowlegs.

Lesser Yellowlegs (*Tringa flavipes*) Common transient, chiefly in the fall; uncommon and irregular winter and late summer visitor on the Coastal Plain. Uncommon transient farther inland.

Solitary Sandpiper (*Tringa solitaria*) Fairly common transient on the Coastal Plain, more common farther inland. Southbound migrants begin arriving in July.

Willet (*Catoptrophorus semipalmatus*) Abundant transient and breeding summer resident in coastal and Chesapeake Bay salt marshes. In winter it is locally uncommon on mudflats and coastal marshes. Farther inland, a rare transient and summer visitor.

Spotted Sandpiper (*Actitis macularia*) On the Coastal Plain, a common transient, uncommon summer resident, and very rare winter visitor. On the Piedmont and in the Mountains and Valleys, a common transient, rare breeding summer resident, and occasional winter visitor.

Upland Sandpiper (*Bartramia longicauda*)n A rare spring and locally uncommon fall transient on the Coastal Plain. On the northern Piedmont and Mountains and Valleys, a rare transient and breeding summer resident at a few sites with extensive grassy fields; declining for many years.

Whimbrel (*Numenius phaeopus*) Common transient chiefly in extensive coastal salt marshes and on mudflats, rare summer and irregular winter visitor along the coast. Farther inland, a very rare transient.

Long-billed Curlew (*Numenius americanus*) A rare visitor in all seasons along the coast and the lower Chesapeake Bay. One inland record, 22 May 1948 at Arlington.

Hudsonian Godwit (*Limosa haemastica*) Locally rare to uncommon transient on mudflats near the coast, with one summer record. Rare transient in Mountains and Valleys.

Bar-tailed Godwit (*Limosa lapponica*)n Two records, both at Chincoteague, 28 December 1973 and 5 to 15 September 1991.

Marbled Godwit (*Limosa fedoa*)n Locally rare to uncommon fall transient and winter resident, rare spring transient and summer visitor on mudflats, chiefly near the coast. One spring record for Mountains and Valleys.

Ruddy Turnstone (*Arenaria interpres*) Common to abundant transient; fairly common winter resident, and uncommon summer visitor on the coast; less common along the Chesapeake Bay. Rare transient farther inland.

Red Knot (*Calidris canutus*) Locally common to abundant transient, uncommon or rare winter and summer visitor, chiefly on open beaches along the coast; rare along the Chesapeake Bay. Rare transient farther inland.

Sanderling (*Calidris alba*) Common to abundant transient, common winter resident, and uncommon summer visitor on coastal beaches; less common along the Chesapeake Bay. Very rare transient farther inland.

Semipalmated Sandpiper (*Calidris pusilla*) Common to abundant transient and uncommon summer visitor on beaches, along impoundments, and on plowed fields along the coast. Uncommon to common transient farther inland. Generally, the Semipalmated arrives in the fall two weeks after the Western Sandpiper does.

Western Sandpiper (*Calidris mauri*) Rare spring and common fall transient, and uncommon to rare winter resident on the coast and the lower Chesapeake Bay. Farther inland it is a common fall transient.

Red-necked Stint (*Calidris ruficollis*) One record: a bird seen at Craney island, 23 July 1994.

Least Sandpiper (*Calidris minutilla*) Common transient and rare winter resident on the coast; less common along the Chesapeake Bay. Uncommon transient farther inland. Often feeds in coastal, grassy areas.

White-rumped Sandpiper (*Calidris fuscicollis*) Much less common than Least or Semipalmated Sandpipers, the White-rumped is only a locally uncommon transient and rare summer visitor to shore, lagoons, and wet grassy areas along the coast; rare along the Chesapeake Bay. Rare and irregular transient farther inland.

Baird's Sandpiper (*Calidris bairdii*)n Scarce and irregular fall transient and occasional summer visitor on mudflats and grassy pool margins along the Eastern Shore. Rare transient farther inland.

Pectoral Sandpiper (*Calidris melanotos*) Uncommon spring and common fall transient and rare winter visitor on the coast; rare along the Chesapeake Bay. Numbers sometimes fluctuate widely from year to year. Uncommon transient farther inland.

Sharp-tailed Sandpiper (*Calidris acuminata*)n Three records: 14 to 24 September 1983 and 16 September 1989, Fairfax County, and 14 to 21 September 1984, Chincoteague.

Purple Sandpiper (*Calidris maritima*)n Uncommon to rare and local winter resident on Chesapeake Bay Bridge-Tunnel islands, at Craney Island, and the lower Chesapeake Bay, where it frequents rock jetties and rocky sea walls; rare elsewhere on the coast. One upper Chesapeake Bay record: Westmoreland County, 10 May 1975.

Dunlin (*Calidris alpina*) Common to abundant transient and winter resident and rare summer visitor near the coast; somewhat less common along the Chesapeake Bay. The most abundant wintering shorebird; it chooses shorelines, mudflats, impoundments, and plowed fields. Uncommon transient farther inland, with a few winter records.

Curlew Sandpiper (*Calidris ferruginea*)n Rare spring, summer, and fall transient to the Eastern Shore, Barrier Islands, and other coastal locations.

Stilt Sandpiper (*Calidris himantopus*) Locally uncommon to common transient on coastal sections of the Coastal Plain, with a few summer records. Rare transient farther inland.

Buff-breasted Sandpiper (*Tryngites subruficollis*)✶ Rare to uncommon fall transient, chiefly near the coast. Farther inland, it is a rare fall migrant. It prefers short-grass and plowed fields.

Ruff (*Philomachus pugnax*)✶ Rare transient and winter visitor near the coast. Farther inland, a rare summer visitor or spring and fall migrant.

Short-billed Dowitcher (*Limnodromus griseus*)n Common to abundant transient and uncommon to rare winter and summer visitor along the coast and the Chesapeake Bay. Both dowitcher species feed on mudflats and tidepools. Uncommon transient farther inland.

Long-billed Dowitcher (*Limnodromus scolopaceus*)✶ Uncommon fall and rare spring transient; uncommon and local to rare winter resident along the coast and the Chesapeake Bay. Rare fall transient farther inland.

Common Snipe (*Gallinago gallinago*) Uncommon to common transient and uncommon winter resident statewide.

Eurasian Woodcock (*Scolopax rusticola*) One old record for Loudoun County in 1873.

American Woodcock (*Scolopax minor*) Common transient and uncommon breeding summer resident throughout the state, preferring moist woods and bottomland forests. Common in winter in scattered coastal locations; rare elsewhere.

Wilson's Phalarope (*Phalaropus tricolor*)n Unlike the other two phalarope species, Wilson's can often be seen associated with land. It is an uncommon to rare, local transient and rare summer visitor to impoundments, tidal edges, and marsh lagoons of the Coastal Plain, especially the Eastern Shore. Elsewhere in the state it is chiefly a rare and irregular transient.

Red-necked Phalarope (*Phalaropus lobatus*) Uncommon to common transient offshore; rare along the coast and on the Chesapeake Bay. Seen chiefly in May and August into September. Rare transient farther inland.

Red Phalarope (*Phalaropus fulicaria*) Rarest of the phalaropes on land, it is an uncommon, irregular transient and winter visitor to offshore Atlantic waters. Very rare transient farther inland.

Pomarine Jaeger (*Stercorarius pomarinus*) Uncommon transient and winter visitor (rarely in summer) along the coast but chiefly offshore. Two inland records: 3 to 9 October 1975, Pulaski County, and 16 to 28 July 1993, Loudoun County.

Parasitic Jaeger (*Stercorarius parasiticus*) The jaeger most likely to be seen from shore. Uncommon to common transient and winter visitor, chiefly offshore but also along the coast and in the Chesapeake Bay. Inland fall records from Fairfax County and Smith Mountain Lake.

Long-tailed Jaeger (*Stercorarius longicaudus*) Rare spring migrant and uncommon fall migrant far offshore. Exceptionally rare near shore. A few summer records along the coast.

Great Skua (*Catharacta skua*) A rare but regular transient and winter visitor (Dec-Mar) far offshore. A few old summer records from the Barrier Islands, but these summer records probably pertained to South Polar Skua , before the distribution and taxonomy of these species were worked out.

South Polar Skua (*Catharacta maccormicki*)n A rare spring (May-Jun) visitor to offshore Atlantic waters.

Laughing Gull (*Larus atricilla*) Common to abundant transient and breeding resident and uncommon winter visitor along the coast and the Chesapeake Bay. It breeds in salt marshes of the Barrier Islands and on a few islands in the upper Chesapeake Bay. Rare spring and uncommon fall migrant throughout the interior.

Franklin's Gull (*Larus pipixcan*) Rare visitor (Jun-Apr, but chiefly winter) to Loudon and Fairfax Counties, Eastern Shore regions, and the lower Chesapeake Bay, where it mixes with flocks of other gulls. One old record (specimen) from the Mountains and Valleys: Blacksburg, 22 October 1898.

Little Gull (*Larus minutus*)✶ Variable, uncommon to rare winter, spring, and summer visitor to the Eastern Shore, Tidewater, and the lower Chesapeake Bay. Often it joins flocks of Bonaparte's Gulls. Rarely found inland (Loudoun and Fairfax Counties).

Black-headed Gull (*Larus ridibundus*) Rare to uncommon transient and winter visitor to the Eastern Shore and Craney Island. Three inland winter records, two near Alexandria and one near Blacksburg.

Bonaparte's Gull (*Larus philadelphia*) Uncommon to common transient, winter resident, and rare summer visitor along the coast and the Chesapeake Bay. Farther inland, rare to uncommon and irregular transient and winter visitor, especially on large impoundments.

Black-tailed Gull (*Larus crassirostris*) One record: a bird seen and photographed on Chesapeake Bay Bridge-Tunnel, 27 December 1996.

Mew Gull (*Larus canus*) Three records: Suffolk, 2 January 1996, and two from Alexandria, 17 November 1974, and 14 and 30 September 1978.

Ring-billed Gull (*Larus delawarensis*) Common to abundant winter resident and transient along beaches, rivers, bays, lakes, fields, and parking lots; rare in summer. The commonest wintering gull statewide.

California Gull (*Larus californicus*) Probably a rare winter visitor among gull concentrations in northern Virginia and Eastern Shore sections, with accepted records from the Fairfax County region, Chesapeake Bay Bridge-Tunnel, and Virginia Beach.

Herring Gull (*Larus argentatus*) Common transient, winter, and summer resident over much the state but especially in coastal areas. Breeding on Barrier Islands and the lower Chesapeake Bay. Less common away from the coast and rare in the Mountains and Valleys.

Thayer's Gull (*Larus thayeri*) Rare fall/winter/spring visitor, chiefly at coastal sites (e.g., Chesapeake Bay Bridge-Tunnel, Virginia Beach landfill), where the species mixes with Herring Gulls. Inland records are from the Fairfax County region.

Iceland Gull (*Larus glaucoides*)n Rare transient and winter visitor, mostly near the coast. Several inland records (fall, winter, spring) from Piedmont lakes and landfills (e.g., Richmond, Lake Anna).

Lesser Black-backed Gull (*Larus fuscus*)n Rare to uncommon transient and winter visitor, mostly along the coast and offshore. Winter observations seem to be increasing in recent years. Inland records from Alexandria area, Prince William County (winter and late spring), Great Dismal Swamp (Dec), Lake Anna (Dec), and Roanoke (Apr).

Glaucous Gull (*Larus hyperboreus*)n Rare transient and winter visitor, mostly near the coast, where it is often found with Herring Gulls on beaches, inlets, nearshore, and offshore. Also rare farther inland, with winter records for Henrico, Prince William, and Arlington Counties, Kerr Reservoir, and Roanoke.

Great Black-backed Gull (*Larus marinus*) Common permanent resident along the coast, the Chesapeake Bay, and its major tributaries. Breeds on Barrier and Chesapeake Bay islands; rare fall and winter visitor on the Piedmont.

Black-legged Kittiwake (*Rissa tridactyla*) Irregular and uncommon to common winter visitor offshore (sometimes seen in the hundreds), but may be seen occasionally in nearshore waters and the lower Chesapeake Bay. One inland record from Fairfax County, October 1956.

Sabine's Gull (*Xema sabini*) A very rare and irregular visitor, May through October, to the Eastern Shore and offshore Atlantic. A scattering of records for Back Bay National Wildlife Refuge, Chesapeake Bay Bridge-Tunnel, and Chincoteague.

Gull-billed Tern (*Sterna nilotica*)n Uncommon to common transient and summer resident in coastal locations and the lower Chesapeake Bay. Breeding chiefly on the Barrier Islands, where it is declining in numbers. Rare farther inland (two sight records in May).

Caspian Tern (*Sterna caspia*) Common transient, rare winter visitor, and rare breeder on the Barrier Islands (only two adults were found in 1993). Farther inland, it is a rare transient or summer visitor.

Royal Tern (*Sterna maxima*) Common to abundant transient and summer resident, and very rare winter visitor on the Coastal Plain. It breeds on the Barrier Islands and on an island in the lower Chesapeake Bay; a rare spring transient inland.

Elegant Tern (*Sterna elegans*) One record: Chincoteague, 20 June 1985.

Sandwich Tern (*Sterna sandvicensis*)n Uncommon transient and summer resident along the coast and in the Chesapeake Bay. Breeds on the Barrier Islands.

Roseate Tern (*Sterna dougallii*) Rare transient and summer visitor near the coast and Chesapeake Bay Bridge-Tunnel. Formerly nested on several Barrier Islands, but no definite breeding record since 1927.

Common Tern (*Sterna hirundo*) Common transient and summer resident, rare winter visitor at coastal locations, the lower Chesapeake Bay, and in offshore waters. Breeds on the Barrier Islands, along the Chesapeake Bay, and at Hampton Roads. Farther inland, an uncommon but regular transient and rare summer visitor.

Arctic Tern (*Sterna paradisaea*) First recorded in May 1972 off Virginia Beach. It is now considered to be a rare to uncommon spring and fall migrant offshore and a rare visitor to near-shore waters.

Forster's Tern (*Sterna forsteri*) Common transient and summer resident, uncommon winter resident along the coast, in the Chesapeake Bay, and in tidal rivers. Breeds in salt marshes of the Eastern Shore and Chesapeake Bay islands. The most common wintering tern. Farther inland, an uncommon transient and rare summer or winter visitor.

Least Tern (*Sterna antillarum*) Common transient and summer resident, breeding on the Barrier Islands (where it is currently decreasing in numbers), along the Chesapeake Bay, and lower tidal rivers; very rare transient farther inland.

Bridled Tern (*Sterna anaethetus*) Uncommon to rare late summer and fall visitor (chiefly Aug-Sep) to offshore Atlantic waters. One record (5 and 6 Sep 1979) from Lake Anna after Hurricane *David*.

Sooty Tern (*Sterna fuscata*) Rare fall transient and summer visitor, mostly well offshore; especially after hurricanes. Several inland records from the Coastal Plain and lower Piedmont following Hurricane *David* in September 1979. Much rarer offshore than Bridled.

White-winged Tern (*Chlidonias leucopterus*) Recorded in the state several times (1963-1980) as a late spring, summer, and early fall visitor. All birds were seen at Chincoteague.

Black Tern (*Chlidonias niger*) Uncommon and irregular spring migrant but fairly common in fall migration on the Eastern Shore, with most birds departing by early September. Irregular and uncommon to rare transient farther inland.

Black Skimmer (*Rynchops niger*) Common to abundant transient and summer resident, uncommon winter visitor along coast and the lower Chesapeake Bay. It breeds commonly on the Barrier Islands (now declining) and rarely on Chesapeake Bay islands and Hampton Roads Bridge-Tunnel islands. One late-spring and one summer record from the Piedmont.

Dovekie (*Alle alle*)✶ Irregular and uncommon to common winter visitor well offshore (Nov-Mar). During that time it is rare in nearshore waters.

Common Murre (*Uria aalge*) One record: a bird seen and photographed 13 February 1994, 50 miles east of Cape Henry.

Thick-billed Murre (*Uria lomvia*) Rare winter visitor along the coast and in offshore waters. Two old inland records: 20 December 1896, Fairfax County, and 22 November 1899, Arlington.

Razorbill (*Alca torda*)✶ Rare to uncommon, irregular fall to early-spring visitor offshore; rarely seen from the coast.

Black Guillemot (*Cepphus grylle*) One record: one seen off the beach at Back Bay, 23 February 1986.

Atlantic Puffin (*Fratercula arctica*)n A rare and irregular winter (Feb-Mar) visitor to offshore waters, with about a dozen recent records, including two in May.

Rock Dove (*Columba livia*) Common to abundant breeding resident throughout the state, especially in urban, suburban, and farmland habitats.

White-winged Dove (*Zenaida asiatica*) Three records, all from the Eastern Shore, 10 August 1984, 19 December 1987, and 26 to 28 July 1991 (photographed).

Mourning Dove (*Zenaida macroura*) Common to abundant breeding resident throughout the state in residential and farmland habitats.

Passenger Pigeon (*Ectopistes migratorius*) Extinct. Formerly abundant transient and irregular winter visitor, chiefly on the Coastal Plain and Piedmont.

Common Ground-Dove (*Columbina passerina*) Rare transient and summer visitor, chiefly at southeastern coastal sites, but also reported at Lynchburg, Augusta County (specimen), and Mountain Lake (Giles County).

Carolina Parakeet (*Conuropsis carolinensis*) Extinct. Formerly an irregular transient, chiefly on the Coastal Plain.

Black-billed Cuckoo (*Coccyzus erythropthalmus*) Rare to uncommon, irregular transient and summer resident of hardwood forests, breeding chiefly in the western Piedmont and Mountains and Valleys.

Yellow-billed Cuckoo (*Coccyzus americanus*) Uncommon to common transient and summer resident of hardwood and mixed forests, breeding throughout the state.

Groove-billed Ani (*Crotophaga sulcirostris*) Two records from the Mountains and Valleys: 20 October-18 November 1979, Tazewell County; 24 and 25 October and 8 to 15 November 1981, Rockingham County.

Barn Owl (*Tyto alba*) Uncommon to fairly common resident, breeding throughout the state in siloes, duck blinds, deserted buildings, hollow trees, and nest-boxes. For foraging it prefers open country, extensive marshes, and weedy fields. The breeding population has apparently declined in recent years.

Eastern Screech-Owl (*Otus asio*) Locally common resident, breeding throughout the state, preferring farms, small woodlots, and wooded residential areas.

Great Horned Owl (*Bubo virginianus*) Locally common resident, breeding throughout the state, occurring in residential areas and farmlands as well as in extensive forested tracts.

Snowy Owl (*Nyctea scandiaca*)n Rare, irregular winter visitor (Nov-Mar) scattered over much of the state, from Virginia Beach to Roanoke. The 28 specimen records show no evidence of cyclical occurrences.

Burrowing Owl (*Speotyto cunicularia*) Three records: Virginia Beach, 22 October 1918 (on an offshore ship); Albemarle County, 10 August-16 October 1983; and a specimen from the Chesapeake Bay Bridge-Tunnel, 11 January 1994.

Barred Owl (*Strix varia*) Locally common resident, breeding throughout the state, preferring heavily wooded bottomland or upland forests.

Long-eared Owl (*Asio otus*)n Rare to uncommon fall transient and winter resident over much of the state. Breeds (or bred) rarely in pine forests of the northern Piedmont and Mountains and Valleys. It forages over open fields and forest edges and roosts in groups in dense coniferous stands.

Short-eared Owl (*Asio flammeus*)n Uncommon to rare transient and winter visitor, foraging over grassy fields of the Piedmont and coastal salt marshes; rare west of the Blue Ridge. Rare in summer; two breeding records (Westmoreland and Loudoun Counties).

Northern Saw-whet Owl (*Aegolius acadicus*)n Rare or uncommon transient and winter visitor statewide, summer resident of high mountain forests; two confirmed breeding records for Mountains and Valleys (Russell County, 29 April 1989, and Highland County, 13 March 1995).

Common Nighthawk (*Chordeiles minor*) Locally common transient and uncommon, local summer resident foraging over cities and towns and open country, breeding locally throughout much of the state, including the Barrier Islands.

Chuck-will's-widow (*Caprimulgus carolinensis*) Common to uncommon transient and breeding summer resident in a variety of forests, chiefly pine forests in southern parts of the state. It is much less common west of the Blue Ridge.

Whip-poor-will (*Caprimulgus vociferus*) Common to uncommon breeding summer resident in hardwood forests over much of the state (much less common on eastern Coastal Plain). Shows signs of a recent population decrease.

Chimney Swift (*Chaetura pelagica*) Common transient and breeding summer resident statewide, foraging over residential and farm areas and open country. It may breed in hollow trees but shows a distinct preference for brick chimneys.

Ruby-throated Hummingbird (*Archilochus colubris*) Common transient and breeding summer resident statewide, preferring residential areas, forest edges, and streamside vegetation. Winter records are known from Norfolk and Newport News.

Rufous Hummingbird (*Selasphorus rufus*) Occasional, about 8 records from late summer into winter, chiefly in eastern and southern parts of the state. Because of a close similarity to Allen's Hummingbird (*Selasphorus sasin*), unless a bird is critically examined in the hand, sight records of this genus should be listed as *Selasphorus* sp.

Belted Kingfisher (*Ceryle alcyon*) Common but local permanent breeding resident over most of the state along streams and lakes.

Lewis's Woodpecker (*Melanerpes lewis*) One record from Loudoun County, January-May 1988.

Red-headed Woodpecker (*Melanerpes erythrocephalus*)✷ Locally uncommon to rare transient and breeding resident statewide, preferring open deciduous and coniferous forests, cultivated areas, towns, parks, and golf courses. More common in southeastern third of state, with some local "pockets" in the northern Piedmont and Mountains and Valleys.

Red-bellied Woodpecker (*Melanerpes carolinus*) Common breeding resident statewide; widespread in forests and woodlands.

Yellow-bellied Sapsucker (*Sphyrapicus varius*) Common to uncommon transient and winter resident statewide, found in a variety of woodlands. A rare breeding bird in the high mountains (Highland County, Mount Rogers); formerly bred in Mountain Lake region of Giles County.

Downy Woodpecker (*Picoides pubescens*) Common breeding resident statewide, found in a wide variety of woodlands, especially hardwood forests.

Hairy Woodpecker (*Picoides villosus*) Uncommon breeding resident statewide (less common on the Coastal Plain), and found in a wide variety of woodlands, including mature hardwood forests. Ratio of sightings compared with the Downy is about 1:5.

Red-cockaded Woodpecker (*Picoides borealis*)✴ Endangered. Declining. Presently a rare breeding resident of Sussex and Southampton Counties, where it is restricted to extensive tracts of open, mature pine woods. One recent record from Lancaster County.

Northern Flicker (*Colaptes auratus*) Common transient and breeding resident statewide, found in open woods, residential areas, farmland, and woodland margins. It is a common fall transient on the coast.

Pileated Woodpecker (*Dryocopus pileatus*) Locally common to uncommon breeding resident statewide, preferring extensive hardwood forests.

Olive-sided Flycatcher (*Contopus cooperi*) Rare late spring and early fall transient, with sightings scattered over the state. A few summer records from the western mountains. It prefers high, exposed snags over open areas.

Eastern Wood-Pewee (*Contopus virens*) Common transient and breeding summer resident statewide in open hardwood and pine forests and their edges, as well as in heavily wooded residential areas.

Yellow-bellied Flycatcher (*Empidonax flaviventris*) Rare transient widespread over the state; has bred on Mount Rogers but not found there in recent years. Prefers wet or swampy places in various types of dense forests.

Acadian Flycatcher (*Empidonax virescens*) Common transient and breeding summer resident statewide, preferring hardwood forests near streams.

Alder Flycatcher (*Empidonax alnorum*) Presumably a rare spring and fairly common fall migrant to wet woodland and meadow edges scattered over the state. May be common in fall along the Eastern Shore, where calling Alder Flycatchers outnumber Willows 7 to 2. Breeding, probable breeding, and summer records have been reported locally close to mountain summits in several western counties (Washington, Tazewell, Scott, Grayson, Bath, and Highland). It prefers moist transitional or disturbed habitats such as mountain meadows with blackberry thickets and alders or swamp borders with open spaces.

Willow Flycatcher (*Empidonax traillii*)n Rare to uncommon transient and uncommon summer resident, breeding mostly in the northern Piedmont and Mountains and Valleys south to at least Lee County, preferring low thickets (often willows) near streams or bodies of water. Much less common in southern and eastern parts of the state.

Least Flycatcher (*Empidonax minimus*) Rare to uncommon transient widespread over the state, breeding locally at high elevations in Mountains and Valleys and Blue Ridge. It prefers open hardwood forests, edges of pastures, and orchards.

Eastern Phoebe (*Sayornis phoebe*) Common transient and breeding summer resident statewide, preferring streamside habitats, bridges, and man-made structures for nesting. Otherwise, it may be found in open country, parks, and along fencelines. It is an uncommon and irregular winter resident throughout state.

Say's Phoebe (*Sayornis saya*) Only five records, with single birds seen at Virginia Beach (Dec and Jan), Highland County (Dec-Apr), Fauquier County (December), and Chesapeake Bay Bridge-Tunnel (September).

Vermilion Flycatcher (*Pyrocephalus rubinus*) Two records: Eastern Shore, immature male 15 January 1993, at edge of flooded soybean field near Birds Nest, remaining nearby until late February; a bird (photographed) at Woodbridge, 13 December 1994 to 1 January 1995.

Ash-throated Flycatcher (*Myiarchus cinerascens*) Occasional late fall and winter visitor, chiefly near the coast. One record in December for the Piedmont in the Haymarket area.

Great Crested Flycatcher (*Myiarchus crinitus*) Common transient and breeding summer resident statewide, found in a variety of open woodlands and forests. One January record at Chesapeake.

Western Kingbird (*Tyrannus verticalis*) Rare to uncommon, local fall transient and winter visitor near the coast, only occasionally found farther inland. Casual in spring and summer. It prefers fencelines, overhead wires, and high, prominent snags.

Eastern Kingbird (*Tyrannus tyrannus*) Common transient and breeding summer resident statewide, preferring forest edges, open country with scattered trees, and roadsides. It is especially common on the Eastern Shore as a fall migrant.

Gray Kingbird (*Tyrannus dominicensis*) Several records: Chincoteague in July and fall, Kiptopeke in November, Chesapeake Bay Bridge-Tunnel in May.

Scissor-tailed Flycatcher (*Tyrannus forficatus*) Rare transient and visitor throughout the year on the Coastal Plain, plus a few spring (Albemarle and Loudoun Counties, Back Bay) and summer (Augusta County) records elsewhere.

Fork-tailed Flycatcher (*Tyrannus savana*) Only three Coastal Plain records: Charles City County, 4 June-August 1988; Chincoteague, 18 and 19 May 1990; False Cape State Park, 12 October 1991 (photographed).

Horned Lark (*Eremophila alpestris*) Uncommon to common resident and locally breeding bird at scattered locations over the state, from the Barrier Islands to the western mountains. Its preferred habitats include short-grass or agricultural fields and bare-ground habitats.

Purple Martin (*Progne subis*) Locally common transient and breeding summer resident statewide, foraging over open farmland, ponds, and fields. Although it is apparently most abundant in the eastern one-third of the state and absent from some Mountains and Valleys counties, its abundance locally is probably affected by the presence of suitable nest-boxes.

Tree Swallow (*Tachycineta bicolor*) Common transient and locally common to uncommon breeding summer resident, especially on the Delmarva peninsula, northern Piedmont, and west of the Blue Ridge. Its preferred breeding habitat is around ponds or lakes with dead trees and stubs. Along the coast it is an abundant fall transient, whereas in winter it is irregularly rare to uncommon.

Northern Rough-winged Swallow (*Stelgidopteryx serripennis*) Common transient and breeding summer resident statewide, but less common in the southeastern one-third of the state. It prefers shores of ponds, lakes, and streams.

Bank Swallow (*Riparia riparia*) Uncommon transient statewide and locally common breeding summer resident, its colonies scattered widely over the state. It prefers banks or bluffs along rivers or lakes for nesting.

Cliff Swallow (*Hirundo pyrrhonota*) Rare to uncommon transient and locally common breeding summer resident, nesting under large bridges and at large concrete dams. Most colonies are currently found from the central Piedmont and Mountains and Valleys northward. It forages over lakes, rivers, fields, and open country.

Barn Swallow (*Hirundo rustica*) Common transient and breeding summer resident statewide, preferring to nest under bridges and in barns or sheds. Rarely has it been found in winter. This is the most common swallow in Virginia.

Blue Jay (*Cyanocitta cristata*) Common transient and breeding resident statewide, using a wide variety of woodlands and residential areas. It is a common to abundant diurnal migrant.

Black-billed Magpie (*Pica pica*) Four records, all of probably escaped individuals from Chincoteague to Roanoke, at various times of the year.

American Crow (*Corvus brachyrhynchos*) Common to abundant resident statewide, preferring open fields, roadsides, and a variety of woodlands. On Christmas counts, the American Crow outnumbers the Fish Crow by 10:1.

Fish Crow (*Corvus ossifragus*) Uncommon to common breeding resident on the Piedmont and Coastal Plain, much less common or absent from southern Piedmont and Mountains and Valleys south of Augusta County. In the Shenandoah Valley, south to Staunton, its numbers have been increasing recently. It is found in a variety of habitats from coastal marshes and along rivers to forest edges and city parks and other residential areas.

Common Raven (*Corvus corax*)n Locally uncommon to fairly common breeding resident on the western Piedmont (especially near the Blue Ridge) and Mountains and Valleys, preferring extensive forested areas. Formerly an uncommon visitor on the Coastal Plain.

Black-capped Chickadee (*Poecile atricapillus*)✶ Resident on the western edge of the Mountains and Valleys region, chiefly from Shenandoah County south to the Mount Rogers area, where it shows a preference for montane hardwood and coniferous forests. It may wander to lower elevations during winter. Elsewhere in the state it is very rare and irregular. Occasionally, fall and winter irruptions occur when Black-capped Chickadees have been reported as locally common in northern and central sections of the Piedmont and Coastal Plain. Hybrid breeding birds (between Black-caps and Carolinas), based on vocalizations and measurements, have been reported from several localized sites in the Mountains and Valleys.

Carolina Chickadee (*Poecile carolinensis*) Common breeding resident over most of the state, especially in hardwood forests at lower elevations. On the western flanks of the Mountains and Valleys province, for example in Augusta and Rockingham Counties, its range closely approaches that of the Black-capped Chickadee.

Boreal Chickadee (*Poecile hudsonicus*) This rare northern visitor has been recorded three times in the state: Alexandria, January-March 1955; Warrenton, November 1969; and Falls Church, March 1978.

Tufted Titmouse (*Baeolophus bicolor*) Common breeding resident state-wide, preferring residential areas and a variety of forests.

Red-breasted Nuthatch (*Sitta canadensis*) Irregular and uncommon to common transient and winter visitor over most of the state. It is a locally rare to uncommon breeding resident at higher-elevation coniferous forests of the Mountains and Valleys. Because of its irruptive nature, the wintering status of this nuthatch varies from year to year.

White-breasted Nuthatch (*Sitta carolinensis*) Uncommon to common breeding resident over most of the state, but much less common on the Eastern Shore and lower Coastal Plain. It prefers mature hardwood forests and residential areas.

Brown-headed Nuthatch (*Sitta pusilla*)n Locally uncommon to common breeding summer resident of southern Coastal Plain and southern Piedmont pine forests; occasional elsewhere in the state. On the Coastal Plain it is often associated with dead snags in high salt marshes.

Brown Creeper (*Certhia americana*) Uncommon transient and winter resident over most of the state. A rare and local breeding summer resident in the northern Piedmont and at widely scattered sites in the Mountains and Valleys, preferring high-elevation mature forests. It is a common fall transient along the coast.

Rock Wren (*Salpinctes obsoletus*) Two records from the Coastal Plain: Chesapeake Bay Bridge-Tunnel, 29 and 30 October 1988 and on Craney Island, 4 November 1990 (photographed) to March 1991.

Carolina Wren (*Thryothorus ludovicianus*) Common breeding resident statewide, preferring brushy and tangled areas in or near woodlands.

Bewick's Wren (*Thryomanes bewickii*)n Formerly widespread but never common, this species is extremely rare today. Its former range was chiefly the Mountains and Valleys but also included scattered sites on the Coastal Plain and Piedmont. It inhabited towns and farmyards, brush piles, and fence rows. The last known breeding record was in Highland County in June 1985.

House Wren (*Troglodytes aedon*) Common transient and breeding summer resident and rare to uncommon winter resident over much of the state, but much less common in the southern Piedmont and Coastal Plain. It is found in residential areas, farmyards, overgrown fields, and hedgerows.

Winter Wren (*Troglodytes troglodytes*) Uncommon to common transient and winter resident statewide, uncommon or rare breeding bird at high elevations in the Mountains and Valleys. It is found in cool coniferous forests, in tangles or thickets in woodlands. The numbers of this species in migration or winter vary widely from year to year.

Sedge Wren (*Cistothorus platensis*)n Rare and local resident in sedge/grass meadows and marshes of the Coastal Plain; uncommon migrant, locally scarce breeder on the Eastern Shore (Accomack County, Virginia Beach), the lower Chesapeake Bay, and the northern Piedmont. A rare to uncommon transient elsewhere in the state. May be decreasing and warrants concern.

Marsh Wren (*Cistothorus palustris*) Rare to common transient statewide. It is a locally common breeder on the Coastal Plain and rarely so in the Piedmont. The bird inhabits salt marshes (cordgrass), cattail marshes, and wet meadows. It is rare to uncommon in winter.

Golden-crowned Kinglet (*Regulus satrapa*) Common transient and uncommon to common winter resident statewide, and a rare, local breeder at higher mountain elevations in coniferous forests. It may be found in a variety of other woodlands at other times of the year.

Ruby-crowned Kinglet (*Regulus calendula*) Common transient and uncommon winter resident statewide; found in a wide variety of woodlands. It is somewhat less common in winter in the Mountains and Valleys.

Blue-gray Gnatcatcher (*Polioptila caerulea*) Common transient and breeding summer resident statewide; primarily found in hardwood forests. A few are found each winter on the southern Coastal Plain and Piedmont.

Northern Wheatear (*Oenanthe oenanthe*) Five sightings of this accidental bird: Chincoteague, March and October; two from Northampton County, October; and Albemarle County, September.

Eastern Bluebird (*Sialia sialis*) Uncommon to locally common breeding resident statewide. It inhabits open country with scattered trees, orchards, roadsides, and residential areas.

Veery (*Catharus fuscescens*) Uncommon to common transient statewide; locally common breeder above 3,000 feet in the Mountains and Valleys, where it inhabits hardwood or coniferous forests.

Gray-cheeked Thrush (*Catharus minimus*) Uncommon transient, more common in the fall, especially on the Coastal Plain. It has been reported in winter from a few widely scattered sites over the state. (**Bicknell's Thrush** [*Catharus bicknelli*], now recognized as a distinct species, is a spring and fall migrant in the state, but its exact status remains uncertain.)

Swainson's Thrush (*Catharus ustulatus*) Uncommon to common transient statewide, especially along the coast in the fall. In summer it is rare in the highest western mountains (Mount Rogers, Tazewell Beartown, Highland County). The only known breeding location is on Mount Rogers in coniferous forests. It has been rarely reported in winter from a few sites scattered over the state.

Hermit Thrush (*Catharus guttatus*) Common transient and fairly common winter resident in woodlands statewide. Summer records are known from high-mountain elevations (Mount Rogers, Whitetop, Tazewell Beartown, Highland County), with breeding reported from Mount Rogers and Highland County in moist coniferous forests.

Wood Thrush (*Hylocichla mustelina*) Common transient and breeding summer resident statewide. It prefers hardwood forests, but may also be found in residential areas and parks. It is a rare winter visitor to southern parts of the state.

American Robin (*Turdus migratorius*) Common to abundant transient and breeding summer resident statewide. It is locally fairly common in winter, especially in the southeastern part of the state. It inhabits open woodlands, residential areas, farmyards, and parks.

Varied Thrush (*Ixoreus naevius*) This accidental species has been found occasionally in the Piedmont (four winter records) and the Mountains and Valleys (four fall/winter records). Many of these were seen at feeders or nearby in association with American Robins.

Gray Catbird (*Dumetella carolinensis*) Common transient and breeding summer resident statewide, but resident along the coast and the Chesapeake Bay. It inhabits dense thickets, fence-rows, and shrubbery of residential areas. Rare and irregular winter resident west of the Coastal Plain.

Northern Mockingbird (*Mimus polyglottos*) Common breeding resident statewide, but decidedly less common at high elevations. It occupies open residential habitats, fence-rows, forest edges, and roadsides.

Sage Thrasher (*Oreoscoptes montanus*) Two records: Loudoun County, December 1962; Chincoteague, October 1985.

Brown Thrasher (*Toxostoma rufum*) Common transient and breeding summer resident statewide, but resident along the coast and the Chesapeake Bay. It inhabits overgrown fields, fence-rows, and thickets. In winter it is much less common, especially in the Mountains and Valleys.

American Pipit (*Anthus rubescens*) Common transient and winter resident on Coastal Plain, uncommon to rare elsewhere in the state. It prefers bare ground or short-grass areas, and, especially, winter-wheat fields along the coast.

Sprague's Pipit (*Anthus spragueii*) Three fall/winter records from Chincoteague and Henrico and Wise Counties. Possibly occurs more often than records would indicate.

Bohemian Waxwing (*Bombycilla garrulus*) Two winter records: Alexandria, February 1967, and Montgomery County, March 1975.

Cedar Waxwing (*Bombycilla cedrorum*) Uncommon to common but irregular transient and winter visitor statewide. It is locally common but an irregular breeding summer resident over much of the state. It is much more common in the western Piedmont and Mountains and Valleys than elsewhere. At least in the breeding season, it shows a preference for forests, forest edges, and residential areas with scattered trees.

Northern Shrike (*Lanius excubitor*)n Rare and irregular winter visitor with about ten records, chiefly in northern parts of the state, especially in Loudoun County.

Loggerhead Shrike (*Lanius ludovicianus*)n Declining in recent years, this shrike is now a rare to uncommon transient, local resident, and breeding summer resident, with most birds now occurring in the southern Piedmont and northern Shenandoah Valley. It appears to be virtually extirpated from the southeastern part of the state. Its habitats include cultivated or open fields with shrubby borders.

European Starling (*Sturnus vulgaris*) Abundant breeding resident statewide in residential areas and farmland.

White-eyed Vireo (*Vireo griseus*) Common transient and breeding summer resident over most of the state, but decidedly less common in northern sections west of the Blue Ridge. Over most of the state, it is a rare winter visitor, but in the Great Dismal Swamp it is found year round. It prefers dense thickets or streamside shrubbery.

Bell's Vireo (*Vireo bellii*) One record: Chesterfield County, 12 August 1962.

Blue-headed Vireo (*Vireo solitarius*) Uncommon to common transient statewide, rare winter visitor, chiefly in southern parts of the state; breeding summer resident mainly from the Blue Ridge westward, inhabiting hardwood or coniferous forests.

Yellow-throated Vireo (*Vireo flavifrons*) Uncommon transient and breeding summer resident of hardwood forests and associated swampland. Although known to breed from the Eastern Shore to the Mountains and Valleys, its actual breeding distribution is somewhat localized over the state.

Warbling Vireo (*Vireo gilvus*) Rare transient and summer visitor on the Coastal Plain; uncommon breeding summer resident in the western Piedmont and west of the Blue Ridge. It is found chiefly in riparian woodlands, especially those with large trees.

Philadelphia Vireo (*Vireo philadelphicus*) Uncommon late-spring migrant to western sections of the state, including the northern Piedmont. Uncommon fall migrant throughout.

Red-eyed Vireo (*Vireo olivaceus*) Abundant transient and breeding summer resident statewide, especially in mature hardwood forests.

Bachman's Warbler (*Vermivora bachmanii*) Four historical records: King William County, August 1892; Augusta County, 5 July 1937; Fairfax County, 8 May to 2 June 1954 and 10 to 31 May 1958.

Blue-winged Warbler (*Vermivora pinus*)n Rare to uncommon transient statewide, uncommon to rare breeding summer resident on the western

Piedmont and Mountains and Valleys, where it inhabits overgrown fields and clear-cuts or streamside shrubbery.

Golden-winged Warbler (*Vermivora chrysoptera*)✳ Rare to uncommon transient statewide. As a breeding bird, it is rare or locally uncommon west of the Blue Ridge, where it occupies abandoned fields with scattered tall saplings. Interbreeding of Blue-winged and Golden-winged Warblers occurs occasionally in the mountains.

Tennessee Warbler (*Vermivora peregrina*) Rare to uncommon spring and common fall transient, especially on the Coastal Plain; farther inland, it is an uncommon migrant.

Orange-crowned Warbler (*Vermivora celata*) Rare transient statewide and rare winter resident on Coastal Plain.

Nashville Warbler (*Vermivora ruficapilla*)n Rare to uncommon transient statewide, irregular and very rare on the Coastal Plain in winter. In summer it has been seen at high elevations in Mountains and Valleys (e.g., Augusta, Highland, and Rockingham Counties and on Mount Rogers), where it is found in shrubby forest openings and second-growth forests.

Northern Parula (*Parula americana*) Common transient and breeding summer resident statewide though patchily distributed. It inhabits swamps, bottomland forests, and riparian woodlands. Very rarely, it has been seen in winter on the Coastal Plain.

Yellow Warbler (*Dendroica petechia*) Common transient and breeding summer resident statewide, although less common on the Coastal Plain and southern Piedmont. It inhabits riparian woodlands, especially stands of willow.

Chestnut-sided Warbler (*Dendroica pensylvanica*) Common to uncommon transient statewide, fairly common breeding summer resident in the Mountains and Valleys above 2,000 feet, favoring second-growth woods and forest edges.

Magnolia Warbler (*Dendroica magnolia*)n Uncommon transient statewide. Singing birds have been observed in summer at local sites on some of the highest mountains, including Highland County, the Mountain Lake area, and in southwest Virginia at Beartown (Tazewell, Russell Counties), Whitetop, and Grayson County. Habitats may include coniferous forests or disturbed mixed coniferous/deciduous forests or second-growth deciduous forests.

Cape May Warbler (*Dendroica tigrina*) Uncommon spring and common fall transient statewide. It has been recorded rarely in winter at widely scattered points in the state.

Black-throated Blue Warbler (*Dendroica caerulescens*) Uncommon to common transient statewide, fairly common breeding summer resident in the Mountains and Valleys from Rockingham County southward. When breeding, it favors forests with a dense understory of mountain laurel or rhododendron. Several winter records are known from the Coastal Plain and Piedmont.

Yellow-rumped Warbler (*Dendroica coronata*) Uncommon to abundant transient and winter resident statewide, but most common on the lower Coastal Plain. It is by far the most common wintering warbler in the state.

Black-throated Gray Warbler (*Dendroica nigrescens*) Five records: Fairfax County, October 1949; Newport News, September 1973, 20 to 31 January and March 1974, January-April 1975.

Black-throated Green Warbler (*Dendroica virens*) Uncommon to common transient statewide. As a breeding bird, it has two disjunct populations, in the Great Dismal Swamp and locally common in the Mountains and Valleys. It prefers swamp forests or mixed coniferous/hardwood forests at high elevations.

Blackburnian Warbler (*Dendroica fusca*) Rare to uncommon transient statewide and a rare winter visitor (Coastal Plain). As a breeding bird, it is sparsely distributed in the Mountains and Valleys, where it prefers hardwood and mixed hardwood/coniferous forests.

Yellow-throated Warbler (*Dendroica dominica*)✳ Rare to uncommon transient statewide. It breeds at widely scattered points in the state, and prefers riverine hardwood or bottomland forests. Rarely, it has been found in winter (southern Coastal Plain and Piedmont).

Pine Warbler (*Dendroica pinus*) Generally a common transient and common breeding summer resident statewide, but distinctly less common in far southwestern Virginia. In winter it is irregular and uncommon, especially in southern parts of the state. It is virtually restricted to pine forests.

Kirtland's Warbler (*Dendroica kirtlandii*) This accidental species has been seen several times: Fairfax County, September and October 1887; Kerr Reservoir, September 1974; and, more recently, in Wise County, 7 to 9 May 1994 (song recorded).

Prairie Warbler (*Dendroica discolor*) Common transient and breeding summer resident statewide but somewhat less common in the northern Shenandoah Valley and southwest Virginia. It is usually found in abandoned fields with scattered saplings, woodland edges, and growths of saplings and shrubs. In winter it is rare on the Coastal Plain.

Palm Warbler (*Dendroica palmarum*) Uncommon spring and common, sometimes abundant, fall transient statewide. It is uncommon or rare in winter, found chiefly near the coast.

Bay-breasted Warbler (*Dendroica castanea*) Statewide, an uncommon transient increasingly more common westward and more common in the fall. Rarely has it been found in winter.

Blackpoll Warbler (*Dendroica striata*) Common late spring and irregularly common fall transient statewide, but decidedly less common in southwest Virginia. Extremely late migrants or non-migrants have been occasionally reported in summer at various places in the state.

Cerulean Warbler (*Dendroica cerulea*)n Uncommon transient especially away from the coast. It breeds locally in extensive hardwood forests along the Blue Ridge, northern Piedmont, and elsewhere in the Mountains and Valleys.

Black-and-white Warbler (*Mniotilta varia*) Uncommon to common transient, uncommon breeding summer resident in mature hardwood forests, and rare winter visitor on the lower Coastal Plain. In the breeding season it is decidedly more common in the Mountains and Valleys.

American Redstart (*Setophaga ruticilla*) Common transient and common to uncommon breeding summer resident statewide but much less common in the central Piedmont and on the Coastal Plain. It prefers open, disturbed hardwood forests.

Prothonotary Warbler (*Protonotaria citrea*)n Rare to uncommon transient and locally common breeding summer resident, chiefly on the Coastal Plain; elsewhere, it is spottily distributed along river systems (rare or absent in the Mountains and Valleys). In the breeding season it prefers swamps or bottomland forests.

Worm-eating Warbler (*Helmitheros vermivorus*) Uncommon to common transient and uncommon, local breeding summer resident, especially in the Mountains and Valleys and western and northern Piedmont. It breeds rarely on the southern Piedmont and Coastal Plain. In the breeding season it favors steep slopes and ravines in mature hardwood forests.

Swainson's Warbler (*Limnothlypis swainsonii*)n Rare and local transient statewide. As a breeding bird, it has two disjunct populations, in bottomland hardwood forests with cane in the Great Dismal Swamp region, and in ravines of hardwood forests with a rhododendron understory chiefly in the far western counties (Buchanan, Dickenson, Wise, Washington). In both locations, the bird is rare or uncommon.

Ovenbird (*Seiurus aurocapillus*) Common to abundant transient and common breeding summer resident statewide, its preferred habitat being hardwood forests with a well-developed understory.

Northern Waterthrush (*Seiurus noveboracensis*)✶ Uncommon to common transient statewide. In the breeding season singing birds have been seen in the Mount Rogers area and in Bath County. Breeding has been confirmed at a high elevation in Highland County. Rarely, it has been found in winter on the southern Coastal Plain and northern Piedmont.

Louisiana Waterthrush (*Seiurus motacilla*) Common transient and breeding summer resident statewide but decidedly less common on the Coastal Plain and southern Piedmont. Its habitat usually includes rocky streams in forests or swampy woodlands.

Kentucky Warbler (*Oporornis formosus*) Uncommon transient and locally common breeding summer resident over much of the state but much less common in lower Piedmont and Coastal Plain. Its habitat choice is mature hardwood forests.

Connecticut Warbler (*Oporornis agilis*) Rare late-spring migrant, especially in western parts of the state. Rare to uncommon fall transient statewide.

Mourning Warbler (*Oporornis philadelphia*)n Rare transient statewide, with summer records at high elevations in Highland, Bath, Giles, and Augusta Counties, where the birds favor blackberry thickets and cut-over, regenerating habitats. Evidence of breeding has been found in Highland and Augusta Counties.

Common Yellowthroat (*Geothlypis trichas*) Common to abundant transient and breeding summer resident statewide in dense thickets, hedgerows, and swampy shrubbery. In winter it is uncommon on the southeastern Coastal Plain and rare farther inland.

Hooded Warbler (*Wilsonia citrina*) Uncommon to common transient and breeding summer resident statewide, although less common on the Eastern Shore, central Coastal Plain, and southern Piedmont. It shows a preference for moist hardwood forests with a well-developed understory.

Wilson's Warbler (*Wilsonia pusilla*) Rare to uncommon transient statewide, but its occurrence is patchy (e.g., more common in southern than northern Mountains and Valleys). It is a very rare winter visitor on the Coastal Plain.

Canada Warbler (*Wilsonia canadensis*) Rare to uncommon transient on the Coastal Plain and Piedmont. In the Mountains and Valleys this species is an uncommon breeding summer resident, especially in high-elevation forests with a dense understory of mountain laurel or rhododendron.

Yellow-breasted Chat (*Icteria virens*) Common transient and locally common breeding summer resident statewide, although it is less common or absent from the lower Eastern Shore and the northern Mountains and Valleys. It prefers overgrown fields, brushy hillsides, or woodland edges, usually at low elevations. It is a rare winter visitor to the lower Coastal Plain and Piedmont.

Summer Tanager (*Piranga rubra*)n Uncommon to common transient and breeding summer resident, especially in southern and eastern parts of the Coastal Plain and Piedmont and far western counties. Its habitats include upland dry hardwood or pine forests. In many places, its range overlaps that of the Scarlet Tanager.

Scarlet Tanager (*Piranga olivacea*) More widespread than the Summer Tanager, this bird is a common transient and breeding summer resident statewide, although somewhat less common on the lower Piedmont and Coastal Plain. It prefers mature hardwood forests.

Western Tanager (*Piranga ludoviciana*) The dozen or so records of this accidental western species have been in spring, fall, and winter from such widely scattered points as Fairfax County, Norfolk, and Wise County. Often, these birds were at feeders.

Northern Cardinal (*Cardinalis cardinalis*) Common to abundant breeding resident statewide. It is found in forest understories, thickets, residential areas, and forest edges.

Rose-breasted Grosbeak (*Pheucticus ludovicianus*) Uncommon transient on the Piedmont and Coastal Plain. From the Blue Ridge westward, it is a common transient and breeding summer resident in mature hardwood forests at higher elevations. It has been found rarely in winter at scattered points of the state.

Black-headed Grosbeak (*Pheucticus melanocephalus*) This accidental western visitor has been seen about a dozen times at widely scattered points in the state, from Chincoteague to Charlottesville to Radford. The records indicate that it may be found at any season except mid-summer.

Blue Grosbeak (*Guiraca caerulea*) Uncommon to common transient and breeding summer resident statewide, chiefly in the Shenandoah Valley, and on the Piedmont and Coastal Plain. It prefers abandoned fields, hedgerows, brushy sites, and woodland edges. Rarely has this bird been found in winter (lower Coastal Plain and Piedmont).

Lazuli Bunting (*Passerina amoena*) This accidental western species has been found twice in the state: Newport News, 7 January to 25 February 1966, and Norfolk, 9 October 1975.

Indigo Bunting (*Passerina cyanea*) Abundant transient and breeding summer resident statewide in open sites, roadsides, overgrown fields, and other shrubby locations, from near sea level to the high mountains in suitable habitat. Rarely has it been found in winter, at widely scattered locations from Chincoteague to Warren County.

Painted Bunting (*Passerina ciris*)n A rare and irregular visitor chiefly to southern parts of the state from Newport News to Augusta County; a recent record from Goochland County. It has been seen at all seasons but chiefly in winter and spring.

Dickcissel (*Spiza americana*)✳ This bird, once a common resident, is now a rare and irregular transient and local winter visitor and summer resident in the state. It currently breeds at widely scattered points from the western Coastal Plain to the Shenandoah Valley, westward as far as Lee County. It is found in open grassy areas, including grain fields.

Green-tailed Towhee (*Pipilo chlorurus*) This accidental visitor from the west has been found in the state three times: Chesapeake, 26 January 1908; Newport News, 26 February to 22 April 1953; and Amelia, 7 to 11 April 1953.

Eastern Towhee (*Pipilo erythrophthalmus*) Common transient and breeding resident statewide but less common in winter. It prefers brushy sites, roadsides, hedgerows, and thickets.

Bachman's Sparrow (*Aimophila aestivalis*)n Formerly a rare transient and breeding summer resident in various habitats statewide; its decline in the last 50 years was probably related to habitat loss. Today it is a rare local breeder in the Piedmont (Caroline, Nottoway, Dinwiddie, Brunswick Counties) and Coastal Plain (Sussex County). Its habitats include cut-over and overgrown sites, open pine forests with sparse understory, and Loblolly Pine/grassland savannas.

American Tree Sparrow (*Spizella arborea*)n An uncommon and somewhat irregular transient and winter visitor or winter resident statewide, but more commonly found in northern and western locations. Its numbers have apparently decreased in recent years.

Chipping Sparrow (*Spizella passerina*) Common transient and breeding summer resident statewide. In winter it is less common and is chiefly restricted to southern parts of the state. Its habitats include residential areas, forest edges, and clearings.

Clay-colored Sparrow (*Spizella pallida*)n Rare fall and occasional spring transient with most records near the coast; much less common farther inland. Very rare in winter.

Field Sparrow (*Spizella pusilla*) Common transient and breeding resident statewide in abandoned or overgrown fields and hedgerows. It is less common in winter.

Vesper Sparrow (*Pooecetes gramineus*) Uncommon to common transient and winter resident statewide. It breeds uncommonly chiefly on the northern Piedmont and Mountains and Valleys, sometimes at high elevations (Highland County). It prefers pastures, meadows, and grassy fields.

Lark Sparrow (*Chondestes grammacus*)n Historically, this bird was a sporadic and rare breeder on the Piedmont and Mountains and Valleys. Today it is a rare transient and winter visitor statewide, and probably no longer breeds in the state.

Black-throated Sparrow (*Amphispiza bilineata*) This accidental western species has been found three times in the state: Norfolk, 7 October 1967; Fairfax County, 17 January to 11 April 1971; and Henrico County, 21 October 1979.

Lark Bunting (*Calamospiza melanocorys*) Five records, chiefly from Virginia Beach and Back Bay from late August to late October. One bird was found at Lexington in February 1932. Because most records were before 1972, its current status is unknown.

Savannah Sparrow (*Passerculus sandwichensis*) Uncommon to common transient and winter resident statewide, but becoming more common eastward in winter. It breeds chiefly and locally at scattered sites along the Blue Ridge and western mountains, often at high elevations in grassy or cultivated fields. In winter it is much more common in southern parts of the Coastal Plain (extensive weedy fields, sand-dunes) and Piedmont. The well-marked "Ipswich" race of this sparrow, once believed to be a distinct species, is an uncommon transient and winter resident of coastal areas (especially sand-dunes) and the lower Chesapeake Bay.

Grasshopper Sparrow (*Ammodramus savannarum*) Uncommon to locally common transient and breeding summer resident statewide, but most common on the Piedmont and valleys of the Mountains and Valleys. On the Eastern Shore and lower Coastal Plain, it is chiefly an uncommon transient.

Its habitats include short-grass pastures or hay and small-grain fields. Winter records are scarce.

Henslow's Sparrow (*Ammodramus henslowii*)n This secretive bird was formerly and locally common at various places in the state, mostly below 3,000 feet. In recent years its numbers have greatly declined so that current breeding sites of small colonies are restricted to local sites in Accomack County and the northern and southern Piedmont. Rarely has it been found in winter in the state. Its preferred habitats include wet clear-cuts, brushy fields, hayfields, cut-over areas with sapling conifers, and wet meadows. Our limited knowledge about its current distribution is at least in part due to its secretive nature.

Le Conte's Sparrow (*Ammodramus leconteii*)n Another species difficult to find, this sparrow is a rare fall transient and winter resident at widespread sites from Chincoteague to Wise County.

Saltmarsh Sharp-tailed Sparrow (*Ammodramus caudacutus*)✳ Uncommon to common transient, winter resident, and locally common breeding summer resident in salt marshes on Eastern Shore and the lower Chesapeake Bay. Elsewhere in the state, it is a rare transient and winter visitor (lower Piedmont). (**Nelson's Sharp-tailed Sparrow** [*Ammodramus nelsoni*], now recognized as a distinct species, is a coastal migrant and probably an uncommon winter resident, but its exact status here remains unclear.)

Seaside Sparrow (*Ammodramus maritimus*) Common transient and breeding summer resident in salt marshes of the Eastern Shore, the lower Chesapeake Bay, and some major river tributaries. In winter it is less common along the coast and the lower Chesapeake Bay.

Fox Sparrow (*Passerella iliaca*) Uncommon transient and somewhat irregular winter resident statewide.

Song Sparrow (*Melospiza melodia*) Common to abundant breeding resident statewide but somewhat less common in the central Coastal Plain and southern Piedmont. Its habitats include residential areas, streamside and pond thickets, and shrubby open country.

Lincoln's Sparrow (*Melospiza lincolnii*) Rare to locally uncommon transient statewide, rare winter visitor especially in the southeastern parts of the state, and occasional winter visitor elsewhere.

Swamp Sparrow (*Melospiza georgiana*)n Uncommon to common transient and winter resident statewide. Breeding has been documented in Highland County and is suspected for Fairfax, Bath, and Washington Counties. This bird prefers emergent vegetation in or near fresh to brackish marshes, and wet meadows.

White-throated Sparrow (*Zonotrichia albicollis*) Common to abundant transient and winter resident statewide. It is found in woodland thickets and edges, hedgerows, and shrubbery in residential areas. It is a rare summer visitor to widely scattered parts of the state.

White-crowned Sparrow (*Zonotrichia leucophrys*) Uncommon to common transient and irregular winter resident statewide, becoming less common in to the east and south. Its habitats include blackberry thickets, edges of large overgrown fields, and hedgerows.

Harris's Sparrow (*Zonotrichia querula*) Rare winter visitor on the Piedmont (three records, Nov-Mar) and Mountains and Valleys (7 records, Nov-May). All records date from the 1960s and 1970s.

Dark-eyed Junco (*Junco hyemalis*) Common to abundant transient and winter resident statewide. It is an uncommon to common breeding summer resident in the Mountains and Valleys above 3,000 feet. Here it chooses open forests, their edges, and roadside clearings.

Lapland Longspur (*Calcarius lapponicus*)n Uncommon and irregular transient and winter resident or visitor statewide, but much more common in northern parts of the state and on the Eastern Shore. It is most often found with Horned Larks in extensive open fields and on beaches.

Chestnut-collared Longspur (*Calcarius ornatus*) Only two records: Roanoke, 13 April 1958 and Chincoteague, 5 June 1977, the latter in breeding plumage.

Snow Bunting (*Plectrophenax nivalis*)n Rare to uncommon transient and rare to uncommon, irregular and local winter resident or visitor, chiefly in northern parts of the state. It is also found on sands and on rocky dikes on the Barrier Islands, Craney Island, and Back Bay NWR.

Bobolink (*Dolichonyx oryzivorus*)n Common transient over much of the state, where its habitats include open meadows, unmowed hay, wheat, and clover fields, and marshes. In summer it is a rare visitor or resident, locally breeding in farming areas, sometimes at high elevations, from Loudoun to Smith Counties.

Red-winged Blackbird (*Agelaius phoeniceus*) Common to abundant transient and breeding resident statewide in marshes, hayfields, roadside ditches, and wet thickets. In winter it is less common in western and northern parts, but may occur in huge flocks on the southern Coastal Plain.

Eastern Meadowlark (*Sturnella magna*) Uncommon to common breeding resident statewide in hayfields and pastures, but decreasing in recent years where development has encroached on its habitat of open country or grassy fields.

Yellow-headed Blackbird (*Xanthocephalus xanthocephalus*) Rare fall, winter, and spring transient over much of the state, especially the Eastern Shore and northern Virginia.

Rusty Blackbird (*Euphagus carolinus*) Uncommon to common transient and winter visitor statewide, but much less common in recent years.

Brewer's Blackbird (*Euphagus cyanocephalus*) Rare and local in fall, winter, and spring in pastures and farming areas throughout the Piedmont and Coastal Plain. Occasionally, it mixes with traveling flocks of other blackbirds.

Boat-tailed Grackle (*Quiscalus major*)n Common breeding resident near the coast and locally along the lower Chesapeake Bay and its major tributaries. It can be found in open woods, salt marshes, residential areas, and estuarine thickets.

Common Grackle (*Quiscalus quiscula*) Common to abundant breeding resident statewide, apparently increasing in recent years. It is found in residential areas, fields, pine forests, forest edges, and juniper groves. Although somewhat less common in winter, its winter flocks may be immense.

Brown-headed Cowbird (*Molothrus ater*) Common breeding summer resident statewide, but irregular and locally common in winter, when its flocks may be very large. Apparently increasing in numbers, it prefers forest edges, fields, and open woods. Apparently, it has increased in numbers over a wide area in recent years, especially in fragmented forest environments.

Orchard Oriole (*Icterus spurius*) Common transient and breeding summer resident statewide; very rare in winter on the Coastal Plain. It is found in roadside trees, orchards, and farmland, where it sometimes occurs with Baltimore Orioles.

Baltimore Oriole (*Icterus galbula*) Uncommon to common transient and breeding summer resident over much of the state, but nearly absent as a breeder on the Coastal Plain and southern Piedmont. Rarely, it is found in winter, with most records from the Tidewater region. It prefers streamside hardwoods, farmyards, and other open-country habitats with trees.

Bullock's Oriole (*Icterus bullockii*) This rare transient has been recorded in late fall and winter at widely scattered points from Loudoun to Lee Counties.

Pine Grosbeak (*Pinicola enucleator*) Extremely rare and erratic transient or winter visitor at scattered localities over the northern and western parts of the state, but only one record from northern Coastal Plain. The most recent record was in 1972 in Shenandoah National Park.

Purple Finch (*Carpodacus purpureus*) Irregular and uncommon to common transient and winter resident statewide. Its known or suspected breeding sites have included Highland County and Mount Rogers at high elevations, and singing males have been seen near Mountain Lake in summer. Its numbers have apparently declined in recent years. At different times of the year, it may be found in a variety of woodlands, residential areas, and high mountain forests.

House Finch (*Carpodacus mexicanus*) Common to abundant breeding resident statewide. It has increased in numbers and expanded its range rapidly in recent years. It is chiefly found in residential areas, especially at feeders with sunflowers. In some locations it shows a preference for nesting in junipers.

Red Crossbill (*Loxia curvirostra*)n Rare, irregular, and even erratic transient and winter visitor statewide, but chiefly in the Mountains and Valleys. Breeding, either known or suspected; has been reported from high elevation forests from Rockingham and Highland Counties south to Whitetop. It may be found in mixed forests but shows a preference for conifers.

White-winged Crossbill (*Loxia leucoptera*) Rare and erratic transient and winter visitor statewide, but chiefly in the Mountains and Valleys. It has not been reported since 1986. When found, it has been in mature stands of pines and Eastern Hemlock.

Common Redpoll (*Carduelis flammea*) Rare and irregular winter visitor statewide, but chiefly at northern locations, where it is sometimes found at feeders. It is more common in some winters (e.g., 1977-1978, 1993-1994) than in others.

Hoary Redpoll (*Carduelis hornemanni*) One record. A bird was visiting a feeder (photographed) in Highland County, 27 February through 1 April 1994.

Pine Siskin (*Carduelis pinus*) Irregular and rare to common transient and winter resident statewide. Its numbers vary from year to year. It has been reported breeding (or suspected to be breeding) in Fairfax, Giles, and Montgomery Counties and on Mount Rogers. Although found in a wide variety of forests and residential areas, Pine Siskins show a preference for conifers.

American Goldfinch (*Carduelis tristis*) Common to abundant breeding resident statewide, although somewhat less common as a breeder in the southern Piedmont and Coastal Plain. It may be found in overgrown fields, forest tree-tops, and residential areas.

Evening Grosbeak (*Coccothraustes vespertinus*) Irregular and rare to abundant transient and winter resident statewide, occasionally occurring in large incursions (e.g., 1977-1978, 1983-1984). Except in the incursion years, it is more numerous in western parts of the state. Summer records are known from Rockbridge and Giles Counties.

House Sparrow (*Passer domesticus*) Common to abundant breeding resident statewide in residential areas and farmland. In recent years it has shown some decrease in numbers, perhaps because of competition with House Finch.

SPECIALTIES OF VIRGINIA

by David Abbott

Here are listed a number of specialties, species that may be of particular interest for birding in Virginia. Although no bird species is unique to the state, some are rare or unusual because within Virginia they are at the northern or the southern limit of their usual ranges. We also know that abundances can vary widely according to season, geographical region, and habitat and food availability. Thus, a bird may be rare throughout the state or found only at certain localities. Still other birds occur erratically (Evening Grosbeak, Common Redpoll), present in some years in large numbers, mostly absent in other years. Further information about the specialties discussed here can be found in other specific sections of this book (the annotated checklist, the pelagic birding section, and the hawk-watching section).

A word about vagrants ("waifs," "accidentals"): Almost anywhere in the state can be productive, but certain locations are most consistent in producing rare or new birds. Examples of these locations are the Potomac River shores at Hunting Creek, the lower Chesapeake Bay, the Chesapeake Bay Bridge-Tunnel, the Eastern Shore, the Virginia Beach area, and, of course, the offshore waters. Although these species are often referred to as "accidentals," it is now thought that the appearances of at least some of these vagrants are part of a larger picture and not simply random accidents. With more observers in the field, records are accumulating, and it becomes clear that many of the occurrences are parts of patterns. The patterns are several and can be catalogued as disorientation (as an immature in fall, for example), spring overshoot, post-breeding dispersal, or cyclic winter invasions. Several species, including several pelagic birds, are now proving to be regular and annual in occurrence.

The interested visiting birder is encouraged to explore relatively less birded areas, including the northwest sections such as Highland County and surrounding areas, the Cumberland region of extreme southwest Virginia, and anywhere along the Virginia/North Carolina boundary. Also, during October and November try the southern part of the Eastern Shore, the Chesapeake Bay Bridge-Tunnel, and False Cape State Park. By exploring Virginia's many varied habitats, a birder here can nearly always see something interesting at almost any time of the year. The rewards of exploring can be exciting!

Pelagic species—See the section on "Pelagic Birding in Virginia" for details on pelagic birds and on trips to find birds that are only rarely seen from shore. Only recently, birds such as Manx Shearwater, Band-rumped Storm-Petrel, and South Polar Skua have proved to be regular in season at Virginia's offshore canyons. In terms of success or failure in finding birds offshore, environmental factors such as weather, currents, food availability, water temperature, Gulf Stream eddies, and salinity can all be important.

Land-based observers can see Sooty Shearwaters reliably in May and June from Back Bay NWR, whereas Wilson's Storm-Petrel is regularly seen in summer from the Chesapeake Bay Bridge-Tunnel and from the shores of the southern Chesapeake Bay. Northern Gannets are regularly seen from shore all along the Atlantic coast and the southern Chesapeake Bay from November to March. Especially following strong easterly winds and "northeasters," rare birds have turned up along the beaches: shearwaters, petrels, alcids, and gulls. During these conditions vantage points include Back Bay NWR, Fort Story in Virginia Beach, Chesapeake Bay Bridge-Tunnel, and Chincoteague NWR. Inland lakes should also be checked for pelagic species immediately after the passage through interior Virginia of a hurricane or a major tropical storm.

Pelicans—Brown Pelicans have been regular and easily seen in the summer since the dramatic incursion of 1982. The nesting colony on Fisherman Island has been increasing in size in recent years. Now look for this conspicuous species at Virginia Beach, CBBT, along the Eastern Shore as far north as Chincoteague NWR, and along most Chesapeake Bay shorelines. Rarely, it has been found inland. The much-less-common American White Pelican has increasingly become a regular rare winter visitor to the Eastern Shore. A few usually turn up in late fall at Chincoteague NWR. Also look for one or more at the southern end of the Delmarva Peninsula (Cape Charles) and at Virginia Beach.

Great Cormorant—Virtually guaranteed during winter along the CBBT. It also occurs irregularly farther south along the immediate coast and the lower Chesapeake Bay and its main tributaries.

Anhinga—Your chances of finding an Anhinga are fairly good during the summer at Stumpy Lake in Virginia Beach, the Great Dismal Swamp, or along the Virginia/North Carolina boundary west to Greensville County. Elsewhere it is of casual occurrence.

White Ibis—A few breed on inaccessible Fisherman Island, but post-breeding birds wander in late summer to marshes, ponds, lakes, and rivers over the state. Good spots for those hoping to see one are Chincoteague NWR, Back Bay, and False Cape.

Tundra Swan—The winter home for the Tundra Swan in Virginia is chiefly the Chesapeake Bay. As flocks move around in late fall and early spring, look for them on the lower bay as well as on inland reservoirs, lakes, and major rivers—for example, the Potomac. Swans may also be found in fields with geese, as well as flying over northern Virginia.

Mute Swan—This resident and occasional breeder is common on the Coastal Plain and Eastern Shore. Pairs are always present at Chincoteague NWR.

Greater White-fronted Goose—A rarity, to be looked for in all migrating flocks of Canada Geese, especially in the eastern Coastal Plain and Piedmont.

Ross's Goose—A rarity but increasing in recent years largely due to the increased vigilance of birders. It has become regular in winter among huge winter flocks of Snow Geese at Back Bay NWR. Other recent records come from Chincoteague NWR and adjacent locations. A word of caution: Ross's and Snow Geese are known to hybridize; close scrutiny is necessary to identify the hybrids.

Eurasian Wigeon—Rare, but it regularly winters along the Eastern Shore, especially where large numbers of American Wigeon are found. It has wintered in Surry County near Hog Island and has passed through Chincoteague NWR and Craney Island during migration.

Sea Ducks—An excellent and reliable spot to see eiders, scoters, and Harlequin Ducks is the CBBT in winter. King and Common Eiders are present most years, and sometimes small flocks winter here. Harlequin Duck winters in small numbers virtually every year along the CBBT. As with the eiders, nearly all birds found here are either young-of-the-year or second-year birds. Also try Fort Story and Rudee Inlet, both in Virginia Beach.

All three scoter species (Black, Surf, and White-winged) winter along the CBBT but may be seen anywhere along the coast from Chincoteague NWR to Back Bay NWR. Large migrating flocks occur along the Atlantic coast during October and November. Surf Scoter is the most common of the three in Virginia. Inland, though, White-winged Scoter is the most likely. Inland, look for migrating scoters on ponds, lakes, reservoirs, and rivers. Almost any large pond or lake has potential during migration. Scoters (mostly Surfs) also winter all along the coasts of the southern Chesapeake Bay, along with Oldsquaws.

Other Waterfowl—Waterfowl in numbers can often be seen during fall migration on nearly any large pond/lake/reservoir. Among the largest in Virginia are Kerr Reservoir, Smith Mountain Lake, Lake Anna, Claytor Lake, Gaston Lake, and Philpott Reservoir, but virtually any suitable pond during migration can be worth a check. Checking bodies of water following the passage of warm or cold fronts or other drastic weather changes, when birds are grounded, can be very productive. Chincoteague NWR is a good place to study dabbling and some diving ducks. Hunting Creek near Alexandria and Hog Island near Richmond are other excellent locations that offer good opportunities and many varieties. Thousands of waterfowl winter on the tidal Rappahannock River. Atlantic Ocean and Chesapeake Bay coastal waters provide excellent views of wintering sea and bay ducks.

Swallow-tailed Kite—You would be fortunate to see this southern species in Virginia. Look for it in spring in the Back Bay NWR vicinity or the Great Dismal Swamp. Other recent sightings have been made in late May in extreme southern Greensville County along the Virginia/North Carolina boundary.

Mississippi Kite—Once considered to be a vagrant (and still rare throughout the state), the Mississippi Kite is either expanding its range or we are just now learning how to find it. It probably breeds in southern Greensville County. During August 1995 near Woodbridge, a recently fledged bird was observed by many people as it was repeatedly fed by an adult. A nest with young was found in 1996. Still, your best chance for seeing this kite would come from driving patiently along the secondary roads of Greensville and Southampton Counties in June or July. Most sightings have been along Route 730 (Low Ground Road) near the Meherrin River. Most of this territory is private property, so please observe the "No Trespassing" signs.

Bald Eagle—This eagle now breeds along major tidewater rivers, near the Chesapeake Bay, and even on some inland lakes. In winter look for it along the Potomac, Rappahannock, and James Rivers. Fall migrants are regularly recorded by hawk-watching stations.

Rough-legged Hawk—Look for this bird in winter in Loudoun County and points west and south to Monterey. It is less likely near the coast, but checking all candidates around Saxis Marsh, Kiptopeke, and Craney Island would be worth your while. Scattered Rough-legs also occur uncommonly on the Piedmont in most winters, south to the James River.

Golden Eagle—Although Golden Eagles have been seen in every month, they are more common in fall migration and winter. The major hawk-watching stations along the Blue Ridge and at Kiptopeke usually report several each fall. The most reliable place to see one is probably the Blue Grass Valley in Highland County, where a few birds winter regularly.

Peregrine Falcon—Because of a successful re-introduction program, breeding pairs are now present at a few places along the coast, on tall buildings in major cities, at big bridges in southeastern Virginia, and at a few mountain sites. As a fall migrant, Peregrines are reasonably common along the Eastern Shore (Kiptopeke State Park and Eastern Shore of Virginia NWR).

Black Rail—You are likely only to hear this bird at Saxis Marsh (Accomack County) during May and June. A few lucky people have seen it in migration in other marshes of coastal areas. Formerly, it was rarely found in freshwater marshes in the Mountains and Valleys, and these marshes (Roanoke, Blacksburg) should be checked again.

Clapper Rail—Salt marshes of the Barrier Islands, the Eastern Shore, the Chesapeake Bay, and its major tributaries are home to the Clapper Rail. It is common in spring, summer, and fall, but uncommon in winter in these areas. Sometimes it is encountered during migration along the CBBT. Best bets are Chincoteague NWR and Saxis Marsh.

King Rail—A common but extremely local summer resident in fresh and brackish marshes. Migrants can sometimes be heard passing over at night almost anywhere in the Piedmont, and over the Coastal Plain during April. It is common at Back Bay NWR and fairly easy to find at Huntley Meadows Park (Fairfax County). This rail also breeds in marshes along the Rappahannock and other Coastal Plain rivers.

Shorebirds—Suitable shorebird habitat varies from year to year, depending on rainfall, the relative heat of the summer, or even the whims of refuge managers. In summer drought conditions, good shorebird habitat can be found along ponds and lakes anywhere in the state. Almost anything can turn up during migration times, and at those times it pays to stop and investigate any possible habitat anywhere in the state. From mid-August to late October is the best time, but do not pass up July, which can produce some exciting shorebirds. Probably the most productive shorebird spot in the state at the moment is Craney Island (the management's strict rules must be closely followed). Curlew Sandpipers, Ruffs, and godwits have been regular at Craney Island. Other great shorebird spots are Chincoteague NWR (a Sharp-tailed Sandpiper and a recent Bar-tailed Godwit), Hog Island, and Hunting Creek in Fairfax County (two Sharp-tailed Sandpiper sightings). Hunting Creek is remarkable for its variety and is the best place in northern Virginia for Baird's Sandpiper, both dowitchers, and Wilson's Phalarope; even godwits and American Avocet have appeared. Inland, always check any suitable farm pond or sewage treatment plant.

American Golden-Plover—This species is rare from late March to May along the coast with a few inland records, too. Following cold fronts and rainstorms, check any sod farm or fallow pasture area throughout the Piedmont, Coastal Plain, and Eastern Shore. Sod farms near Dulles International Airport have also been productive.

Wilson's Plover—Although fairly common in summer, this plover is found chiefly on the Barrier Islands, to which human access is restricted. Look for it in late summer along the lower Chesapeake Bay and the coast from Cape Henry south to Back Bay NWR.

Piping Plover—Also mostly found in summer on the Barrier Islands. Transients are most likely to be seen along the coast and the lower Chesapeake Bay. The species can also be found during the breeding season on Craney Island, but all breeding areas are off-limits to human traffic. Still, while avoiding the roped-off breeding areas, you may see one or two Piping Plovers along some of the unrestricted dikes.

Black-necked Stilt—Its abundance is variable from year to year; during some years there are several, though other years may have none. During summer your best bets are along the causeway to Chincoteague and at Craney Island.

American Avocet—Try any coastal impoundment or salt-marsh edge around Chincoteague NWR or Craney Island from October to December or April and May. Rare elsewhere in the state.

Upland Sandpiper—This uncommon migrant has been seen from the northern Shenandoah Valley and the Piedmont to the Eastern Shore. Among the most reliable breeding sites are the rolling pasture lands around Lucketts in Loudoun County, east of Berryville, and in northern Rockingham County. In August it is worthwhile to stop and check the NASA grounds along Route 175 west of the Chincoteague causeway.

Marbled Godwit—One of the best spots in the state for this rarity is the harbor in the little fishing village of Oyster in Northampton County from October to March. Check it at low tide, and also plan to check nearby Willis Harbor.

Purple Sandpiper—The best place in Virginia to see this species is along the CBBT islands from November to May. They may also be seen in small numbers during the same period on jetties and rocky sea walls at Rudee Inlet, Virginia Beach, and Craney Island.

Buff-breasted Sandpiper—Look for this bird from mid-August into October along the Eastern Shore, but inland generally not before early September. Good places are Chincoteague NWR, fields along US-13 between Chincoteague and Cape Charles, and fields around Oyster, Cape Charles, and Kiptopeke. On September days, try the sod and turf farms near Ashburn and Waxpool in Loudoun County, or the hydrilla mats in Hunting Creek.

Little Gull—To determine your chances of seeing a Little Gull, all you have to do is calculate the numbers of Bonaparte's Gulls; the more the better. Little Gulls will often be present December to March from Fort Story to Back Bay NWR and in the lower Chesapeake Bay when Bonaparte's are plentiful. When thousands of Bonaparte's are present, Littles can reach double-digits. It pays to watch migrating Bonaparte's which stop on inland lakes and ponds.

Iceland, Glaucous, and Lesser Black-backed Gulls—Look for these birds from December into April in the eastern portions of the state and offshore. Lesser Black-backed is by far the most likely of the trio. Search among Herring Gulls. Try landfills, Hunting Creek, Four Mile Run, Atlantic beaches (especially Back Bay NWR), CBBT, and Fort Story.

Gull-billed Tern—An uncommon summer resident, this tern can be found mainly along Atlantic coastal marshes and farm fields. Look for it at Chincoteague NWR, Craney Island, and Back Bay NWR.

Sandwich Tern—The best places to see this uncommon summer resident, other than on the inaccessible Barrier Islands, are Craney Island, the lower Chesapeake Bay, and Back Bay NWR.

Alcids—Dovekie, Razorbill, and Atlantic Puffin are uncommon and very local offshore from January to March as far south as Back Bay. Offshore trips in February can produce these....and maybe a murre. Dovekies and Razorbills sometimes show up in mid-winter along the CBBT and at Rudee Inlet.

Owls—If your visit is during winter and you have called the various bird lines for recent sightings, you have probably noticed that usually there are few records of wintering owls, with the exception of

Short-eared and Snowy Owls. These and other species of owls are hard to find. Search for Long-eared Owls in groves of conifers in northern Virginia and the northern Piedmont. Saw-whet breeds, or probably breeds, at several high-elevation sites in our western mountains (Highland, Bath, Alleghany, Russell, and Washington Counties). Both Long-eared and Northern Saw-whet Owls should be looked for in winter among the extensive pine tracts at Chincoteague NWR and southern Assateague Island. If a Snowy Owl has been seen, the sighting will probably be mentioned on one or both of the Virginia bird lines. Although decidedly irregular in occurrence, this species can show up anywhere from November to March. As for Short-eared Owls, in winter Short-ears may be seen occasionally over salt marshes of the Eastern Shore south to Back Bay. Sometimes on late winter afternoons they have been noted in Loudoun and Prince William Counties at airports, and down the Shenandoah Valley to the Staunton region near or over fallow fields.

Red-headed Woodpecker—The best chance for seeing this uncommon and local bird is on the Coastal Plain around Williamsburg in dead trees or snags, especially in flooded timberland. Sky Meadows and Huntley Meadows parks and Mason Neck are reliable northern Virginia sites.

Red-cockaded Woodpecker—This endangered bird may be found by driving the roads through extensive pine forests in Sussex and Southampton Counties at dawn and dusk while listening for their distinctive call. Most of the land there is private property.

Willow Flycatcher—Uncommon and local summer resident in the willows or alders around the edges of marshes and ponds in the Mountains and Valleys and northern Piedmont; often associated with Yellow Warbler. The numerous reliable sites include Dyke Marsh in Alexandria, the Lucketts area of Loudoun County, Goose Creek Valley near Montvale, Bedford County, and the Mount Rogers area, Smyth/Grayson/Washington Counties. Inquiries to local birders should be made to find the site nearest to you.

Common Raven—It should be easy to find a raven at any season along the Skyline Drive (Shenandoah National Park) and from any number of overlooks along the Blue Ridge Parkway and on ridges west of the Shenandoah Valley. At times, it can also be found along the western Piedmont and in the Shenandoah Valley.

Black-capped Chickadee—Common resident in the highlands from Shenandoah County south to Mount Rogers. Observe birds carefully and listen to their songs because hybrids with Carolina Chickadees have been reported from many locations, especially along the flanks of the western mountains. Irregular winter observations have been reported from northern Virginia and southward into the central Piedmont.

Brown-headed Nuthatch—Locally common in pinelands along the North Carolina boundary as far west as Henry County. A good spot in all seasons is the area around Kerr Reservoir, especially Palmer Point and North Bend Park (near the Dam). Also good is Occoneechee State Park just east of Clarksville and Stumpy Lake. On the Eastern Shore your best bet is the Wildlife Drive or the Pony Trail at Chincoteague NWR.

Bewick's Wren—Although this wren was once widespread over the state, it may no longer breed here, but it may still persist in the southwestern mountains. If you feel like exploring, try the open, high-elevation areas from Alleghany County south to Grayson County and westward to the Kentucky state line. Report any sightings immediately to the bird line.

Sedge Wren—It has been known to breed irregularly at Saxis Marsh. Back Bay NWR is the best spot in the state in late fall and winter. It may also winter occasionally around Tom's Cove at Chincoteague NWR.

Northern Shrike—This rare, unpredictable winter visitor has been found chiefly in open country in the northern third of the state. Try, for example, open fields in the Lucketts area of Loudoun County.

Loggerhead Shrike—It may still be found reliably in a few rural areas in the Piedmont and Southern sections, as well as in the Shenandoah Valley, in the Kerr Reservoir area, and in the Holston River Valley in the southwest. The closer you get to North Carolina, the better. Also, try Lucketts, Gleedsville, and other suitable locations in Loudoun County, as well as the Nokesville area in Prince William County and Louisa County. As you drive, scan the hedgerows, power lines, and fences.

Vireos and Warblers—Most of the state offers excellent opportunities to see migrants. Both spring and fall offer good chances to see the more common migrants and breeders, and a mid-May morning with a low cloud-ceiling following a southern weather front can be very rewarding. Spring migrants can occur just about anywhere, but some of the best areas are oak woodlands just as the leaves are forming and the catkins (flowers) are fully developed. It is easiest to find just the right stage of development on forest service roads in the mountains, such as Warbler Road, but avoid areas in the north being sprayed to control Gypsy Moths. There are still plenty of areas in the Northern Virginia Piedmont worth exploring, as well as the Great Dismal Swamp NWR (spring) and Kiptopeke State Park (fall).

Blue-winged and Golden-winged Warblers and their hybrids—Both species are rare to uncommon statewide migrants with breeding confined mostly to the Mountains and Valleys at moderate to high elevations. They prefer to nest in young clear-cuts and regenerating fields. "Brewster's" Warbler has been seen as a migrant and also paired with a Blue-wing; "Lawrence's" Warbler is a rare migrant.

Nashville Warbler—Although a rare or uncommon migrant statewide, in summer Nashvilles have been seen at high-elevation sites in Augusta, Highland, Rockingham, and Smyth Counties, where breeding needs to be documented. Look for it in forest openings or second-growth forests.

Magnolia Warbler—As a migrant, this warbler is widespread over the state. Its occurrence in summer, however, is confined to high-elevation sites from Highland to Grayson County, where breeding, or suspected breeding, takes place in disturbed forest sites. Look for it especially in patches of second-growth deciduous forests.

Yellow-throated Warbler—Fairly common along river bottoms, especially in sycamores, in the Piedmont north to Great Falls Park (Fairfax County) and Coastal Plain (for example, along the James and Rappahannock Rivers). It is much less common in the mountains, but look for it on pine bluffs in southwest Virginia, such as those at Breaks Interstate Park.

Cerulean Warbler—Look for this bird among the tall deciduous trees of the Shenandoah Valley and the Blue Ridge Mountains, particularly near rivers and stretches of mature hardwood forests.

Prothonotary Warbler—A southern specialty of swamps and wooded floodplains, this species is most common as a breeder and migrant on the Coastal Plain but is less common along rivers into the western Piedmont (James and Potomac Rivers).

Swainson's Warbler—Your best chances to see this bird are along Washington and Jericho Ditches in the Great Dismal Swamp, where it is a common breeder, and at Breaks Interstate Park in Dickenson County. Great Falls National Park (Fairfax County) has had several records over the years, with the most recent one being two singing birds present for nearly two months during the summer of 1995. Another western locale to try Lee County, where the extensive rhododendron thickets near Lake Keokee and Cumberland Gap National Historical Park can be productive.

Northern Waterthrush—An uncommon migrant statewide along standing or slow-flowing water, it is a very rare nester at high elevations (above 3,500 feet) in a few locations. Look for it in northwestern Highland County and Grayson Highlands Recreation Area.

Mourning Warbler—Migrants are seen at widely scattered locations in the state. Try to find birds during the breeding season at the high elevations of Augusta, Bath, and Highland Counties. They seem to prefer open woods or wood margins with extensive thickets, especially regenerating montane forests with blackberry thickets. These are successional habitats, so the birds may not be in the same areas from year to year. Some reliable areas have been located along Forest Road 55 near the summit of Paddy's Knob.

Summer Tanager—A southern specialty that is most common along the lower Coastal Plain and Piedmont, where it prefers open woodlands. Good spots for breeders are Seashore State Park in Virginia Beach, parks along the Kerr Reservoir, and in Charlotte County along the Staunton River.

Painted Bunting—This rare southern specialty has been found at almost any season, mostly in the southern one-third of the state. Specific locations are not predictable, so follow sightings on the bird lines.

Dickcissel—This bird can probably be found somewhere in the state every breeding season. It is attracted to places which emulate its typical prairie habitat, such as extensive weedy hay or grain fields. It is regularly found during the summer in the Shenandoah Valley and on the Coastal Plain.

In winter the bird may turn up in farmland following a heavy snow, often in company with House Sparrows.

Bachman's Sparrow—This specialized bird of southern pine savannas seems to prefer fields of 3 to 6 feet tall pine seedlings and broomsedge in this, the northernmost part of its current range. It can be found in one of these successional habitats for only a few years, before the habitat becomes unsuitable for it. Listen for its distinctive song at dawn and dusk along county roads through the right habitat in Brunswick, Dinwiddie, Sussex, and Greensville Counties. Be aware that most of this property is private.

American Tree Sparrow—From Thanksgiving Day through mid-March, look for this sparrow in weedy fields and thicket borders of woods in northern parts of the state, such as near the Potomac River in Fairfax and Loudoun Counties. In some winters, it moves farther southward and can become fairly common in other parts of the state.

Clay-colored Sparrow—Your best locations for seeing this bird are coastal sections of Accomack County (Chincoteague NWR), Northampton County (Wise Point, Eastern Shore NWR, Kiptopeke State Park), the CBBT islands, Back Bay NWR, and False Cape State Park). The best month is October.

Lark Sparrow—Comments for the Clay-colored also apply for the Lark Sparrow, except that the Lark is an earlier migrant (from August on). Look among the grassy dunes of Chincoteague NWR and Assateague Island, the CBBT islands, and Back Bay NWR.

Henslow's Sparrow—A secretive bird, Henslow's Sparrow is often difficult to find. Nighttime, as well as dawn and dusk, are best for locating singing males. From May to July try Saxis Marsh on the Eastern Shore and weedy meadows, predominately in broomsedge, throughout the Coastal Plain and Piedmont. As with Bachman's, breeding sites may change from year to year.

Le Conte's Sparrow—Recently, Le Conte's has proven to be a regular winter visitor to wet grassy meadows, predominantly broomsedge, to extreme southeastern Virginia, especially Back Bay NWR. Sometimes recorded in October on the CBBT islands.

Saltmarsh Sharp-tailed Sparrow—Uncommon to common transient in Atlantic coast and Chesapeake Bay salt marshes and rare in inland marshes. It breeds locally in a few salt marshes; try Chincoteague NWR, the Saxis area, and Grandview Beach. (**Nelson's Sharp-tailed Sparrow** [Ammodramus nelsoni] is a spring and fall migrant and a probable uncommon winter resident through the coastal areas, but its exact status remains unclear.)

Swamp Sparrow—To find this rare bird during the breeding season, try the marshes at high elevations of Bath, Highland, and Washington Counties or even eastern Fairfax County, where it is believed to nest.

Lapland Longspur—Look for this longspur from Thanksgiving Day to early March, often in flocks of American Pipits and Horned Larks, from northern sections of the state to the Eastern Shore. Try the Lucketts area (Loudoun County), Calmes Neck, Northampton County, and the CBBT islands. Listen for their distinctive notes as flocks pass overhead. After heavy snows, they often show up in barnyards and feedlots in flocks of Horned Larks.

Snow Bunting—Look for small flocks of these tundra birds in extensive flat fields or barren areas from November through March. They are often seen on sand-dunes on the Eastern Shore or at Back Bay NWR, at Craney Island, or around the shoreline of large reservoirs such as Lake Anna or Kerr Reservoir. Snow Buntings can also be found in mixed flocks with longspurs, pipits, and Horned Larks.

Bobolink—In addition to being a common transient in the state, Bobolinks breed locally in grain fields, often at high elevations, at widely scattered sites from Loudoun and Clarke Counties to Highland and Tazewell (Burkes Garden) Counties.

Boat-tailed Grackle—A year-round resident of salt marsh environs all along the Atlantic coast and the lower Chesapeake Bay; also check residential areas and estuarine thickets near Chincoteague NWR, the north toll booths of the CBBT, Back Bay NWR, and coastal Mathews County.

Red Crossbill—Virginia has a resident population on Shenandoah Mountain in Highland County. Near the top on Route 250 is always worth checking where, in winter, the birds can sometimes be seen coming to the road for grit. Elsewhere in the state, crossbills can be seen with some degree of regularity in the higher mountains from Highland County to Mount Rogers and Whitetop and erratically in winter at widely scattered points of the Piedmont and Coastal Plain.

OTHER ANIMALS OF VIRGINIA

BUTTERFLIES OF VIRGINIA

Paul A. Opler [1]

Pipevine Swallowtail (*Battus philenor*). Common, statewide.
Zebra Swallowtail (*Eurytides marcellus*). Common, statewide.
Black Swallowtail (*Papilio polyxenes*). Common, statewide.
Giant Swallowtail (*Papilio cresphontes*). Uncommon, statewide.
Eastern Tiger Swallowtail (*Papilio glaucus*). Common, statewide.
Spicebush Swallowtail (*Papilio troilus*). Common, statewide.
Palamedes Swallowtail (*Papilio palamedes*). Common, Coastal Plain.
Checkered White (*Pontia protodice*). Uncommon, statewide.
West Virginia White (*Pieris virginiensis*). Uncommon, Mountains and Valleys.
Cabbage White (*Pieris rapae*). Very common, introduced.
Great Southern White (*Ascia monuste*). Rare, statewide.
Olympia Marble (*Euchloe olympia*). Uncommon, Mountains and Valleys.
Falcate Orangetip (*Anthocharis midea*). Common, statewide.
Clouded Sulphur (*Colias philodice*). Common, statewide.
Orange Sulphur (*Colias eurytheme*). Common, statewide.
Pink-edged Sulphur (*Colias interior*). Rare, Mountains and Valleys.
Southern Dogface (*Colias cesonia*). Rare, statewide.
Cloudless Sulphur (*Phoebis sennae*). Rare, statewide.
Orange-barred Sulphur (*Phoebis philea*). Rare, vagrant.
Barred Yellow (*Eurema daira*). Rare, vagrant.
Little Yellow (*Eurema lisa*). Uncommon, statewide.
Sleepy Orange (*Eurema nicippe*). Uncommon, statewide.
Dainty Sulphur (*Nathalis iole*). Rare, vagrant.
Harvester (*Feniseca tarquinius*). Uncommon, statewide.
American Copper (*Lycaena phlaeas*). Common, statewide.
Great Purple Hairstreak (*Atlides halesus*). Uncommon, Coastal Plain.
Coral Hairstreak (*Satyrium titus*). Common, statewide.
Edwards' Hairstreak (*Satyrium edwardsii*). Uncommon, Mountains and Valleys.
Banded Hairstreak (*Satyrium calanus*). Common, statewide.
Hickory Hairstreak (*Satyrium caryaevorum*). Uncommon, statewide.
King's Hairstreak (*Satyrium kingi*). Rare, Coastal Plain.
Striped Hairstreak (*Satyrium liparops*). Uncommon, statewide.
Southern Hairstreak (*Satyrium favonius*). Uncommon, statewide.
Brown Elfin (*Callophrys augustinus*). Uncommon, statewide.
Hoary Elfin (*Callophrys polios*). Rare, Mountains and Valleys.
Frosted Elfin (*Callophrys irus*). Rare, statewide.
Henry's Elfin (*Callophrys henrici*). Uncommon, statewide.
Eastern Pine Elfin. (*Callophrys niphon*). Common, statewide.
Juniper Hairstreak (*Callophrys gryneus*). Common, statewide.

1   3354 Valley Oak Dr., Loveland, CO 80358-8921

Hessel's Hairstreak (*Callophrys hesseli*). Rare, southeastern Coastal Plain.
White M Hairstreak (*Parrhasius m-album*). Rare, statewide.
Gray Hairstreak (*Strymon melinus*). Common, statewide.
Red-banded Hairstreak (*Calycopis cecrops*). Common, statewide.
Early Hairstreak (*Erora laeta*). Rare, Mountains and Valleys.
Eastern Tailed-Blue (*Everes comyntas*). Common, statewide.
Spring Azure (*Celastrina ladon*). Common, statewide.
Appalachian Azure (*Celastrina neglectamajor*). Uncommon, Mountains and Valleys.
Dusky Azure (*Celastrina nigra* [=*ebinina*]). Uncommon, Mountains and Valleys.
Silvery Blue (*Glaucopsyche lygdamus*). Uncommon, Mountains and Valleys.
Little Metalmark (*Calephelis virginiensis*). Rare, southeastern Coastal Plain.
Northern Metalmark (*Calephelis borealis*). Rare, Mountains and Valleys.
American Snout (*Libytheana carinenta*). Uncommon, statewide.
Gulf Fritillary (*Agraulis vanillae*). Rare, statewide.
Variegated Fritillary (*Euptoieta claudia*). Uncommon, statewide.
Diana Fritillary (*Speyeria diana*). Uncommon, Mountains and Valleys.
Great Spangled Fritillary (*Speyeria cybele*). Common, statewide.
Aphrodite Fritillary (*Speyeria aphrodite*). Common, statewide.
Regal Fritillary (*Speyeria idalia*). Extirpated in Virginia.
Atlantis Fritillary (*Speyeria atlantis*). Rare, Mountains and Valleys.
Silver-bordered Fritillary (*Boloria selene*). Rare, Mountains and Valleys.
Meadow Fritillary (*Boloria bellona*). Common, statewide.
Gorgone Checkerspot (*Chylosyne gorgone*). Extirpated in Virginia.
Pearl Crescent (*Phyciodes tharos*). Common, statewide.
Northern Crescent (*Phyciodes selenis*). Rare, Mountains and Valleys.
Tawny Crescent (*Phyciodes batesii*). Extirpated in Virginia.
Baltimore Checkerspot (*Euphydryas phaeton*). Uncommon, statewide.
Question Mark (*Polygonia interrogationis*). Common, statewide.
Eastern Comma (*Polygonia comma*). Common, statewide.
Green Comma (*Polygonia faunus*). Rare, Mountains and Valleys.
Gray Comma (*Polygonia progne*). Uncommon, Mountains and Valleys.
Mourning Cloak (*Nymphalis antiopa*). Common, statewide.
American Lady (*Vanessa virginiensis*). Common, statewide.
Painted Lady (*Vanessa cardui*). Uncommon, statewide.
Red Admiral (*Vanessa atalanta*). Common, statewide.
Common Buckeye (*Junonia coenia*). Uncommon, statewide.
Red-spotted Purple (*Limenitis arthemis*). Common, statewide.
Viceroy (*Limenitis archippus*). Common, statewide.
Goatweed Leafwig (*Anaea andria*). Rare, Mountains and Valleys.
Hackberry Emperor (*Asterocampa celtis*). Uncommon, statewide.
Tawny Emperor (*Asterocampa clyton*). Uncommon, statewide.
Southern Pearly-Eye (*Enodia portlandia*). Uncommon, southeastern Coastal Plain.
Northern Pearly-Eye (*Enodia anthedon*). Uncommon, statewide.
Creole Pearly-Eye (*Enodia creola*). Uncommon, southeastern Coastal Plain.
Appalachian Brown (*Satyrodes appalachia*). Common, statewide.
Gemmed Satyr (*Cyllopsis gemma*). Uncommon, statewide.
Carolina Satyr (*Hermeuptychia sosybius*). Rare, statewide.
Georgia Satyr (*Neonympha areolata*). Rare, Coastal Plain.
Little Wood-Satyr (*Megisto cymela*). Common, statewide.

Common Wood-Nymph (*Cercyonis pegala*). Common, statewide.
Monarch (*Danaus plexippus*). Common, statewide.
Silver-spotted Skipper (*Epargyreus clarus*). Common, statewide.
Long-tailed Skipper (*Urbanus proteus*). Rare, statewide.
Golden-banded Skipper (*Autochton cellus*). Rare, statewide.
Hoary Edge (*Achalarus lyciades*). Uncommon, statewide.
Northern Cloudywing (*Thorybes pylades*). Common, statewide.
Southern Cloudywing (*Thorybes bathyllus*). Common, statewide.
Confused Cloudywing (*Thorybes confusis*). Rare, statewide.
Hayhurst's Scallopwing (*Staphylus mazans*). Uncommon, statewide.
Dreamy Duskywing (*Erynnis icelus*). Common, statewide.
Sleepy Duskywing (*Erynnis brizo*). Common, statewide.
Juvenal's Duskywing (*Erynnis juvenalis*). Common, statewide.
Horace's Duskywing (*Erynnis horatius*). Common, statewide.
Columbine Duskywing (*Erynnis lucilius*). Rare, Mountains and Valleys.
Wild Indigo Duskywing (*Erynnis baptisiae*). Common, statewide.
Persius Duskywing (*Erynnis persius*). Rare, Mountains and Valleys.
Grizzled Skipper (*Pyrgus centaureae*). Rare, statewide.
Common Checkered-Skipper (*Pyrgus communis*). Common, statewide.
Common Sootywing (*Pholisora catullus*). Common, statewide.
Swarthy Skipper (*Nastra lherminier*). Common, statewide.
Clouded Skipper (*Lerema accius*). Uncommon, statewide.
Least Skipper (*Ancyloxypha numitor*). Common, statewide.
European Skipper (*Thymelicus lineola*). Introduced, Mountains and Valleys.
Fiery Skipper (*Hylephila phyleus*). Uncommon, statewide.
Leonard's Skipper (*Hesperia leonardus*). Uncommon, statewide.
Cobweb Skipper (*Hesperia metea*). Uncommon, statewide.
Dotted Skipper (*Hesperia attalus*). Rare, Piedmont.
Indian Skipper (*Hesperia sassacus*). Uncommon, Mountains and Valleys.
Peck's Skipper (*Polites peckius*). Common, statewide.
Tawny-edged Skipper (*Polites themistocles*). Common, statewide.
Crossline Skipper (*Polites origenes*). Common, statewide.
Long Dash (*Polites mystic*). Rare, Mountains and Valleys.
Southern Broken-Dash (*Wallengrenia otho*). Uncommon, southeastern Coastal Plain.
Northern Broken-Dash (*Wallengrenia egeremet*). Common, statewide.
Little Glassywing (*Pompeius verna*). Common, statewide.
Sachem (*Atalopedes campestris*). Common, statewide.
Delaware Skipper (*Anatrytone logan*). Uncommon, statewide.
Rare Skipper (*Problema bulenta*). Rare, Coastal Plain.
Hobomok Skipper (*Poanes hobomok*). Uncommon, statewide.
Zabulon Skipper (*Poanes zabulon*). Rare, statewide.
Aaron's Skipper (*Poanes aaroni*). Uncommon, Coastal Plain.
Yehl Skipper (*Poanes yehl*). Rare, southeastern Coastal Plain.
Broad-winged Skipper (*Poanes viator*). Common, statewide.
Palatka Skipper (*Euphyes pilatka*). Rare, southeastern Coastal Plain.
Dion Skipper (*Euphyes dion*). Rare, statewide.
Dukes' Skipper (*Euphyes dukesi*). Rare, southeastern Coastal Plain.
Black Dash (*Euphyes conspicua*). Rare, Mountains and Valleys.
Two-spotted Skipper (*Euphyes bimacula*). Rare, southeastern Coastal Plain.

Dun Skipper (*Euphyes vestris*). Common, statewide.
Dusted Skipper (*Atrytonopsis hianna*). Uncommon, statewide.
Pepper and Salt Skipper (*Atrytonopsis hegon*). Rare, statewide.
Lace-winged Roadside-Skipper (*Atrytonopsis aesculapius*). Rare, Coastal Plain.
Carolina Roadside-Skipper (*Atrytonopsis carolina*). Rare, southeastern Coastal Plain.
Reversed Roadside-Skipper (*Atrytonopsis reversa*). Rare, southeastern Coastal Plain.
Common Roadside-Skipper (*Amblyscirtes vialis*). Uncommon, statewide.
Dusky Roadside-Skipper (*Amblyscirtes alternata*). Rare, southeastern Coastal Plain.
Eufala Skipper (*Lerodea eufala*). Rare, Coastal Plain.
Brazilian Skipper (*Calpodes ethlius*). Rare vagrant.
Salt Marsh Skipper (*Panoquina panoquin*). Uncommon, Coastal Plain.
Ocola Skipper (*Panoquina ocola*). Uncommon vagrant.

AMPHIBIANS AND REPTILES OF VIRGINIA
Joseph C. Mitchell [2]

AMPHIBIANS

Frogs and Toads

Northern Cricket Frog (*Acris crepitans*). Common east of Blue Ridge Mountains, uncommon westward.
Southern Cricket Frog (*Acris gryllus*). Common, southeast.
American Toad (*Bufo americanus*). Common, statewide.
Oak Toad (*Bufo quercicus*). Rare, southeast only.
Southern Toad (*Bufo terrestris*). Common, southeast only.
Woodhouse's Toad (*Bufo woodhousii*). Common, statewide.
Eastern Narrowmouth Toad (*Gastrophryne carolinensis*). Common east of Blue Ridge Mountains; rare, southwest corner.
Cope's Gray Treefrog (*Hyla chrysoscelis*). Common, Coastal Plain, eastern Piedmont, southwestern Mountains and Valleys.
Green Treefrog (*Hyla cinerea*). Common, Coastal Plain.
Pine Woods Treefrog (*Hyla femoralis*). Locally common, Coastal Plain.
Barking Treefrog (*Hyla gratiosa*). State threatened; rare, southeast only.
Squirrel Treefrog (*Hyla squirella*). Uncommon, southeast only.
Eastern Gray Treefrog (*Hyla versicolor*). Common, western Piedmont, Mountains and Valleys north of New River.
Mountain Chorus Frog (*Pseudacris brachyphona*). Locally common, southwest only.
Brimley's Chorus Frog (*Pseudacris brimleyi*). Locally common, southeast only.
Spring Peeper (*Pseudacris crucifer*). Common, statewide.
Little Grass Frog (*Pseudacris ocularis*). Rare, southeast only.
Upland Chorus Frog (*Pseudacris triseriata*). Common, statewide.
Bullfrog (*Rana catesbeiana*). Common, statewide.
Green Frog (*Rana clamitans*). Common, statewide.
Pickerel Frog (*Rana palustris*). Common, statewide.
Wood Frog (*Rana sylvatica*). Common, northern and western Virginia.

[2] Department of Biology, University of Richmond, Richmond, VA 23173

Southern Leopard Frog (*Rana sphenocephala*). Common, Coastal Plain; uncommon, parts of Piedmont.

Carpenter Frog (*Rana virgatipes*). Rare, Coastal Plain.

Eastern Spadefoot (*Scaphiopus holbrookii*). Locally common, statewide.

Salamanders

Jefferson Salamander (*Ambystoma jeffersonianum*). Uncommon, northern Blue Ridge and western mountains.

Mabee's Salamander (*Ambystoma mabeei*). State threatened; rare, southeast only.

Spotted Salamander (*Ambystoma maculatum*). Common, statewide but declining.

Marbled Salamander (*Ambystoma opacum*). Common, east of Blue Ridge Mountains, uncommon west.

Mole Salamander (*Ambystoma talpoideum*). Rare, southern Piedmont.

Tiger Salamander (*Ambystoma tigrinum*). State endangered, rare, Coastal Plain, Shenandoah Valley.

Two-toed Amphiuma (*Amphiuma means*). Common, southeast only.

Green Salamander (*Aneides aeneus*). Uncommon, southwest only.

Hellbender (*Cryptobranchus alleganiensis*). Uncommon, southwest only.

Southern Dusky Salamander (*Desmognathus auriculatus*). Uncommon, southeast only.

Dusky Salamander (*Desmognathus fuscus*). Common, mountains; locally common, Piedmont.

Seal Salamander (*Desmognathus monticola*). Common, mountains.

Mountain Dusky Salamander (*Desmognathus ochrophaeus*). Common, southwest and western Virginia.

Black-bellied Salamander (*Desmognathus quadramaculatus*). Common, southwest only.

Black Mountain Salamander (*Desmognathus welteri*). Uncommon, southwest only.

Pigmy Salamander (*Desmognathus wrighti*). Rare, southwest only.

Northern Two-lined Salamander (*Eurycea bislineata*). Common, northern Virginia.

Southern Two-lined Salamander (*Eurycea cirrigera*). Common, southern Virginia.

Blue Ridge Two-lined Salamander (*Eurycea wilderae*). Rare, southwest only.

Three-lined Salamander (*Eurycea guttolineata*). Uncommon, Coastal Plain and Piedmont.

Longtailed Salamander (*Eurycea longicauda*). Common, Mountains and Valleys.

Cave Salamander (*Eurycea lucifuga*). Rare, southwest only.

Spring Salamander (*Gyrinophilus porphyriticus*). Common, Mountains and Valleys.

Four-toed Salamander (*Hemidactylium scutatum*). Locally common, east of Blue Ridge Mountains; rare, western mountains.

Shovel-nosed Salamander (*Leurognathus marmoratus*). Rare, southwest only.

Mudpuppy (*Necturus maculosus*). Rare, southwest only.

Dwarf Waterdog (*Necturus punctatus*). Rare, southeast only.

Eastern Newt (*Notophthalmus viridescens*). Common, statewide.

Red-backed Salamander (*Plethodon cinereus*). Common, statewide.

Atlantic Coastal Slimy Salamander (*Plethodon chlorobryonis*). Common, southeast only

White-spotted Slimy Salamander (*Plethodon cylindraceus*). Common, Piedmont, upper Coastal Plain, northern Mountains and Valleys.

Zigzag Salamander (*Plethodon dorsalis*). Rare, southwest only.

Northern Slimy Salamander (*Plethodon glutinosus*). Common, western mountains.

Valley and Ridge Salamander (*Plethodon hoffmani*). Uncommon, western mountains.

Peaks of Otter Salamander (*Plethodon hubrichti*). Rare, Blue Ridge Mountains only.

Jordan's Salamander (*Plethodon jordani*). Uncommon, southwest only.

Cumberland Plateau Woodland Salamander (*Plethodon kentucki*). Common, far southwest only.
Cow Knob Salamander (*Plethodon punctatus*). Rare, western mountains only.
Ravine Salamander (*Plethodon richmondi*). Common, southwest only.
Shenandoah Salamander (*Plethodon shenandoah*). Federal endangered; Blue Ridge Mountains only.
Wehrle's Salamander (*Plethodon wehrlei*). Uncommon, southwest mountains only.
Weller's Salamander (*Plethodon welleri*). Rare, southwest mountains only.
Yonahlossee Salamander (*Plethodon yonahlossee*). Uncommon, southwest mountains only.
Mud Salamander (*Pseudotriton montanus*). Uncommon, Piedmont, Coastal Plain.
Red Salamander (*Pseudotriton ruber*). Uncommon, statewide.
Many-lined Salamander (*Stereochilus marginatus*). Rare, southeast only.
Lesser Siren (*Siren intermedia*). Rare, southeast only.
Greater Siren (*Siren lacertina*). Rare, Coastal Plain.

REPTILES

Turtles

Spiny Softshell (*Apalone spinifera*). Uncommon; native southwest, introduced southeast.
Loggerhead Sea Turtle (*Caretta caretta*). Federal threatened; uncommon, seasonal in Chesapeake Bay.
Green Turtle (*Chelonia mydas*). Federal endangered; rare, seasonal in Chesapeake Bay.
Snapping Turtle (*Chelydra serpentina*). Common, statewide.
Painted Turtle (*Chrysemys picta*). Common, statewide.
Spotted Turtle (*Clemmys guttata*). Uncommon, declining, east of Blue Ridge Mountains and parts of Shenandoah Valley.
Wood Turtle (*Clemmys insculpta*). State threatened; northern counties.
Bog Turtle (*Clemmys muhlenbergii*). State endangered; southwest only.
Chicken Turtle (*Deirochelys reticularia*). State endangered; southeast only.
Leatherback (*Dermochelys coriacea*). Federal endangered; seasonal in Chesapeake Bay.
Hawksbill (*Eretmochelys imbricata*). Federal endangered; seasonal in Chesapeake Bay.
Map Turtle (*Graptemys geographica*). Common, southwest only.
Striped Mud Turtle (*Kinosternon baurii*). Common, Coastal Plain.
Common Mud Turtle (*Kinosternon subrubrum*). Common, east of Blue Ridge Mountains.
Kemp's Ridley (*Lepidochelys kempii*). Federal endangered; seasonal in Chesapeake Bay.
Diamondback Terrapin (*Malaclemys terrapin*). Locally common but declining, in estuaries along coastline.
River Cooter (*Pseudemys concinna*). Common, Piedmont.
Florida Cooter (*Pseudemys floridana*). Uncommon, southeast only.
Red-bellied Turtle (*Pseudemys rubriventris*). Common, Coastal Plain to Shenandoah Valley.
Loggerhead Musk Turtle (*Sternotherus minor*). Uncommon, southwest only.
Stinkpot (*Sternotherus odoratus*). Common, statewide.
Eastern Box Turtle (*Terrapene carolina*). Common, but declining, statewide.
Slider (*Trachemys scripta*) Common, southeast, rare, southwest; midwestern subspecies introduced, urban areas statewide.

Lizards

Six-lined Racerunner (*Cnemidophorus sexlineatus*). Common, east of Blue Ridge Mountains.
Coal Skink (*Eumeces anthracinus*). Rare, Mountains and Valleys.

Five-lined Skink (*Eumeces fasciatus*). Common, statewide.
Southeastern Five-lined Skink (*Eumeces inexpectatus*). Locally common, east of Blue Ridge Mountains.
Broad-headed Skink (*Eumeces laticeps*). Locally common, east of Blue Ridge Mountains.
Slender Glass Lizard (*Ophisaurus attenuatus*). Uncommon, east of Blue Ridge Mountains.
Eastern Glass Lizard (*Ophisaurus ventralis*). State threatened; southeast only.
Fence Lizard (*Sceloporus undulatus*). Common, statewide.
Ground Skink (*Scincella lateralis*). Locally common, east of Blue Ridge Mountains.

Snakes

Copperhead (*Agkistrodon contortrix*). Common, statewide.
Cottonmouth (*Agkistrodon piscivorus*). Uncommon, southeast only.
Timber Rattlesnake (*Crotalus horridus*). Uncommon, mountains; populations in southeast endangered.
Worm Snake (*Carphophis amoenus*). Common, statewide.
Scarlet Snake (*Cemophora coccinea*). Rare, Coastal Plain and eastern Piedmont.
Black Racer (*Coluber constrictor*). Common, statewide.
Ringneck Snake (*Diadophis punctatus*). Common, statewide.
Corn Snake (*Elaphe guttata*). Uncommon, Piedmont and mountains north of New River.
Rat Snake (*Elaphe obsoleta*). Common, statewide.
Mud Snake (*Farancia abacura*). Rare, southeast only.
Rainbow Snake (*Farancia erytrogramma*). Uncommon, Coastal Plain.
Eastern Hognose Snake (*Heterodon platirhinos*). Uncommon, statewide.
Prairie Kingsnake (*Lampropeltis calligaster*). Uncommon, east of Blue Ridge Mountains.
Common Kingsnake (*Lampropeltis getula*). Uncommon; statewide, except New River drainage.
Milk Snake (*Lampropeltis triangulum*). Locally common, mountains; rare, Piedmont and Coastal Plain.
Plain-bellied Water Snake (*Nerodia erythrogaster*). Common, southeast only.
Northern Water Snake (*Nerodia sipedon*). Common, statewide.
Brown Water Snake (*Nerodia taxispilota*). Locally common, southeast only.
Rough Green Snake (*Opheodrys aestivus*). Locally common, statewide.
Smooth Green Snake (*Opheodrys vernalis*). Uncommon, Mountains and Valleys.
Pine Snake (*Pituophis melanoleucus*). Rare, Mountains and Valleys.
Glossy Crayfish Snake (*Regina rigida*). Rare, Coastal Plain.
Queen Snake (*Regina septemvittata*). Locally common, Piedmont and southwest.
Brown Snake (*Storeria dekayi*). Common, Coastal Plain and eastern Piedmont; rare, mountains.
Red-bellied Snake (*Storeria occipitomaculata*). Uncommon, statewide except absent southwest.
Southeastern Crowned Snake (*Tantilla coronata*). Rare, southern Piedmont and Coastal Plain.
Ribbon Snake (*Thamnophis sauritus*). Uncommon, statewide.
Garter Snake (*Thamnophis sirtalis*). Common, statewide.
Rough Earth Snake (*Virginia striatula*). Locally common, southeast.
Smooth Earth Snake (*Virginia valeriae*). Locally common, statewide.

MAMMALS FOUND IN VIRGINIA

by Charles O. Handley, Jr. [3]

Virginia Opossum (*Didelphis virginiana*). Abundant, statewide.

Masked Shrew (*Sorex cinereus*). Abundant, mountains; rare, Eastern Shore.

Rock Shrew (*Sorex dispar*). Uncommon, mountains.

Smoky Shrew (*Sorex fumeus*). Common, mountains.

Pygmy Shrew (*Sorex hoyi*). Uncommon, statewide (except Eastern Shore).

Southeastern Shrew (*Sorex longirostris*). Threatened (Dismal Swamp); common, Coastal Plain (except Eastern Shore) and Piedmont; rare, mountains.

Water Shrew (*Sorex palustris*). Endangered; rare, mountains.

Northern Short-tailed Shrew (*Blarina brevicauda*). Abundant, Eastern Shore, Dismal Swamp, northern Coastal Plain, northern Piedmont, mountains.

Southern Short-tailed Shrew (*Blarina carolinensis*). Common, Coastal Plain (except Eastern Shore), southern Piedmont.

Least Shrew (*Cryptotis parva*). Common, statewide.

Hairy-tailed Mole (*Parascalops breweri*). Common, high mountains.

Eastern Mole (*Scalopus aquaticus*). Common, statewide (except high mountains).

Star-nosed Mole (*Condylura cristata*). Uncommon, statewide.

Gray Myotis (*Myotis grisescens*). Endangered; rare, southwestern mountains.

Eastern Small-footed Myotis (*Myotis leibii*). Rare, mountains.

Little Brown Myotis (*Myotis lucifugus*). Common, statewide.

Northern Myotis (*Myotis septentrionalis*). Uncommon, statewide.

Social Myotis (*Myotis sodalis*). Endangered; rare, mountains.

Northern Red Bat (*Lasiurus borealis*). Common, statewide.

Hoary Bat (*Lasiurus cinereus*). Rare, statewide.

Northern Yellow Bat (*Lasiurus intermedius*). Rare; one record from southeast.

Seminole Bat (*Lasiurus seminolus*). Rare; one record from southeast.

Silver-haired Bat (*Lasionycteris noctivagans*). Uncommon, statewide.

Eastern Pipistrelle (*Pipistrellus subflavus*). Common, statewide.

Big Brown Bat (*Eptesicus fuscus*). Abundant, statewide.

Evening Bat (*Nycticeius humeralis*). Common, statewide (except high mountains).

Rafinesque's Big-eared Bat (*Plecotus rafinesquii*). Endangered; rare, southeast.

Townsend's Big-eared Bat (*Plecotus townsendii*). Endangered; rare, southern mountains.

Eastern Cottontail (*Sylvilagus floridanus*). Abundant, statewide.

Marsh Rabbit (*Sylvilagus palustris*). Uncommon, southeast only.

Appalachian Cottontail (*Sylvilagus obscurus*). Common, mountains.

Snowshoe Hare (*Lepus americanus*). Endangered; rare, mountains.

Eastern Chipmunk (*Tamias striatus*). Common, statewide.

Woodchuck (*Marmota monax*). Common, statewide.

Eastern Gray Squirrel (*Sciurus carolinensis*). Abundant, statewide.

Eastern Fox Squirrel (*Sciurus niger*). Rare, Assateague and southeast; common, mountains.

Red Squirrel (*Tamiasciurus hudsonicus*). Common, northern Piedmont and mountains.

Northern Flying Squirrel (*Glaucomys sabrinus*). Endangered; rare, high mountains.

Southern Flying Squirrel (*Glaucomys volans*). Common, statewide.

American Beaver (*Castor canadensis*). Common, statewide.

Marsh Rice Rat (*Oryzomys palustris*). Common, Coastal Plain and southern Piedmont.

3   Division of Mammals, National Museum of Natural History, Washington, DC 20560

Eastern Harvest Mouse (*Reithrodontomys humulis*). Common, statewide (except Eastern Shore).

Cotton Mouse (*Peromyscus gossypinus*). Rare, southeast only.

White-footed Mouse (*Peromyscus leucopus*). Abundant, statewide.

Deer Mouse (*Peromyscus maniculatus*). Abundant, northern Piedmont and mountains.

Golden Mouse (*Ochrotomys nuttalli*). Common, southern parts of state.

Hispid Cotton Rat (*Sigmodon hispidus*). Common, southern Coastal Plain and Piedmont.

Eastern Woodrat (*Neotoma floridana*). Common, mountains.

Norway Rat (*Rattus norvegicus*). Abundant, statewide.

Black Rat (*Rattus rattus*). Common, southeast harbors, and rare, mountains.

House Mouse (*Mus musculus*). Abundant, statewide.

Southern Red-backed Vole (*Clethrionomys gapperi*). Abundant, mountains.

Rock Vole (*Microtus chrotorrhinus*). Endangered; rare, mountains.

Meadow Vole (*Microtus pennsylvanicus*). Abundant, statewide.

Woodland Vole (*Microtus pinetorum*). Common, statewide.

Common Muskrat (*Ondatra zibethicus*). Common, statewide.

Southern Lemming Vole (*Synaptomys cooperi*). Uncommon, Dismal Swamp and mountains.

Meadow Jumping Mouse (*Zapus hudsonius*). Common, statewide.

Woodland Jumping Mouse (*Napaeozapus insignis*). Common, mountains.

Common Porcupine (*Erethizon dorsatum*). Historical, mountains.

Nutria (*Myocastor coypus*). Introduced; uncommon, Coastal Plain.

Coyote (*Canis latrans*). Uncommon, mountains.

Gray Wolf (*Canis lupus*). Historical, statewide.

Red Wolf *(Canis niger)*. Historical, southeast.

Red Fox (*Vulpes vulpes*). Common, statewide.

Common Gray Fox (*Urocyon cinereoargenteus*). Common, statewide.

Black Bear (*Ursus americanus*). Uncommon, Dismal Swamp and mountains.

Harbor Seal (*Phoca vitulina*). Uncommon, ocean.

Gray Seal (*Halichoerus grypus*). Uncommon, ocean.

Harp Seal (*Pagophilus groenlandicus*). Rare, ocean.

Hooded Seal (*Cystophora cristata*). Rare, ocean and estuaries.

Common Raccoon (*Procyon lotor*). Abundant, statewide.

Fisher (*Martes pennanti*). Endangered; mostly historical; introduced, mountains.

Long-tailed Weasel (*Mustela frenata*). Common, statewide.

Least Weasel (*Mustela nivalis*). Uncommon, statewide.

Mink (*Mustela vison*). Common, statewide.

Eastern Spotted Skunk (*Spilogale putorius*). Rare, mountains.

Striped Skunk (*Mephitis mephitis*). Common, statewide.

Northern River Otter (*Lutra canadensis*). Common, Coastal Plain and Piedmont; rare, mountains.

Mountain Lion (*Felis concolor*). Endangered; mostly historical; possibly re-introduced in mountains.

Bobcat (*Felis rufus*). Common, mountains; uncommon Piedmont and Coastal Plain (except Eastern Shore).

Minke Whale (*Balaenoptera acutorostrata*). Uncommon, ocean and estuaries.

Sei Whale (*Balaenoptera borealis*). Endangered; rare, ocean.

Bryde's Whale (*Balaenoptera edeni*). Rare, ocean and estuaries.

Blue Whale (*Balaenoptera musculus*). Endangered; rare, ocean.

Fin Whale (*Balaenoptera physalus*). Endangered; common, ocean.

Humpback Whale (*Megaptera novaeangliae*). Endangered; uncommon, ocean.
Black Right Whale (*Balaena glacialis*). Endangered; rare, ocean.
Rough-toothed Dolphin (*Steno bredanensis*). Uncommon, ocean.
Bottle-nosed Dolphin (*Tursiops truncatus*). Common, ocean and estuaries.
Striped Dolphin (*Stenella coeruleoalba*). Uncommon, ocean.
Atlantic Spotted Dolphin (*Stenella frontalis*). Uncommon, ocean.
Pantropical Spotted Dolphin (*Stenella attenuata*). Rare, ocean.
Saddle-backed Dolphin (*Delphinus delphis*). Rare, ocean.
Atlantic White-sided Dolphin (*Lagenorhynchus acutus*). Rare, ocean.
Risso's Dolphin (*Grampus griseus*). Common, ocean.
Short-finned Pilot Whale (*Globicephala macrorhynchus*). Common, ocean.
Long-finned Pilot Whale (*Globicephala melas*). Common, ocean.
Harbor Porpoise (*Phocoena phocoena*). Common, ocean and estuaries.
Goose-beaked Whale (*Ziphius cavirostris*). Uncommon, ocean.
Dense-beaked Whale (*Mesoplodon densirostris*). Rare, ocean.
Gervais' Beaked Whale (*Mesoplodon europaeus*). Rare, ocean.
True's Beaked Whale (*Mesoplodon mirus*). Rare, ocean.
Pygmy Sperm Whale (*Kogia breviceps*). Uncommon, ocean.
Dwarf Sperm Whale (*Kogia simus*). Uncommon, ocean.
Sperm Whale (*Physeter macrocephalus*). Endangered; uncommon, ocean.
Manatee (*Trichechus manatus*). Endangered; rare, ocean and estuaries.
Elk (*Cervus elaphus*). Historical; statewide.
Sika Deer (*Cervus nippon*). Introduced, Assateague.
White-tailed Deer (*Odocoileus virginianus*). Abundant, statewide.
American Bison (*Bos bison*). Historical; Piedmont and mountains.

Suggested References

Birds

Augusta Bird Club. *Birds of Augusta County, Virginia* (Updated 1994). Augusta Bird Club, Staunton, VA.

Feduccia, Alan. *Birds of Colonial Williamsburg: a Historical Portfolio* (1989). Colonial Williamsburg Foundation Publ., Williamsburg, VA.

Hansrote, Charles J., Jr. *The Birds of Lynchburg, Virginia, and Vicinity* (1987). Lynchburg Bird Club, Lynchburg, VA.

Johnston, David W. *Mountaintop Birds. A Century of Bird Studies at Mountain Lake* (1997). McDonald and Woodward Publ. Co., Blacksburg, VA.

Johnston, David W., and Roger B. Clapp. *Birds of Prey in Virginia: An Addendum to Specimen Records* (1993). Virginia Avifauna No. 5, Gloucester, VA.

Johnston, David W., and William J. Ehmann. *Birds of Prey in Virginia: A History of Specimen Records from 1853 to 1988.* (1990). Virginia Avifauna No. 4, Lynchburg, VA.

Kain, Teta (ed.). *Virginia's Birdlife: An Annotated Checklist* (1987). Virginia Avifauna No. 3.

Meanley, Brooke. *Birdlife at Chincoteague and the Virginia Barrier Islands* (1981). Tidewater Publishers, Centreville, MD.

Meanley, Brooke. *Birds and Marshes of the Chesapeake Bay Country* (1975). Tidewater Publishers, Cambridge, MD.

Simpson, Marcus B., Jr. *Birds of the Blue Ridge Mountains* (1992). University of North Carolina Press, Chapel Hill, NC.

Wauer, Roland H. *The Visitor's Guide to the Birds of the Eastern National Parks,. United States and Canada* (1992). John Muir Publications, Santa Fe, NM.

Wilds, Claudia. *Finding Birds in the National Capital Area* (1992). 2nd ed. Smithsonian Institution Press, Washington, DC.

Geology and History

Brooks, Maurice. *The Appalachians* (1965). Seneca Books, Inc., Morgantown, WV.

Frye, K. *Roadside Geology of Virginia* (1986). Mountain Press Publ. Co., Missoula, MT.

James River Project Committee. *The James River Basin: Past, Present, and Future* (1950). Virginia Academy of Science, Richmond, VA.

Plants

Gupton, O.W., and F. C. Swope. *Wildflowers of the Shenandoah Valley and Blue Ridge Mountains* (1979). University Press of Virginia, Charlottesville, VA.

Harvill, A. M., Jr., T. R. Bradley, C. E. Stevens, T. F. Wieboldt, D. M. E. Ware, and D. W. Ogle. *Atlas of the Virginia Flora* (1986). 2nd. Ed., Virginia Botanical Associates, Farmville, VA.

Insects

Opler, Paul A. *A Field Guide to Eastern Butterflies* (1992). Houghton Mifflin Co., New York.

Opler, Paul A., and G. O. Krizek. *Butterflies East of the Great Plains* (1984). Johns Hopkins University Press, Baltimore, MD.

Pyle, Robert Michael. *The Audubon Society Field Guide to North American Butterflies.* (1981). Alfred A. Knopf, New York.

FISHES

Jenkins, R. E., and N. M. Burkhead. *Freshwater Fishes of Virginia* (1944). American Fisheries Society, Bethesda, MD.

REPTILES

Mitchell, Joseph C. *The Reptiles of Virginia* (1994). Smithsonian Institution Press, Washington, DC.

MAMMALS

Handley, Charles O., Jr., and Clyde P. Patton. *Wild Mammals of Virginia* (1947). Commission of Game and Inland Fisheries, Richmond, VA.

NATURAL HISTORY

Badger, C. J. *A Naturalist's Guide to the Virginia Coast* (1996). Stackpole Books, Mechanicsburg, PA.

Conners, John A. *Shenandoah National Park. An Interpretive Guide* (1988). McDonald and Woodward Publ. Co., Blacksburg, VA.

Duda, Mark D. *Virginia Wildlife Viewing Guide* (1994). Falcon Press Publ. Co., Helena, MT.

Godfrey, M. A. *A Sierra Club Naturalist's Guide to the Piedmont* (1980). Sierra Club, San Francisco, CA.

Heatwole, Henry. *Guide to Shenandoah National Park* (1992). Fourth edition. Shenandoah Natural History Association, Luray, VA.

Meanley, Brooke. *The Great Dismal Swamp* (1973). Audubon Naturalist Society, Washington, DC.

Terwilliger, Karen (coord.). *Virginia's Endangered Species* (1991). McDonald and Woodward Publ. Co., Blacksburg, VA.

Terwilliger, Karen, and John R. Tate (coord.). *A Guide to Endangered and Threatened Species in Virginia* (1995). McDonald and Woodward Publ. Co., Blacksburg, VA.

Winegar, G., and D. Winegar. *Natural Wonders of Virginia: A Guide to Parks, Preserves, & Wild Places* (1994). Country Roads Press, Castine, ME.

HIKING

Adkins, Leonard M. *Walking the Blue Ridge: A Guide to the Trails of the Blue Ridge Parkway* (1991). University of North Carolina Press, Chapel Hill, NC.

De Hart, Allen. *Hiking the Old Dominion: The Trails of Virginia* (1984). Sierra Club, San Francisco, CA.

Johnson, Randy. *The Hiker's Guide to Virginia* (1992). Falcon Press, Helena, MT.

GEOGRAPHY

Virginia Atlas and Gazetteer (1989). DeLorme Mapping Co., Freeport, ME.

NOTES

AMERICAN BIRDING ASSOCIATION SALES

ABA Sales is the largest birding supply business of its kind in North America. We carry a full line of bird field guides, bird identification guides, and other birding books. The FREE 96-page, annotated catalog features top-notch optical equipment for birders as well as helpful birding accessories. You'll also find bird-song tapes and Cds, videos, CD-ROMs, and computer listing programs for Macintosh and PC.

ABA Sales distributes the *ABA/Lane Birdfinding Guide Series*. Thes books specialize in accurate, detailed instructions for North America's most productive locations. Please see the following page for a list of the other guides in this series.

ABA Sales
Phone 800/634-7736
or 719/578-0607

Fax 800/590-2473
or 719/578-9705

Email: abasales@abasales.com

Web Site: www.americanbirding.org

273

OTHER ABA BIRDFINDING GUIDES

A Birder's Guide to the Rio Grande Valley
Mark Lockwood, James Paton,
Barry R. Zimmer, and William B. McKinney
September 1999 — $23.95

A Birder's Guide to Southern California
Brad Schram
August 1998 — $23.95

A Birder's Guide to the Bahama Islands
Anthony W. White
June 1998 — $26.95

A Birder's Guide to Idaho
Dan Svingen and Kas Dumroese
October 1997 — $18.95

A Birder's Guide to Colorado
Harold R. Holt
February 1997 – $21.95

A Birder's Guide to Florida
Bill Pranty
May 1996 – $21.95

A Birder's Guide to New Hampshire
Alan Delorey
January 1996 – $18.95

Birdfinder: A Birder's Guide to Planning North American Trips
Jerry A. Cooper
November 1995 – $21.95

A Birder's Guide to Southeastern Arizona
Rick Taylor
August 1995 – $21.95

A Birder's Guide to Arkansas
Mel White
May 1995 – $18.95

A Birder's Guide to Eastern Massachusetts
Bird Observer
August 1994 – $18.95

A Birder's Guide to Churchill
Bonnie Chartier
January 1994 – $17.95

A Birder's Guide to the Texas Coast
Harold R. Holt
May 1993 – $21.95

A Birder's Guide to Wyoming
Oliver K. Scott
February 1993 – $18.95

THE VIRGINIA SOCIETY
OF ORNITHOLOGY

The Virginia Society of Ornithology (VSO) was founded in 1929 for the purpose of encouraging bird study in Virginia. More than two dozen local bird clubs throughout the state are now affiliated with the VSO.

Activities undertaken by the VSO include the following:

1. An annual meeting (usually in the spring) is held in a different part of the state each year. It features talks on ornithological subjects and field trips to nearby areas.

2. Other forays or field trips lasting a day or more are scheduled throughout the year so as to include all seasons and to cover the major physiographic regions of the state.

3. A journal, *The Raven*, is published annually or semi-annually, containing articles about Virginia birds and news of the activities of the Society and its chapters.

4. A newsletter is published quarterly, containing current news items of interest to members and information about upcoming events, field trips, and pertinent conservation issues.

5. Study projects (nesting studies, winter bird population surveys, etc.) are encouraged, in order to make genuine contributions to ornithological knowledge.

6. Published periodically are lengthy major contributions to Virginia ornithology, such as a checklist of birds found in the state, raptor surveys, and egg dates.

In addition to these activities, for over 30 years VSO members have banded birds each autumn on the Eastern Shore at Kiptopeke. The bird records committee for the state (VARCOM) was established by the VSO to verify reports of rare species in the state. The committee collects and stores photographs, recordings, and other documentation. The VSO also manages a state-wide birding hotline (804/238-2713) for anyone who would like to know or report sightings of rare or unusual birds in the state.

The VSO periodically presents three special awards: the Jackson M. Abbott Conservation Award, the J.J. Murray Award for ornithological research, and the James W. Eike Service Award.

Annual dues for the VSO are $15 for active members, $25 for sustaining members, $50 or more for contributing members, $400 for life members, and $20 for family members.

Inquiries about membership and publications should be addressed to the VSO office listed on the other side of this page.

Walter Weber

THE VIRGINIA SOCIETY OF ORNITHOLOGY

MEMBERSHIP

FORM

Membership Category

- ☐ Active—$15
- ☐ Family—$20
- ☐ Sustaining—$25
- ☐ Contributing—$50 or more
- ☐ Life—$400

Name_____

Address _____

_____

City _____

State, ZIP_____

Phone _____

Return this form with check made payable to VSO to:

The Virginia Society of Ornithology
1230 Viewmont Drive
Evington, VA 24550
www.ecoventures-travel.com/vso

AMERICAN BIRDING ASSOCIATION

ABA is the organization of North American birders, and its mission is to bring all the excitement, challenge, and wonder of birds and birding to you. As an ABA member you will get the information you need to increase your birding skills so that you can make the most of your time in the field.

ABA supports the interests of birders of all ages and experiences, and promotes birding publications, projects, and partnerships. It focuses on bird identification and birdfinding skills and the development and dissemination of information on bird conservation. ABA also champions ethical birding practices.

Each year members receive six issues of ABA's award-winning magazine *Birding* and twelve issues of *Winging It*, a monthly newsletter. ABA conducts regular conferences and biennial conventions in the continent's best birding locations, publishes a yearly *Membership Directory and Yellow Pages*, compiles an annual *Directory of Volunteer Opportunities for Birders*, and offers discount prices for many bird books, optical gear, and other birding equipment through ABA Sales. The organization's *ABA/Lane Birdfinding Guide Series* sets the standard for accuracy and excellence in its field.

ABA is engaged in bird conservation through such institutions and activities as Partners in Flight and the American Bird Conservancy's Policy Council. ABA also actively promotes the economic and environmental values of birding.

ABA encourages birding among young people by sponsoring birding camp scholorships and "ABA/Leica Young Birder of the Year" competition, and by publishing *A Bird's-Eye View*, a newsletter by and for its younger members.

In cooperation with the National Audubon Society, ABA also publishes *North American Birds*, a quarterly which reviews all imrportant bird sightings and significant population trends for the US, Canada, and the West Indies.

In short, ABA works to ensure that birds and birding have the healthy future that they deserve. In the words of the late Roger Tory Peterson, the American Birding Association is "the best value in the birding community." The American Birding Association gives active birders what they want. Consider joining today. You will find a membership form on the other side of this page.

American Birding Association Membership Services
PO Box 6599
Colorado Springs, CO 80934
telephone 800/850-2473 or 719/578-1614
fax 719/578-1480
e-mail: member@aba.org
web site: http://www.americanbirding.org

AMERICAN BIRDING ASSOCIATION
Membership Application

All memberships include six issues of **Birding** magazine, monthly issues of **Winging It** newsletter, and full participation in all ABA activities.

MEMBERSHIP CLASSES AND DUES:

- ❏ Individual - US $40.00 / yr
- ❏ Individual - Canada *$50.00 / yr
- ❏ Individual - Int'l $50.00 / yr
- ❏ Student - US $20.00 / yr
- ❏ Student - Canada* $30.00 / yr

- ❏ Family - US $47.00 / yr
- ❏ Family - Canada * $58.00 / yr
- ❏ Family - Int'l $58.00 / yr
- ❏ Student - Int'l $30.00 / yr
- ❏ Student newsletter $6.00 / yr (individuals add $6.00)

- ❏ *Century Club Membership:* Hooded Merganser $140 / yr
- ❏ *Century Club Membership:* Mountain Plover $300 / yr
- ❏ *Century Club Membership:* Violet-crowned Hummingbird $500 / yr

* *Canadian dues include GST*
All membership dues include $30 for **Birding** *magazine and $10 for* **Winging It** *newsletter*

APPLICATION TYPE:

❏ New Membership   ❏ Renewal   ❏ Gift

MEMBER INFORMATION:

Name _____

Address _____

City, State, ZIP _____

Phone _____

PAYMENT INFORMATION:

❏ Check or Money Order enclosed (US funds only)

❏ Charge to VISA / MasterCard / Discover (circle one)

Account Number _____

Exp Date _____ Signature _____

Send this completed form with payment to: **ABA Membership
PO Box 6599
Colorado Springs, CO 80934**

VA 12/99

278

INDEX

A

Accotink Bay 99
Albatross
  Yellow-nosed 211
Alexandria 89-91, 227, 235
Anhinga 34, 39, 53-54, 56, 94, 213, 250
Ani
  Groove-billed 230
Appalachian Trail 113, 166, 182
Apple Orchard Mountain 166-167
Arlington 83-86
Assateague Island 25, 255, 258
Avocet
  American 29, 58, 76, 92, 94, 119, 155, 175, 223, 253

B

Barrier Islands 214-215, 222-223, 225-226, 228-229, 231, 246, 252-254
Beach
  Nude 30
Beartown 237, 239
Belle Haven Picnic Area 91-93
Berryville 254
Big Meadows 124
Birds Nest 233
Bittern
  American 68, 94, 96, 143, 177-178, 213
  Least 62, 65-66, 77, 79, 94, 119, 154, 178, 213
Blackbird
  Brewer's 10, 56, 124, 135-136, 247
  Red-winged 72, 94, 181, 246
  Rusty 56, 60, 69, 74, 247
  Yellow-headed 10, 30, 38, 43, 76, 175, 247
Blacksburg 226-227
Blue Grass Valley 135-136, 252
Blue Ridge 252
Blue Ridge Parkway 161, 165-167, 169-173, 255
Bluebird
  Eastern 50, 74-75, 77, 95, 105, 112, 124, 131-132, 139, 148, 150, 170, 236
Bobolink 62, 69, 75, 81, 107, 115, 136, 150, 175, 183, 246, 259
Bobwhite
  Northern 4, 72, 107, 124, 132, 221
Booby
  Brown 30, 34, 43, 212
Brant 29, 33, 216
Breaks Interstate Park 195-197
Brookneal 149
Bufflehead 49, 69, 73, 78-79, 93, 102, 104-105, 133, 139, 145, 148, 181, 218
Bunting
  Indigo 3, 56, 72, 77, 79, 81, 84, 86, 90, 95, 104, 107, 122, 141, 150, 154, 159, 243
  Lark 60, 63, 244
  Lazuli 243
  Painted 7, 243, 257

  Snow 7, 9, 25, 30, 34, 39, 54, 58, 60, 63, 68, 73, 82, 108, 119, 155, 176, 194, 246, 259
Burkes Garden 182-183, 259

C

Calmes Neck 259
Canvasback 4, 57, 72-73, 77-79, 94, 102, 133, 158, 217
Cape Charles 212, 250, 254
Cape Henry 212, 229, 253
Cardinal
  Northern 4, 59, 86, 93, 131, 139, 148, 150, 157, 243
Catbird
  Gray 4, 59, 67, 69, 86, 93, 131-132, 147, 170, 237
Cedar Island 222
Charlottesville 128, 243
Chat
  Yellow-breasted 7, 50, 77, 79, 112, 131, 141, 143, 147, 154, 166, 172, 181, 242
Chesapeake Bay 25, 66, 212, 214, 217-218, 222, 224-226, 228, 245, 249-254, 258
Chesapeake Bay Bridge-Tunnel 26, 36, 39, 41-43, 207, 212-213, 217-218, 225, 227-228, 230, 233, 235, 249-252, 254, 258-259
Chickadee
  Black-capped 39, 135, 137, 180, 182, 185, 188, 234, 255
  Boreal 235
  Carolina 46, 50, 78-79, 81, 84, 86, 93, 127-128, 142, 180, 235, 255
Chincoteague 31, 203, 209
Chuck-will's-widow 37, 141, 231
Clinch Mountain 191-192
Clinch Valley College 192-193
Colonial Parkway 72-73
Coot
  American 76, 119, 133, 148, 154, 222
Cormorant
  Double-crested 33, 53, 60, 72, 77, 79, 93, 101, 104, 118-119, 139, 145, 157, 176, 190, 213
  Great 33, 39, 60, 68-69, 73, 94, 213, 250

ABBREVIATED TABLE OF CONTENTS	
Introduction	**1-23**
Eastern Shore	**24-43**
Coastal Plain	**44-79**
Northern Virginia	**80-113**
Central Virginia	**114-139**
Southern Piedmont	**140-159**
Southern Mountains/Valleys	**160-197**
Hawk-watching	**198-202**
Pelagic Birding	**203-209**
Annotated Checklist	**210-248**
Virginia Specialties	**249-259**

Cowbird
Brown-headed 93, 180, 247
Crake
Paint-billed 222
Crane
Sandhill 4, 30, 39, 63, 105, 190, 200, 222
Craney Island Landfill 58, 223, 225, 227, 246, 251-254, 259
Creeper
Brown 4, 53, 60, 72, 78-79, 84, 86, 90, 104, 136, 139, 148, 179-180, 186-187, 235
Crossbill
Red 39, 115, 135, 137, 155, 161, 179-180, 185-187, 248, 259
White-winged 124, 185-186, 248
Crow
American 90, 234
Fish 46, 93, 234
Cuckoo
Black-billed 17, 55, 108, 131, 161, 172, 230
Yellow-billed 69, 72, 77, 79, 84, 87, 128, 147, 230
Curlew
Long-billed 30, 34, 224

D
Daleville Ponds 177-178
Danville 214
Delmarva Peninsula 25, 234, 250
Dickcissel 10, 38-39, 76, 81, 94, 108, 141, 243, 257
Dove
Mourning 229
Rock 229
White-winged 229
Dovekie 26, 34, 203, 229, 254
Dowitcher
Long-billed 175, 225, 253
Short-billed 33, 58, 92, 175, 225, 253
Duck
American Black 29, 51, 53, 60, 62, 65, 69, 71, 73, 76, 93, 99, 102, 105, 118, 133, 139, 143, 145, 171, 181, 216
Harlequin 10, 34, 68, 119, 217, 251
Ring-necked 49, 54, 56, 71, 73-74, 76, 102, 105, 133, 139, 148, 158, 217
Ruddy 57, 72-73, 78-79, 93-94, 102, 133, 148, 218
Wood 49-51, 53, 56, 62, 65, 71-74, 77-79, 86, 93-94, 99, 102, 115, 118, 143, 147-148, 171, 176, 181-182, 188, 216
Dunlin 30, 33-34, 37, 58-60, 62, 65, 67, 78, 108, 157, 175, 225
Dyke Marsh 91-94, 255

E
Eagle
Bald 22, 37, 46, 50-51, 53-54, 59-60, 62, 66, 69, 72-73, 75-79, 86, 93-94, 99-102, 108, 111, 118, 122, 139, 145, 148, 151, 154-155, 157-158, 176, 181, 183, 190, 192, 199, 219, 252
Golden 7, 10, 39, 81, 102, 110, 113, 115, 122-123, 136, 139, 161, 180, 182-183, 185-187, 192, 197, 199, 220, 252
Eastern Shore Birding Festival 25, 35
Egret
Cattle 28, 33, 49, 77, 108, 139, 214

Great 28, 33, 49, 54, 60, 77, 93, 102, 118, 132, 213
Little 30, 214
Reddish 30, 214
Snowy 28, 33, 49, 60, 93, 175, 214
Eider
Common 10, 34, 217, 251
King 10, 34, 68, 217, 251

F
Falcon
Peregrine 22, 26, 29-30, 38, 58, 62, 65, 68-69, 96, 110, 113, 121-122, 175, 180, 190, 199-200, 220, 252
Fallingwater Cascades 167
Falls Church 235
Finch
House 81, 248
Purple 105, 115, 129, 135-136, 162, 176, 185, 247
Fisherman Island 35, 215, 220, 250
Flamingo
Greater 215
Flicker
Northern 38, 54, 69, 157, 232
Floyd Fields 167
Flycatcher
Acadian 50, 56, 71-72, 74, 77, 79, 81, 86, 93, 96, 102, 104, 122, 143, 232
Alder 136, 185, 187, 232
Ash-throated 10, 25, 39, 233
Fork-tailed 62-63, 233
Great Crested 46, 50, 72, 74, 77, 81, 86, 90, 93, 143, 169, 233
Least 89, 136-137, 161, 172, 179-180, 182, 185, 195, 232
Olive-sided 39, 63, 66, 96, 99, 104-105, 145, 185, 232
Scissor-tailed 5, 63, 65, 233
Vermilion 233
Willow 94, 107, 111-112, 139, 161, 182, 187, 192, 232, 255
Yellow-bellied 162, 181, 185, 232
Fort Belvoir 97
Fort Hill 158-159
Fort Story 59-60, 207, 250-251, 254
Four Mile Run 83, 254
Frigatebird
Magnificent 26, 34, 43, 63, 73, 213
Front Royal 121
Fulmar
Northern 205-206, 211

G
Gadwall 29, 60, 69, 71, 78, 133, 158, 217
Gallinule
Purple 30, 43, 63, 178, 222
Gannet
Northern 30, 39, 59-60, 62-63, 65, 73, 205, 212, 250
George Washington Parkway 94
Gleedsville 256
Gnatcatcher
Blue-gray 86, 93, 104, 145, 170, 236
Godwit
Bar-tailed 30, 224, 253

Hudsonian 29, 94, 224
Marbled 10, 29, 33-34, 36, 62, 76, 94, 224, 253-254
Golden-Plover
American 25, 29, 38, 58, 62, 75, 92, 119, 157, 175, 190, 222, 253
Goldeneye
Barrow's 43, 218
Common 57, 60, 68, 73, 79, 102, 133, 181, 218
Goldfinch
American 78-79, 93, 248
Goose
Barnacle 216
Canada 29, 49, 51, 56, 62, 65, 69, 73-76, 78-79, 93, 102, 104, 118, 133, 215-216, 251
Greater White-fronted 39, 76, 79, 155, 215, 251
Ross's 10, 30, 63, 66, 216, 251
Snow 29, 51, 56, 62-63, 65, 76, 108, 112, 119, 133, 215, 251
Goose Creek Valley 255
Gose Mill Pond 182-183
Goshawk
Northern 10, 39, 94, 108, 110, 113, 136, 161, 187, 193, 199-200, 219
Grackle
Boat-tailed 26, 67, 73, 94, 247, 259
Common 72, 93, 247
Grandview Beach 66, 68, 258
Grayson Highlands Recreation Area 257
Grebe
Clark's 211
Eared 43, 58, 62-63, 94, 119, 190, 211
Horned 34, 68, 72-73, 77, 79, 119, 124, 133, 148, 154-155, 158, 190, 210
Pied-billed 67, 71-74, 96, 119, 133, 145, 147-148, 155, 158, 188, 190, 210
Red-necked 34, 60, 73, 93, 119, 133, 139, 149, 155, 190, 192, 211
Western 58, 73, 155, 211
Grosbeak
Black-headed 25, 39, 76, 128, 243
Blue 56, 72, 75, 77, 79, 81, 95-96, 104, 111, 141, 145, 150, 154, 159, 173, 175, 243
Evening 7, 81, 115, 129, 136, 139, 145, 248-249
Pine 124, 247
Rose-breasted 81, 84, 86-87, 89-90, 122, 125, 128-129, 136, 143, 165-166, 168-169, 171-172, 175, 179, 187-188, 193, 195, 243
Grottoes 129
Ground-Dove
Common 230
Grouse
Ruffed 4, 110-111, 113, 115, 122-123, 132, 135-137, 139, 161, 166, 170, 172, 176, 180, 193, 200, 221
Guillemot
Black 229
Gulf Stream 203, 206, 212
Gull
Black-headed 34, 43, 73, 94, 227
Black-tailed 68, 227
Bonaparte's 34, 39, 42, 51, 60, 63, 68, 72, 77, 79, 93, 119, 148, 155, 158, 227, 254

California 227
Franklin's 58, 69, 226
Glaucous 10, 30, 34, 58, 68, 73-74, 76, 145, 155, 205, 227, 254
Great Black-backed 28, 33, 51, 93, 119, 145, 227
Herring 28, 33, 51, 72, 86, 93, 119, 145, 148, 155, 158, 205, 227, 254
Iceland 9-10, 30, 34, 73, 205, 227, 254
Laughing 28, 33, 37, 51, 57, 67, 72-73, 93, 118, 190, 226
Lesser Black-backed 10, 60, 62, 69, 92, 94, 119, 175, 205, 227, 254
Little 25, 34, 43, 58, 60, 63, 68-69, 94, 226, 254
Mew 227
Ring-billed 51, 72, 74, 86, 93, 118-119, 145, 158, 175, 227
Sabine's 30, 43, 63, 155, 206, 228
Thayer's 43, 227
Gyrfalcon 81, 200, 221
H
Hampton 66
Hampton Roads 228
Harrier
Northern 38, 62, 65, 67, 76, 108, 111, 122, 142, 155, 158-159, 199, 219
Harrisonburg 131-132
Hawk
Broad-winged 9, 56, 81, 104-105, 110, 113, 115, 122, 171, 175, 192, 199, 220
Cooper's 29, 38, 60, 62, 65, 76, 90, 155, 158-159, 175, 199-200, 219
Ferruginous 220
Red-shouldered 49, 53, 56, 60, 74, 86, 90, 104, 122, 127, 145, 148, 155, 158-159, 193, 199, 220
Red-tailed 72, 81, 86, 104, 111, 122-123, 127, 145, 148, 155, 158-159, 180, 199, 220
Rough-legged 31, 58, 76, 82, 94, 108, 115, 119, 124, 155, 158-159, 182-183, 199, 220, 252
Sharp-shinned 29, 38, 60, 62, 65, 67, 76, 90, 110, 113, 155, 158-159, 175, 199-200, 219
Swainson's 39, 110, 200, 220
Hawk Migration Association of North America 201
Hawk-watch
Harvey's Knob 168, 201

ABBREVIATED TABLE OF CONTENTS
Introduction 1-23
Eastern Shore 24-43
Coastal Plain 44-79
Northern Virginia 80-113
Central Virginia 114-139
Southern Piedmont 140-159
Southern Mountains/Valleys 160-197
Hawk-watching 198-202
Pelagic Birding 203-209
Annotated Checklist 210-248
Virginia Specialties 249-259

Hawksbill Mountain 122, 202
Kiptopeke State Park 200
Linden Fire Tower 202
Mary's Rock 202
Mendota Fire Tower 191-192, 201
Rockfish Gap 165, 201
Shenandoah National Park 202
Snickers Gap 201
State Park 201
Stony Man 202
Hawksbill Mountain 121
Haymarket 233
Heron
Great Blue 28, 33, 53-54, 56-57, 69, 72, 75, 77, 79, 86, 93, 100, 102, 112, 118, 133, 147, 159, 175, 178, 200, 213
Green 28, 33, 56, 72-73, 77, 79, 86, 112, 147, 175, 177, 214
Little Blue 28, 33, 49, 93, 96, 214
Tricolored 28, 33, 154, 214
High Knob Recreation Area 194
Highland County 115, 134-136, 231, 233, 237, 239, 246-249, 252, 257-258
Hog Island 251, 253
Hog Island Waterfowl Management Area 75-76
Hopewell 213
Hummingbird
Allen's 231
Ruby-throated 4, 93, 110, 113, 128, 231
Rufous 7, 231
Humpback Rocks 166
Humpback Rocks Visitor Center 170
Hunting Creek 91, 93, 249, 251, 253-254
Hurricane
Bertha 42, 207
David 229
Fran 155, 207
Hazel 212
I
Ibis
Glossy 28, 33, 49, 53, 67, 84, 96, 154, 159, 215
White 29, 33, 49, 62, 65, 74, 76, 94, 175-176, 190, 215, 250
White-faced 30, 215
Ivy Creek Natural Area 127-128
J
Jaeger
Long-tailed 30, 205-206, 226
Parasitic 94, 155, 205-207, 226
Pomarine 42, 155, 205-207, 226
Jamestown 72
Jamestown Island 68-69
Jay
Blue 38, 86, 110, 113, 234
Jolly Pond 70-71
Junco
Carolina (Dark-eyed) 4
Dark-eyed 4, 84, 86, 111, 115, 123, 131, 135, 137, 139, 150, 161, 166, 168, 170, 172, 180, 183, 185-187, 194-195, 246

K
Kestrel 11, 202
American 4, 38, 67, 81, 90, 108, 110, 127, 175, 192, 199-200, 220
Killdeer 4, 92, 94, 112, 133, 175, 178, 223
Kingbird
Eastern 38, 62, 75, 90, 93, 104, 147, 177, 233
Gray 30, 39, 43, 233
Western 25, 38-39, 62, 65, 155, 175, 233
Kingfisher
Belted 73, 111, 133, 166, 175, 178, 231
Kinglet
Golden-crowned 4, 69, 84, 86, 104, 115, 136-137, 162, 179-180, 185-187, 236
Ruby-crowned 69, 84, 86, 104, 236
Kiptopeke 233, 252, 254
Kite
Mississippi 37, 46, 56, 66, 124, 155, 200, 219, 252
Swallow-tailed 37, 56, 66, 76, 219, 251
White-tailed 219
Kittiwake
Black-legged 34, 60, 94, 155, 205, 207, 228
Knot
Red 33, 60, 62, 65, 67, 92, 224
L
Lake
Anna 117-119, 210, 227, 229, 251, 259
Buggs Island 151
Carvins Cove Reservoir 176-177
Claytor 251
Drummond 55, 213
Gaston 251
John H. Kerr Reservoir 142, 151, 153-155, 210, 223, 227, 251, 255-257, 259
Keokee 257
Kerr Reservoir 207
Laurel Bed 188
Moomaw 138-139
Mountain 178, 180, 219, 230-231, 239, 247, 259
Philpott Reservoir 251
Silver 132-133
Smith Mountain 226, 251
South Holston 189-190
Stumpy 53-54, 213, 250
Swift Creek Reservoir 148-149
Lark
Horned 39, 75, 108, 111, 115, 135-136, 141, 154, 169, 182-183, 185, 233, 258-259
Limpkin 222
Linden Fire Tower 113
Locust Springs Picnic Area 135
Longspur
Chestnut-collared 30, 246
Lapland 7, 10, 25, 30, 34, 39, 58, 60, 63, 68, 73, 82, 108, 246, 258
Loon
Common 29, 34, 56, 59-60, 68, 72-73, 77, 79, 93-94, 118-119, 133, 139, 148, 158, 177, 210
Pacific 39, 63, 210

Red-throated 29, 34, 59-60, 68, 119, 210
Lucketts 81, 107-108, 254-256, 259
Lynchburg 222, 230
M
Magpie
  Black-billed 234
Mallard 29, 49, 51, 53-54, 56, 60, 62, 65, 69, 71, 73, 76, 93, 102, 118, 133, 139, 143, 145, 158, 181, 216
Martin
  Purple 66, 107, 147, 233
Meadowlark
  Eastern 3, 81, 107, 111, 124, 141, 246
Mendota Fire Tower 191-192
Merganser
  Common 54, 76, 93-94, 102, 104-105, 145, 148, 158, 176, 218
  Hooded 54, 73, 76, 78, 93-94, 102, 105, 115, 133, 147-148, 158, 175, 181, 218
  Red-breasted 28, 30, 34, 39, 62, 65, 68, 73, 77-78, 93-94, 142, 148, 154, 218
Merlin 26, 29, 34, 38, 54, 62, 65, 67-68, 96, 108, 110, 113, 132, 178, 180, 190, 199, 220
Milam Gap 122
Mockingbird
  Northern 4, 93, 237
Mole Hill 132
Monterey 134, 136
Montvale 255
Moorhen
  Common 63, 66, 104, 133, 222
Mount Rogers 161, 185-187, 219, 231-232, 235, 237, 241, 247-248, 255, 259
Mount Rogers National Recreation Area 185
Murre
  Common 229
  Thick-billed 30, 229
N
National Fish Hatchery
  Harrison Lake 49
National Monument
  George Washington Birthplace 76-78
National Park
  Shenandoah 81, 121-125, 255
National Wildlife Refuge
  Back Bay 61-63, 207, 210-211, 215-216, 219, 228, 246, 250-251, 253-254, 256, 258-259
  Chincoteague 25, 27-30, 207, 214-216, 220, 223-224, 233, 246, 250-256, 258-259
  Eastern Shore of Virginia 25, 35-36, 220, 252, 258-259
  Fisherman Island 36
  Great Dismal Swamp 46, 55-56, 219, 227, 238, 240, 250-251, 256-257
  Mason Neck 100-102, 255
  Presquile 51
Newport News 213, 243
Night-Heron
  Black-crowned 28, 33, 53, 84, 93, 214
  Yellow-crowned 28, 33, 53, 84, 96, 175, 214
Nighthawk
  Common 37, 105, 147, 171, 231
Nokesville 256
Norfolk 53, 64, 214, 243

Norfolk (submarine) Canyon 203, 209, 212
North Cove Recreation Area 176
Norton 193
Nuthatch
  Brown-headed 3, 25, 30, 39, 46, 53, 60, 69, 74-76, 141, 148, 153, 235, 255
  Red-breasted 4, 39, 78, 86, 89, 115, 136-137, 145, 161, 185-186, 195, 235
  White-breasted 46, 50, 60, 78, 81, 93, 104, 128, 142, 166, 235
O
Observatory Mountain 128
Ocean City, Maryland 203
Oldsquaw 26, 30, 34, 39, 60, 68, 77, 79, 94, 119, 142, 149, 190, 217, 251
Oriole
  Baltimore 4, 38, 77, 81, 84, 86-87, 89, 93-94, 104, 127-128, 131-132, 145, 165, 171, 177, 181, 183, 247
  Bullock's 247
  Orchard 69, 75, 77, 79, 89, 93-94, 96, 104, 127, 154, 177, 247
Osprey 37-38, 56, 62, 65, 67, 69, 71-73, 75, 77, 79, 86, 93, 101-102, 104, 108, 111, 118-119, 143, 145, 148, 177-178, 181, 192, 199, 219
Otter Creek Trail 166
Ovenbird 46, 53, 59, 69, 74, 77, 79, 89, 93, 102, 105, 113, 122, 129, 137, 143, 147, 157, 169, 172, 176, 179, 181, 241
Owl
  Barn 230
  Barred 50, 56, 71, 77, 79, 93, 96, 99, 104, 122, 125, 155, 166, 176, 179, 195, 230
  Burrowing 230
  Great Horned 39, 69, 71, 77, 79, 93, 99, 104, 122, 155, 176, 194-195, 230
  Long-eared 10, 39, 90, 132, 135, 183, 230, 255
  Northern Saw-whet 10, 38-39, 94, 135-136, 185, 187, 231, 255
  Short-eared 10, 31, 34, 51, 58, 68, 76, 108, 119, 124, 142, 155, 183, 230, 255
  Snowy 7, 30, 63, 82, 230, 255
Oyster 36, 254
Oystercatcher
  American 28, 30, 34, 36, 223
P
Paddy's Knob 257

ABBREVIATED TABLE OF CONTENTS
Introduction 1-23
Eastern Shore 24-43
Coastal Plain 44-79
Northern Virginia 80-113
Central Virginia 114-139
Southern Piedmont 140-159
Southern Mountains/Valleys 160-197
Hawk-watching 198-202
Pelagic Birding 203-209
Annotated Checklist 210-248
Virginia Specialties 249-259

Parakeet
Carolina 3-4, 230
Monk 60
Park
Accotink Bay Wildlife Refuge 97, 99
Breaks Interstate 195-197, 257
Chinquapin 89-90
Cumberland Gap National Historical 257
Flag Rock 193-194
Fort Hunt 94
G. Richard Thompson Wildlife Management Area 112
Glencarlyn 83-84
Grand Caverns Regional 129
Great Falls National 105, 257
High Knob Recreation Area 194-195
Huntley Meadows 95-96, 253, 255
James River 143, 145
Jones Point 94
Long Branch Nature Area 83-84
Lubber Run 86-87
Montgomery Hall 131
Monticello 90-91
Natural Chimneys Regional 131-132
Newport News City 74
North Bend 151
Pohick Bay Regional 100
Point of Rocks 50
Potomac Overlook Regional 85-86
Riverbend 105
Scotts Run Nature Preserve 103-104
Parula
Northern 50-51, 56, 59, 69, 71-74, 93, 99, 102, 125, 137, 143, 147, 150, 166, 172, 181, 239
Peaks of Otter Recreation Area 167
Pelican
American White 10, 26, 30, 34, 39, 76, 212, 250
Brown 33, 36-37, 62, 65, 67, 69, 73, 119, 200, 213, 250
Petrel
Black-capped 8, 42, 155, 206-207, 211
Cape Verde 155
Herald 42, 155
Phalarope
Red 30, 76, 94, 155, 175, 205-207, 226
Red-necked 94, 155, 175, 205-207, 226
Wilson's 58, 75, 94, 175, 226, 253
Pheasant
Ring-necked 107, 221
Phoebe
Eastern 84, 104, 132, 233
Say's 39, 136, 233
Pigeon
Passenger 3, 6, 229
Pintail
Northern 51, 62, 65, 73, 76, 93, 105, 133, 139, 216
White-cheeked 30, 216

Pioneer Farm Exhibit 169
Pipit
American 9, 25, 39, 73, 75, 108, 154-155, 175, 190, 237, 258
Sprague's 30, 238
Plover
Black-bellied 30, 33-34, 60, 62, 65, 67, 75, 119, 157, 175, 190, 222
Mountain 30, 223
Piping 22, 26, 33, 58-59, 62, 65, 67-68, 175, 223, 253
Semipalmated 33, 60, 62, 65, 75, 115, 175, 222
Snowy 34, 222
Wilson's 22, 26, 33, 58, 62, 65, 222, 253
Poor Man's (submarine) Canyon 203, 209
Puffin
Atlantic 43, 203, 229, 254

R
Radford 243
Ragged Island Wildlife Management Area 56-57
Rail
Black 25, 31, 43, 68, 221, 252
Clapper 28, 34, 46, 57, 66-68, 73, 221, 252
King 62-63, 96, 154, 221, 252
Virginia 31, 63, 68, 96, 124, 155, 221
Yellow 43, 68-69, 221
Ramseys Draft 137
Raven
Common 81, 108, 110, 113, 123, 135, 161, 166, 170, 176, 179-180, 182, 185-188, 195-196, 200, 234, 255
Razorbill 60, 203, 207, 229, 254
Red Hill Shrine 149-150
Redhead 74, 94, 133, 139, 217
Redpoll
Common 7, 60, 84, 90, 108, 115, 136, 193, 248-249
Hoary 136, 248
Redstart
American 4, 50-51, 89-90, 93, 113, 115, 122, 131, 137, 143, 147, 169, 172, 181, 241
Richmond 49, 143, 148, 227
River
Appomattox 50
Dan 156
Holston 256
James 45, 51, 56, 72, 143, 166, 171-172, 252, 257
Meherrin 46, 219, 252
New 180
North 131
Potomac 45, 76, 78, 81, 91, 93, 101-102, 105, 107, 249-250, 252, 257-258
Rappahannock 45, 251-253, 257
Staunton 156-158, 257
York 45, 73
Roanoke 176-177, 227, 246
Roanoke Sewage Treatment Plant 174-175
Robin
American 5, 38, 60, 69, 86, 93, 131-132, 139, 237
Rockfish Gap 169
Rocky Knob Recreation Area 168

Rudee Inlet 64, 251, 254
Ruff 5, 25, 29-30, 62, 76, 92, 225, 253
Russell Fork 196-197

S

Saddle Overlook 169
Sandbridge Beach 207
Sanderling 37, 58-60, 62, 67, 92, 119, 157, 175, 190, 224
Sandpiper 147
   Baird's 29, 62, 65, 175, 188, 225, 253
   Buff-breasted 29, 38, 58, 75, 92, 175, 225, 254
   Curlew 29-30, 58, 94, 225, 253
   Least 49, 53, 60, 75, 112, 118, 157, 175, 224
   Pectoral 62, 65, 75, 118, 157, 175, 225
   Purple 25-26, 68, 225, 254
   Semipalmated 49, 53, 58, 60, 75, 92, 118, 157, 175, 224
   Sharp-tailed 30, 94, 225, 253
   Solitary 49, 53, 75, 84, 92, 112, 115, 118, 147, 157, 175, 223
   Spotted 49, 53, 75, 78, 92, 112, 115, 118, 143, 151, 157, 175, 181, 223
   Stilt 58, 62, 65, 75, 225
   Upland 22, 30, 38, 56, 75, 81, 107-108, 124, 223, 253
   Western 36, 49, 53, 60, 75, 175, 190, 224
   White-rumped 58, 62, 65, 75, 119, 175, 224
Sapsucker
   Yellow-bellied 60, 90, 111, 135, 145, 148, 231
Saxis Marsh 25, 31, 252, 256, 258
Scaup
   Greater 102, 133, 139, 217
   Lesser 69, 73, 93-94, 102, 133, 139, 147-148, 158, 217
Scoter
   Black 68, 218, 251
   Surf 68, 78-79, 149, 190, 218, 251
   White-winged 68, 145, 176, 218, 251
Screech-Owl
   Eastern 39, 60, 69, 99, 104, 155, 176, 230
Shearwater
   Audubon's 42, 206, 212
   Cory's 42, 63, 155, 205-206, 211
   Greater 34, 42, 63, 94, 205-207, 211
   Manx 63, 205, 207, 212, 249
   Sooty 34, 43, 62, 205-207, 211, 250
Shenandoah Mountain 137, 259
Shenandoah Valley 243, 253, 255, 257
Shoveler
   Northern 60, 93, 133, 216
Shrike
   Loggerhead 22, 108, 115, 155, 178, 238, 256
   Northern 7, 30, 81, 108, 124, 238, 256
Siskin
   Pine 7, 81, 86, 108, 115, 136, 145, 162, 179-180, 187, 248
Skimmer
   Black 10, 37, 67, 94, 155, 229
Skua
   Great 205, 226
   South Polar 34, 205, 226, 249

Skyland 122
Skyline Drive 81, 121-122, 255
Snickers Gap 109-110, 220
Snipe
   Common 4, 73, 94, 99, 108, 111, 119, 157, 175, 178, 183, 225
Sora 5, 63, 96, 145, 177-178, 222
South Holston Lake 189-190
Sparrow
   American Tree 76, 82, 96, 108, 244, 258
   Bachman's 22, 124, 141, 148, 154, 244, 258
   Black-throated 244
   Chipping 53, 62, 72, 78-79, 89, 111, 159, 244
   Clay-colored 29, 38-39, 58, 62, 155, 244, 258
   Field 3, 54, 72, 78-79, 89, 93, 124, 150, 159, 244
   Fox 53, 69, 71, 73, 86, 93, 142, 158-159, 175, 245
   Grasshopper 3, 51, 62, 65, 81, 107, 111, 141, 150-151, 169-170, 245
   Harris's 155, 246
   Henslow's 22, 25, 31, 39, 43, 54, 112, 141, 148, 154-155, 159, 175, 245, 258
   House 248, 258
   Lark 10, 29, 38-39, 58, 60, 62-63, 65, 119, 244, 258
   Le Conte's 10, 25-26, 39, 43, 58, 63, 73, 175, 245, 258
   Lincoln's 38-39, 63, 84, 87, 96, 104, 131, 178, 192, 245
   Nelson's Sharp-tailed 36, 66, 68, 245, 258
   Saltmarsh Sharp-tailed 25, 36, 42, 62, 65-66, 68, 178, 245, 258
   Savannah 60, 68, 81, 89, 111, 115, 135, 142, 183, 244
   Seaside 25, 36, 42, 46, 56-57, 62, 65-67, 245
   Song 50, 84, 86, 89, 93, 124, 148, 158-159, 245
   Swamp 50, 53, 68, 72-74, 96, 99, 104, 115, 136, 145, 159, 178, 246, 258
   Vesper 81, 108, 111, 115, 135, 142, 183, 244
   White-crowned 9, 53, 82, 89, 93, 108, 111, 133, 142, 151, 155, 158-159, 178, 246
   White-throated 9, 50, 53, 69, 84, 86, 93, 104, 123, 131, 133, 137, 139, 142, 150, 158-159, 246
Spring Creek 190
Starling
   European 238

ABBREVIATED TABLE OF CONTENTS

Introduction	1-23
Eastern Shore	24-43
Coastal Plain	44-79
Northern Virginia	80-113
Central Virginia	114-139
Southern Piedmont	140-159
Southern Mountains/Valleys	160-197
Hawk-watching	198-202
Pelagic Birding	203-209
Annotated Checklist	210-248
Virginia Specialties	249-259

State Park
Breaks Interstate 195-197
False Cape 64-66, 258
First Landing/Seashore 59-60, 257
Grayson Highlands 185, 187
Kiptopeke 25, 35-39, 252, 256, 258
Lake Anna 119
Mason Neck 100-102
New River Trail 180-181
North Bend 154
Occoneechee 151, 255
Pocahontas 147-148
Shot Tower 180-181
Sky Meadows 110-112, 255
Staunton River 156-158
Staunton River Battlefield 151, 158-159
Westmoreland 78-79
York River 71-72
Staunton 129, 131
Stilt
Black-necked 29, 58, 65, 175, 223, 253
Stint
Red-necked 224
Stork
Wood 5, 58, 63, 66, 76, 154-155, 215
Storm-Petrel
Band-rumped 42, 206, 212, 249
Leach's 42, 205-206, 212
White-faced 206, 212
Wilson's 34, 42, 205-207, 212, 250
Sunset Field Overlook 166, 171
Swallow
Bank 51, 75, 107, 175, 234
Barn 66, 73, 75, 107, 124, 132, 166, 171, 175, 234
Cliff 75, 94, 107, 111, 118, 136, 154, 166, 171, 175, 234
Northern Rough-winged 75, 107, 132-133, 175, 234
Tree 50, 75, 107, 112, 133, 171, 175, 182, 188, 234
Swan
Mute 29, 73, 215, 250
Tundra 56, 62, 65, 73-74, 78-79, 102, 104, 119, 133, 148, 158, 176, 215, 250
Swift
Chimney 4, 86, 231

T
T. M. Gathright Wildlife Management Area 138
Tanager
Scarlet 3, 50, 53, 72, 74, 77, 79, 81, 84, 86-87, 89, 102, 105, 122, 125, 127, 131, 137, 141, 143, 147, 154, 166, 168-172, 176, 179, 181, 187, 242
Summer 3, 46, 50, 53, 71-72, 74, 77, 79, 89, 105, 108, 127, 141, 147-148, 150, 154, 242, 257
Western 63, 94, 243
Tanner's Ridge Overlook 122
Teal
Blue-winged 4, 53, 60, 62, 65, 75, 94, 99, 115, 118, 133, 171, 181, 216

Green-winged 60, 62, 65, 76, 93-94, 99, 112, 115, 133, 216
Tern
Arctic 205, 228
Black 29, 62, 65, 69, 92-93, 118, 132, 145, 154, 157, 190, 229
Bridled 42, 73, 115, 119, 206, 229
Caspian 33, 51, 58, 67, 73, 75, 77-79, 92-93, 115, 118, 132, 154, 157, 190, 228
Common 28, 33, 37, 57, 67, 118, 132, 157, 190, 228
Elegant 30, 228
Forster's 28, 33, 37, 66-67, 73, 75, 78-79, 92-93, 118, 132, 157, 190, 228
Gull-billed 22, 28, 33, 37, 58, 228, 254
Least 28, 33, 37, 57-58, 67, 75, 228
Roseate 22, 42, 62, 73, 228
Royal 28, 33, 36-37, 57-58, 67, 73, 75, 78-79, 228
Sandwich 28, 33, 58, 119, 155, 228, 254
Sooty 8, 30, 34, 42, 73, 94, 115, 119, 155, 206-207, 229
White-winged 30, 229
Thrasher
Brown 5, 59, 81, 94, 131, 237
Sage 25, 30, 237
Thrush
Bicknell's 236
Gray-cheeked 50, 60, 86, 89-90, 96, 137, 143, 181, 236
Hermit 39, 50, 56, 60, 69, 71-72, 78-79, 86, 89-90, 115, 131, 136, 145, 182, 185-186, 237
Swainson's 60, 86, 89, 143, 162, 181, 185, 237
Varied 136, 237
Wood 46, 59, 77, 84, 86, 89-90, 96, 102, 104-105, 122, 137, 145, 166, 181, 237
Titmouse
Tufted 78-79, 81, 93, 235
Tom's Cove 29, 256
Towhee
Eastern 3, 56, 69, 84, 86, 94, 122, 124, 131-132, 150, 159, 244
Green-tailed 243
Townsend 36
Trail
Appalachian 121
Elk Run 167
Flat Top Mountain 167
Johnson Farm Loop 167
Limberlost 122
of the Trees 166, 171
Rock Castle Gorge National Recreation 169
South River Falls 122, 125
W & OD 83
Tropicbird
White-tailed 206, 212
Turkey
Wild 4, 49, 71, 86, 105, 110-111, 113, 115, 122-123, 127-128, 136-137, 139, 142, 148, 158, 167, 169-170, 172, 176, 180, 194-196, 200, 221
Turnstone
Ruddy 60, 67, 119, 155, 190, 224

V

VARCOM 15, 209-210

Veery 60, 86, 122, 136, 143, 161, 165-166, 168, 170, 172, 179, 181-182, 186, 188, 195, 236

Vireo

Bell's 238

Blue-headed 10, 56, 60, 93, 115, 122, 136, 139, 157, 166, 168-169, 172, 176, 179, 186, 188, 194-195, 238

Philadelphia 29, 59, 65, 87, 93, 99, 131, 238

Red-eyed 3, 46, 50, 53, 56, 60, 72, 77, 79, 84, 86, 93, 104, 128, 139, 157, 179, 181, 239

Warbling 60, 81, 93, 105, 108, 111-112, 157, 166, 171, 173, 181-182, 238

White-eyed 10, 50, 53, 56, 60, 72, 77, 79, 86, 112, 131, 141, 147, 157, 175, 177, 181, 238

Yellow-throated 50, 59, 69, 71, 102, 104-105, 107, 125, 147-148, 150, 157, 166, 169-170, 238

Virginia Beach 64, 203, 207, 211, 227-228, 233, 236, 244, 249-250, 254

Virginia Coast Reserve Barrier Islands 33-34

Vulture

Black 170, 218

Turkey 170, 219

W

Wachapreague 203, 209

Warbler

"Brewster's" 145, 192

"Lawrence's" 128

Bachman's 5, 22, 99, 239

Bay-breasted 9, 55, 60, 90, 104-105, 172, 192-195, 241

Black-and-white 60, 77, 89, 115, 125, 128-129, 131, 157, 172, 176, 181, 241

Black-throated Blue 4, 50, 84, 86-87, 89, 91, 104, 122, 125, 136, 150, 161, 166-170, 172, 179, 188, 194-195, 197, 240

Black-throated Gray 240

Black-throated Green 3, 46, 50, 53, 59, 77, 89, 93, 104, 115, 129, 131, 136-137, 143, 161, 169, 171-172, 178-179, 181, 186, 188, 194-195, 197, 240

Blackburnian 60, 86, 90, 93, 105, 115, 122, 125, 131, 136-137, 147, 157, 161, 167-168, 172, 179, 181, 186, 195, 240

Blackpoll 9, 84, 86-87, 89, 104, 143, 157, 172, 181, 241

Blue-winged 50, 55, 84, 86-87, 104, 143, 147, 161, 172, 182, 239, 256

Canada 77, 87, 104, 115, 136-137, 143, 165-166, 168, 172, 179, 181-182, 195, 242

Cape May 7, 59, 87, 89, 104, 129, 131, 150, 172, 181, 187, 193-195, 240

Cerulean 81, 104-105, 113, 125, 129, 131, 136, 157, 165-170, 172, 181, 195, 241, 257

Chestnut-sided 4, 55, 60, 89-90, 115, 122, 135, 147, 157, 166, 169-170, 172, 179, 181, 187-188, 192, 194-195, 239

Connecticut 29, 60, 65, 84, 93, 96, 99, 124, 131, 242

Golden-winged 17, 50, 55, 60, 84, 87, 89, 135-136, 139, 172, 179, 192, 239, 256

Hooded 17, 50, 56, 71, 77, 79, 81, 90, 105, 113, 122, 125, 128-129, 136, 147, 169, 172, 176, 181, 192, 194, 242

Kentucky 56, 59, 71-72, 77, 79, 81, 90, 104-105, 113, 125, 131, 136, 167, 169, 172, 181, 192, 194, 242

Kirtland's 22, 155, 240

Magnolia 59, 89-90, 93, 104, 115, 131, 135-136, 143, 147, 162, 180-181, 185, 187, 195, 239, 256

Mourning 55, 60, 89, 93, 96, 112, 115, 131, 135-136, 180, 242, 257

Nashville 86, 131, 136, 162, 175, 239, 256

Orange-crowned 39, 53, 56, 63, 65, 84, 131, 181, 239

Palm 39, 63, 87, 89, 99, 151, 157, 159, 181, 240

Pine 3, 46, 49-50, 53, 57, 69, 72, 74, 77-79, 90, 99, 132, 137, 141, 147, 154, 157-158, 166, 172, 176, 240

Prairie 3, 77, 79, 81, 99, 147, 150, 154, 172, 240

Prothonotary 46, 49-51, 53, 56, 69, 71, 74, 77, 79, 81, 96, 99, 143, 157, 165-166, 171, 173, 241, 257

Swainson 197

Swainson's 5, 46, 56, 94, 105, 161, 196, 241, 257

Tennessee 90, 104, 172, 187, 192-195, 239

Wilson's 87, 104, 131, 181, 192, 242

Worm-eating 56, 59, 81, 91, 104-105, 113, 125, 136, 139, 147, 157, 161, 168-169, 172, 176, 179, 181, 197, 241

Yellow 50, 67, 77, 79, 94, 111, 143, 150, 166, 173, 181, 239, 255

Yellow-rumped 9, 57, 63, 74, 78-79, 172, 181, 240

Yellow-throated 49, 53, 59, 69-70, 72-74, 77, 79, 102, 104-105, 139, 141, 143, 147, 150, 154, 165-166, 171, 173, 181, 197, 240, 257

Warbler Road 166, 171-173, 256

Warrenton 235

Washington (submarine) Canyon 203, 209, 212

Waterthrush

Louisiana 49, 53, 59, 69-70, 72, 74, 78, 84, 87, 89, 104-105, 111, 125, 129, 137, 157, 166, 169, 172, 176, 181, 242

Northern 53, 56, 59, 69, 84, 87, 89, 115, 136, 157, 241, 257

Waxwing

Bohemian 238

Cedar 38, 50, 77, 79, 81, 86, 89, 93, 110, 113, 129, 131, 135, 139, 145, 169, 179, 182, 200, 238

ABBREVIATED TABLE OF CONTENTS

Introduction	**1-23**
Eastern Shore	**24-43**
Coastal Plain	**44-79**
Northern Virginia	**80-113**
Central Virginia	**114-139**
Southern Piedmont	**140-159**
Southern Mountains/Valleys	**160-197**
Hawk-watching	**198-202**
Pelagic Birding	**203-209**
Annotated Checklist	**210-248**
Virginia Specialties	**249-259**

Weyer's Cave 221
Wheatear
  Northern 25, 30, 39, 236
Whimbrel 30, 33-34, 37, 59, 62, 65, 175, 224
Whip-poor-will 71, 86, 115, 122, 141, 147-148, 176, 231
Whistling-Duck
  Fulvous 29, 39, 58, 62-63, 65-66, 76, 105, 175, 215
Whitetop Mountain 161, 185-187, 237, 239, 248, 259
Wigeon
  American 54, 58, 60, 71, 74, 78, 102, 105, 133, 148, 217, 251
  Eurasian 10, 30, 58, 60, 71, 73-74, 76, 133, 217, 251
Wildlife Center of Virginia 221
Willet 30, 34, 36-37, 59, 62, 65, 67, 92, 223
Williamsburg 70, 75, 255
Willis Harbor 254
Wise 192
Wise Point 258
Wood-Pewee
  Eastern 72, 77, 104, 232
Woodbridge 219, 233, 252
Woodcock
  American 36, 39, 96, 102, 124, 132, 170, 192, 225
  Eurasian 225
Woodpecker
  Downy 54, 57, 69, 74, 90, 104, 142, 157, 232
  Hairy 54, 60, 69, 74, 84, 86, 90, 104, 157, 232
  Lewis's 108, 231
  Pileated 56, 60, 74, 81, 84, 86, 105, 110-111, 113, 127, 157, 193, 200, 232
  Red-bellied 46, 54, 57, 60, 69, 74, 90, 127-128, 142, 157, 231
  Red-cockaded 22, 46, 232, 255
  Red-headed 37, 39, 69, 74, 91, 96, 99, 102, 110-111, 113, 133, 148, 157-159, 182-183, 191, 200, 231, 255
Wren
  Bewick's 22, 124, 135-136, 162, 187, 235, 256
  Carolina 5, 84, 86, 93, 132, 148, 235
  House 81, 86, 89, 104, 236
  Marsh 25, 31, 42, 46, 56-57, 62, 65-68, 72-73, 77, 79, 94, 112, 118, 143, 154, 177-178, 236
  Rock 26, 43, 58, 235
  Sedge 25, 31, 42, 62, 65-66, 68, 236, 256
  Winter 4, 56, 84, 90, 96, 104-105, 125, 132, 137, 148, 165-166, 168, 172, 178-180, 186, 236
Y
Yellowlegs
  Greater 49, 53, 58, 75, 92, 118, 175, 223
  Lesser 49, 53, 58, 75, 92, 112, 118, 175, 223
Yellowthroat
  Common 53, 59, 67, 69, 77, 79, 89, 124, 141-142, 172, 181, 242

ABOUT THE ARTISTS

Georges Dremeaux is a jewelry designer in New York City whose first love is bird illustration. Besides appearing in several of the *ABA Birdfinding Guides*, Georges' work can also be found in *The* Audubon Handbook, Eastern and Western editions, *The Audubon Society Master Guide to Birding*, Volume I, and in a number of issues of *Birding*. Georges also works regularly for the Wildlife Conservation Society (The Bronx Zoo) as an illustrator of identification labels for the various bird and mammal exhibits.

Ali Wieboldt grew up in rural central Virginia with parents who were birdwatchers and banders. There were also many artists in the family, and her earliest recollections of art projects were of copying birds from the field guides. She graduated from UNC-Charlotte with a degree in Creative Arts with an emphasis in Ceramics and Art Education. Ali finished an MFA in Metals/Jewelry from James Madison University in 1984. She draws some, but her studio emphasis is the creation of fine art jewelry that incorporates small paintings of birds and animals.

Gail D. Yovanovich is an illustrator and photographer specializing in birds. Her artwork, photographs, and articles have appeared in numerous publications, including *Birding* magazine, and many of the *ABA Birdfinding Guides*. She has also designed patches and T-shirts for the Houston Audubon Society. A former Texas resident now living in New Jersey, Gail also serves on the Texas Bird Records Committee of the Texas Ornithological Society.